Foreword

OVER THE COURSE of her life and reign more than 300 women served Queen Elizabeth in a position of attendance. Sadly, the names of some of these women are lost forever and the identities of others will never be known. There are huge gaps in the historical record and even identifying some of the Queen's most important attendants is difficult. For example, almost nothing is known about Elizabeth Norwich, Lady Carew, a senior attendant for half a century, as there are no known letters to her or from her, no known portraits, and little is said about her in surviving documents. All that seems to remain of her life is her resting place in death and even on her tomb the original inscription has been lost. Telling the personal stories of the Queen's women is therefore fraught with difficulty and, unfortunately, it is not much easier to tell their professional stories either as few documents survive to give us an insight into their daily duties.

Adding to the above difficulties is the lack of interest there has been historically in the Queen's women; the attention has primarily been on her men. Yet some of the Queen's women were significant figures at court and had just as much influence and sway as the more famous men around her. Indeed, the women of the Queen's inner circle were of immense importance in her life and were far more than just personal attendants. By blood, or by bond, they were the Queen's 'family'; her closest companions, her trusted confidantes, and her all important support network in a treacherous political world. Many of these bonds were made in the dangerous years before Elizabeth became queen, bonds that shaped her character, bonds that endured a lifetime, and bonds that make Elizabeth's childhood the key to understanding her inner circle of women as queen.

Because so many women served Elizabeth over the course of her life it is impossible to tell all their stories in one book. This book therefore focuses on those women who were most important in her life and reign, giving especial attention to the small number of women who, consecutively, managed her domestic staff, starting with her Lady Mistress, who headed her nursey, and ending with her Chief Gentlewomen of the Privy Chamber. These women were: Margaret Bourchier, Baroness Bryan; Blanche Milborne, Lady Herbert of Troy Parva; Kateryn Champernon Astley; Elizabeth Oxenbridge, Lady Tyrwhit; Blanche Parry; and Mary Radclyffe. This book also presents an overview of all the main positions of attendance, the three principal being Ladies and Gentlewomen of the Privy Chamber, Maids of Honour, and Ladies of Honour, and describes the nature of these roles and the duties involved as far as they can presently be understood. There is still a tremendous amount to learn about the roles of the Queen's women and future research will hopefully shed more light on their professional responsibilities.

The appendices of this book contains a list of all the women presently known to have served Elizabeth over the course of her life and reign. The women are listed chronologically by position and brief biographical information about each one can be found in the *Index of Women*.

In terms of dates, names, titles, job titles, and quotes, the following conventions have been used in this book:

Dates – all dates have been modernised. In Tudor times the New Year officially began on 25 March, not on 1 January when it was celebrated, so the date of the Queen's coronation would have been 15 January 1558 to her people, not 1559.

Names – in general, women are referred to by their maiden name, unless this is unknown or they are better known by their married name. Where known, first names are generally spelled as the woman herself spelled it unless the spelling makes the name difficult to recognise, i.e. 'Dorythe' (Dorothy). Although there are merits to modernising first names, by doing so we not only lose a piece of a person's identity, but we lose a piece of history, as there were many variations of popular names and many different pronunciations. For example, the name 'Katherine' went through a transformation in the sixteenth century, changing from the old medieval form of 'Kateryn' or 'Katryn' (pronounced Kat-eh-Rin and Kat-Rin or Kate-eh-Rin and Kate-Rin) to the modern form of 'Katherine' and 'Kathryn' with the 'Kath' pronunciation. These two different forms still exist in Wales where the names Catrin (pronounced Cat-Rin) and Catherine are considered distinct from each other. Queen Elizabeth's older women generally had the older form of the name, spelt in various ways, whilst her younger women generally had the newer. Whether Mistress Astley, Elizabeth's childhood governess, was known to the Queen as 'Kat' or 'Kate' is presently impossible to say, as both diminutives were popular in the sixteenth century, but as her Christian name was 'Kateryn' not 'Katherine', and as 'Kat-eh-Rin' was probably the more common pronunciation, the name 'Kat', by which she is popularly known, has been used in this book. The name 'Joan' also had many variants in the sixteenth century ranging from Joan to Jane to Joanne to Johanna. The sixteenth century name 'Johan' is usually modernised to 'Joan' (pronounced Jone) but it was recognised as distinct from 'Joan' by contemporary historian William Camden, who tells us in his book *Remains* (1623) that the name Jenet was 'a diminutive from Joan as little and pretty Jhoan [Johan]'. This suggests that Johan, like Jenet, was two syllables and was probably pronounced like Joanne (Jo-Anne) or Johanne (Jo-Han). In this book, therefore, the name 'Johan' is modernised to 'Joanne'. The name Elizabeth too had variants, ranging from Isabelle to Ellsabeth, and it is surprising how popular the spelling 'Elyzabeth' was, especially amongst the Queen's women, and where known this spelling has been retained.

ELIZABETH I's
~ LADIES ~
GENTLEWOMEN
AND MAIDS

For my parents and sister, with love and gratitude.

ELIZABETH I's
~ LADIES ~
GENTLEWOMEN AND MAIDS
THE WOMEN WHO SERVED ~ THE TUDOR QUEEN ~

HEATHER SHANETTE

PEN & SWORD
HISTORY
AN IMPRINT OF PEN & SWORD BOOKS LTD.
YORKSHIRE - PHILADELPHIA

First published in Great Britain in 2025 by
PEN AND SWORD HISTORY
An imprint of
Pen & Sword Books Ltd
Yorkshire – Philadelphia

ISBN 978 1 39909 461 0

Typeset in Times New Roman 10/12 by
SJmagic DESIGN SERVICES, India.
Printed and bound in the UK by CPI Group (UK) Ltd.

The Publisher's authorised representative in the EU for product safety is
Authorised Rep Compliance Ltd., Ground Floor, 71 Lower Baggot Street,
Dublin D02 P593, Ireland.
www.arccompliance.com

For a complete list of Pen & Sword titles please contact
PEN & SWORD BOOKS LIMITED
George House, Units 12 & 13, Beevor Street, Off Pontefract Road,
Barnsley, South Yorkshire, S71 1HN, England
E-mail: enquiries@pen-and-sword.co.uk
Website: www.pen-and-sword.co.uk

or

PEN AND SWORD BOOKS
1950 Lawrence Rd, Havertown, PA 19083, USA
E-mail: uspen-and-sword@casematepublishers.com
Website: www.penandswordbooks.com

MIX
Paper | Supporting
responsible forestry
FSC® C013604

Contents

Acknowledgements

THIS BOOK WOULD not have been possible without the help of many people. I would therefore like to say a heartfelt thankyou to: Sarah-Beth Watkins and Claire Hopkins, my Pen and Sword editors, for their support and encouragement; Sarah J. Hodder, my copyeditor, for her helpful comments and suggestions; the staff of the National Archives, the British Library and Kent Archives for all their help in locating and copying documents; Sarah Whale and the staff of Hatfield House for the same; Essex Record Office for their help in tracking down Lady Denny's Will; Simon Neal for translating and transcribing sixteenth century documents; Lord De L'Isle for graciously permitting me to access the Gamage/Sidney pedigree; Dr A. Cynfael Lake for giving me permission to quote from a Welsh elegy by Lewys Morgannwg; and Drea Leed of elizabethancostume.net for her help with wardrobe records. I would also like to thank the Marquess of Salisbury, Lord Hastings, the Hon. Edward Tollemache, Agecroft Hall and Gardens, Lady Hawkins' School, Oliver D. Harris and Michael Day for kindly permitting me to reproduce pictures in their collection.

Cover: Rainbow Portrait of Elizabeth I, *c*.1600, embellished. Reproduced with permission of the Marquess of Salisbury, Hatfield House.

Titles – Elizabeth is referred to as Princess Elizabeth before her accession. Although she was declared illegitimate before her third birthday, and was subsequently known as Lady Elizabeth, the title of princess was still used by some of her contemporaries and appears, for example, in her household account book of 1551 to 1552: 'The house of the right excellent Princess the Lady Elizabeth Her Grace'. Women of the nobility are either referred to by their full title, such as Countess of Lennox, or their shortened title, such as Lady Lennox.

Job Titles – most job titles held by women at court have been capitalised. This is due to the prestige and/or exclusivity of these positions. As the term 'ladies-in-waiting' was not in common use in the sixteenth century (the term became popular in the eighteenth century) it has not been used in this book.

Quotes – sixteenth-century text has generally been modernised and occasionally tenses have been changed for easier reading. Sources are referenced unless obvious.

As to the definition of a lady, gentlewoman and maid, they are as follows in this book:

Lady – titled noblewoman by birth or marriage (i.e. an earl's daughter or an earl's wife) or a knight's wife.

Gentlewoman – an untitled woman from the aristocracy.

Maid – an unmarried young woman who was a lady or a gentlewoman.

Additionally, in the context of this book 'livery' means uniforms, clothes, or materials for uniforms/clothes provided to staff by the monarch rather than general living provisions.

Christening

ON 10 SEPTEMBER 1533 the newborn daughter of King Henry VIII and his second wife, Anne Boleyn, made her first public appearance. The occasion was her christening, just three days after her birth, and the venue was the Church of the Observant Friars, Greenwich. Famously unwanted, as her father was desperate for a male heir, celebrations for her birth had been muted. The celebratory jousting tournament had been cancelled and an air of mourning had fallen over the court as though there had been a death, not a birth. 'The King's mistress was delivered of a girl', wrote the Spanish Ambassador, Eustace Chapuys, who did not recognise the King's second marriage, 'to the great disappointment and sorrow of the King, of the lady herself, and of others of her party, and to the great shame and confusion of physicians, astrologers, wizards and witches, all of whom affirmed it would be a boy'.[1] From that moment onwards, a dark shadow fell over the King's new marriage. For Anne had failed. Instead of giving the King his much longed for son, a son she had promised with all her heart, she had given him what he already had, a daughter. Nevertheless, the King, for the sake of public appearance, put on a brave face and gave his new daughter a magnificent christening.

Agnes Tilney, Dowager Duchess of Norfolk, Anne Boleyn's step-grandmother, was chosen for the all-important role of chief godmother, and in glorious procession she carried the King's baby daughter, who was clad in a gown of white satin and wrapped in a 'mantle of purple velvet with a long train furred with ermine', from the Palace of Greenwich, where she had been born, to the Church of the Observant Friars for the christening. Heading the procession was a host of esquires, gentlemen, chaplains, aldermen, bishops, barons, courtiers, councillors and noblemen, some of them carrying unlit torches, and heading the royal party was Henry Bourchier, Earl of Essex, carrying a silver gilt (gold-plated silver) basin that was to be used in the ceremony. Then came Henry Courtenay, Marquess of Exeter, the King's first cousin, carrying an unlit taper of virgin wax, then came Henry Grey, Marquess of Dorset, carrying a gold salt cellar, also to be used in the ceremony, and then came Lady Mary Howard, Anne Boleyn's first cousin, carrying the chrisom-cloth. To the right of Lady Norfolk was her step-son, Thomas Howard, Duke of Norfolk, Anne Boleyn's uncle, and to her left was Charles Brandon, Duke of Suffolk, widower of Mary Tudor, Henry VIII's sister. The long train of the royal baby's mantle was borne by Margaret Finch, Countess of Kent, with the assistance of Thomas Boleyn, Earl of Wiltshire, Anne Boleyn's father, and Edward Stanley, Earl of Derby, her uncle by marriage.[2]

Over the royal baby was a 'rich canopy' borne by George Boleyn, Viscount Rochford, Anne Boleyn's brother, with the help of her uncles, Lord William Howard and Lord Thomas Howard, and John Hussey, Baron Hussey of Sleaford. Behind the royal baby walked 'many ladies and gentlewomen' – her first female escort.

When Lady Norfolk reached the church door she was met by John Stokesley, Bishop of London, the man who was to christen the King's daughter, and together with the infant's two other godparents, Thomas Cranmer, Archbishop of Canterbury, and Margaret Wotton, Dowager Marchioness of Dorset, she chose the baby's name.[3] Typically, babies were named after their chief godparent, as the chief godparent was male if the child was male and female if the child was female, but as the baby in Lady Norfolk's arms was a princess, and the realm's only recognised heir, a royal name was chosen, the name of the King's mother: Elizabeth. The name also happened to be that of the Queen's mother. The baby princess was then taken to a private space that was heated by 'a pan of fire' and undressed by her godmothers for the ceremony. Then, completely naked, she was carried to the font, given a little salt from the cellar to protect her from evil, gently immersed in the warmed waters three times during the ceremony, anointed with holy oil, and then wrapped in the beautiful chrisom-cloth. As a symbol of her salvation the unlit taper carried by the Marquess of Exeter was lit, followed by all the torches held by the gentlemen present, and then the Garter King of Arms, Sir Thomas Wriothesley, cried aloud: 'God of his infinite goodness send prosperous life, and long, to the high and mighty Princess of England, Elizabeth'.

To the sound of trumpets the 'high and mighty' Princess Elizabeth was then carried by her chief godmother to the altar to be confirmed in the Christian faith by the Archbishop of Canterbury. For this second ceremony, Gertrude Blount, Marchioness of Exeter, was godmother. A devout Catholic, and a close friend of Katherine of Aragon, the King's discarded first wife, Lady Exeter allegedly only accepted the role to avoid the King's wrath, but whatever her personal feelings, she played the part to perfection and gave her new goddaughter 'three standing bowls graven, all gilt, with a cover'. The newly named Princess Elizabeth also received gifts from her three other godparents: a 'cup of gold fretted with pearl' from Lady Norfolk, 'three gilt bowls pounced with a cover' from Lady Dorset, and a 'cup of gold' from the Archbishop of Canterbury.

Following the christening and confirmation, refreshments were served to the guests and then Princess Elizabeth, once again fully dressed in her satin gown and velvet mantle, was carried back to the Palace of Greenwich in another stately procession. This time the processional route glittered with the glow of five hundred torches carried by the King's guard, and around the little princess more torches burned in the afternoon sun. Immediately in front of her walked four noblemen, carrying the gifts she had received from her four godparents, and immediately behind her walked the ladies and gentlewomen of the court as before.[4] Upon arriving at the palace, Lady Norfolk, in whose arms the princess still lay, carried the newly christened royal to the Queen's bedchamber door. This was her last duty of the day, and when it was done, she left the baby girl who would, unbeknown to herself and to everyone else present, grow up to be one of history's greatest queens, in the care of her recovering mother and her Lady Mistress.

Chapter One

Lady Mistress

THE LADY MISTRESS was a woman of great importance in the early lives of Henry VIII's children. There is still much to learn about this prestigious position, and the women who held the title in the Tudor period, but the Lady Mistress presided over the royal nursery and her full title was either 'Lady Mistress of the King's Nursery' or, if there was just one child in the nursery, 'Lady Mistress to the Prince or Princess'. The Tudor royal nursery was modelled upon the Yorkist royal nursery that Henry VIII's mother, Elizabeth of York, had grown up in. The first Tudor queen had been the eldest of many children born to Edward IV and his wife, Elizabeth Woodville, and when she was setting up a royal nursery for her first child, Prince Arthur, she was helped by her mother and by the woman who had headed the nursery of her younger siblings, in the role of Lady Mistress – Elizabeth Tyrrell, Lady Darcy. A few years later the new king and queen put together a volume of Household Ordinances that outlined in great detail what was to happen at the birth of a royal baby and how the royal nursery was to be staffed and furnished.[1] Henry VIII followed these ordinances closely, and when it came time to choosing a Lady Mistress for his first child with Katherine of Aragon, he chose the woman who had headed his own nursery, Elizabeth Jerningham, Lady Denton.

The Tudor royal nursery consisted of a suite of richly furnished rooms that included a 'rocking chamber', in which the royal baby slept in a grand cradle; a 'privy chamber', which was a lavish day room; and a stately 'presence chamber' in which a 'great cradle of estate' was on display. This was typically a magnificent cradle of silver gilt, more than five feet long, that was adorned with precious stones, dynastic emblems, painted figures, pommels, and elaborate pillars. In this shimmering cradle, upon luxurious bedding, the royal baby, wrapped in rich swaddling bands, was shown to important visitors.[2]

The Lady Mistress had a small team of staff to help her care for the royal baby: a wet nurse, who had the important job of breastfeeding the royal baby as it was not fashionable in this period for aristocratic women to suckle their own children; a laundress, who washed the baby's clothes and bedding; and four 'rockers' who took it in turns to rock the royal cradle and to assist the nurse. The wet nurse, obviously still lactating from a recent pregnancy, was always a young married woman from a respectable family who was in good health and of impeccable moral character. The latter was considered of paramount importance as the wet nurse was thought able to pass on personality traits to the baby through her milk. As the royal baby's health depended on hers, the wet nurse's diet was highly restricted and everything she ate or drank had to be tested for poison. There were also a few gentlemen attached to the nursery who were responsible for security, general provisions and maintenance. In return for their service the nursery staff received wages, bed and board, and livery.[3] As the women in attendance were from the aristocracy they usually had servants of their own and these too would receive bed and board. The Lady Mistress, who had sumptuous lodgings, was particularly well rewarded, receiving in due course a generous annuity of £50–£70 and a tun of wine every year for life.[4]

By the reign of Henry VIII the Lady Mistress was so highly respected and esteemed that her 'office and fee' had seemingly become a lifelong honour. When Princess Mary was born in 1516, Lady Denton was unable to take up her position as Lady Mistress, perhaps due to ill health, but rather than appointing a new Lady Mistress, the King appointed an acting one instead, Margaret Bourchier, Baroness Bryan, who was only to officially have the 'office and fee' of Lady Mistress after Lady Denton's death.[5] This means that when Lady Denton died, Baroness Bryan became the court's official Lady Mistress, and as the 'office and fee' is likely to have been a lifelong honour for her too, there was probably no other official Lady Mistress for the rest of the King's reign.

As the Lady Mistress had the immense responsibility of raising the King's children she was always of mature years and well experienced in childcare. The Lady Mistress also had to be completely trustworthy, of unswerving loyalty to the King, of sound moral character, learned and accomplished, and a superb organiser and communicator. Had there been any doubts about the continued suitability of Baroness Bryan for the role after the King's controversial divorce from Katherine of Aragon then the King would not have hesitated in depriving her of office, but in what is one of history's many ironies, the incumbent Lady Mistress was Anne Boleyn's aunt.

Margaret Bourchier, Baroness Bryan

Margaret Bourchier was born in the troubled years of the Wars of the Roses and was the eldest daughter of Sir Humphrey Bourchier, a man with royal blood in his veins, and his wife, Elizabeth Tilney, Lady Bourchier. At the time of her birth, in the late 1460s, Margaret's grandmother, namesake, and probable godmother, Margaret Bourchier, Baroness Berners, was serving the royal family of Edward IV in a role that was none other than Lady Mistress to Princess Elizabeth of York.[6] As a child, Margaret may even have been a companion to the princess and her two younger sisters, Mary and Cecily of York, for both her parents were in attendance upon their mother and it was normal practice for the children of very favoured courtiers to be raised in the royal nursery. Margaret and the princesses also shared a great aunt and uncle, for Margaret's great uncle, Henry Bourchier, Earl of Essex, grandfather of his namesake who led the royal party at Elizabeth's christening, was married to Isabel of York, a great aunt to the princesses. Baroness Berners is usually credited with educating the princesses, especially Elizabeth of York who was 9 years old when the baroness died in 1475, and the learned matron may also have educated her own granddaughter.

4

Sadly for Margaret, her father did not survive the Wars of the Roses. When King Edward temporarily lost the throne in the autumn of 1470, her father took up arms to help him win it back but was killed in the Battle of Barnet the following spring. The battle was a triumphant victory for King Edward, and the fallen soldier was given a hero's burial, but his young wife was now a widow with three small children to raise. As was customary, Lady Bourchier mourned her husband for a year, but then went on to make a marriage that would change the course of history. For the following year she married Thomas Howard, Earl of Surrey, future Duke of Norfolk, and through two of their children, Edmund and Elizabeth, they became the grandparents of two queens: Katheryn Howard, Henry VIII's fifth wife, and Anne Boleyn.

When Margaret was still a child she was betrothed to a boy named John Sandys, son and heir of Sir William Sandys of The Vyne. Whether or not the marriage went ahead is uncertain, but by the 1490s John Sandys was dead and Margaret was married to Sir Thomas Bryan of Ashridge, a Knight of the Body to Henry VII. The couple had at least five children together and by the reign of Henry VIII both Margaret and her husband were in the service of Katherine of Aragon. Margaret was attending upon the Queen whilst her husband was her Vice-Chamberlain. When it came time for the King and Queen to select a new Lady Mistress in 1516, due to Lady Denton's failing health, Margaret was chosen, perhaps because of her kinship to Baroness Berners, and, according to her own testimony, she was made a baroness *suo jure* at the same time. This means she was made a baroness in her own right, a very rare honour for a woman.[7]

Margaret remained Princess Mary's Lady Mistress until 1519 when she was replaced by Margaret Pole, Countess of Salisbury, who had been appointed the princess's Lady Governess. This change was probably due to the birth of Henry Fitzroy, the King's illegitimate son who was born to his mistress, Bessie Blount, that summer. The King considered the boy a potential heir, even though he was illegitimate, so it is likely that he wanted him to be raised by the court's official Lady Mistress. Indeed, Baroness Bryan's own words 'and so I have been a [mistress] to the children His Grace have had since' strongly suggests that she took care of another child between Mary and Elizabeth.[8] For Mary, the change may have been distressing, as she was probably very attached to Baroness Bryan, but it was in no way denigrating as Lady Salisbury was one of the greatest peeresses in the land. A Plantagenet by birth, she was the daughter of George, Duke of Clarence, the famous brother of Edward IV and Richard III who supposedly ended his days in a vat of wine, so she was of royal blood and a cousin of the King's. Indeed, she was a far more prestigious attendant than Baroness Bryan and this may have been an additional factor in the King's decision. At only 3 years of age, Mary still needed nursery care, as in Tudor times children did not generally leave their nursery until they were 6 years of age, but she was old enough to forgo a Lady Mistress for a Lady Governess and to begin her schooling. In reward for her service to the princess, Baroness Bryan was granted an annuity of £50 and the customary gift of a tun of wine a year. By now she was the wife of a man named David Zouche, for Sir Thomas had passed away in the winter of 1517, but she retained the name of Bryan and continued to be known as Lady or Baroness Bryan.

History is silent on the early years of Henry Fitzroy, but the boy thrived and grew, and at 6 years of age, when he left his nursery and the care of women, he was created Duke of Richmond and given his own household. For the next few years Baroness Bryan probably lived in semi-retirement with her new husband. Her three surviving children, Margaret, Elizabeth and Francis, were now all grown up and were well favoured by the King. Margaret had married Sir Henry Guildford, former Master of the Horse; Elizabeth had married Sir Nicholas Carew, successor to Sir Henry as Master of the Horse; and Francis, now a knight, was one of the King's right-hand men. Famous for wearing a patch over an eye following a jousting accident, Francis was a Gentleman of the Privy Chamber, an ambassador, a constable of several castles, and a member of parliament. Unfortunately for Baroness Bryan, who was a woman of honour, her son, like many of the men around Henry VIII, was a man of few principles and little loyalty. He led a dissolute life and on account of his moral depravity became known as 'the Vicar of Hell', meaning 'agent of the Devil'. Baroness Bryan is also said to have raised a little girl named Lettice Peniston who would go on to marry three times and live to become the grandmother of one of the most famous women in Tudor history: Lettice Knollys, Countess of Essex and Leicester.

When, by 1527, the King had decided to divorce Katherine of Aragon and marry again, Baroness Bryan may initially have felt awkward when the woman he had chosen for his new wife was her niece, Anne Boleyn. After all, she had served Queen Katherine faithfully for years and had raised Princess Mary for the first three years of her life. However, Baroness Bryan was a pragmatist and a realist, so whatever her thoughts on 'the King's great matter', she kept them to herself and supported her niece when she eventually married the King. By now, the baroness was in her mid-sixties, an advanced age in Tudor times, but as she was still in good health and of sound mind there was no reason why she could not fulfil her duties as Lady Mistress when Elizabeth was born.

For the first few weeks of her life, Elizabeth lived with her parents at Greenwich Palace where a suite of rooms had been transformed into the royal nursery. The Household Ordinances of her grandparents advised that new royal infants should be taken to their nursery immediately after their christening, so 'the high and mighty Princess Elizabeth' was probably taken there within hours of that momentous event. In these early weeks, the number of staff attending to Elizabeth was small, to minimise the risk of infection, and Baroness Bryan's principal assistant was the all-important wet nurse, Agnes Pendred. Very little is known about Agnes, but she was clearly young as she was still bearing children twenty years later, and she was married to a Welshman named David Pendred.[9] The names of Elizabeth's four rockers are not recorded but Joanne Hilton, variously named 'Anne' or 'Agnes' in early records, was probably the nursery's laundress.

When Elizabeth was three months old she was sent to live in the small, but stately, Palace of Hatfield in Hertfordshire. This red-brick palace had been built in the late fifteenth century by John Morton, Bishop of Ely, and it consisted of four wings around a large central courtyard. The royal nursery is thought to have occupied the southern wing, which was fronted by beautiful gardens, and beyond lay glorious deer parks and woodland. King Henry employed a household of people to care for his new daughter, and

Sir John Shelton, husband of Anne Boleyn's paternal aunt and namesake, Anne Boleyn, Lady Shelton, was put in charge. Elizabeth travelled in style to her new home, a move that was overseen by her mother and Baroness Bryan, and she arrived about ten days before Christmas. This was the busiest time at court, with hundreds of people arriving for the festivities, possibly bringing contagions with them, so court was not the best place for a baby to be. It was also normal for royal children to have their own establishment.

For Baroness Bryan, the move meant adjusting to a new way of life, but as an experienced Lady Mistress she was accustomed to moving from palace to palace as all royal residences had to be vacated after a few months of occupation for 'airing and sweetening'. At Hatfield the baroness was reunited with Princess Mary, who had been sent to live in her half-sister's residence as punishment for refusing to accept 'the great divorce' and her subsequent bastard status, but given the circumstance the reunion was far from a happy one. Although it was reported in Catholic circles that Mary had been sent to Hatfield to be a 'lady's maid' to Elizabeth, and the King had threatened as much in an attempt to 'subdue her spirit', in actuality this is unlikely. The true motive was probably to impress upon Mary that Elizabeth was now the King's heir and to break her resistance and resolve. It was a cruel twist of fate, but King Henry was becoming a monster of a man, ruthless and savage, and completely different to the generous and joyful boy who had taken the throne in 1509. The woman charged with breaking the princess's resolve was her new Lady Governess, Lady Shelton, as Lady Salisbury had been dismissed. This was another humiliation for Mary, and she felt it deeply, but things could have been far worse for at least Lady Shelton treated her well. Indeed, within weeks of her appointment Lady Shelton was in trouble for treating Mary with 'too much respect and kindness' and was told that she should treat her as the bastard she is. Lady Shelton, who did not agree, bravely replied that 'even if the princess were only the bastard of a poor gentleman she deserves honour and good treatment for her goodness and virtues'.[10] In the weeks that followed, Baroness Bryan also endeavoured to persuade Mary to give up her futile and dangerous resistance to the King, but Mary, fiercely loyal to her mother and fighting for her birthright, would not. She continued to defy her father and when it came time for the household to move to Eltham in the spring, she flatly refused to go, which resulted in Lady Shelton having to have her 'put by force' into a litter so the move could proceed. By the autumn, when the household was at Hunsdon, things were no better and Baroness Bryan, who was still trying to convince the princess to give up her resistance, received a visit from Lady Shelton, on behalf of the King, regarding a letter that her daughter, Lady Carew, had sent to the princess. Baroness Bryan confirmed that she had delivered a letter to Mary from her daughter, whose husband was sympathetic to Katherine of Aragon, a letter which allegedly 'desired her, for the passion of Christ, in all things to follow the King's pleasure otherwise she was utterly undone'.[11]

By the time Elizabeth reached her first birthday she was probably on her way to being fully weaned. This meant that the time was coming to say goodbye to her wet nurse, Agnes Pendred, and the parting, when it came, was surely the first of many emotional wrenches for Elizabeth. In Agnes's place a dry nurse was probably appointed, whose duties were general nursing needs, such as assisting with bathing and toileting, and sleeping with Elizabeth every night. Unfortunately, the name of this dry nurse is unknown, but may have been Elyzabeth Cavendish, a younger daughter of Thomas Cavendish of Overhall, late Clerk of the Pipe to the King (senior financial officer). For her year of nursing, Agnes Pendred was awarded an annuity of £40, a considerable amount for the time.[12]

For as long as there was hope of Anne Boleyn bearing a prince, Elizabeth was safe from her father's dark side, but all that changed in January 1536 when Katherine of Aragon died. By now, Henry and Anne had been married for three years and the King was growing impatient for a son. At first, he and Anne had rejoiced at the news of Katherine's death, for Anne was pregnant and the future looked bright, but at the end of January Anne suffered a miscarriage. The King was devastated, especially as the baby was said to be male, and in his despair he concluded that his second marriage was as cursed as his first one. Long gone were the 'fervents of love' he had once felt for his 'own darling' and, according to Ambassador Chapuys, the King was secretly saying that he wanted out of a marriage he had been 'seduced and forced into' by sorcery and witchcraft so he could take a third wife.[13] Anne's days were now numbered but few could have imagined how swift and how brutal her removal would be. Within weeks rumours were circulating that she had been unfaithful to the King with many lovers, even with her own brother, and she was soon arrested, imprisoned in the Tower of London, and condemned to death as a whore. On 19 May, at 9 o'clock in the morning, the Queen of England, attended by four women, was led out of her rooms in the Tower to the green outside where, upon a scaffold, her head was struck from her body with a sword. 'No one ever showed more courage or greater readiness to meet death than she did', wrote Ambassador Chapuys to the Emperor Charles later that day, words of high praise from a man who had always called her 'the concubine' and her daughter 'the little bastard'. Anne maintained her innocence to the end, as did all but one of the men condemned to share her fate, that one probably only 'confessing' under torture. 'Although most people here are glad of the execution of the concubine', Ambassador Chapuys wrote, 'a few find fault, and grumble at the manner in which the proceedings against her have been conducted'. He himself may have been one for he informed the Emperor that he had been told 'in great secrecy' that Anne had sworn 'before and after receiving the Holy Sacrament' and 'on peril of her soul's damnation' that she was innocent.[14]

With her mother's death a light went out in Elizabeth's life forever. Although she was too young to feel the loss of her mother right away, for Anne, like all royal parents, was a somewhat absent figure in her life, visiting her only occasionally, her mother had always loved her and had always made sure that she was well cared for and had beautiful clothes to wear. Now Elizabeth's future was entirely in the hands of her tyrannical father, and in the dark weeks that followed her mother's execution, no one knew what that future looked like. Would the King still provide for her? Would he even still acknowledge her as his daughter when her mother had been put to death as an adulteress and strumpet? Was it because he doubted she was his daughter that he had annulled his marriage to her mother and declared her a bastard? Or had he done this merely to clear the path to the throne for the children he hoped to have with his new wife, Jane Seymour? Not even Baroness Bryan knew what was to become of her great niece and by the summer tensions in Elizabeth's household were intolerable. Sir John was struggling to finance the household, Baroness Bryan was struggling to manage the nursery, and Princess Mary, who was still in residence, was in close confinement. Rather than restoring the former Princess of Wales in all rights and dignities, as the girl had hoped following Anne's demise, the King was more determined than ever to get her to acknowledge her bastard status. Mary held out as long as she could, but when the King started to turn his ire on her supporters, she had no choice but to yield, although she did so at the expense of her conscience and her mind was troubled. Baroness Bryan's mind was troubled too. Not only was she grieving for her niece and nephew, for Anne Boleyn's brother had been one of the five men executed for adultery with the Queen, but her husband had recently died, Henry Fitzroy was also dying, and her notorious son was of no comfort. The beleaguered baroness was undoubtedly also worried about another great niece, Mary Norris, who was probably in attendance upon Elizabeth, as her father, Sir Henry Norris, was also amongst those executed as one of the Queen's supposed lovers. With her father's death, Mary became an orphan, as her mother, Mary Fiennes, Baroness Bryan's niece, had died some years before.

By August, Baroness Bryan was at her wits end and could stay silent no longer. In a letter to Thomas Cromwell, the King's chief advisor, she beseeched him to 'be a good lord to me in the greatest need that ever I was' and voiced her concerns about Elizabeth's welfare and about the breakdown of order within her household. 'Now that my Lady Elizabeth is put from that degree she was afore', she wrote, 'and what degree she is at now I know not but by hearsay, I know not how to order her nor myself, nor none of hers that I have the rule of, that is, her women and her grooms'. She begged Cromwell for clarity in the matter and asked him to 'be a good lord' to Elizabeth and to see that she 'may have what is needful for her' because at present she had 'neither gown nor kirtle, nor petticoat, nor no manner of linen for smocks, nor kerchiefs [head coverings], sleeves, rails [capes], body-stychets [binding cloths], handkerchiefs, mufflers [scarves], nor begens [caps]'. All these the child desperately needed and Baroness Bryan could 'drive off' the necessity no longer. Further, she informed Cromwell that Sir John wanted to have Elizabeth 'dine and sup every day at the board of estate' (high table in the great hall) of which the Lady Mistress did not approve:

> Alas, my lord, it is not meet for a child of her age to keep such rule yet. I promise you, my lord, I dare not take it upon me to keep her in health if she keep that rule. For there she shall see divers meats and fruits and wine: which would be hard for me to restrain Her Grace from. You know, my lord, there is no place of correction there, and she is yet too young to correct greatly. I know well that if she be there I shall neither bring her up to the King's honour nor to hers, nor to her health, nor my poor honesty.

The baroness wished that 'my lady may have a mess of meat in her own lodging, with a good dish or two, that is meet for Her Grace to eat'. Not only would this be better for the child's health, but would be economical as the mess would be sufficient for 'all her women, a gentleman usher, and a groom'. This is how Princess

Mary had been raised and Baroness Bryan wanted everything 'ordered in all things as Her Grace was afore'. As Sir John 'will not be content with this' she wanted him to believe that it was 'the King's pleasure' and not 'my desire'. She also wished that 'Your Lordship will see the house honourably ordered' and to let her know 'what your order is'.[15] This long and heartfelt letter did some good. Sir John was promptly told that Elizabeth was to dine in her lodgings on the King's command and, no doubt, the urgent matter of the child's clothes was also dealt with.

By the autumn there had been some return to the order that Baroness Bryan craved. Elizabeth was still to be known as the King's daughter, although she was legally illegitimate and excluded from the line of succession, and her household, still under the stewardship of Sir John Shelton, was to be a joint one with Princess Mary's. Also young Mary Norris, if she was in attendance at this time, was permitted to remain in attendance. There were still problems to iron out, not least staffing issues in the nursery, but soon there were bigger things to worry about as the north of England had risen in revolt against the King's religious reforms. The rebellion, known as the Pilgrimage of Grace, was the most serious uprising of the Tudor age and was triggered by the King's closure of all the small monasteries and convents. As thousands of outraged men gathered together in the north to march south, the King, who was facing a considerable threat, withdrew to Windsor Castle, his most secure residence, and sent for both his daughters to join him there. Baroness Bryan therefore had to prepare Elizabeth for the journey upon short notice and accompany her to the castle. It was the first time since Anne Boleyn's execution that Henry was to see his daughter, and Baroness Bryan may have been nervous about the kind of reception the little girl would receive, but the King was apparently 'very affectionate to her' and was said to 'love her much'. Princess Mary also received a warm welcome and was treated as 'first after the Queen'.[16]

The Pilgrimage of Grace was over within weeks and life for Baroness Bryan and Princess Elizabeth returned to the 'new normal'. But change was on the horizon. The following October the King's third wife succeeded where his first two had failed and gave birth to a healthy baby boy at Hampton Court Palace. As official Lady Mistress, the little prince, who was named Edward, now became Baroness Bryan's responsibility, and she was in residence at the time of his birth. Had the prince been Anne Boleyn's son, then he would have joined Elizabeth in her nursery, and Baroness Bryan would have been Lady Mistress to both children, but because Elizabeth was now illegitimate, and Edward was the King's heir, this was impossible. Consequently, Baroness Bryan had to part from Elizabeth, who was also at Hampton Court for the birth, in order to take up her responsibilities to the prince. For the baroness, this cannot have been easy, even though she was experienced in parting from children she had cared for, but just because she was leaving Elizabeth's nursery, does not mean she was leaving her life. As heartless as the King could be, he wanted his children to have a relationship with each other, so he intended to make the joint household of Elizabeth and Mary a satellite of Edward's much grander one. With Elizabeth living under the same roof as her new half-brother, at least for most of the year, there would be ample opportunity for Baroness Bryan to see her great niece. For Elizabeth, however, losing her beloved Lady Mistress, the centre of her world, was undoubtedly traumatic, even if she did still see her great aunt regularly. The emotional impact was surely greater than that of her mother's execution, or that of her stepmother's death just two weeks after Prince Edward's birth, for her mother and stepmother had been fleeting presences in her life, Baroness Bryan a constant. Elizabeth was also losing the Sheltons, another constant fixture, as the King wanted a fresh start for his family so dismissed them.

Baroness Bryan soon settled into her new role, and from the letters she sent to Thomas Cromwell over the years, it is clear that she was proud of the little prince who 'danced and played so wantonly that he could not stand still'.[17] However, it is unlikely that she remained with the prince until he was 6 years of age. The Exeter Conspiracy of 1538, which was an alleged attempt by the Courtenay and Pole families to replace the King with his first cousin, Henry Courtenay, Marquess of Exeter, probably ended her career. The Marquess was swiftly executed, and prominent members of the Pole family, including Princess Mary's former Lady Governess, Margaret Pole, Countess of Salisbury, were imprisoned in the Tower of London. Baroness Bryan's son-in-law, Sir Nicholas Carew, was amongst those charged with treason, and in the March of 1539 he was beheaded. This left his wife and young children with almost nothing, not even their home, for Carew Manor in Beddington, their main residence, was seized by the Crown. Baroness Bryan used the little influence she had to secure some manors for her daughter, telling Cromwell in a letter that her 'poor daughter' was 'not used to strait living' and 'it would grieve me in my old days to lose her', but her family's star had fallen and her son's dismissal from the Privy Chamber extinguished it.[18] Wanting to retire, or 'encouraged' to do so by Cromwell and the King, for her position had become untenable, Baroness Bryan probably left the prince's nursery in the autumn of 1539. Like Lady Denton before her, however, she seemingly remained the court's official Lady Mistress, and she may have been permitted to see the prince from time to time, especially when her son recovered the King's favour.

Very little is known about Baroness Bryan's last years. She may have attended upon Kateryn Parr, the King's sixth wife, as a 'Lady Bryan' is recorded as one of her ladies in official records, but this 'Lady Bryan' was probably the baroness's daughter-in-law, Philippa Spice.[19] But wherever the baroness spent her last years, she lived to see the prince she had cared for become king. Sadly, by reason of long life, she outlived all her children, even her beloved daughter, Lady Carew, who died in 1546, but Lettice lived on, who was probably like a daughter to her, and she also had the comfort of grandchildren. One day, her two granddaughters, Anne and Mary Carew, would serve at the court of the Virgin Queen, and one day their children would have a role to play, but all this lay in the future, a future that Baroness Bryan would not see. In the summer of 1552, in her ninth decade of life, she passed away. The year before she had made a will, and in this will she recalled her time as Lady Mistress, asking the Boy King to finally grant her a formal discharge 'for all such things I had, of His Majesty's, in my charge or custody during the time of my daily attendance upon His Highness'. She also asked if her next due half-year's annuity could be paid to her executor 'towards the payment of my debts and reward of my servants' in appreciation of 'my poor service, done as well unto His Majesty in his tender age, as also unto his dearly beloved sisters, the Lady Mary's Grace and the Lady Elizabeth's Grace'.[20]

Chapter Two

Governesses

IN TUDOR TIMES a governess was a woman who looked after children in *loco parentis*. Unlike the 'Lady Mistress of the King's Nursery' who, by the reign of Henry VIII, looked after children in their infancy, the governess was either responsible for the 'governance' of older children, meaning she had overall responsibility for their upbringing and education, or she presided over their household. Because he did not have a mother, or a stepmother for the first few years of his life, Prince Edward had both a Lady Mistress and a Lady Governess until he was 6 years of age. His Lady Mistress, Baroness Bryan, presided over his nursery, whilst his Lady Governess, Anne Pakenham, Lady Sidney, presided over his household along with her husband, Sir William Sidney, Chamberlain to the little prince. Elizabeth may also have had both a Lady Mistress and a Lady Governess for a time. After the execution of her mother, her great aunt, Anne Boleyn, Lady Shelton, may have been made governess of her household, remaining in post until the reorganisation of the household following the birth of Prince Edward. Princess Mary, on the other hand, did not have a Lady Governess until she left the care of her Lady Mistress at 3 years of age.

In the early Tudor period the Lady Mistress was sometimes called the Lady Governess, and vice versa, as was the case in the Household Ordinances of Henry VII, but by the reign of Henry VIII, when the 'office and fee' of Lady Mistress had seemingly become a lifelong honour, the two were generally seen as distinct roles. Lady Salisbury, for example, is consistently referred to as Lady Governess in contemporary sources, not as Lady Mistress.[1] The role of Lady Governess was also not for life and there could be several Lady Governesses at the same time.

When Princess Mary, as Princess of Wales, was sent to live in the Welsh Marches in 1525, detailed instructions were drawn up regarding her sojourn, and these directives give us a rare and fascinating insight into the duties of the Lady Governess:

> …the Countess of Salisbury, being Lady Governess, shall according to the singular confidence that the King's Highness hath in her, give most tender regard to all such things as concern the person of the said princess, her honourable education and training in all virtuous demeanour. That is to say, at due times to serve God, from whom all grace and goodness proceedeth. Semblably at seasons convenient to use moderate exercise for taking open air in gardens, sweet and wholesome places and walks, which may confer unto her health, solace and comfort, as by the said Lady Governess shall be thought

most convenient. And likewise to pass her time most seasons at her virginals, or other instruments musical, so that the same be not too much, and without fatigation or weariness to intend to her learning of Latin tongue and French. At other seasons to dance, and amongst the residue to have good respect unto her diet, which is meet to be pure, well prepared, dressed and served, with comfortable, joyous and merry communication in all honourable and virtuous manner, and likewise unto the cleanliness and well wearing of her garments and apparel, both of her chambers and body, so that everything about her be pure, sweet, clean and wholesome as to so great a princess doeth appertain, and all corruptions, evil airs and things noisome and unpleasant to be forborne and eschewed.[2]

It is very likely that following the birth of Prince Edward in 1537 the same changes were made to Elizabeth's care as had been made to Mary's following the birth of Henry Fitzroy in 1519. Therefore, Baroness Bryan's replacement in Elizabeth's life, Blanche Milborne, Lady Herbert of Troy Parva (Lady Troy), is likely to have been Elizabeth's Lady Governess rather than her Lady Mistress. Unfortunately, it is not very clear from primary sources just how long she remained in the role. It is possible she was still Elizabeth's official Lady Governess when Henry VIII died, as she tops the list of women in attendance upon Elizabeth at his funeral, but had this been the case, then she, not Kateryn Champernon Astley, would have been in charge of Elizabeth in the household of Kateryn Parr as Lady Troy accompanied Elizabeth there. Also, Elizabeth told Sir Robert Tyrwhit in 1549 that Mistress Astley 'was put by the King's Majesty her father to be her mistress', suggesting that Mistress Astley had been in charge of the princess for some years.[3] Mistress Astley was certainly Elizabeth's governess by 1548, but because she was not a titled lady she could not be known as Lady Governess. Instead, she was simply known as Elizabeth's 'governess' or 'mistress'. It is therefore likely that Lady Troy retired as Elizabeth's Lady Governess when she became acting Lady Mistress to Prince Edward. That she was the prince's acting Lady Mistress is almost certain as Lewys Morgannwg, a Welsh bard who wrote an elegy to Lady Troy after her death, tells us:

Gorchweidwad cyn ymadaw
Tŷ Harri Wyth a'i blant draw.
I Edwart Frenin ydoedd,
Uwch ei faeth, goruchaf oedd,
Waetio yr oedd at ei Ras,
Gywirddoeth wraig o urddas.

In her last years a guardian
To Henry VIII's children.
Supreme to Edward the King,
In charge of his upbringing,
His Grace she waited upon,
A wise, dignified matron.[4]

It is difficult to see what other position she could have held that made her 'supreme' for the number of staff attending on the young prince was small. This was necessary to reduce the risk of infectious disease. According to Sir Henry Sidney, who served the prince as a boy companion from the age of 10, Edward's care was almost entirely in the hands of the Sidney family:

> ...my near kinswoman being his only nurse, my father being his Chamberlain, my mother his governess, my aunt by my mother's side in such place as among meaner [poorer] personages is called a dry nurse, for from the time he left sucking she continually lay in bed with him, so long as he remained in woman's government.[5]

Sybil Penn, now one of Hampton's Court's most famous ghosts, is usually said to have been the prince's dry nurse, and 'Mother Jak', a somewhat mysterious figure, his wet nurse, but the reverse is likely true. Sybil Penn was not a sister, stepsister, or sister-in-law to Anne Pakenham, Lady Sidney, but 'Mother Jak' probably was. Her identity has never been discovered but it is not difficult to imagine 'Mistress Pakenham' becoming 'Mother Jak' to a little boy as 'Mistress Pakenham' is something of a mouthful for a child to say. Therefore 'Mother Jak' was probably an unmarried sister of Lady Sidney. In this way, she was far more suited to the role of dry nurse than Sybil Penn, who was a married woman, and the fact that Sybil Penn was granted an annuity of £40 in 1539, 'in consideration of her services as nurse to Prince Edward', the same amount as Agnes Pendred, is further evidence that she was the Prince's wet nurse. Also a letter written by Sir Henry Sidney's father in 1538 supports this conclusion:

> I have received your letters for me to signify to you the ability of my wife's sister for the room [position] of the prince's dry nurse, to weigh the charge that shall be committed to her and to write plainly if I thought the thing meet for her. I doubt not but that she is every way an apt woman for the same, and there shall be no lack of good will in her.[6]

Blanche Milborne, Lady Herbert of Troy Parva

Born in the reign of Edward IV, in the middle years of the Wars of the Roses, Blanche Milborne, Lady Herbert of Troy Parva, is one of the Tudor period's most overlooked figures. Her parents were Simon Milborne, once Sheriff of Herefordshire, and Jane Baskerville, only child and heiress of Ralph Baskerville. Blanche grew up in a large, female dominated family, for she was one of at least eleven sisters, and in her teens or early twenties she married James Whitney, son of Robert Whitney, Lord of Whitney in Herefordshire. The couple lived, at least some of the time, in the Manor of Icomb, a medieval house in the Cotswolds that Blanche's parents had given her as a dowry. Over the next few years she and James had at least three children together, Robert, James and Elizabeth, but by the autumn of 1500 Blanche was a widow.

Following the death of her husband, Blanche married, as his second wife, William Herbert of Troy Parva. Although he was an illegitimate son of William 'the black' Herbert, first Earl of Pembroke, he was an acknowledged son and a prominent member of the powerful Herbert family. His rather illustrious title was derived from the name of his palatial manor, Troy Parva, which lay near the village of Mitchel Troy in Monmouthshire, Wales. The name Troy Parva means 'Little Troy' in Latin and the manor is said to have had a famous garden on account of William's interest in horticulture.[7] William was a lot older than Blanche, perhaps by twenty years, but the marriage is thought to have been happy and within three or four years Blanche had borne William two sons: Charles, his much needed heir, and Thomas. Sadly, little is known about these years of Blanche's life, but her marriage to William was crucial in elevating her to court circles. For although William himself was not a courtier, as a member of the Herbert family he had a very personal connection to the King. This connection went all the way back to the Wars of the Roses when William's father, one of the most powerful men in Wales, fought for the House of York. In 1461, after Edward IV of York had taken the throne from Henry VI of Lancaster, William's father, then a knight, besieged Pembroke Castle, a Lancastrian stronghold in the hands of Jasper Tudor, Earl of Pembroke, and forced the earl to surrender. He then took the earl's 4-year-old nephew, Henry Tudor, into his custody, and the boy was later made his ward. This little Henry was, of course, the future monarch, Henry VII. Sir William took the child to Raglan Castle, his principal residence, and for the next few years Henry lived there with the Herbert family. In reward for Sir William's siege of Pembroke Castle, the King gave him the castle, and in 1468 made him Earl of Pembroke. The following year, however, the new earl was taken prisoner at the Battle of Edgecote and was executed. Anne Herbert, his wife, fled with Henry and her own children to Weobly in Herefordshire, but soon Jasper Tudor was back on the scene and regained custody of his nephew.

Years later, when he was king, Henry looked back on his time with the Herberts fondly. Although they were of a rival house, the Herberts had taken good care of him, treating him like a member of the family and providing him with a stellar education. Henry was grateful, especially considering the fate of the Princes in the Tower who, if the voice of history speaks true, were killed by their own uncle, of the same house, in the name of power. Henry therefore invited his former guardian, Anne Herbert, to court and personally thanked her for taking such good care of him. He also knighted her son, Walter, who had deserted the Yorkists at Bosworth to fight alongside his boyhood companion. The Herberts, then, were highly thought of by the King and were personally acquainted with him.

In 1502, not long after their wedding, William and Blanche had the honour of hosting the King and Queen at their home, Troy Parva, when the royal couple visited on their way to stay with Sir Walter and his wife at Raglan Castle. The visit was a proud moment in the history of Troy Parva and was commemorated for years to come by the renaming of several chambers in honour of the King and

Queen. William remained in royal favour into the reign of Henry VIII and in 1516 he received a knighthood. From them on, Blanche became known as Lady Herbert of Troy Parva, or Lady Troy for short. By now, the Herbert family influence had waned. All William's legitimate brothers were dead, the earldom and castle of Pembroke had been lost, and Raglan Castle, along with other Herbert strongholds, had fallen to the Somerset family by way of marriage. Raglan Castle was now owned by Charles Somerset, Earl of Worcester, former husband of William's niece, Elizabeth Herbert, who had inherited the castle after Sir Walter's death. Charles Somerset was related to the King and was a man of great importance at court for he was the Lord Chamberlain. Sir William and Lady Troy were on good terms with the earl, who was probably godfather to their son, Charles, and in the event that his own line died out, Sir William intended to make the earl's son, Henry Somerset, Lord Herbert, his heir, for Lord Herbert was his great nephew. Henry's wife was no less a person than the King's first cousin, Margaret Courtenay, daughter of Princess Catherine of York, the King's maternal aunt. So, despite the decline of the Herbert family fortune, Sir William still had very powerful connections right at the heart of court.

In 1524, when Blanche was middle-aged, her husband died. He had lived a long and prosperous life and left her a wealthy widow, trusting that she would 'keep herself sole'.[8] How Blanche spent the next few years is something of a mystery, but as a woman of influence in the Welsh Marches, she is likely to have attended the court of Princess Mary between 1525 and 1527 when, in her role as Princess of Wales, the 9-year-old royal took up residence in the Welsh Marches, residing primarily at Ludlow Castle and Tickenhill Palace in Bewdley. When Princess Mary was recalled to London, and the King began his history-making quest to divorce her mother, Lady Troy probably began attending the royal court in the company of Elizabeth Browne, Countess of Worcester, the new wife of Henry Somerset, Lord Herbert, who was now Earl of Worcester after his father's death in 1526. Elizabeth Browne was a woman of considerable standing at court. Not only was she a close friend of the King's prospective bride, Anne Boleyn, but her late sister had been the wife of Sir Charles Brandon, who was now married to the King's favourite sister, Mary Tudor, Queen Dowager of France.

By the time Princess Elizabeth was born in the September of 1533, Lady Troy was a respected figure at court. She was accomplished, learned, cultured and dignified. She could speak two or three languages, was unwaveringly loyal to the Tudors, and she had a pleasant and pragmatic personality that endeared people to her. She was also the mother of four fine sons, a fact that is sure to have impressed Henry VIII. What role Lady Troy played in Elizabeth's life during Baroness Bryan's time as Lady Mistress is unclear, but in 1601 a man named John Notte claimed that 'my mother was chosen and brought to the court by my Lady Herbert of Troy to have been Her Majesty's nurse, and had been chosen before all other had her gracious mother [Anne Boleyn] had her own will therein'.[9] If this is true, then Lady Troy was involved in selecting staff for the nursery, and although she may not have had this particular recommendation acted upon, perhaps she was responsible for the appointment of her sister's daughter, Blanche Parry, as a rocker or nursemaid. As Baroness Bryan would have needed a deputy in the nursery, for she would not have been able to be present all the time, perhaps Lady Troy was her deputy, serving as acting Lady Mistress in her absence. But, whatever her role, when Baroness Bryan transferred to Prince Edward's nursery in 1537, Lady Troy was chosen to replace her, probably in the role of Lady Governess. Not only did she have all the personal qualities needed for the role but she had the necessary experience, for according to Lewys Morgannwg she had worked as a governess in her youth. Sadly, the bard does not give details of time, place or persons, but perhaps she had worked for the Herberts or Somersets.

Although it is not known exactly when Baroness Bryan relinquished full responsibility for Elizabeth, Lady Troy was already taking charge of the princess during Prince Edward's christening which, like Elizabeth's, took place three days after his birth:

> Lady Elizabeth went with her sister, Lady Mary, and Lady Herbert
> of Troy to bear the [prince's] train.[10]

By now, Elizabeth had a good relationship with her half-sister. Mary's feelings towards the child had softened following the execution of her mother and, having a natural fondness for children, she could not resist mothering the little girl and giving her gifts of beautiful clothes, just as Anne Boleyn had done before. Mary also had a good relationship with Lady Troy, for the two had history, and as Lady Troy was probably more conservative than reformist in religion, there were no obvious points of conflict.

Following a time of mourning for Queen Jane, the dysfunctional family of Henry VIII entered a rare period of domestic tranquillity. Now that he had his precious son, the King was in no rush to remarry, and now that he and Princess Mary were reconciled, there were no family quarrels. As Elizabeth was still only 4 years of age, she still needed nursery care, so the new Lady Governess was assisted in her duties by Kateryn Champernon, who had joined the nursery in Baroness Bryan's time, Elyzabeth Cavendish, who may have been the dry nurse, Mary Norris, who was still in attendance, and Elyzabeth Grey, Lady Gerald. Formerly the Countess of Kildare, Lady Gerald was the King's first cousin as her father was Thomas Grey, Marquess of Dorset, maternal half-brother of Elizabeth of York. She was well thought of by the King, and high in his favour, even though she had married Gerald Fitzgerald, 9th Earl of Kildare, against her family's wishes. The earl, who was loyal to the King, had served as Lord Deputy of Ireland for a time, but in 1534 his loyalty had come into question and he was imprisoned in the Tower of London. Lady Gerald, then known as Lady Kildare, had stayed with her husband in the Tower, tenderly nursing him as he had been crippled by a gunshot wound in a recent battle, but the weak and sick earl is said to have died of a broken heart when his son, known as Silken Thomas, raised a rebellion in Ireland for his sake. This rebellion was eventually crushed, by no less a person than Lord Leonard Grey, Lady Gerald's brother, but Silken Thomas was executed and the earldom of Kildare was stripped from the Fitzgeralds. With her stepson's death, Lady Gerald's 12-year-old son, Gerald Fitzgerald, became the family's new figurehead, but Lady Gerald had little contact with her son as he spent the next few years on the run in Ireland. Her younger son, Edward, however, was mysteriously abandoned at her home in Lancashire, and the devoted mother was successful in her quest to have custody of the boy so he could be 'brought up in virtue'.[11] Just when Lady Gerald joined Elizabeth's nursery is unclear, but it is almost certain that in 1534, when she arrived in England from Ireland, she left her daughter, Elyzabeth Fitzgerald, who was about 7 years of age, in the princess's nursery to be brought up alongside her. This little girl was probably still there in 1538, when her mother was in attendance, and, ironically, she, Mary Norris and Princess Elizabeth all had something sinister in common – they had all lost a parent in the terrifying fortress that was the Tower of London and they all had a parent buried there.

In addition to having charge of Elizabeth's ladies and gentlewomen, Lady Troy was also in charge of the rest of the nursery staff which had grown to include: two chamberers, Jane Broadbelt and Alice Huntercombe, who probably had some responsibility for Elizabeth's clothes and for keeping her nursery clean and tidy; Joanne Hilton, the resident laundress; three gentlemen, Thomas Tyrell (Torell), Robert Porter and Richard Sandes; two yeomen, Gabriel Tenant and David Morgan (a probable grandson); two grooms of the chamber, Richard Foster and William Russell; a chaplain, Sir Raffe Taylor; and a woodbearer, known only as Christopher. Blanche Parry was also still in attendance, by her own later testimony, and there were probably other members of staff who do not appear in surviving records.

Under Lady Troy's care, Elizabeth blossomed into a confident and clever child, but by the summer of 1539 change was once again on the horizon. With Lady Troy poised to replace Baroness Bryan as Lady Mistress to the prince, and with Elizabeth fast approaching her milestone sixth birthday, which marked the end of her nursery years, a new way of life was dawning for the princess. For Lady Troy, the timing of Baroness Bryan's retirement was probably a good one, for she was better suited to the task of caring for younger children than of educating older ones, but the kind-hearted woman had become very attached to Elizabeth so leaving her in favour of the prince cannot have been easy, especially if Elizabeth had not taken Baroness Bryan's departure very well when the prince was born. But of course, Lady Troy, like Baroness Bryan, was not going very far, as the two royal children continued to share an establishment, so she would still get to see Elizabeth regularly.

In 1544, when Prince Edward's nursey was disbanded and his women dismissed, Lady Troy resumed attending upon Elizabeth, perhaps after spending that summer and Christmas at Troy Parva. Although she may have remained Elizabeth's official Lady Governess, even after transferring to the prince's nursery, as this is unlikely she probably returned to the princess's service as one of her lady attendants. This would allow her to spend time with the little girl she adored whilst taking things easier in a state of semi-retirement. After all, she was now in her seventies, and although in good health, was probably happy for Kateryn Champernon to have the stress and worry of managing Elizabeth's domestic needs and demanding educational schedule. But whatever Lady Troy's exact position, she continued to be Elizabeth's most prestigious attendant and for the next few years was an important presence in her life. She was given the honour of being Elizabeth's principal bedfellow and she continued to have an influence over the women appointed to serve her. One of these was her own granddaughter, Blanche Whitney, who entered the princess's service sometime after the death of her father, Robert Whitney, Lady Troy's eldest son, in 1541. Lady Troy also secured a position for another granddaughter of hers, Anne Morgan, in the service of Princess Mary.[12] However, it would not be for serving Princess Mary that Anne would be remembered, for in 1545 she married Elizabeth's first cousin, Henry Carey, future Baron Hunsdon and son of Mary Boleyn, and Anne would become one of the Virgin Queen's most important and long-serving ladies.

In the January of 1547, after years of crippling health problems that saw him balloon in size, King Henry VIII died at Whitehall Palace. The following month he was given a magnificent funeral and laid to rest in Windsor Castle beside his favourite wife, the one to have given him a prince, Jane Seymour. Lady Troy, like all Elizabeth's servants, was given black livery for the occasion, and as well as topping the list of 'ladies and gentlewomen attending upon my Lady Elizabeth's Grace', she received a higher allowance of black cloth than everyone else. After the funeral, Lady Troy continued to attend upon Elizabeth, and for a while lived with her in the household of Kateryn Parr, but as Lady Troy was never questioned regarding the sordid saga of the 'Lord High Admiral' that played out there, she probably retired in the winter of that year.

For the rest of her life Lady Troy lived in the home she had shared with her late husband, Troy Parva. The house now belonged to her son, Charles, but she had a furnished apartment within it where she could live independently.[13] Depending on the state of her health, she may have visited Elizabeth from time to time, especially in the summer when the weather was better for travelling, but even if she was not able to travel, she surely kept in touch with Elizabeth, and the women of her world, by letter. In her retirement, Lady Troy was receiving an annuity of £40, an annuity that had been granted to her by Henry VIII, possibly when she retired from Elizabeth's nursery or when Edward's was disbanded, and she was also receiving a small annuity of £7 from Elizabeth, perhaps as a token of appreciation for her many years of dedicated service.[14]

Lady Troy outlived the Boy King she had looked after, and is thought to have lived well into the reign of Queen Mary, but, like Baroness Bryan, she did not live to see Elizabeth become queen. At some point between the years 1552 and 1557, probably closer to the latter, she passed away at her home in Troy Parva. No doubt the news of her passing was met with sincere grief by the future queen as Lady Troy had played a huge part in her life. According to Lewys Morgannwg, Lady Troy was a woman of grace, wisdom, kindness and charity, a woman who 'gave meals to the poor and feeble' (i dlawd gwan didlawd giniaw) and 'fed with her own hand the old blind' (i'r dall hen rhôi fwyd â'i llaw).[15] These values she no doubt instilled in the little red-headed girl she helped to raise, values that made her a queen for the poor as well as for the rich, and the first leader in world history to introduce the welfare state.

Kateryn Champernon Astley (Part One)

Kateryn Champernon, better known in history as 'Kat Ashley' or 'Kat Astley', was the eldest daughter of Sir Philip Champernon of Modbury in Devon and his wife, Kateryn Carew.[16] While her exact date of birth is unknown, she was probably born between 1500 and 1506 in the Manor of Aston Rowant, at the foot of the Chiltern Hills in Oxfordshire, where her parents were living at the time.[17] The Champernons were of Norman descent, hailing from Cambernon in Normandy, and they first came to England with William the Conqueror. By the late fifteenth century they were firmly established in Devon and had married into many of the county's leading families, including the powerful Courtenays. In fact, Sir Philip's mother, Margaret, was a Courtenay, and through her he was a first cousin of William Courtenay, husband of Henry VIII's illustrious aunt, Catherine of York. The Champernons therefore had friends and relatives in very high places and during the reign of Henry VIII they reached the height of their influence and success. Very little is known about Sir Philip's court career, but he served the King as an Esquire of the Body and was made High Sheriff of Devon in 1526. He was knighted soon after, and following the dissolution of the monasteries was amongst the King's friends and favourites to benefit from grants of land.

Kat probably spent most of her childhood in Devon, living with her parents and siblings in Modbury Manor, an ancient, castellated mansion that had been in her family since the early fourteenth century. Her parents had inherited the manor in 1503, upon the death of Sir John Champernon, Kat's grandfather, and by the 1510s it was their principal residence. Kat had at least seven siblings, but as her mother had been a young bride, there was a generation between the eldest and the youngest.[18] Kat therefore grew up with the first of her siblings, Joan, Frances and John. When she was 10 or 11 years of age, she may have left home for Tiverton Castle. This magnificent, moated fortress was the home of Catherine of York, widowed since 1511, and the Plantagenet princess kept a sophisticated court at the castle. Famously taking a vow of celibacy after her husband's death, Princess Catherine was devoutly religious, but she also loved music, banqueting, fine clothes and horse riding. She kept a number of animals at the castle and had a small library of printed books and manuscripts. In attendance on her person were seven maidens and it is quite possible that Kat and her sisters were amongst those who served over the years. At Tiverton, in such a prestigious setting, Kat would have acquired all the social graces and feminine skills needed to succeed at the royal court and an education beyond what was typical for a gentlewoman.

Sadly, nothing at all is known about Kat's life before she entered Elizabeth's service in the summer or autumn of 1536. Her sisters, Joan and Frances, married young, Joan marrying Robert Gamage of Coity Castle in Wales, and Frances marrying Roger Budockside, a ward of Princess Catherine's son, Henry Courtenay, future Marquess of Exeter, but Kat remained single. Perhaps she stayed on at Tiverton Castle, attending upon Princess Catherine until her death in 1527; perhaps she went on to serve in the household of her son; perhaps she attended upon her own grandmother, Kateryn Huddesfield, Lady Carew, who is thought to have lived into the 1530s; or perhaps she served in the household of Katherine of Aragon or Anne Boleyn, both of whom died in 1536. Kat may also have returned to Modbury Manor to educate her own younger siblings, perhaps explaining her close bond with them, or perhaps, like Lady Troy, she become a governess to a noble family. Although very unlikely, it is also possible that Kat was in a convent until the smaller ones closed that summer. The closest convent to Modbury was Cornworthy Priory, which had housed a community of Augustinian nuns since the thirteenth century, and it was dissolved in the spring/summer of 1536.[19] It was not unusual in families with lots of daughters for one or more to enter a convent as finding husbands (and expensive dowries) for all of them was difficult, and by her late teens Kat had three more sisters: Elizabeth, Catherine and Joanne. In Tudor times it was not uncommon for younger siblings to share a name with older siblings, especially when there was a decade or more between them, but the fact that there were two Champernon girls named 'Katherine' and two named 'Joan' has led to great confusion over their identities.[20]

Whatever the truth of Kat's past, she arrived in Elizabeth's nursery amidst all the turmoil in the princess's household following the execution of Anne Boleyn. Her arrival was undoubtedly a relief to Baroness Bryan, who may have been struggling with staff shortages on top of everything else, and she received a warm welcome as is evident from a letter she was forced to write to Cromwell a few weeks later:

> Right honourable and my singular good lord, after my duty remembered, this may be most humbly to thank Your Lordship for the great goodness I find in you divers ways: which is not only that you were the very mean to prefer me to the room that I am in, and, by your letters, in the same the better accepted and regarded, much more than I am worthy to be, but also as I right well perceive by my friends Your Lordship persevereth in your goodness in reporting the best of me to the King's Grace, wherein I have good cause to think myself as much bound to Your Lordship as I am to my father or any friend that I have living.

The reason for this letter was the financial hardship Kat was facing due to a lack of salary. Why she was not receiving a wage is unclear, but her troubles are a further indication of the chaos in Elizabeth's household following the execution of her mother. Struggling to make ends meet Kat had no choice but to ask Cromwell for help:

> As much as it hath pleased the King's Majesty, by your mean, to call me to that room, which I am not able to maintain [i.e. continue

in] to his honour unless His Grace appoint me some yearly stipend towards my living. I thought therefore meet, most humbly, to desire Your Lordship to have me in remembrance for the same to the King's Highness at such convenient time as you think best. I would have been loath to have troubled Your Lordship with this rude writing except very necessity had moved me so to do, and loath I will be to charge my father, who hath as much to do with that little living he hath as any man that I know.[21]

Kat's letter clearly met with success, for she remained in post, but just how much she received as her 'yearly stipend' is unknown. Evidently Kat felt indebted to Cromwell for her position, so she must have been appointed upon his recommendation, but undoubtedly others played a part in her appointment too. Her father, Sir Philip, was a man of some influence, and her brother, John, was a trusted courtier who was married to Kateryn Blount, half-sister of Elizabeth's godmother, Gertrude Blount, Marchioness of Exeter. Kat also had other family connections that made her a suitable attendant. Through her mother, she was a second cousin to Sir William Carey, late husband of Mary Boleyn, and she was a sister-in-law to Robert Gamage, brother of Margrett Gamage, wife of Elizabeth's great uncle, William Howard, future Baron Howard of Effingham.[22]

Elizabeth soon came to think the world of Kat, who was jolly and kind, and Kat came to love her dearly. With Baroness Bryan now in her late sixties, and Lady Troy not much younger when she took over, it was probably left to Kat to take care of Elizabeth on a practical level. In this way, it was probably Kat who took charge of dressing her, bathing her, and of nursing her when she was sick, and when she began her schooling, Kat is likely to have assisted Lady Troy in teaching her. Kat was an excellent teacher, for she was learned and accomplished and possibly experienced, and Lady Troy may have left her to teach Elizabeth, and young Mistress Fitzgerald, 'subjects' whilst she taught them 'accomplishments'.

When Lady Troy left to become Lady Mistress to Prince Edward, probably in the last quarter of 1539, Kat was put in charge of Elizabeth. By now, Kat was in her mid to late thirties, considerably younger than the matrons usually appointed, and as an untitled, unmarried woman, was not the obvious choice to replace Lady Troy. However, it was not always easy to find a titled woman willing to take on the responsibility of raising a royal, as Cardinal Wolsey had discovered when he was tasked with finding a temporary Lady Governess for Princess Mary in 1521, and with Elizabeth being the daughter of a disgraced queen, the task would be all the harder. But Kat was up for the challenge and she had a powerful new advocate at court, Anthony Denny, who had recently married her sister, Joanne, and replaced Sir Francis Bryan in the Privy Chamber. The King may also have been moved to appoint Kat if she had been educated by his aunt, Catherine of York, giving her a royal qualification, and perhaps Elizabeth's great affection for the west country woman played a part, especially if, as new evidence suggests, the King was consumed by guilt for killing her mother.[23] Although homely, rather than glamorous, Kat was about the same age as Anne Boleyn, and with her dark hair and eyes she may have reminded the King of his former bride. Of course, it was the King's wives that Elizabeth called 'mother', and she famously had four stepmothers in her young life, but it was with Kat that she came to have the deepest bond, a bond that was akin to mother and daughter. Indeed, Kat loved Elizabeth so much that she probably sacrificed her own romantic happiness to wait until she was beyond childbearing age to marry so she could keep her position and not have to part from her beloved princess.

Kat's promotion to governess probably coincided with Elizabeth's milestone sixth birthday. This meant that changes had to be made to the princess's care to cater for the needs of an older child, and as well as beginning her education in earnest, Elizabeth also began to have horse riding lessons. Kat herself is not known to have had a passion for horses, though her future husband, John Astley, certainly did, but Blanche Parry, who was now promoted to gentlewoman attendant at last, is thought to have been a keen rider. As a new decade dawned, a decade of mixed fortunes, Blanche became Kat's principal assistant. Lady Gerald and Elyzabeth Cavendish had retired, the latter to marry a man named Richard Snow, and Mary Norris left that winter to become a Maid of Honour to the King's fourth wife, Anne of Cleves. This left Elizabeth with only three gentlewomen attendants: Blanche, Elyzabeth Fitzgerald, who had taken her mother's place, and new recruit Mary Hill. Mary, who was not much older than Elizabeth, was a daughter of Richard Hill, the King's late Sergeant of the Cellar, and she owed her appointment entirely to her mother who had repeatedly petitioned the King on her behalf. Unsuccessful at first, on the grounds that Mary 'had too much youth about her' and because 'Her Grace was full furnished', Mistress Hill's persistence eventually paid off and Mary was chosen to serve over the daughters of Lady Lisle (who had sent Kat's sister a gift in the hope of good effect) and over many other girls whose mothers 'have had nay in like suit'.[24] Because of her tender age, Mary was more of a companion than a servant, and she and Elizabeth soon became very close. The two little girls probably did everything together, from schooling to dancing to horse riding, and in most activities they were probably joined by Elyzabeth Fitzgerald who was no more than 13 or 14 years of age. Indeed, Kat and Blanche were Elizabeth's only adult attendants, aside from her chamberers and other lower ranking staff, so the two women had to develop a good working relationship in order to take care of all Elizabeth's needs and those of her young attendants. This they managed to do, both united in their love for Elizabeth, and their working relationship was so successful that it lasted decades.

For a while, Elizabeth's new world was a good one. She enjoyed her lessons in the schoolroom, for she was a bright and curious child who loved to learn, and she proved to be a natural upon a horse. The King's fifth marriage to Katheryn Howard, her mother's first cousin, also bettered her world, for the teenage queen made much of her little stepdaughter in public and showered her with gifts in private. Elizabeth came to adore her stepmother, who was fun-loving and vivacious, so when Queen Katheryn was suddenly gone from her life by the fall of an axe, Elizabeth's world was shattered. The difficult task of telling Elizabeth about her stepmother's fate probably fell to Kat, unless Princess Mary or another relative told her, and with everyone talking about Katheryn, and comparing her case to Anne Boleyn's, it may have been impossible to keep from Elizabeth the terrible truth about her own mother's death. However, if the King had ordered a silence concerning her mother, a silence it would be perilous to break, then Kat and Blanche, and all those around the little princess, would have had to do their best to keep her in ignorance. That there was a 'hush, hush' over Anne Boleyn is almost certain, for even years later, when Elizabeth was in her teens, Thomas Seymour, Lord High Admiral, sarcastically said to one of her gentlemen 'no words of Boleyn'.[25] Unfathomably, then, Elizabeth may have been an adult, or almost so, before she learnt the truth about her mother, but in the long corridors of power at court, and in the shadows of servants, she may have heard whispers over the years, whispers that created a horror story in her mind, and it is, perhaps, significant that from the time of Katheryn's death she allegedly said she would never marry.[26]

By the time King Henry married his sixth wife, Kateryn Parr, in the July of 1543, Elyzabeth Fitzgerald had blossomed into a beautiful and witty young lady. At 16 going on 17, she had outgrown the confines of Elizabeth's world, so was chosen to serve Queen Kateryn as a Maid of Honour. While at court, Elyzabeth caught the eye of Henry Howard, Earl of Surrey, who forever immortalised her as 'Fair Geraldine' in a poem:

> From Tuscan came my lady's worthy race.
> Fair Florence was sometime her ancient seat.
> The western isle, whose pleasant shore doth face
> Wild Camber's cliffs, first gave her lively heat.
> Fostered she was with milk of Irish breast:
> Her sire an earl, her dame of prince's blood.
> From tender years, in Britain did she rest,
> With a king's child, who tasteth ghostly food.
> Hunsdon did first present her to mine eyen:
> Bright is her hue, and Geraldine she hight [called].
> Hampton me taught to wish her first for mine,
> And Windsor, alas, doth chase me from her sight.
> Her beauty of kind, her virtues from above;
> Happy is he that can obtain her love.[27]

It was not the Earl of Surrey, however, that Elyzabeth went on to marry, for by 1544 she was the wife of Sir Anthony Browne, the King's Master of the Horse. A widower with several children, Sir Anthony was decades older than his bride, but the marriage was seemingly happy and Elyzabeth bore him two sons. Sadly, the two boys died in infancy.

The year 1545, which began unremarkably for Elizabeth and her women, became a memorable one in Tudor history for it was the year Henry VIII's famous flagship, *The Mary Rose*, sunk between Portsmouth and the Isle of Wight in the Battle of the Solent. This was a sea skirmish fought between the invading fleets of Francis I of France and Henry VIII's defending warships. The battle was inconclusive, and the invasion failed, but the sinking of *The Mary Rose*, with the loss of all its crew, made history. For Kat, and especially for young Mary Norris, the loss was personal, for the ship's captain, Sir George Carew, was Kat's first cousin and Mary's husband. The couple had married in the summer of 1541 and Mary, now Lady Carew, had received a chain of beads with 'crosses, pillars, and tassels' from Queen Katheryn as a wedding present.[28] Mary was with the King on the Battlements of Southsea Castle, watching as the English fleet set sail for battle, when *The Mary Rose* suddenly capsized and sank beneath the waves. Overcome with grief, knowing her beloved husband could not survive, she 'fell into a swooning' and had to be comforted by the King.[29] The year 1545 also changed Kat's life forever for it was the year her father died. Not long after the sinking of *The Mary Rose* he made his will and passed away that winter. Although he had six daughters, at least five still living, only Kat is mentioned in his will, perhaps because she was the eldest and the only one still unmarried. Sir Philip declared that 'Katherine Champernon, my daughter', was to be executor of his will, along with her mother and uncle (another Sir George Carew) but on the understanding that 'neither the said Sir George, nor yet the said Katherine, shall have any part or meddling with my goods or chattels unless my said wife die before my will be performed'.[30] Lady Champernon was the main beneficiary of the will along with Kat's only surviving brother, Arthur. Sadly, John had died some years before, but he had fathered at least one child with his wife, a little boy named Henry, who at 7 years of age succeeded his grandfather as Lord of Modbury.

The following year was a much better one for Kat and Mary. It was a year of new beginnings and of surprising romances. Kat married John Astley, a man somewhat younger than herself, who was attending upon Prince Edward, whilst Mary had a new suitor, Kat's younger brother, Arthur. Although John Astley and Princess Elizabeth were not related by blood, they considered themselves kin as they shared an aunt by marriage: Elizabeth Wood, Lady Boleyn, wife of Elizabeth's great uncle, Sir James Boleyn, and sister to John's mother, Anne Wood. Upon her marriage to John, Kat's surname changed, but as spellings had not yet been standardised, she is known to history by two surnames: Astley and Ashley. Astley was the name eventually adopted by the family, and by Kat herself, but in contemporary records she is more commonly referred to as 'Mistress Ashley'. Upon her marriage to Arthur, Mary retired from the court scene to live permanently in Devon, and although she may have visited court from time to time, she was not a part of Elizabeth's story when she became queen.

By now, Elizabeth was 13 years of age and had grown into an accomplished and attractive young lady who excelled at her studies. Kat continued to oversee her education, and to have a role in teaching her, but the princess now had her own schoolmaster, William Grindal. The eminent scholar was a protégé of Roger Ascham, and in an undated letter to Kat, Ascham praised the hardworking governess for her efforts with Elizabeth:

> Gentle Mrs Astley, would God my wit wist [knew] what words would express the thanks you have deserved of all true English hearts for that noble imp [Elizabeth], by your labour and wisdom so flourishing

in all godly godliness, the fruit whereof doth even now redound to Her Grace's high honour and profit, of singular commendations amongst men, and desert at God's hands, to the rejoicing of all that hear it, to the example of all that will follow, and to me, although the least amongst the most, yet one that knoweth it best.

He also offered words of advice on how best to tutor Elizabeth so she would 'come to that end in perfectness' which 'her wit, painfulness in her study, true trade of her teaching, and your diligent overseeing doth most constantly promise'. His advice was to take a gentle approach to learning, to teach little by little, for 'if you pour much drink at once into a goblet, the most part will dash out and run over; if you pour it softly you may fill it even to the top'. In concluding his letter, he asked Kat to 'commend me to my good Lady of Troy', who was once again in attendance, 'and all that company of godly gentlewomen'.[31]

The honeymoon for Kat was soon over, however, as the death of Henry VIII in the January of 1547 ushered in a very difficult decade for her and Elizabeth. Yet, the difficulties to come could not have been predicted in the spring of that year when Elizabeth's stepmother, the widowed queen, Kateryn Parr, was made her guardian. Now known as the Queen Dowager, Kateryn was the longest lasting of Henry's wives after Katherine of Aragon, and during their marriage she had worked hard to foster a relationship with his children and to improve theirs with their father by having them at court often. Kateryn had also been a tender nurse to Henry in his final agonising years. There was every reason to hope, then, that Elizabeth would continue 'flourishing in all godly godliness' in the household of the Queen Dowager, who was considered pious, virtuous and studious, but the usually wise Kateryn Parr made a rather foolish decision that spring when she secretly married her former beau, Thomas Seymour, Lord High Admiral. The admiral was irresistibly handsome, confident and charming, and was popular with the ladies. Kat considered him quite the catch, and ever since Elizabeth had reached the age of marriageability, which was 12 for a girl and 14 for a boy, she had actively encouraged the match. But Elizabeth's father had made no moves that way, and now that the admiral's nephew, Prince Edward, was king, the admiral knew he would never be permitted to marry Elizabeth by his brother, Edward Seymour, Duke of Somerset, who was now Lord Protector of England as the Boy King was too young to rule. There was something of a rivalry between the two brothers, both wanting power and prestige, and they did not get along. As he could not have Elizabeth, the admiral rekindled his relationship with the Queen Dowager, for he wanted a high profile marriage, and he successfully convinced her to marry him even though she was in formal mourning for the King. By now, Elizabeth was living with her stepmother in Chelsea Place, a manor gifted to Kateryn by the King, and as the flirtatious admiral knew he had been championed as a potential husband for Elizabeth by her governess, the three of them living under one roof was a recipe for disaster.

Much has been written about 'the Seymour affair', but everything known about this troubling episode in Elizabeth's history comes from testimonies gathered months later. In the January of 1549, Thomas Seymour, now a widower as Kateryn

Parr had died in childbirth a few months earlier, was arrested and sent to the Tower of London on suspicion of treason. The Lord Protector had been very reluctant to arrest his brother, despite their poor relationship, but the accusations against the admiral were piling up and it was even said that he was scheming to kidnap the King and seize power. A full scale investigation into the admiral's activities ensued and, unfortunately for Kat, one of the people of most interest to the Privy Council was herself. Not long after the admiral's arrest, a party of men arrived at Hatfield Palace, where Elizabeth was residing, placed the 15-year-old princess under house arrest and took Kat away for questioning. Thomas Parry, the princess's cofferer (accountant) and a distant relative of Blanche's, was taken too, and they were imprisoned in a part of Westminster known as Petty Calais (on account of the French wool merchants who lived there). Upon arrival they were subjected to a gruelling interrogation of all their dealings with the admiral. Had he intended to marry Elizabeth? Had they colluded with him to arrange a secret marriage? Was he planning to seize the throne in Elizabeth's name? Kat presumably proclaimed her innocence, as did Thomas Parry, but otherwise she said nothing. Meanwhile, Kat's husband, who happened to be in London, was seized and thrown into The Fleet, a major prison on the bank of the River Fleet. After days of futile questioning, Thomas Parry was taken to the Tower of London, and Kat soon followed. It must have been with terror that she entered the foreboding fortress, for it had only been eight years since Princess Mary's 'second mother', the Countess of Salisbury, had been put to death in one of the most bloody and brutal executions in the Tower's history. But Kat was a brave woman and she maintained her silence, even though she was thrown into a prison cell so horribly cold that she could not sleep by night, or see by day, for she had to block its glassless window with straw to keep out the freezing winter wind. Thomas Parry, however, who had been a wreck since his capture, finally cracked, perhaps after threats of torture, and began talking.

When Kat was told that Thomas Parry had 'confessed' she could not believe it. Only when she was brought face to face with him, and he told her in person that he 'stood fast' to all he had said, did she accept it. As angry as she was frightened, she allegedly called him a 'false wretch' as he had 'promised he would never confess unto death'.[32] Fortunately, his statement was more scandalous than it was incriminating, but scandalous was dangerous, and there was just enough meat on the bones of his words to give the interrogators something to make a meal of. For Thomas alleged there was a mutual 'good will' between Elizabeth and the admiral to marry and that the admiral had been considered as a husband for Elizabeth during her father's lifetime. He said that Mistress Astley had a very favourable opinion of the admiral, though dared not speak of him for fear of losing her position, and that she wanted him to marry Elizabeth more than any other man. He also said that Mistress Astley had told him that the Queen Dowager was jealous of Elizabeth and had once caught the princess in an embrace with the admiral. He also divulged that the admiral had enquired about Elizabeth's lands, possessions and wealth, and confessed that he (Parry) now feared he had been used 'for an instrument to serve their purposes.'[33] Kat was now in serious trouble, for these allegations might be seen as evidence that she had plotted with the admiral, and she could no longer afford to stay silent. For however foolish she had been in encouraging a match between Elizabeth and the admiral in the days of Henry VIII, perhaps even later, she had done so with the best of intentions, genuinely believing he would be a good husband for Elizabeth. Whether she still believed that after everything that had happened in the Queen Dowager's household is unclear, for the testimonies are contradictory, but there is probably a lot of truth in Kat's self-confessed answer to Parry when he told her the admiral was 'a worthy gentleman' to marry Elizabeth if it was 'the council's pleasure'. 'So think I', Kat had replied, 'if it were the council's mind, but else I had rather he were hanged'.[34]

In a series of statements Kat admitted having talked to Elizabeth about marrying the admiral. She admitted having told the admiral in the late king's reign that she wished the two of them were married and that she had said the same to Elizabeth many times. She confessed to having discussed the admiral with Thomas Parry and Mary Hill (now Mistress Cheke on account of her marriage to John Cheke, the renowned scholar) but she emphatically denied having been involved in any marriage plot, or of having had any 'communication or conference' with the admiral on the matter in recent months. Kat also emphatically denied having ever considered a marriage for Elizabeth without the council's consent. In fact, she claimed to have been extremely cautious in her dealings with the admiral since the death of the Queen Dowager, not least because several people, including 'her brother Denny', had warned her of the danger she was in 'if she did anything other than according to the council's mind'. Consequently, she had forbidden the admiral from coming to visit Elizabeth, unless he came with the council's consent, and she had forbidden Thomas Parry from speaking to him and from going to his house. She also told her interrogators of the admiral's improper conduct towards Elizabeth while he was her guardian and how she had been forced to admonish him many times. She told how he had repeatedly come to Elizabeth's bedchamber in the mornings, sometimes 'in his nightgown' and 'barelegged in his slippers', and had taken such liberties with her as to try and 'kiss her in her bed' or 'strike her upon the back or on the buttocks familiarly'. Kat made it clear that it was the admiral, not Elizabeth, who had behaved scandalously, and that she and Elizabeth had done everything within their power to discourage him, even making sure that Elizabeth was 'up at her book' before he came. She also corrected Parry's story about the Queen Dowager having found Elizabeth and the admiral together in an embrace, giving her own, rather different, version of events. According to her statement, when she and Elizabeth were staying with Kateryn Parr at Hanworth House, the Queen Dowager told her one day that she had looked in at a window and 'seen my Lady Elizabeth cast her arms about a man's neck'. Kat duly asked Elizabeth about this, but the princess 'denied it weeping', and all her women denied it, and Kat knew it could not be true 'for there came no man but Grindal, the schoolmaster'. She could only conclude that the Queen Dowager had made up the story because she was jealous and suspicious of her husband's interest in Elizabeth and wanted the princess to be watched more closely.[35]

Meanwhile, back at Hatfield, Elizabeth and her servants were being interrogated by Sir Robert Tyrwhit. Sir Robert was not a Privy Councillor, but he was a trusted courtier and politician, and he had served Kateryn Parr as her Master of the Horse. He was also connected to the Parrs through marriage as his cousin, Sir Edward de Burgh, had been the Queen Dowager's first husband. For all these reasons, he was judged the best person to question Elizabeth, but to his frustration and dismay he could get nothing from her. He tried every possible approach, from bullying to beguiling, but nothing worked. He even forged a letter to Blanche Parry from a friend of hers, a letter in which he said 'Mistress Ashley and her cofferer was put into the Tower' when in fact they were still at Petty Calais, in the hope that Elizabeth would break. This ploy met with some success, for after she had 'wept very tenderly a long time', Elizabeth told Sir Robert that she was now willing to tell him 'certain things' she had previously forgotten to mention, but to Sir Robert's disappointment these 'certain things' were of no great consequence. In a letter to the Lord Protector, Sir Robert wrote:

> After all this I did require her to consider her honour and the peril that might ensue, for she was but a subject; and I further declared what a woman Mistress Ashley was, with a long circumstance, saying that if she would open all things herself, that all the evil and shame would be ascribed to them, and her youth considered both with the King's Majesty, Your Grace, and the whole council, but in no way will she confess any practise by Mistress Ashley or the cofferer concerning my Lord Admiral; and yet I do see it in her face that she is guilty, and do perceive as yet she will abide more storms before she accuses Mistress Ashley.[36]

Sir Robert believed that he had a potential helper in Elyzabeth Fitzgerald, now Lady Browne, who had been visiting Elizabeth when he arrived. Believing 'there is no body may do more good to cause her to confess the truth than she, nor, in good faith, I think there is no body hath better will that she should do so than she hath, nor can wiser counsel her to it than she can', Sir Robert wanted Elyzabeth returned as she had been taken into custody along with Mary Hill, Mistress Cheke. In his assessment of Lady Browne, Sir Robert was clearly deluded, as Elyzabeth was devoted to her former mistress and would never act against her interests, but the 'Fair Geraldine' was clearly a very smooth operator who had the same effect on men as the Lord Admiral had on women. Indeed, according to the testimony of a man named William Wightman, the Lord Admiral considered using Lady Browne to further his agenda because 'she was wise and able to compass matters'. Because of this testimony, Sir Robert's request for Elyzabeth's return may have been denied, for she was seemingly held in custody for some time along with Mistress Cheke, who Sir Robert said 'may be well forborne'.[37]

It was only when he showed Elizabeth the confessions of her governess and cofferer, which she carefully examined to make sure of their signatures, that Elizabeth, 'much abashed and half breathless', was willing to make her own confession. But again, to Sir Robert's dismay, her statement was 'not so full of matter as I would it were', for despite giving details of her conversations with

Kat about the admiral, she would in no way confess 'that either Mistress Ashley or Parry willed her to any practice with my Lord Admiral either by message or writing'.[38] He was not having much luck with her servants either, for all he was getting from her women were stories about how small Elizabeth's bedchamber had been at Chelsea Place, so small that Kat had 'put out' Lady Troy, who was still her principal bedfellow, in favour of Blanche Parry, and then put out Blanche Parry and the pallet bed and taken the role upon herself. In Sir Robert's opinion, and he clearly did not have sound judgement, this was because Kat 'could not abide to have nobody lay there but only herself'. However, if this had been the case then Kat would never have permitted Lady Troy to be Elizabeth's sleeping companion 'for about two years'.[39] A more likely explanation is that Kat was so concerned about the admiral's early morning visits that she wanted to be present when he came – and not just present but sleeping in Elizabeth's bed just in case he crept in at ungodly hours. She was there when he tried to kiss Elizabeth in the bed, for she sent him away 'for shame', she was there when Kateryn Parr accompanied him and they both tickled Elizabeth in the bed, and she was there when the admiral came 'barelegged in his slippers'. It is evident from her testimonies, and from her letter to Sir Thomas Smith, Secretary of State, that she had been extremely worried about the admiral's behaviour and the damage it was doing to Elizabeth's reputation:

> As touching my lord's boldness in her chamber, the Lord I take to record, I spoke so ugly to him, and said that it was complained of to my lords of the council, but he would swear 'What do I? I would they all saw it!' that I could not make him leave it. At last I told the Queen of it, who made a small matter of it to me, and said she would come with him herself, and so she did ever after.[40]

Kat was completely helpless to resolve the situation for she was just the governess, the servant, and was expected to know her place and to obey the wishes of Elizabeth's guardians. All she could do was be present when the admiral visited, to ensure that nothing improper happened, and to try and think of ways of removing Elizabeth from the situation. It is therefore no coincidence that King Edward received a letter from his half-sister that winter asking if she could stay at court for an extended period over Christmas. The King agreed, so Kat, for a little while at least, had a much needed break. It was probably at this point that Lady Troy retired to Troy Parva, for the Queen Dowager's household was not a good place to be and all the tension was unhealthy for an old lady. The admiral's antics continued as soon as Elizabeth was back under his roof, but by the following May Kateryn Parr was pregnant and matters came to a head. Not in the best of health, perhaps due to the stress in the household, the Queen Dowager decided it was better for everyone if Elizabeth left. By now, Elizabeth's relationship with her stepmother had painfully deteriorated, for Kateryn was jealous of her young and attractive stepdaughter, even if she knew in her heart that the fault lay with her husband, and this had tarnished her love for Elizabeth. No doubt the decision was music to Kat's ears and

30

she hurried the princess to Cheshunt Manor in Hertfordshire, the grand home of her own sister, Joanne, now Lady Denny on account of her husband's knighthood.

Although Sir Robert, and many Privy Councillors, were still convinced that Mistress Astley and Thomas Parry had colluded with the admiral to bring about a secret marriage between him and Elizabeth, they had no proof. For despite their best efforts, their interrogations had dug up nothing but a lot of scandalous dirt. Consequently, neither Kat nor Thomas Parry could be charged with a crime, so it was ultimately only the admiral who was charged with planning 'by crafty and secret means' to marry Elizabeth to 'the danger' and 'great peril' of the King.[41] Kat was out of the woods, but she was not out of prison, and she was continuing to suffer. In her letter to Sir Thomas Smith, written before the admiral's conviction, she requested him to ask the Lord Protector to 'have pity on me and to forgive this my great folly that would either talk or speak of marriage to such a personage as she is, for punishment whereof I have suffered great sorrow and punishment and shame that never will out of my heart'. It was not only Kat who was shamed, for Elizabeth's reputation was in tatters. People were saying everywhere that she was pregnant with the Lord Admiral's child, a slander that could ruin her forever. Whether Sir Thomas ever did petition the Lord Protector on Kat's behalf is unknown, but one person certainly did, Elizabeth herself:

> My lord, I have a request to make unto Your Grace, which fear has made me omit till this time for two causes: the one because I saw that my request for the rumours which were spread abroad of me took so little place, which thing, when I considered, I thought I should little profit in any other suit, howbeit, now I understand that there is a Proclamation for them (for the which I give Your Grace and the rest of the council most humble thanks) I am the bolder to speak for another thing; and the other was because peradventure Your Lordship, and the rest of the council, will think that I favour her evil doing for whom I shall speak for, which is for Kateryn Ashley, that it would please Your Grace and the rest of the council to be good unto her. Which thing I do not to favour her in any evil (for that I would be sorry to do) but for these considerations which follow, the which hope doth teach me in saying that I ought not to doubt but that Your Grace and the rest of the council will think that I do it for other considerations. First, because she hath been with me a long time, and many years, and hath taken great labour and pain in bringing of me up in learning and honesty, and therefore I ought of very duty speak for her, for Saint Gregory sayeth that we are more bound to them that bringeth us up well than to our parents, for our parents do that which is natural for them, that is bringeth us into this world, but our bringers up are a cause to make us live well in it. The second is because I think that whatsoever she hath done in my Lord Admiral's matter, as concerning the marriage of me, she did it because knowing him to be one of the council, she thought he would not go about any

such thing without he had the council's consent thereunto; for I have heard her many times say that she would never have me marry in any place without Your Grace's and the council's consent. The third cause is because that it shall, and doth, make men think that I am not clear of the deed myself, but that it is pardoned in me because of my youth, because she that I loved so well is in such a place. Thus hope, prevailing more with me than fear, hath won the battle; and I have at this time gone forth with it. Which I pray God be taken no other ways than it is meant. Also, if I may be so bold, not offending, I beseech Your Grace, and the rest of the council, to be good to Master Ashley, her husband, which because he is my kinsman I would be glad he should do well.[42]

Kat was released within days of Elizabeth's letter, but, for now, there would be no happy reunion for the two. The Privy Council had decided that Mistress Astley was unfit to be a royal governess and they officially informed Elizabeth of this by letter: 'Katheryn Ashley, who heretofore hath had the special charge to see to the good education and government of your person, hath showed herself far unmeet to occupy any such place longer about Your Grace'. Instead they appointed Lady Tyrwhit, Sir Robert's wife, 'to remain about you in lieu of the said Ashley, and to commit unto her the same charge about your person that Ashley had'.[43] Elizabeth was devastated, Kat too, for she had promised that 'if it were possible that I might be with Her Grace again … never would I speak nor wish of marriage, no, not to win all the world', but the King's advisors were resolved and Kat's days as Elizabeth's governess were over.

Elizabeth Oxenbridge, Lady Tyrwhit

Historically, Lady Tyrwhit has not received much attention from historians as she was only Elizabeth's governess for a very short time. Yet, during that time she was invested with as much authority over Elizabeth as Lady Troy and Kat Astley had formerly had. Although Elizabeth was 15 years of age, she was still considered a child in law, for the age of marriageability was not the age of adulthood, and even when a girl married at 12 it was not usual for the marriage to be consummated until she was in her mid to late teens. With Kat in prison, and Lady Troy in retirement, Elizabeth was left without a governess, so Elizabeth Oxenbridge, Lady Tyrwhit, was appointed to the role. The result, initially, was domestic fireworks.

Lady Tyrwhit was the daughter of Sir Goddard Oxenbridge, Sheriff of Surrey and Sussex, and his second wife, Anne Fiennes, who was related to Mary Norris. The family home was Brede Place, a medieval manor in the village of Brede in Sussex, and for reasons that are not altogether clear, Sir Goddard has become attached to a notorious village legend: The Brede Ogre. According to this legend, Sir Goddard was a giant of a man who roamed the streets of Brede every night looking for children to eat for supper. Conventional weapons could not kill him, so the story goes, for he had super human powers that made him impervious to metal, so only objects made of wood could harm him. Afraid, the children of Brede came together to kill the terrifying ogre, and accomplished this by getting him drunk and cutting him in half with a wooden saw, only to learn, to their horror, that death could not end his tyranny, for in death he returned to the place he had died as an angry ghost, a place known in Brede as Groaning Bridge.[44] This macabre legend may have begun in Sir Goddard's lifetime, for he was a man of huge stature who may have been feared by the superstitious villagers, but in all likelihood it originated years later. In his lifetime, Sir Goddard is thought to have been a kind and pious man who held firm to his Catholic faith after the break with Rome. Lady Tyrwhit was one of several siblings and through her paternal aunt, Magdalen Oxenbridge, she was the first cousin of Baroness Bryan's ill-fated son-in-law, Sir Nicholas Carew. As Sir Nicholas's glittering court career drew to an end, her own began, for in 1537, the year of her father's death, she was chosen to serve Jane Seymour as one of her women. A year or two later she married Robert Tyrwhit, a childless widower who had been raised at court, and then went on to serve all three of Henry VIII's last wives. With her husband, Lady Tyrwhit had three children, but only one survived infancy, a daughter named Katherine.

Like Lady Troy and Kat Astley, Lady Tyrwhit was an accomplished and well educated woman. She was a religious reformist, with a passion for collecting and composing prayers, psalms and hymns, and was once described by her husband as 'half a scripture woman'. On account of her evangelical views, she was implicated in a plot by religious conservatives, led by Stephen Gardiner, Bishop of Winchester, to bring down the King's last wife, Kateryn Parr, and she only narrowly avoided arrest. The Queen was becoming increasingly reformist in her views, as were her ladies, and the conservatives saw her as a considerable threat. Bishop Gardiner attempted to associate the Queen and her ladies with a radical reformist named Anne Askew, who had been arrested several times for preaching sermons in London, and in an attempt to get Anne to name the Queen or her ladies as her patrons she was tortured in the Tower of London, even though it was illegal to torture a woman. Anne gave no names, despite the horrific injuries she received at the cruel hands of the Lord Chancellor, Henry Wriothesley, and Sir Richard Rich, but plans were drawn up regardless to arrest the Queen and three of her ladies: Anne Parr, Countess of Pembroke, the Queen's sister; Maud Parr, Lady Lane, the Queen's cousin; and Lady Tyrwhit. Fortunately for all concerned, the Queen got wind of the plot and was able to persuade her husband, the King, that she was nothing but 'a silly, poor woman' who had debated religion with him only to profit from his wisdom and to distract him from his pain.

Lady Tyrwhit was one of Kateryn Parr's closest friends and continued to attend her after the King's death. She was therefore well acquainted with Princess Elizabeth, for they had lived together for many months in the Queen Dowager's household, and she was attending upon Kateryn Parr when she died.[45] Lady Tyrwhit was well acquainted with Kat Astley too, for Kat, by her own admission, had discussed the problem of the Lord High Admiral with her after the Queen Dowager's death, and had been told by Lady Tyrwhit that 'men did think that my

Lord Admiral kept the Queen's maidens together to wait upon the Lady Elizabeth, whom he intended to marry shortly, as the bruit [rumour] went'.[46]

When, in the January of 1549, Kat was arrested and sent to the Tower of London on suspicion of treason, the Lord Protector and the Privy Council had the difficult task of finding Elizabeth a new governess. Perhaps believing it was impossible, considering the scandal around the princess and the fact that two governesses in living memory had ended up in the Tower of London, the council used a sneaky tactic to recruit Lady Tyrwhit. Instead of asking her directly, they called her before them and rebuked her for not having taken upon herself the office of governess to the princess in the absence of Mistress Astley. Of course, Lady Tyrwhit was never going to take the office upon herself, no woman would have dared, but by making it clear to her that she was expected to do so, and by expressing dismay that she had not already done so, they were effectively giving her no choice. So off Lady Tyrwhit went to Hatfield to take up the role of Lady Governess to the princess, and as the princess's new Lady Governess, it was up to her to break the news of Kat's dismissal. Elizabeth, upon hearing the news, exploded. According to Sir Robert she yelled that 'Mistress Ashley was her mistress, and that she had not so demeaned herself that the council should now need to put any more mistresses unto her'. Lady Tyrwhit replied that 'if she did allow Mistress Ashley to be her mistress, she need not be ashamed to have any honest woman in that place'. Criticising Kat was not the best way to begin, even if Lady Tyrwhit sincerely believed that the former governess was not an 'honest woman', and her words did nothing to comfort Elizabeth who was so distraught that 'she wept all that night and loured all the next day'.[47] It was only when she received the Privy Council's official letter of explanation that Elizabeth pulled herself together. For as devastating as the confirmation of Kat's dismissal was, there was nothing in the letter to suggest that the council bore her any ill will or that they thought badly of her. Quite the contrary, they said they wished her well and hoped she would 'prosper in all virtue and honour'. Regarding Lady Tyrwhit, they believed she would 'endeavour herself from henceforth in all things to the weal [well-being] and honour of Your Grace', and they asked Elizabeth to 'accept her service thankfully and follow her good advices from time to time, especially in such matters as we have at this time appointed her to move unto you'. The 'such matters' was Thomas Seymour. Sir Robert's dealings with Elizabeth had convinced him that 'nothing is gotten off her but by great policy' so it was hoped that Lady Tyrwhit would succeed where her husband was failing and entice something out of Elizabeth that would incriminate Kat and Thomas Parry. But whenever 'Mistress Ashley was touched' in conversation Elizabeth would come to her defence 'vehemently'.[48]

After reading the Privy Council's letter, Elizabeth wished to write to the Lord Protector on the matter but Sir Robert advised her to only do so if she was willing to signify her acceptance of the Privy Council's decision. Elizabeth was not willing and told him that 'the world would note her to be a great offender, having so hastily a governess appointed her'. Sir Robert answered that if she cared for her honour she would be glad of having a governess. In his opinion she was 'very loath to have a governess', and in a letter of his own to the Lord Protector, he told him that 'she fully hopes to recover her old mistress again' and 'the love yet she beareth her is to be wondered at'.[49] He also added the snide remark that in his opinion she needed two governesses, not one. Ignoring Sir Robert's advice, Elizabeth wrote to the Lord Protector of her dissatisfaction, but as she had been warned, the letter was not well received, and she had to write again explaining herself:

> ...you write that I seem to stand in mine own wit in being so well assured of mine own self ... the cause why that I was sorry that there should be any such about me, was because that I thought the people will say that I deserved, through my lewd demeanour, to have such a one, and not that I mislike anything that Your Lordship or the council shall think good...or that I take upon me to rule myself, for I know that they are most deceived that trusteth most in themselves.[50]

Reluctantly, Elizabeth had to accept she had lost this particular battle, and resign herself to having Lady Tyrwhit instead of Kat, but it was a difficult adjustment to make for she missed her former governess terribly. As for Lady Tyrwhit, who may have been no happier about her new role, she did her best to do what was expected of her. From her perspective, Elizabeth had been badly governed by Mistress Astley, resulting in a girl who was wilful, disobedient, and tarnished by scandal.

By the summer, Elizabeth was severely depressed. She was still only 15 years of age but her whole world was in ruins. The two women she had depended on her entire life, Kat Astley and Lady Troy, were gone, and she had no one around her, except for Blanche Parry and a couple of other attendants, who cared for her at all. Also people were still gossiping about her and the admiral, who had been executed as a traitor, and except for her half-siblings and a few other relatives, none of whom she saw often, she was completely alone in the world. On top of all this, she may finally have learnt the truth about her mother's death. The strain, anguish and worry of the last weeks and months began to show on her health, which had already been compromised by sickness the previous year, and she declined rapidly. Indeed, the Lord Protector was so concerned that he sent King Edward's physician, Dr Thomas Bill, to attend her. Under his care Elizabeth improved but there was only one person who could lift her spirits. So, probably upon the good doctor's advice, a much missed Kat Astley was summoned to the princess's bedside. From then on, Elizabeth's recovery was swift, and the relieved Lord Protector permitted Kat to return to her service. Lady Tyrwhit, for now, was still in charge, but Elizabeth's world was suddenly a lot brighter, and soon Thomas Parry was back in his former role.

Although Elizabeth despised Sir Robert, she seems to have warmed to Lady Tyrwhit, who treated her kindly, and seems to have been the same stellar pupil for her as she had been for Kat. Sadly, William Grindal, her schoolmaster, had died of the plague the year before, so his mentor, Roger Ascham, was now her tutor. Elizabeth was now approaching her sixteenth birthday, a milestone age at which she would reach her majority. This came to pass on 7 September 1549, and there was probably no other birthday she was ever as glad to reach, for being an adult meant she was now responsible for her own affairs, at least in theory, and no longer in need of a governess. But, on account of her royal status, the reality was somewhat different. Princess Mary had had to endure the rule of a Lady Governess, in the form of Lady Shelton, for some years after reaching her majority, for she was not given her independence until she conformed to her father's wishes, and Elizabeth too did not achieve her independence right away. But as long as she behaved herself and conformed to the wishes of the Lord Protector and the Privy Council, and as long as she continued rehabilitating her damaged reputation, independence would come, as it did the following year. Roger Ascham, who knew her so well, made the following appraisal of the future queen as she reached this milestone age:

> The Lady Elizabeth has accomplished her sixteenth year; and so much solidity of understanding, such courtesy united with dignity, have never been observed at so early an age. She has the most ardent love of true religion and of the best kind of literature. The constitution of her mind is exempt from female weakness, and she is endued with a masculine power of application. No apprehension can be quicker than hers, no memory more retentive. French and Italian she speaks like English; Latin, with fluency, propriety, and judgement; she also spoke Greek with me, frequently, willingly, and moderately well. Nothing can be more elegant than her handwriting, whether in the Greek or Roman character. In music she is very skilful, but does not greatly delight. With respect to personal decoration, she greatly prefers a simple elegance to show and splendour, so despising the outward adorning of plaiting the hair and of wearing of gold, that in the whole manner of her life she rather resembles Hippolyta than Phaedra.[51]

Lady Tyrwhit's time as Lady Governess probably came to an end that winter when Elizabeth was invited to court for the Christmas festivities. After a year in the shadows, this invitation was a sign that her rehabilitation was complete, and Elizabeth arrived at court with great pomp and ceremony. Thereafter, Lady Tyrwhit retired from the court scene and lived a quiet life in the country. Her husband continued to hold a number of high profile positions, but his career had reached its zenith and was on the descent. Sir Robert did not enjoy royal favour during Elizabeth's reign, for reasons that are obvious, and Lady Tyrwhit is not known to have attended court. However, it was with some fondness that Queen Elizabeth remembered her final governess. During the dark days of Queen Mary's reign, when Elizabeth was imprisoned in the Tower of London, Lady Tyrwhit is said to have sent her a tiny book of prayers called a girdle book, a courageous gesture made to encourage the imprisoned princess and to remind her that she was now the hope of the reformists. This book still exists and is made of solid gold with enamelled figures of biblical scenes and with quotes on the front and back. Girdle books were popular in the 1540s amongst the ladies of Kateryn Parr's circle and were worn as a symbol of their adherence to the new religion. Elizabeth is said to have cherished this book all her life and to have bequeathed it upon her death to 'a woman of her bedchamber'. Although doubts have risen in recent years about the truth of this story, it is very likely true. In 1788, when John Nichols published his mammoth work *The Progresses and Public Processions of Queen Elizabeth*, the girdle book was in the possession of a Reverend George Ashby of Barrow in Suffolk. Nichols stated that there was a blank leaf inside the book on which was written: 'This book of Private Prayer was presented by the Lady Eliz. Tirwitt to Queen Eliz. during her confinement in the Tower, and the Queen generally wore it hanging by a gold chaine to her girdle; and att her death left it by will to one of her women of her bedchamber'. Nichols further informs us that 'Mr Ashby's mother received this book soon after her marriage in 1720 from her husband's father, George Ashby of Quenby ... as a choice heir-loom. He was born 1656; his father 1629; and his grandfather was married 1625. These four, or at most a fifth, are all the hands through which the book could have passed from 1603 to 1788'.[52] According to the British Museum, who now own the book, it stayed with the Ashby family until 1791. Afterwards it had several owners before being donated to the museum in 1894. The blank leaf described by Nichols no longer exists but the book definitely dates from the 1540s and a connection between the Ashbys and two 'women of the bedchamber' can be found. The likely history for the book, then, is as follows:

> Lady Tyrwhit (who may have been left the book by Kateryn Parr) gave the book to Princess Elizabeth.
>
> Queen Elizabeth gave the book at her death to either Mary Shelton, Lady Scudamore, her second cousin, or to Margaret Vaughan, Lady Hawkins, who had a great interest in religious learning.
>
> Lady Scudamore or Lady Hawkins left the book to Margaret Devereux, Lady Littleton (d.1625), who was related to the Queen and who was a first cousin-in-law to Lady Scudamore and a second cousin to Lady Hawkins.[53]
>
> Lady Littleton bequeathed the book to her granddaughter, Mary Shuckburgh, daughter of Sir Edward Littleton of Pillaton (d. 1629).
>
> Mary Shuckburgh bequeathed the book to her daughter, Mary Ashby, who was the wife of George Ashby of Quenby.

Nichols ultimately missed the connection to the Queen's 'women of the bedchamber' because he was following the male, not the female, line.[54]

Lady Tyrwhit died in 1578, having outlived her husband and her daughter, and was buried in the parish church of Leighton Bromswold, where she and Sir Robert had lived for many years. Upon her tomb, which she shares with her husband, are worn effigies of them both, along with figures of their children: Katherine, who predeceased them both, and two swaddled babies. But before Lady Tyrwhit died, a collection of prayers and hymns that she composed, probably many years

37

earlier, was published. This work was entitled *Lady Tyrwhit's Morning and Evening Prayers with Divers Psalms, Hymns and Meditations*. Only one copy of this original publication survives, and that copy is inside Queen Elizabeth's girdle book. For in the 1570s the contents of the girdle book were updated to include this volume alongside prayers by Kateryn Parr and a work by an unknown author. However, another version of Lady Tyrwhit's book appeared a few years later in Thomas Bentley's anthology of religious works by women entitled *The Monument of Matrons*. In this publication are a list of 'godly sentences' composed by Lady Tyrwhit which give a great insight into her character, for example:

> Think about the needy once a day.
> Further the just suit of the poor.
> Be at peace with all men.
> Hastily judge not anybody.
> Kill anger with patience.
> Favour the friendless.
> Be not unthankful.
> Trust not the world.
> Rather take hurt than do any.
> Let your mind be occupied well.
> Once you were not here.
> Away you must and turn to dust.

Lady Tyrwhit probably incorporated several of these *Prayers, Psalms, Hymns and Meditations* into Elizabeth's daily routine when she was her governess, and one of her 'godly sentences' may have resounded so much with the young princess that it later inspired her famous Latin motto *Semper Eadem* – Be Always One.[55]

Chapter Three

The Hatfield Flock

THE YEAR 1550, which in Tudor times formally began on 25 March, was a new beginning for Princess Elizabeth. Her inheritance of lands worth £3000 a year, as stipulated in her father's will, was finally settled upon her and she was now as independent as any adult heir to the throne could ever hope to be. She was able to organise her own household, to select her own servants, and to oversee her own financial affairs. Elizabeth was now a very wealthy and influential young lady and that summer she acquired, in her own right, a palace that would forever come to be associated with her youth: the Palace of Hatfield. The palace had been granted to John Dudley, Earl of Warwick, soon to be Duke of Northumberland, an ambitious man who had ousted the Lord Protector and assumed the title of Lord President of the Council, but when Elizabeth made her interest in the palace known, the Lord President agreed to give it to her in exchange for lands in Lincolnshire. Elizabeth immediately made the palace her principal residence and it would remain so until she became queen. During her reign, those women and men who served her there referred to themselves as 'the Hatfield flock'.[1]

Now that Elizabeth was the head of her household, her staffing arrangements reflected this new independent status and her palatial home was structured like a mini royal court. Presiding over the household was Sir Henry Parker, the princess's first Chamberlain, a man who was closely connected to her through his wife and sister. His wife was Elizabeth Calthorpe, a daughter of Jane Boleyn, Lady Calthorpe, an aunt of Anne Boleyn's who had briefly been Lady Governess to Princess Mary in the early 1520s, and his sister was the late Jane Parker, Lady Rochford, wife to Anne Boleyn's executed brother. Lady Parker probably lived with her husband at Hatfield and would have been the most important lady of the household after Elizabeth. Anne Rede, Lady Fortescue, who was married to Thomas Parry, still cofferer, was another lady of the household and she too had a connection to Elizabeth as her first husband, Sir Adrian Fortescue, was a relative. Sir Henry Parker died in 1552 and was replaced with Sir Walter Buckler, formerly Kateryn Parr's private secretary, but he too died not long after taking up the position and was replaced with Sir Nicholas Le Strange, a distant cousin of Elizabeth's who was also related to Kateryn Parr.

As an adult woman, Elizabeth no longer needed a governess so, like all 'great ladies', she was attended by a number of gentlewomen and maids. The chief of her gentlewomen was her former governess, Kat Astley. With Lady Tyrwhit having long since left the household, Kat was once again in charge, and although Elizabeth was now her own mistress, she relied heavily upon Kat to organise her life, including her day to day routine, her attendants, her wardrobe, her medical and personal needs, and her travel arrangements. In many ways, Kat's job was the same as before, except now she was employed by Elizabeth, not by the King or the Privy Council, and she no longer had any authority over the princess or any responsibility for her education. In reality, however, Elizabeth still looked to her for the maternal care she had always given and their personal relationship stayed the same. Kat's husband, John, was also given a prominent role in the princess's new household, perhaps as chief of her gentlemen attendants. Assisting Mistress Astley in her duties were the princess's two Blanches: Blanche Parry and Blanche Whitney. Kat received a salary of approximately £15 a year whilst Blanche Parry received £10 and Blanche Whitney £6 13s 4d.[2] They also received bed and board for themselves and their servants, stabling for their horses, and possibly livery. Joanne Hilton continued to serve as laundress but the two chamberers, Jane Broadbelt and Alice Huntercombe, had seemingly retired. In their place was Dorothy Broadbelt, probably Jane's daughter, Elyzabeth Marbury, a likely successor to a Mistress Poore who had served the princess for a time, and new recruit Elizabeth Sondes, a probable niece of 'Richard Sannds', the princess's gentlemen attendant, and a daughter of Anthony Sondes, a wealthy Kent landowner.[3]

The fashionable number of maiden attendants for 'great ladies' was between four and eight and Elizabeth's preference was for six. These maids, some of them already in attendance, acted as the princess's companions and escorts and some of the first were Elizabeth Norwich, Elizabeth Neville, Elizabeth Clyffe, Bridget Skipwith, Elyzabeth St Loe, Isabella Markham, and Anne Poyntz. Of these girls, Elizabeth Neville and Elizabeth Norwich were the longest serving. Both had been attending the princess for at least three years and during the troublesome episode of the Lord High Admiral, Elizabeth Norwich took over from Kat as the princess's sleeping companion when she visited court.[4] Elizabeth Neville was the daughter of Sir Edward Neville, another once favoured courtier sent to the block by Henry VIII, and the granddaughter of Sir Andrew Windsor, once Keeper of the Great Wardrobe. Elizabeth Norwich's parentage is less certain, but according to an old Latin transcript of her tomb's now lost inscription, she was the daughter of 'John Norwich of Brampton in the County of Northamptonshire, soldier'. This John Norwich was probably the son of Simon Norwich of Brampton and Margaret Tyrrell. Margaret Tyrrell was reputedly a 'cousin to Lady Cheney', who was Anne Parr, aunt of Kateryn Parr, which would explain how Elizabeth ended up serving a princess. Her mother was probably John's first wife, known only as Anne Cobham, for he must have fathered Elizabeth young as his parents did not marry until 1512.[5] Susan Norwich, a gentlewoman in attendance upon Kateryn Parr, may have been her aunt or sister, but it is also possible that she and 'Anne Cobham' are one and the same if her name was pronounced 'Suzanne' (compilers of pedigrees were not always accurate).

Elizabeth Clyffe and the other girls had joined the princess's service more recently. Mistress Clyffe (and Bridget Skipwith it seems) had formerly attended upon Kateryn Parr. A daughter of Richard Clyffe, Clerk of the Cheque, she had been granted an annuity by Thomas Seymour the day after his wife's funeral for £6 13s 4d 'out of the manor or lordship of Nun Monkton for life'. Bridget Skipwith must have received a similar annuity for in the reign of Queen Mary both she and Elizabeth Clyffe, described as 'servants to the Princess Elizabeth', took a case to the Court of Requests concerning 'rent in Nun Monkton', suggesting that their annuities were not being honoured.[6] Bridget, a daughter of Sir William Skipwith of South Ormsby and his second wife, Alice Dymoke, was probably appointed by the Tyrwhits. Her father's first wife had been Elizabeth Tyrwhit, paternal aunt of Sir Robert Tyrwhit, and it is likely that her godmother was Sir Robert's first wife, Bridget Wiltshire, Lady Wingfield, one of Anne Boleyn's favourite ladies.[7] Bridget had several siblings, including a sister named Margaret who was married to Kat's first cousin, Sir Peter Carew, so Bridget was undoubtedly an acceptable appointment all around. Bridget was also related to Isabella Markham, a daughter of Sir John Markham, Lieutenant of the Tower of London, who probably joined the princess's service at about this time, as they shared a set of great grandparents in Sir William and Agnes Skipwith. Elyzabeth St Loe owed her appointment to her brother, Sir William St Loe, a soldier and courtier who was now in charge of the princess's security, whilst Anne Poyntz probably owed her appointment to Kat as her father, Sir Nicholas Poyntz, was a first cousin of Kat's mother. Anne was also related to Elizabeth through her great grandmother, Margaret Woodville, who was a niece of Elizabeth Woodville, wife of Edward IV. Like all the young ladies attending upon Elizabeth, Anne was of the new religion, and an interesting and touching exchange between mistress and maid has been captured for posterity in a copy of Myles Coverdale's *New Testament* that Elizabeth is thought to have given Anne. On a blank page at the beginning of the book Elizabeth has quoted four lines from a poem believed to have been written by John Harington:

> Among good things I prove and find
> The quiet life doth much abound
> And sure to the contented mind
> There is no riches may be found.[8]

And underneath this verse the princess instinctively wrote 'Your loving friend, Elizabeth' only to quickly change it to 'Your loving mistress, Elizabeth' when she remembered her position. Yet there is something very poignant about this 'mistake', for it reminds us that beneath all the royal pomp Elizabeth was still only a teenage girl, and like every other teenage girl she longed for friends. On the page opposite Anne replied to her mistress with a verse that may be of her own composition:

> More swift than swallows flight
> Our young days fly away,
> Then age calls for his right

And death will have no stay.
Both day by night and night by day
Our course changes to and fro,
So life by death and death by life
Shall bring us all to well or woe.

And confidently, without ceremony, she signed it 'Your friend, Anne Poyntz'.

There was something very prophetic in Anne's words for all too soon the idyllic quiet life that the princess and her maidens had come to enjoy at Hatfield came to a dramatic end. In the summer of 1553, just weeks before Elizabeth's twentieth birthday, her half-brother, King Edward VI, died. It is often said that the young monarch was a sickly child whom no one expected to live, but in recent years this view has been challenged. At the time, and for years afterwards, it was said that Edward had died 'not without suspicion of poison', and Kat had certainly expected him to live as she had once told Elizabeth that 'it was impossible for my Lord Admiral to have Her Grace till the King's Majesty came to his own rule'.[9] But if Edward's death came as a shock to many people, the subsequent announcement that Lady Jane Grey was now the rightful queen of the realm was a greater. Lady Jane was, at the time, a fairly minor royal, being only the daughter of Henry VIII's niece, Frances Brandon, Duchess of Suffolk, and both Princess Mary and Princess Elizabeth came before her in the line of succession, to which they had been restored by an Act of Parliament in 1543. But in a desperate attempt to stop Mary becoming queen and restoring the country to the Catholic faith, the Lord President and the Privy Council, perhaps with the encouragement of the King, removed both Henry VIII's daughters from the line of succession and settled the crown upon Lady Jane. But Mary, who had always fought so hard for her birthright, was not going to let Lady Jane take her throne without a fight. Within days she had mustered an army strong enough to challenge the usurping queen and within two weeks had defeated her. Soon after, a triumphant Mary, now queen, rode into London to a cheering crowd and Elizabeth, who was now the heir presumptive, was given the first place of honour behind her. The moment was one of great victory for the two cast off daughters of Henry VIII, a moment of sister solidarity, but sadly a moment of unity that would be all too brief. That winter Queen Mary announced her decision to marry Prince Philip of Spain, a man who would one day rule the mighty Spanish Empire, and this announcement struck terror into the heart of every English Protestant. Even some Catholics were horrified as they wanted Mary to marry a native English nobleman. The result was a rebellion against the marriage led by Sir Thomas Wyatt, a descendant of Sir Geoffrey Boleyn, Elizabeth's great, great grandfather, with the support of Sir James Croft, Sir Peter Carew, and Henry Grey, Duke of Suffolk, Lady Jane's father. The rebellion failed, like most rebellions, but unfortunately for Elizabeth, the rebels had intended to depose the Queen and place her on the throne instead, upon condition that she marry her second cousin, Edward Courtenay, Earl of Devon, the grandson of Princess Catherine of York. This implicated Elizabeth and Courtenay in the rebellion, even though it is unlikely that either were involved, and for the second time in her young life Elizabeth was at the centre of a treasonous marriage plot.

Prisoner Princess

At the time of Wyatt's Rebellion, Elizabeth was staying at Ashridge Palace, another favourite childhood home that was now hers, and according to John Foxe, who later published an account of these events in his hugely influential book *Acts and Monuments*, Elizabeth was 'sick in her bed' and 'very feeble and weak' when Queen Mary's men arrived unexpectedly one night to take her to London.[10] Kat Astley was probably the 'lady' who met the men as they were 'ascending up to Her Grace's chamber', for she would have wished to know what was going on, only to be told that they must speak with Elizabeth. The lady told them to come back in the morning, for it was late and the princess was ill, but the men insisted on speaking with her and pushed passed the lady to enter the bedchamber. When there, they told Elizabeth that they were under strict orders to bring her to London 'alive or dead'. Seeing that she was ill, they spoke to her doctors, but on being told it was safe for her to make the journey, they ordered Elizabeth to be ready the next morning. So, at nine o'clock the next day, Elizabeth, 'very faint and feeble and in such case that she was ready to swoon three or four times', was helped into the Queen's litter to begin what would be a long and arduous journey to London. She finally reached the capital eleven days later and upon arriving at Whitehall Palace, where the Queen was residing, was immediately 'shut up and kept a close prisoner' within an allocated apartment.

For now, Elizabeth still had the company of all her gentlewomen and maids, but two weeks later, after being formally charged with treason by Stephen Gardiner, Bishop of Winchester, and told that she was to be sent forthwith to the Tower of London, the distraught princess was separated from all but three of her women. One of these three women was Elizabeth Sondes, her chamberer, but unfortunately the names of the other two are unrecorded. However, Blanche Parry was almost certainly one, and by a process of elimination the third was Blanche Whitney. Lady Troy, who was probably still alive, had always been on good terms with Mary, so it is likely that Mary looked favourably upon her relations who had never given her cause for concern and were not related to the rebels. Kat Astley, on the other hand, was known to be a Protestant and was related to both Sir Peter Carew and Edward Courtenay. Consequently, she was placed in the custody of Sir Roger Cholmley, former Chief Justice of the King's Bench, who lived in Highgate. Elizabeth Norwich, Dorothy Broadbelt and Elyzabeth Marbury were certainly not with the princess whilst Anne Poyntz, Bridget Skipwith and Elyzabeth St Loe were connected to the rebels or to 'suspicious' people. Anne was Sir Peter Carew's cousin, Bridget was Sir Peter Carew's sister-in-law, and Elyzabeth St Loe's brother was in the Tower accused of abetting the rebels. As for the other girls, Elizabeth Clyffe was probably unacceptable on the grounds that she had served Kateryn Parr, for the Queen Dowager was known to have surrounded herself with reformists, Elizabeth Neville had probably already retired to marry Thomas Eynns, Secretary of the Council of the North, and Isabella Markham's father, no longer Lieutenant of the Tower, was a known Protestant. In the place of these dismissed attendants, the Queen appointed three of her own women. The chief of these was seemingly Lady Grey. Although she has never been identified with certainty, she was probably Anne Jerningham, Lady Grey, sister of Sir Henry Jerningham, one of the Queen's strongest supporters and married to one of her favourite ladies, Frances Baynham.[11] The names of the other two women are not known but may have been Mary Thomeo and Dorothy Broughton, two of the Queen's women who are known to have been in attendance later.[12] Of course, Elizabeth protested her innocence to those who accused her, and begged for an audience with the Queen to protest the same, but even though she was allowed to write to her sister, the letter did no more than buy her some time. The following morning, which was Palm Sunday, the princess's worst nightmare came true as she was put on a barge with 'three of the Queen's gentlewomen and three of her own', along with 'her gentleman-usher and two of her grooms', and taken by water to the 'notorious and doleful place' that was the Tower of London.

Within a week of her imprisonment, perhaps in the same suite of rooms that her mother had spent her last days, to increase Elizabeth's terror, the princess was deprived of one of her three gentlewomen.[13] Now that the country was Catholic again, everyone was expected to attend Mass, but Elizabeth Sondes, a devout reformist, refused to go. As a result, the defiant young girl was removed from Elizabeth's service and replaced with a woman named Mistress Coldburn. Sadly, nothing is known about Mistress Coldburn, but as she replaced one of Elizabeth's women she may have been of 'the Hatfield flock'.

According to Foxe, Elizabeth spent her first month in the Tower closely confined, meaning she was kept from everyone, except her attendants, and from walking in the Tower's grounds. Concerned for her health, which was still fragile, Elizabeth asked if she might 'walk but into the Queen's lodging' (a sumptuous and spacious apartment that was clearly close-by) but her request was denied. However, her custodians had a change of heart and agreed that she could walk into the lodgings so long as 'the Lord Chamberlain and three of the Queen's gentlewomen did accompany her, the windows being shut, and she not suffered to look out at any of them'. Eventually, Elizabeth was permitted to 'walk in a little garden', which she found 'pleasant and acceptable', and was visited there by a little boy bearing flowers – until the little boy, who lived at the Tower, was told he could visit 'no more'.

Although she has gone down in history as Bloody Mary, a cruel and vengeful queen, Mary did not have a cruel heart, though she did cruel things in the name of her religion. Despite the way Anne Boleyn had supplanted her beloved mother, and despite the terrible circumstances of Elizabeth's birth, Mary had always been a kind sister to Elizabeth, looking after her when she was little and spending time with her when she was grown. Indeed, according to Foxe, in the days of King

Edward, Mary would 'go no whither but would have her [Elizabeth] by the hand' and would 'send for her to dinner and supper'. Everything changed, however, when Mary became queen, for despite Elizabeth's personal loyalty, she was an existential threat, an attractive alternative queen that religious reformists would never stop plotting to place on the throne. All those feelings of bitterness and resentment that Mary had felt as a teenager towards Anne Boleyn came flooding back and poisoned her love for Elizabeth. Yet, even in these dark and dangerous days, Mary would not move against her sister without due proof, and on the anniversary of Anne Boleyn's execution, an execution that had taken place right where Elizabeth now was, some tenderness for her sister evidently returned as the Queen sent word that Elizabeth, whose guilt could not be established, was to be released from the Tower that day into the custody of Sir Henry Bedingfield.

Sir Henry Bedingfield, of Oxburgh Hall, Norfolk, was one of Queen Mary's strongest supporters. He was a first cousin to Lady Grey and his father had been the custodian of Katherine of Aragon in her final years. Sir Henry was instructed to take Elizabeth to Woodstock Manor, an old royal residence in Oxfordshire, and to keep her there under guard. As Elizabeth did not know Sir Henry at all, not being in the least familiar with him, she was terrified that he was going to assassinate her in the seclusion of a country estate, however, the princess quickly learnt that Sir Henry was a man of conscience who could be trusted with her safety. Nevertheless, he was a very strict custodian and kept Elizabeth locked up in her allocated rooms for most of the day. It was a miserable existence for the princess, and it lasted for months, but what made it worse was the absence of Kat Astley and so many of her other beloved women.

Mistress Coldburn does not appear to have accompanied Elizabeth to Woodstock. The women known to have attended her there are Lady Grey, who wished to retire but had to wait for a suitable replacement; Dorothy Broughton, who did not stay long as she was recalled to court to be Mother of the Maids; Mary Thomeo, who served alongside her husband; and Margaret Morton, 'one of Her Highness's women' who replaced Dorothy Broughton. Another woman who may have attended upon Elizabeth at the manor is Bridget Southwell. From a Catholic family, Bridget was educated at a convent and is said to have been fluent in Latin. Married to a man whose father, Sir Richard Southwell, was on Queen Mary's Privy Council, she may have been the Queen's choice of language tutor for Elizabeth when the princess complained to Sir Henry Bedingfield that she was 'likely to lose' all the languages she had learnt due to a 'lack of conference'. The princess's request for her own tutor, John Picton, 'who taught her many tongues in her youth', was probably denied as the council 'knew not the man'.[14]

Elizabeth Sondes, who had been dismissed for refusing to go to Mass, had somehow managed to sneak back into Elizabeth's service and was with her for a time at Woodstock. However, word had reached Mary's ears of the girl's 'evil opinions' and the Queen had concluded that she was 'not fit to remain about our said sister's person'. Consequently, the girl was dismissed again and the Queen told Sir Henry to persuade Elizabeth 'by the best manner you can' to 'accept in her place Elyzabeth Marbury, another of her women who shall be sent thither for that purpose'.[15] Of course, Elizabeth could not easily be persuaded to forgo Mistress Sondes, and she complained loudly to Sir Henry, but when it became clear that the Queen was resolved, Elizabeth asked if she could have Dorothy Broadbelt or Elizabeth Norwich instead of Elyzabeth Marbury. Sir Henry, caught between a rock and a hard place, duly submitted her request to the Queen, but was promptly told that 'Elyzabeth Marbury is already come thither for that purpose' and that Mistress Sondes should be sent away as soon as possible.[16] From Mary's point of view, Elizabeth was being deliberately awkward, for Mistress Marbury was 'one of her women', but from Elizabeth's point of view, she was probably not as close to Mistress Marbury, who was older and married, as she was to the other girls who were single women of her own age. When this request was also denied, Elizabeth told Sir Henry that she wanted Dorothy Broadbelt, Elizabeth Norwich *and* Elyzabeth Marbury, but her words fell on deaf ears and at 'two of the clock', on a June afternoon, Elizabeth Sondes was dragged away from her mistress with wails of 'great mourning'. The girl was taken to Thomas Parry's house in the town, from where he was administering Elizabeth's affairs, and then conveyed to her uncle's house in London or to her father's house in Kent. Knowing she stood 'in great jeopardy of further trial', Elizabeth soon fled the country and joined the exiled Protestant community in Geneva, a wise decision given that Sir Henry Bedingfield, upon her departure, informed the Privy Council that she was 'a woman meet to be looked unto for her obstinate disposition'.[17]

Very little is known about Elyzabeth Marbury, who now resumed her place as one of the princess's attendants, albeit it in changed and difficult circumstances, but she had been brought to Woodstock by her husband, Thomas, and had arrived before Sir Henry had received official word that she was to 'wait upon Her Grace in the stead of Elizabeth Sondes'. Consequently, the confused gaoler had advised Thomas to 'stay himself and his wife hereabouts' until the matter could be cleared up, which Sir Henry hoped could be done quickly for 'they are very poor folks and unable to bear their own charge'.[18] It has been noted that many of the women attending Elizabeth in the years after her father's death were from humbler backgrounds than would normally be the case for a princess. In the eyes of some past historians who valued 'good blood and breeding', this was a disadvantage, but for a princess whose world was very small, existing mostly of the same circle of women in the same circle of royal residences, it surely helped to broaden her mind to be surrounded by women from very different backgrounds and from very different parts of the country. These women could tell her stories of their childhoods, of the towns and villages beyond the royal circuit, of seasides and mountains that she would never see, and of the many kinds of people who lived and worked on the land. Elizabeth proved to be a very charismatic queen with a rare common touch, and no doubt her upbringing, and all the women who played a part in it, contributed to the great monarch she became.

For almost a year Elizabeth languished in the dilapidated and depressing manor of Woodstock, but finally in the spring of 1555 she was summoned to court. The Queen, who believed herself to be pregnant, was staying at Hampton Court Palace, and Elizabeth was brought there quietly and discreetly for the royal birth. Impending motherhood had lessened Mary's fear of Elizabeth, for the Queen was convinced that she was having a boy, a son and heir who would one day be King of England and of Spain, so she saw her charismatic and popular sister as much less of a threat. There were political reasons too in having Elizabeth at the palace, for the Queen might not survive the birth, resulting in a fragile regency by Philip of Spain if the baby lived, or the accession of Elizabeth if it died. Having one eye on the future as well as one on the present, Philip wanted to make a friend of Elizabeth, for although she was a reformist, he believed it was better for Spanish interests if she ascended the throne rather than Mary, Queen of Scots, who was betrothed to the French King's heir. However, the Queen's impending birth turned out to be not so imminent after all as she was suffering from a phantom pregnancy, meaning her profound longing for a baby had caused her body to produce all the usual symptoms of pregnancy, including a visual bump, but with no real baby to deliver. Many of those around the Queen began to suspect this was the case, for it was not an unusual occurrence in this era, but no one knew for sure, not even the royal doctors, so the waiting game continued. Meanwhile, after weeks of seclusion at court, Elizabeth, who had not been permitted to see the Queen, was finally taken from her lodgings, under the cover of darkness which made her fear assassination, to the royal apartment. The Queen, who cannot have looked well, for her mental agitation was increasing by the day, greeted her, but the meeting was tense and awkward as both sisters felt wronged by the other. However, the Queen was willing to reconcile as there was no proof that Elizabeth had conspired against her. So, the two sisters made up, for the moment, and Elizabeth, although obligated to remain at court while the saga of the Queen's pregnancy continued, was set at liberty. It was a moment, perhaps, she never thought would come, for the Reaper had stood over her many times in the last fifteen months, holding up a sword that was running with her mother's blood. But now she was free, and her freedom also bought someone else's, someone very close to her heart: Kat Astley. At the end of May a warrant was issued to Sir Roger Cholmley instructing him to 'set at liberty Katheryn Ashley who hath of long time remained in his custody'.[19]

Princess of the Palace

By the autumn the Hatfield flock were back together again. Elizabeth and Kat were reunited, Dorothy Broadbelt and Elizabeth Norwich were back in service, as were Elizabeth Clyffe, Bridget Skipwith, Isabella Markham, and Elyzabeth St Loe. Some familiar faces were missing, as Anne Poyntz had got married and Elizabeth Sondes was still in exile, but as the old flock gathered together at Hatfield for the first time in months, it must have felt like old times. Of course, with old servants gone, new ones were needed, and it was probably at this time that a young Gloucestershire girl entered Elizabeth's service who would live to become one of her most important ladies: Francis Newton, future Baroness Cobham. Frances was the daughter of Sir John Newton of Barrs Court, a man of Welsh descent whose surname was originally Cradoc, and she was a first cousin of Anne Poyntz. Her mother, Margaret, was a full sister of Anne's father, Sir Nicholas Poyntz, meaning that Frances, like Anne, was a third cousin to Elizabeth and a second cousin to Kat. She and Kat shared a great grandfather in Sir William Huddesfield, a man of some importance in the early Tudor period as he was Attorney General to Henry VII. Sir William had two wives: first, Elizabeth Bosome, widow of Sir Baldwin de Fulford, with whom he fathered Kat's grandmother, Kateryn Huddesfield, Lady Carew; and second, Katherine Courtenay, daughter of Sir Philip Courtenay of Powderham, with whom he fathered Frances's grandmother, Elizabeth Huddesfield, Lady Poyntz. Frances was about 16 years of age in the winter of 1555 and she was probably selected by Kat to replace Elizabeth Sondes as chamberer. Nothing is presently known of Frances's childhood but she was one of twenty siblings and probably grew up in Barrs Court Manor, an old manor of stone that was enlarged and moated by the Newtons to make a stately family home.

Another new face at this time was Margaret Willoughby, a 12 or 13-year-old orphan who joined Elizabeth's service as a maid. Her mother, Anne Grey, an aunt of Lady Jane Grey and a second cousin of Elizabeth's, had died in 1548, and her father, Sir Henry Willoughby, had been killed the following year suppressing a revolt about land enclosures in Norfolk. After their deaths, Margaret and her younger brother, Francis, had been placed in the care of their maternal uncle, George Medley of Tilty in Essex, but following his imprisonment in the Tower of London for supporting the enthronement of Lady Jane Grey, Margaret went to live for a while with her aunt, Frances Brandon, Duchess of Suffolk. The duchess, who had always been close to the Queen, had managed to survive the fall of her family, and had even managed to persuade the Queen to spare the lives of her husband and daughter, blaming the Duke of Northumberland alone for the coup, but the involvement of her husband in Wyatt's Rebellion undid all her hard work and condemned the duke and Lady Jane to a traitor's death. But yet again Frances survived, as did her two youngest daughters, Katherine and Mary, and within months of the executions Frances was attending the Queen. Keen to build bridges with Elizabeth too, the duchess was probably instrumental in securing for Margaret her place in the princess's service, and at the end of October the young girl left her uncle's house at Tilty, where she was once again living, to start her long journey to Hatfield via London.[20]

For a little while 'the quiet life' returned to the Palace of Hatfield, and no doubt Christmas was celebrated with much joy and merriment that year, despite the absence of loved ones. As winter gave way to spring, the princess and her maids were able to venture further into the glorious park that surrounded the palace, and they spent many an hour walking and riding in the woodland when they were not studying, embroidering, playing musical instruments or dancing. But even as Elizabeth and her women began to relax back into their old life, a plot was hatching that would once again shatter their world. This plot, led by a man named Sir Henry Dudley, another member of the Grey family who was Elizabeth's second cousin, was largely orchestrated abroad and had similar aims to the Wyatt Rebellion. Wanting to end the rule of Mary and Philip, who were

Catholic tyrants in their eyes, the conspirators planned to depose the couple and replace them with Elizabeth and Courtenay. This meant that Elizabeth was once again implicated in a traitorous plot, which was discovered by the spring, and once again she was the subject of an exhaustive investigation. Fortunately, her arch enemy, Stephen Gardiner, was dead, and the Queen's husband, now King of Spain, was still a friend, so the princess was not arrested. However, at the end of May her house in London was searched and a hoard of 'scandalous books against the [Catholic] religion and against the King and Queen, which were scattered about some months ago' were discovered. The owner was said to be the princess's chief gentlewoman, still called governess by some dignitaries, Kateryn Astley.[21] A few days later, according to Foxe, 'Queen Mary's men' arrived at the princess's residence, which may have been the Manor of Lemar in Wheathampstead, a village five miles from Hatfield, and 'took away from Her Grace, Mistress Ashley to the Fleet, and three other of her gentlewomen to the Tower'.[22] This was not quite an accurate account of events, as it was three gentlemen who were taken to the Tower, not three gentlewomen, but Kat was certainly arrested and imprisoned for a third time. The Queen seemed to accept Elizabeth's innocence, despite these arrests, even sending her sister words of comfort and an expensive ring 'as a token of loving salutation', but still Mary took it in hand to reorganise her sister's household and to place her under the watchful eye of a governor and a governess.[23] The governor was Sir Thomas Pope, a Privy Councillor 'of good name' who knew Elizabeth well, having previously served in her household, whilst the governess was 'a widowed gentlewoman' whose name is not known. Elizabeth accepted them both graciously, for there was little else she could do, but undoubtedly she was devastated at being separated from Kat yet again and profoundly worried about what was to become of her former governess. This was, after all, the 'burning time' in which the Queen and her government burnt reformists alive at the stake. The princess may also have lost several other women temporarily as the Venetian Ambassador reported that Elizabeth had 'none but the Queen's dependents about her person' and was effectively 'in ward and custody, though in such decorous and honourable form as is becoming'.[24]

This 'honourable' custody lasted for six months, six anxious months that were spent mostly at Hatfield, but by the autumn the crisis had passed. Sir Thomas Pope was discharged from his role as governor, much to his relief, and the 'widowed gentlewoman' presumably left with him. At the same time Elizabeth's servants were released from imprisonment, including Kat who finally left the Fleet in October, but in what must have been a crushing blow, the former governess was told that she could never see Elizabeth again. Elizabeth's reaction to this news is unrecorded, but she too was surely heartbroken, and from that moment on until Mary's death, the two women had to depend on mutual acquaintances to learn how the other fared. With Kat permanently dismissed, with no hope of reinstatement this time, Elizabeth was forced to adjust to life without her, and this meant appointing a new chief gentlewoman. For such an important, intimate role, there was only one candidate, the woman who had been with her since birth and had weathered every single political storm so far, her loyal and devoted Blanche

Parry. So Mistress Parry was probably put in charge and a new era began for the diminished Hatfield Flock.

Unfortunately, this new era did not begin well. Although Elizabeth received an invitation to court that Christmas, an invitation that was surely very welcome after a year in the wilderness, the visit was a complete disaster. First, just when Elizabeth reached the vicinity of London, one of her gentlewomen fell ill with smallpox. Panic likely ensued, as smallpox was a dreaded disease that not only killed but often left survivors horribly disfigured for life, and the princess's personal staff were reduced to a bare minimum. Margaret Willoughby, who had only just returned from a visit to her uncle's home in Tilty, was amongst the servants dismissed, and the young girl had to spend a week lodging in London at her uncle's expense.[25] The crisis was over quickly, so the outbreak may have been an isolated case, but sadly the infected gentlewoman died. Unfortunately, her name is not known, but this gentlewoman was probably Blanche Whitney.[26] For Elizabeth, this was clearly a devastating blow, as the two women were undoubtedly close, and the princess was surely in very low spirits as she made her formal entry into London at the end of November and took up residence at Somerset House, her main home in the capital. Finally, after a brutal journey, she had reached her destination, but, to the bewilderment of many, within days she was gone again. The reason, it seems, was a quarrel with the Queen. According to French intelligence:

> ...the Queen sent for the Lady Elizabeth to the court, and proposed to her to marry her to the Duke of Savoy, to which she [Elizabeth] replied that the afflictions suffered by her were such that they had not only ridded her of any wish for a husband, but that they had induced her to desire nothing but death, and then by a flood of tears she brought them also to the eyes of the Queen, who seeing that she still persisted in this opinion of not choosing to marry, dismissed her from the court, and purposed assembling Parliament to have her declared illegitimate.[27]

And so, the princess and her entourage made the arduous journey back to Hatfield in what would have been very cold weather, for the world had entered a mini ice age and winters were so harsh that sometimes the River Thames froze over. Christmas that year was no doubt a subdued affair. Kat was gone, smallpox had taken another valued member of the flock, and the new year promised nothing but more misery if the Queen persisted in pursuing the Savoy marriage. That Elizabeth had a genuine deep seated aversion to marriage is generally accepted, and is hardly surprising given the way her father had treated his six wives and the miserable marriage she had witnessed between Kateryn Parr and Thomas Seymour. To her mind, the single, celibate life was the better option, for the women around her who never married, like Blanche Parry, seemed to fare better than those who did. Being married meant putting your life at the mercy of a man, of always being subservient to his will, of spending year after year pregnant, waiting and hoping for that all important son, of being judged a failure if there was none, and ultimately of dying in the attempt.

Even her sister, who had been so keen to marry, was all the worse for it, languishing in deep despair for the absence of her husband, who never had the same strength of feeling for her, and, in her desperation to have a son, imagining herself pregnant to the mockery of the world. It was not a life Elizabeth wanted, and with every fibre of her being it was a life she was determined she would never live.

As predicted, much of 1557 was spent on the 'Savoy marriage', which was passionately promoted by King Philip, who firmly believed the marriage would safeguard Spanish interests in England should his wife die, as the duke was his first cousin. However, Queen Mary had lost all enthusiasm for the match and was becoming increasingly agitated at any mention of Elizabeth succeeding her. To her, it was absolutely unthinkable that the daughter of Anne Boleyn, the 'great whore' who had caused herself and her mother so much heartache and humiliation, would one day wear their father's crown. So the marriage negotiations came to nothing, much to the relief of Elizabeth and her supporters, who may have been plotting to smuggle her out of England rather than see her married to the Catholic duke. Over the next eighteen months, as the Queen's health declined, the political wheel brought the crown ever closer to the young red-headed woman of Hatfield, yet life in that old bishop's palace went on very much as before.

By the November of 1558 Queen Mary was dying. Although her health had been poor for some time, and she was struggling with depression following another phantom pregnancy, the panic in Spain when they received word of her condition suggests that she was not expected to die. But the world was in the grip of a deadly influenza pandemic that was killing thousands of people, and a second wave of the 'new sickness' reached England by late summer. As the virus swept through the country it claimed many lives, especially amongst the elderly, the infirm and the poor, and probably infected the Queen who fell dangerously ill at the end of October. Two weeks later she was on her deathbed, as was her chief advisor, Cardinal Reginald Pole, son of her beloved governess, Lady Salisbury, and within hours of each other both monarch and minister were dead.

According to legend, Princess Elizabeth was resting beneath an old oak tree in the grounds of Hatfield Palace when the news came that she was now queen of the realm. After years in the shadows, years of being obscured by the dazzling light of the crown, that glittering diadem of power was now hers. Although her life would never be her own again, for she would have to live it before the eyes of the world and the scrutiny of history, her life had never truly been her own for she had always been at the mercy of her tyrannical father, her puppet brother's guardians, or her suspicious sister. Now, at long last, she was free, and she held not only her own destiny, but the destiny of millions in her hands. Overwhelmed by the moment, Elizabeth is said to have dropped to her knees and uttered in Latin: 'This is the Lord's doing and it is marvellous in our eyes'. Witnessing this historic scene, in which they played a part, were her attending gentlewomen and maids. The names of those present are not recorded, but perhaps Blanche Parry, Elizabeth Norwich and Dorothy Broadbelt were amongst them, and in this moment of profound magnitude, these loyal and devoted women, who had served a princess for many years, suddenly found themselves attending a queen.

Chapter Four

Stars in the Presence of the Sun

IN THE GOLDEN days running up to her snowy coronation, on 15 January 1559, the new Queen of England, Wales and Ireland began to shape what would become one of the most famous courts in history. As the news of her accession spread far and wide, old friends, relations and servants flocked to Hatfield whilst those in exile abroad made plans to return. Hopes were high that better times lay ahead, for Mary's reign had been difficult and deadly for many of Elizabeth's supporters, and with lucrative court positions suddenly available, dynastic fortunes might dramatically improve. The first two weeks of her reign Elizabeth spent in the familiar palace that had been her sanctuary for so long, selecting advisors and ministers of state, while also appointing the women and men who would attend upon her in public and in private. Now that she was queen, Elizabeth was to be magnificently attended by ladies and knights; gentlewomen and gentlemen; maids and grooms; esquires and pages; as well as by fifty Gentlemen Pensioners, who were the monarch's ceremonial bodyguard, and the Yeomen of the Guard, who were the monarch's official bodyguard. It would be some years before Elizabeth became the glamourous queen of legend, for in these early years she still dressed modestly and the spectacular ruffs that would make her an icon had not yet come into fashion, but from the onset of her reign her court was gloriously majestic and her magnificence of palace and person truly fostered in her people the notion that she was Gloriana, a divine empress appointed by God to rule them.

Some years into the Queen's reign, a French visitor to court, whose name has been lost to history, was asked by the Queen what he thought of her ladies. The visitor, evidently an experienced courtier, replied: 'It is hard to judge of stars in the presence of the sun'.[1] This answer surely pleased and perfectly sums up the court position of the Queen's ladies, gentlewomen and maids. For if the Queen was the sun of her kingdom, the leading lady of the stage, her attending women were the chorus, stars who glittered in their own right but never in the presence of the sun. This royal sun in splendour, a symbol of the Yorkist kings from whom the Queen was descended, and of her grandmother, Elizabeth of York, in whom she may have taken pride, adorned many of her gorgeous gowns in the later years of her reign. In Hatfield House, which lies next to the remains of the old palace where her reign began, hangs a painting of the Queen from about 1600 in which she is idealised as an embodiment of this sun. Cloaked in flaming orange she holds a rainbow in her hand, and above the rainbow are the Latin words *Non Sine Sole Iris*: No rainbow without the sun.[2]

Elizabeth, as the sun of the Elizabethan world, ruled her realm with the help of trusted advisors known as Privy Councillors, from the royal palace. The Privy Council met several times a week, in a room called the Council Chamber, and for most of the Queen's reign it was headed by Sir William Cecil (Baron Burghley from 1571), a man of Welsh descent who was connected to Blanche Parry. A genius administrator, he worked tirelessly for queen and country, and was first made Secretary of State and then, in 1572, Lord High Treasurer. Other important Officers of State were the Lord Chancellor, who was usually also Lord Keeper of the Great Seal (a wax seal authenticating important state documents) and the Lord High Admiral, who was in charge of naval defence. While the Queen did not have an official residence, as she moved in between a number of royal palaces throughout the year, most of them in or near London, all her palaces were magnificent structures that embodied the majesty of the monarch. One of the Queen's favourite palaces was Greenwich, the place of her birth that was said to be particularly pleasant in summer, and another was Richmond in Surrey, which was an impressive building of turreted towers that had been built by her grandfather, the founder of the Tudor dynasty, Henry VII. There was also Hampton Court Palace, St James's Palace, Windsor Castle, and the most spectacular palace of all, Nonsuch near Cheam. This palace, once described as 'an excess of magnificence and elegance, even to ostentation' had been built by Henry VIII to be the greatest palace in the world.[3] For most of the Queen's reign it was in private hands, but in the early 1590s the Queen reacquired it and immediately the palace became one of her favourite residences. Aside from its splendour, the palace had gorgeous gardens ornamented with fountains, statues and trellises, and was surrounded by an especially delightful deer park. But the palace in which the Queen spent most of her time was Whitehall in Westminster. This enormous palace was not only conveniently located, being close to the Houses of Parliament, the Law Courts, and the Great Wardrobe, which stockpiled all kinds of fabrics and furs for the Queen's use, but it was one of the biggest palaces in Europe and its enormous size made accommodating the royal court easier. At any given time there were over a thousand people living or working at court and finding suitable lodgings for everyone was a struggle. Sometimes it was impossible and visitors, or foreign ambassadors, had to lodge in houses nearby.

The Tudor court was a very structured place and had an internal filtering system that separated the high ranking 'upstairs' courtiers and statesmen from the humble 'below stairs' workers. This filtering system meant that, in theory, someone could spend their whole life working at the palace but never see the Queen. There were three important officials to manage the huge royal court: the Lord Chamberlain, the Lord Steward, and the Master of the Horse. These officials, always men, were personally chosen by the Queen and had many staff to help them. The Master of the Horse, the least of these officials, was responsible, as the name suggests, for the Queen's horses, for the royal stables and all its staff, the horses of everyone at court, and the horses used for transport, ceremony and sport. The Lord Steward, the second most important official, was responsible for the household 'below stairs' known as the *Domus Providencie* or, in English, 'the Household'. This included the kitchen and bakehouse; the boiling house and pastry; the pantry and larder; the cellar and buttery; the wafery, spicery and confectionary; the poultry, scalding house and acatery (for meat); the ewery and pitcher house (for jugs and pots); the chaundry (for candles) and laundry; the scullery and wood yard; the gardens and the grounds. The Lord Chamberlain, the most important of the three officials, presided over the household 'above stairs' known as the *Domus Magnificencie* or 'the Chamber'. This was the absolute centre of court, the glittering core around which everything rotated, for the Chamber was a maze of state and private rooms where the Queen lived, worked, worshipped and entertained. Although the size and layout of the Chamber differed from residence to residence, as no two royal palaces were the same, there was a general flow of rooms common to them all. First there was the Great Chamber, a grand reception hall where the Lord Chamberlain, Lord Steward, and Master of the Horse dined along with other high ranking courtiers; second, the Guard or Watching Chamber, where Yeomen of the Guard controlled access to the Presence Chamber (in some palaces, like Hampton Court, this was combined with the Great Chamber to form the Great Watching Chamber); and third, the Presence Chamber. Sometimes called 'the throne room', the Presence Chamber was a magnificent hall that displayed the royal throne beneath an enormous canopy of state. From this throne, which was elevated upon a dais, the Queen held audiences, welcomed ambassadors and statesmen, made speeches, entertained, and officially dined. Beyond the Presence Chamber was the most exclusive zone of the Tudor palace, the private area of the Chamber known as the Privy Chamber. This was where the monarch lived in a magnificent suite of rooms and access to the Privy Chamber was strictly controlled. Also within the *Domus Magnificencie* was the Council Chamber and the Chapel Royal where the Queen worshipped with her courtiers at least once a week. The rooms of the Chamber were lavish and sumptuous, full of rich furnishings and glittering tapestries, whilst the rooms of the *Domus Providencie*, which were generally not seen by visitors to court, were plain and simple. There were visual differences too in the staff of both divisions. Whereas the grooms and pages of the Chamber wore red velvet coats embroidered with the Queen's cypher (ER) in gold, and her Yeomen of the Guard wore similar red coats adorned with the Queen's badge (Tudor rose with crown), the staff of the Household wore inexpensive livery in the dynastic colours of the Tudor dynasty, white and green. Bridging the *Domus Providencie* and the *Domus Magnificencie* was an enormous and glorious hall known as the Great Hall. This was not only where all 'below stairs' staff dined twice a day, but it was also where lesser courtiers dined, and where all visitors to court congregated if they did not have right of access to the Chamber. It was also where the Queen herself occasionally entertained and where plays, dances or masques were often held.

The staff of the *Domus Providencie* changed little with a new reign, as the monarch was not personally acquainted with most of the workers, but changes were always made to the staff of the *Domus Magnificencie*. This is because every new monarch already had a team of staff to attend upon them, as well as family members or friends that they wanted to appoint to key positions. However, there was always a degree of overlapping, even during this time of deep religious division, for there were important families that the new monarch could not afford to offend, and courtiers who were flexible enough in their convictions to loyally serve a Catholic or Protestant monarch. One of these was the Queen's great uncle, William Howard, Baron Howard of Effingham, who had carried the canopy at her christening. A Catholic at heart, like most of the Howards, he was trusted enough by Queen Mary to be made Lord High Admiral in 1554 after Edward Clinton, Baron Clinton, was dismissed from the post on account of his religion. In 1558 Lord Clinton was restored to the role, for reasons that are not too clear, but perhaps William had lost the Queen's trust on account of his passionate support for Elizabeth's right to succeed her. However, he retained enough of the Queen's trust to be granted the 'reversion of the office of Lord Chamberlain', meaning he would be the next Lord Chamberlain after the death, dismissal or retirement of the incumbent. For Elizabeth, this arrangement was perfect, as there was no one better than her great uncle, whose loyalty had been tried and tested, for the position, so when the incumbent, Edward Hastings, Baron Hastings of Loughborough, retired upon Queen Mary's death, the new queen was only too glad to make Lord Effingham her new Lord Chamberlain.

Upon William's appointment to the role, his wife, Margrett Gamage, daughter of Welshman, Sir Thomas Gamage of Coity Castle, and whose brother, Robert, was married to Kat's sister, Joan, became the court's 'Lady Chamberlain', a courtesy title bestowed upon the Lord Chamberlain's wife.[4] This made her one of the most influential women at court and she also served as a Lady of Honour and as a Lady of the Privy Chamber. She and William had been married for many years and were the parents of at least eight children, three boys and five girls. Their two eldest daughters, Mary and Dougles, were amongst the Queen's first official Maids of Honour, and their three youngest daughters, Katheryn, Frances and Martha, all under 10 years of age at this time, would serve the Queen in the future as a Maid of Honour or in the Privy Chamber. William also had a daughter from his first marriage, Agnes, who was married to William Paulet, a grandson of William Paulet, Marquess of Winchester, the Queen's first Lord High Treasurer, and in due course she would serve as a Chief Lady of Honour.

The Queen's de facto Lord Chancellor for the first two decades of her reign was Sir Nicholas Bacon, brother-in-law of Sir William Cecil. His wife, Anne, was one of the five 'learned daughters' of Sir Anthony Cooke, a renowned Humanist scholar who tutored Edward VI, and she became a prominent woman at court, although her exact role is not clear. In the post of Lord High Admiral, the Queen retained Lord Clinton, whose position was also perfect as he happened to be the second husband of her dear friend and cousin, Elyzabeth Fitzgerald. Widowed in 1548, Elyzabeth had married the baron in the autumn of 1552 and was his third wife. His first wife had been Bessie Blount, mother of Henry VIII's illegitimate son, Henry Fitzroy, and his second wife had been Ursula Stourton, a first cousin of John Dudley, Duke of Northumberland. By his two wives, Lord Clinton had several children, but he and Elyzabeth are not known to have had any together. However, Elyzabeth was a good stepmother to his children and to the many children of her first husband. During the troubles of Queen Mary's reign, Elyzabeth had stayed loyal to her old mistress, despite her husband's high profile position, and the Spanish Ambassador informed his master just months before Elizabeth's accession that 'the Admiral's wife was brought up with her [Elizabeth] and is devoted to her'.[5] As the wife of the Lord Admiral, Elyzabeth was known by the courtesy title of 'Lady Admiral', and in addition to serving the new queen as a Lady of Honour, she was also made a Lady of the Privy Chamber.

Regardless of what position a woman held, the *Domus Magnificencie* was where she was based. No women at all worked 'below stairs', not even in the kitchens, and in the reign of a king all the 'upstairs staff' were male too, except for a few laundresses or seamstresses, those women who worked in the royal nursery and those who attended upon the queen consort in her own *Domus Magnificencie*. The reign of Queen Mary, then, the first crowned queen regnant in English history, saw a revolution in the way that the royal court was staffed. For in a time when women were subjected to rigorous moral scrutiny, it was essential, for the sake of the Queen's honour and modesty, that the majority of her personal attendants were female. This completely changed the court's dynamic and placed women, not men, at the top of the pyramid of power, for women, not men, now held most of the important positions of attendance, and positions of attendance were highly coveted as they gave much sought after access to the sovereign. In the privacy of a domestic setting, the Queen's women could influence her opinion, advance private suits, and lobby for positions of power for family and friends. The importance of this should not be underestimated, for in the reign of a king women were almost completely excluded from the political arena and were almost entirely dependent on the men around them, or on the queen consort, or on his mistress of the moment, to bring a matter to the king's attention. Now it was women, not men, who had the monarch's ear, and this made the women highly influential figures at court and moved them from the wings of power to centre stage. Courtiers, statesmen, and ambassadors all sought out Queen Mary's women, and then Queen Elizabeth's, in the hope of furthering their causes or to gauge the Queen's mood, and sometimes in an attempt to win their support in a matter would give them a gift.

But of course, the importance of Queen Elizabeth's women should not be measured or defined solely by how powerful or politically influential they were. While the Queen surely discussed politics with a few of her most trusted women, valuing their opinions and insight, her serving women were not in a political role and this was made clear to them from the onset of her reign. Politics was a man's world and then, like now, was divisive and toxic. The Queen, who always presented herself as an 'exceptional' woman, ruling by the grace of God only, did not want to leave a heated meeting with her advisors only to be badgered on political matters by her women. In her private spaces she wanted to relax, to be entertained, to discuss more pleasant subjects. The Queen had a diverse range of interests and studied classical texts, under the tutelage of eminent scholars, for up to three hours a day. Also, it must be remembered that her court was not just the political centre of the country, it was also the cultural. Consequently, the Queen liked to be surrounded by brilliant, well-educated women who not only appreciated literature and music, mythology and history, alchemy and astrology, languages and philosophy, needlework and art, but who could also enjoy horse riding and hunting, dancing and masques, pageants and plays, sporting events and jousts. After all, this was the age of the Renaissance, a time of the Humanist movement, which saw men and women push their intellectual capacities to the limit. The Queen's love of the arts, her passion for learning, her reputation as a scholar, her ability to speak several languages fluently, her fame as a horsewoman, her skills as a musician, and her knowledge of history, geography, philosophy, theology, science and astronomy, meant that aristocratic fathers were very keen to educate their daughters to the highest possible standard so they could impress the Queen and partake in her court's sophisticated cultural life. As a result there were more female intellectuals in the sixteenth century than there ever had been before or would be again for centuries. Indeed, the Queen's ladies and gentlewomen were renowned for their accomplishments which were perfectly summed up by their contemporary, William Harrison:

> Truly, it is a rare thing with us now to hear of a courtier which hath but his own language. And to say how many gentlewomen and ladies there are that besides sound knowledge of the Greek and Latin tongues are thereto no less skilful in the Spanish, Italian, and French... Our ancient ladies of the court do shun and avoid idleness, some of them exercising their fingers with the needle, others in caulwork, divers in spinning of silk, some in continual reading either of the Holy Scriptures, or histories of our own or foreign nations about us, and divers in writing volumes of their own, or translating of other men's into our English and Latin tongue, whilst the youngest sort in the meantime apply their lutes, citherns, pricksong, and all kind of music, which they use only for recreation's sake when they have leisure, and are free from attendance upon the Queen's Majesty or such as they belong unto. How many of the eldest sort also are skilful in surgery and distillation of waters, besides sundry other artificial practices pertaining to the overture and commendations of their bodies, I might easily declare, but I pass over such manner of dealing, lest I should seem to glaver and curry favour with some of them. Nevertheless, this I will generally say of them all, that each of them are cunning in something whereby they keep themselves occupied in the court.[6]

But once a man was on the throne again, and once the great intellectual movement of the Renaissance was over, women returned to the margins and the desire to highly educate them waned.

The three main positions of attendance for women were Ladies and Gentlewomen of the Privy Chamber, Maids of Honour, and Ladies of Honour. There were few other roles. At the beginning of the Queen's reign she had at least twelve 'ladies of the household', who may have been attendant upon Queen Mary or upon herself at Hatfield, but at some point in her reign, perhaps very early on (as the title may have inferred they were of *the* Household rather than the Chamber), these were seemingly absorbed into the Ladies of Honour.[7] There were also about a dozen 'gentlewomen of the household' at the beginning of the reign, but unfortunately nothing is presently known about their role, and by the end of the Queen's reign they were simply known as 'the Queen's women'. However, as Sybil Penn, King Edward's former nurse, was one of these gentlewomen, and she is known to have personally attended upon the Queen in her apartment, these gentlewomen may have assisted the Privy Chamber women by performing some of the more menial tasks of attendance. The Queen also had at least two laundresses. The most important of these was the Mistress Laundress, and over the course of her long reign the Queen had three: Joanne Hilton, her laundress of old, Elyzabeth Smythson, and Anne Twist. The Mistress Laundress was responsible for washing the Queen's personal laundry, which included clothing and bedlinen, and was therefore in a position of some trust. Dirty laundry could tell a lot about the Queen's state of health, such as when and how often she menstruated, which was of great interest to foreign suitors who were considering matrimony, so the Mistress Laundress possessed intimate knowledge about the Queen which made her a figure of some importance at court. The Mistress Laundress did not receive a great wage, for her salary was only £4 a year, a rate comparable to labourers, but she did receive bed and board, along with the usual perks of service, and livery. This livery consisted of 'three yards of puke for a gown', puke being a woollen cloth of reddish (but sometimes greenish) brown, 'three yards of black velvet' for bordering and trimming the gown; 'seven yards of grosgrain silk' for lining the gown; and 'seven yards of tawny camlet for a kirtle'.[8] In Tudor times, gowns, also known as surcoats, were worn by both sexes and were outer-garments worn over doublets and hose for men and over kirtles for women, kirtles being dresses. Women tended to wear gowns more than men, however, as men were considered fully dressed in doublets and hose. The second laundress of importance was the Laundress of the Board. Unfortunately, not as much is known about this laundress, as she was not as important as the Mistress Laundress, but she received the same livery, at least at the beginning of the reign, and was responsible for washing the Queen's tablecloths.[9] Before being promoted to Mistress Laundress, Elyzabeth Smythson served in the role, and she may have been succeeded by Eleanor Cobham who was in post when the Queen died. The Queen also employed women to make items of clothing and accessories for her, such as stockings and ruffs, but these women did not necessarily live at court. The Queen also had her own starcher, Cecilia Bone, who was succeeded by her daughter, Elizabeth Greene.

Surviving court records suggest that laundresses were the only female attendants, aside from Chamberers (see *Of Her Majesty's Privy Chamber*), to routinely receive livery. No livery warrants exist for any other group of female attendants, unlike those surviving from the reign of Queen Mary which detail liveries of black velvet for her Ladies and Gentlewomen of the Privy Chamber. The records may be lost, or are yet to be discovered, but the probability is that most of the Queen's women did not receive livery, except for her coronation and later for her funeral. After all, Maids of Honour had always provided their own clothes, so there was no reason why Ladies and Gentlewomen of the Privy Chamber could not do the same. However, despite the probable absence of livery, it is very likely that the Queen expected her women to dress in certain fashions and colours. Indeed, the Queen's ladies, gentlewomen and maids were exempt from some of the sumptuary laws, which dictated what people of different social ranks could wear, so that they could glorify their mistress by wearing materials reserved for royalty or nobility. For example, according to the 1577 Royal Proclamation *Enforcing Statutes of Apparel*, no woman below the rank of baroness was permitted to wear velvet of 'crimson, carnation or blue', furs of 'black genet or luserns [lynx]', or 'embroidery, wreath-lace, or passamayne lace of gold or silver', except 'the wives of Knights of the Order and of the Privy Council' and 'the Ladies and Gentlewomen of the Privy Chamber, Bedchamber, and Maids of Honour'. The statute also permitted 'such as be the Queen's women' to wear gowns, cloaks, kirtles, furs and cauls in fabrics like damask, silk, taffeta, satin and velvet otherwise restricted to the nobility. For those less affluent, who struggled to dress themselves to this standard, the Queen often made personal gifts of gowns and kirtles, either from her own wardrobe or tailor-made. In terms of colour, the Queen seems to have preferred her women to wear white, the colour of chastity and one of her four colours (white, green, red and black), at least by the end of her reign. Black, the Queen's favourite colour to wear, as it perfectly showcased the rainbow glitz of her glamourous gems, was probably also a staple colour for her women as it not only signified wealth, due to the costliness of the dye, but was needed in times of mourning. But black and white were not the only colours worn by the Queen's women. They wore a rainbow of colours, as did the Queen herself who had garments in her wardrobe ranging from silver and gold to various shades of red, orange, green, blue, purple, pink and brown.[10]

In addition to their wages, all the Queen's resident women received bed and board for themselves and a certain number of servants, stabling for their horses, and the use of royal carriages. Many of the Queen's women, regardless of salary status, also received a gift from the Queen at New Year. Christmas was the highlight of the Tudor court calendar and was celebrated with great gusto. The season began in mid-November, when dark nights brought courtiers back to London from their country estates, and reached its height during the Twelve Days of Christmas. The Queen spent staggering sums of money each year on food, drink, decorations and gifts, and paid no heed to those reformists who wanted to 'ban Christmas'. Indeed, no queen ever celebrated Christmas as lavishly as Good Queen Bess, whose court festivities were no less extravagant than her father's. Over the Twelve Days of Christmas, which began on 26 December and ended on Twelfth Night, 6 January, there would be feasting, dancing, sugar-banquets, plays, masques and all kinds of revelry.[11] These were busy days for the Queen's women, not just because of all the outfit changes she needed, but because of the New Year's gift exchange which took place on New Year's Day. This was the day that gifts were exchanged in Tudor times, and on that day the Queen would exchange gifts with courtiers, servants, ministers of state, bishops and various other people. These gifts were not given to the Queen in person, the ceremony would take too long, but were delivered by the givers, or their servants, to a room in the palace that was set aside for the occasion. Every year the Queen received hundreds of gifts from money to jewels to clothing and confectionary, and all the gifts would be placed on a long table in her gallery, a table up to forty feet in length, so she could pick out those she wanted to keep. The rest would be taken away by her Privy Chamber staff for use elsewhere or for safekeeping. Not all gifts given to the Queen were accepted by the Queen, for if a courtier was out of favour his or her gift might be rejected, but most gifts were accepted. The gifts given in return by the Queen, which were generally collected by servants from a specified location, were typically items of gilt-plate such as cups, bowls, pots, salt cellars, and spoons, and the weight of the item depended on a person's rank or importance to the Queen. Highly favoured Ladies of Honour might receive a gift weighing in excess of forty ounces whereas the Mistress Laundress generally received a gift weighing seven.[12]

Upon being appointed to the Queen's service every woman had to swear an oath of allegiance before the Lord Chamberlain. Oaths were taken very seriously in this religious and superstitious age and acted as an assurance of loyalty. However, there was an element of ceremonial formality about the 'swearing in' of the Queen's women as the majority of those chosen to serve came from a small clique of loyal families. The Queen had many enemies and it was absolutely vital that all her attendants, male or female, could be trusted. For this reason her circle was a closed one and gaining access was almost impossible without being related or connected to someone who was already in it. Once chosen to serve, a woman or girl would receive a written or verbal invitation from the Queen – a very high honour – and if so inclined, or permitted to do so by her parents or guardians, she would take up her position in due course. For invitations to serve were just that, invitations not commandments, but just how easy it was for a woman or girl to decline an invitation without causing offence is not clear. However, as more women and girls wanted to serve than there were places for, and as all candidates were well vetted for suitability and eagerness to serve beforehand, the problem did not occur very often.

All those 'sworn the Queen's woman' were expected to follow court rules, to conduct themselves honourably, and to be of virtuous character. In the sixteenth century, virtuous character for women meant being chaste, obedient, and silent. Women, regardless of their social status, were considered inferior to men, morally, intellectually and emotionally, and were expected to know their place as men's subordinates. It was for this reason that Henry VIII had been desperate for a male heir as he had been conditioned to believe that a woman was incapable of governing. Leaving the throne to a woman was not unprecedented, as Henry I had left his crown to his daughter, Matilda, his only legitimate child, but the outcome had been civil war. The governing lords were not willing to accept a queen regnant and had crowned his nephew, Stephen of Blois, instead, resulting in two decades of anarchy as Matilda and her supporters fought Stephen for the throne. Without a son to succeed him, Henry VIII feared that history would repeat itself, after all, he too had a powerful nephew, King James V of Scotland, who could easily make a challenge for the crown. Although few Tudor women were 'silent' and 'obedient', for the period is full of formidable women who knew how to assert themselves (much to the lamentation of moralists), most were chaste. For maidens, this meant virginity until marriage; for wives, it meant being faithful to their husbands; and for widows it meant being celibate until they remarried. If a woman, especially a maiden, was anything other than chaste then she risked complete ruin – and not just her own ruin but that of her entire family. As hard as it might be to imagine in our more liberal age, 'seducing a virgin' was morally criminal, and all over the country women and their lovers were regularly hauled before church courts to answer for their sexual sins. Those found guilty of fornication or adultery were often punished by 'carting, ducking, and doing of open penance in sheets' (i.e. they were humiliated by being made to stand in white sheets in public places). For those living at court, or within a certain radius of the court, the Knight Marshal, a royal officer, was in charge of moral order, and he had the power to sentence sexual offenders to 'a dragging over the Thames between Lambeth and Westminster at the tail of a boat'.[13] This rarely, if ever, happened, but as a woman, served by women, Queen Elizabeth could not afford to wink at sexual sins amongst her attendants the way her father had done. Sexual scandals had brought down two queens in her childhood, her mother, Anne Boleyn, and her cousin, Katheryn Howard, and during her reign, a scandal of sex and murder saw Mary, Queen of Scots, kicked off her throne. It was therefore imperative that the women who served Elizabeth upheld the moral standards of the day, standards that applied to the Queen too, for any scandal that befell them also befell the Queen.

Over the centuries, it has been said that Queen Elizabeth was a very strict and stern mistress to work for. However, there is no evidence that she was any stricter with her women than any other Tudor queen. All Tudor queens were strict with their women, as the conduct of their women was publicly seen as a reflection of their own moral character. According to William Latymer, Anne Boleyn's chaplain, Elizabeth's mother 'many times' moved her ladies and maids 'to modesty and chastity', forbidding them 'vain toys and poetical fancies' and commanding that 'all trifles and wanton poesies should be eschewed upon her displeasure'. When one of her gentlewomen was discovered to have written 'idle poesies' in a book of prayer, Anne was said to have called the girl before her and 'wonderful rebuked her that would permit such wanton toys in her book of prayers, which she termed a mirror or glass wherein she might learn to address her wandering thoughts'.[14] There are no such stories about Queen Elizabeth, who is known to have disliked Puritan strictness, and she allowed her women a great deal of freedom to pursue their own interests, as declared by William Harrison, and, to the disgust of some Victorians, allowed her Maids of Honour to watch plays (like Shakespeare's) with 'very broad [bawdy] allusions'. In that way, Elizabeth was probably less strict with her women than her mother, and some of the other Tudor queens, who had more time on their hands, as consorts not monarchs, to monitor and discipline their women. Elizabeth did not have the time, for she had a country to rule, and depended upon the women themselves, and upon her senior female staff, for their good conduct.

The Queen's women lived and worked in a majestic world, a world of glittering magnificence and stately splendour, but as privileged as the women were to belong to this world, it was not always an easy one to live in. 'To be a king and wear a crown is a thing more glorious to them that see it than it is pleasant to them that bear it', Queen Elizabeth once declared, and there is no reason to doubt the sincerity of her words.[15] The glory, the opulence, the lavishness, they were all part of the spectacle of monarchy, a necessary show of prestige, a regal backdrop to the stage of power in which the Queen took the limelight. 'Such as come hither from beyond the seas', wrote Francis Osborne, one of the Queen's first historians who was born at the end of her reign, 'calculate the strength, wisdom and honour of a nation by the apparitions they behold at court'. The Queen, therefore, went to great lengths to ensure that her court was visually splendid, right down to the 'stature, strength and birth' of her menial attendants, so that foreign powers would see that 'though a feminine planet governed the fate of England' there was 'little hope to any foreign malignity of operating with success'.[16] The part Elizabeth had to play was not an easy one, and it was not one she had chosen, but it was a part she played for all it was worth. But the diamonds, the pearls, the gold, the silver, the emeralds, the rubies, and all the endless streams of jewels that came her way, could not possibly have meant as much to her on a personal level, except perhaps for a few items of sentimental value, as her critics have claimed. They were all part of the persona of 'being' a queen and 'wearing' a crown, and every item of jewellery had to be accounted for as they belonged to the state as much as to the monarch. The huge palaces of endless corridors and draughty chambers were not always the most comfortable places to live, and there were always throngs of people clamouring for the Queen's attention or jostling with each other for position. Ambition, envy and betrayal were never far away and every courtier had to watch their back. Even those women devoted to the Queen were not immune from family scandals for at least two of her favourite ladies had to temporarily leave court due to treacherous intrigues by family members. At all times the Queen's staff had to be security conscious, for the risk to the Queen of assassination was very real, and behind the glamour of their surroundings were locks and bars on every door, some doors having 'double locks, bolts, staples, and rings'.[17]

Life could also be difficult for those women who fell short of the moral standards of the day and caused a scandal. The Queen, regardless of her personal feelings towards the women, had no choice but to publicly punish them in order to deflect the scandal away from herself. Consequently, those young women who got themselves pregnant, whether out of wedlock or within secret wedlock, were usually sent to the Tower of London along with their lovers or secret husbands. For most of the Queen's reign, however, scandals of this nature were rare. It was only in the 1590s, when court discipline had broken down, that scandals became more common. Most people are a product of their time, and behave in ways that are expected, so most of the Queen's women lived by the morals of the day. Indeed, most of them would have genuinely believed in preserving their virginity until they were married, and in being chaste in their widowhood, and in protecting their 'virtue' at all costs. For those women who married without the Queen's consent, which was a breach of court protocol, but were not pregnant, the punishment was usually a brief period of house arrest in the custody of a Lady of the Privy

Chamber, but scandals of this kind were also uncommon until the 1590s. It is therefore necessary to keep these scandals in perspective, for as interesting as they are, they are not representative of the Queen's women in general, and giving them too much attention distorts the picture of what life in the Queen's service was like for the majority of her women. Most of the Queen's women passed through her service without scandal, retiring quietly upon marriage or dying in her service due to old age or sickness. Of course, this makes their stories harder to write than the stories of their scandalous colleagues, for scandals make headlines and headlines make history, but when thinking of the Queen's ladies, gentlewomen and maids, it is just as important, if not more so, to remember those many quiet souls who served their sovereign loyally and honourably.

No doubt those women who did best in the Queen's service not only enjoyed the hustle and bustle of court life but knew how to be discrete and diplomatic. The Queen's own motto, *See and Say Nothing*, was a good rule to live by. The Queen's most successful women also needed to be able to stay calm under pressure, for there were times when tensions were very high, and to be able to weather storms without creating more tempests. But above all, the Queen's women, regardless of their role, had to know their place. As much as they might shine in their own right, and some of them dazzled, they had to remember at all times, and in all things, that the Queen was the sun of their world, the golden light of their lives, and they, as the silver stars of her court, were never to outshine her.

Chapter Five

Ladies of Honour

CORONATIONS IN TUDOR times were magnificent public spectacles and Queen Elizabeth's was no different. On Thursday 12 January she arrived at the Tower of London for the traditional 'coronation vigil', which was a two day period of religious observance that included making Knights of the Bath, and then on Saturday afternoon, the eve of her coronation, she made her way in glorious procession through the streets of London to the Palace of Westminster. The new queen was seated in a 'chair of honour' within a glorious litter adorned with glittering cloth of gold, a fabric containing real gold that was so expensive that a yard of the finest cost more than a labourer's annual salary, and she was wearing a circlet of gold upon her head and a furred mantle of cloth of gold and silver over a robe and kirtle of the same.[1] The litter was carried by two decorated mules, the first drawn by Lord Gyles Paulet, son of the Marquess of Winchester, and the second by Lord Ambrose Dudley, eldest son of the executed Duke of Northumberland. Sheltering the Queen from the falling flurries of snow was a fringed canopy of gold borne by four knights; flanking the Queen were footmen and equerries; and on the outermost row were her illustrious Gentlemen Pensioners bearing their famous gilt battle-axes. The men wore liveries of red, the colour of coronations, and before the Queen, to the sound of trumpets and drums, came a legion of heralds, gentlemen, knights, peers and statesmen, all wearing liveries of red. Directly behind the Queen, ceremoniously leading her horse, known as the palfrey of honour, was the new Master of the Horse, Lord Robert Dudley, future Earl of Leicester, and directly behind him in great splendour came the 'goodly and beautiful' Ladies of Honour.

Ladies of Honour, sometimes called 'great ladies of the court' or 'Ladies of the Presence', were first and foremost ceremonial escorts. They followed behind the Queen in formal processions and they varied in number from forty or more for state events to just a dozen or less for routine court ceremonies. The majority were ladies of estate, meaning they were peeresses, but some were dames (wives of knights in the sixteenth century) and a small number were the titled daughters of nobles. They were always positioned according to rank, the highest first, the least last, and when they were at court they were based in the magnificent Presence Chamber, hence why they were sometimes called 'Ladies of the Presence'. Although ladies of estate were automatically Ladies of Honour by virtue of their position, in reality a Lady of Honour had to be in favour with the Queen and she had to be a regular visitor to court so she could participate in ceremonies. Most ladies of estate were probably

Ladies of Honour at some point in their lives, if only to keep on the right side of the Queen. As the role was purely honorary, and because participating in state events was, in many ways, a duty of their exalted position in society, the Ladies of Honour were not paid, but they did receive the usual perks of service when at court. Some of the ladies were at court often, for court was, for many, the centre of their social world, whilst others only visited for state events or for the Christmas festivities.

Fronting the ladies was always a Chief Lady of Honour. A Chief Lady of Honour was the highest ranking of the ladies present or the closest in royal blood to the Queen. She usually had the privilege of holding up the Queen's train, sometimes with the assistance of another lady or nobleman, and she would often sit beside the Queen in public. Notable Chief Ladies of Honour over the years were Margaret Douglas, Countess of Lennox, daughter of Margaret Tudor, Henry VIII's eldest sister; Frances Brandon, Duchess of Suffolk, daughter of Mary Tudor, Henry VIII's youngest sister; Ladies Katherine and Mary Grey, daughters of Lady Suffolk; Margaret Clifford, Countess of Derby, granddaughter of Mary Tudor; Elisabeth Parr and Helena Snakenborg, Marchionesses of Northampton; and Agnes Howard and Lucy Cecil, Marchionesses of Winchester.

Because of her father's tortuous marital history, and the poisonous legacy of the split with Rome, the Queen's relationship with her royal cousins was very strained. Lady Lennox, a devout Catholic, had always been hostile to Elizabeth as the daughter of Anne Boleyn, and when Elizabeth was brought to Whitehall Palace in the reign of Queen Mary, under suspicion of treason, it is said that Lady Lennox, who occupied the apartment above hers, deliberately turned one of the rooms into a kitchen and tortured her royal cousin day and night with the continuous 'casting down of logs, pots, and vessels'.[2] Elizabeth is said to have been so traumatised by the experience that forever afterwards she insisted that the rooms of her private apartment, and any lodgings she was to stay in when travelling, were 'far from heat or noise', suggesting that Lady Lennox's kitchen was as hot as it was noisy.[3] Consequently, Elizabeth's relationship with the countess was poor, and when she heard of Elizabeth's accession, the terrified countess fled London for the safety of her northern estates. Elizabeth's relationship with Lady Suffolk was better, for they shared the same religion and had always got on well, but when it came to the crunch Elizabeth could not trust her either for the duchess had been complicit in the Duke of Northumberland's plot to settle the crown upon her daughter, Lady Jane Grey. Both granddaughters of Henry VII were ambitious for their children and both, in their different ways, were a considerable threat. Nevertheless, Elizabeth was keen on improving her relations with the two women and invited both to partake in her coronation as Ladies of Honour.

As Elizabeth was wary of her Tudor cousins, it suited her to keep them in a public role. That way she could give them the honour that their royal blood demanded, for as Chief Ladies of Honour they fulfilled some of the duties traditionally performed by a royal consort, but without having to admit them into her private world. For unless a Lady of Honour was also a Lady of the Privy Chamber, as some of the Queen's women held more than one role, they did not have automatic right of access to the Privy Chamber where the Queen resided. However, being excluded from the illustrious Privy Chamber could and did cause offence. For example, Lady Katherine Grey, who served as both a Lady and Maid of Honour, told a foreign ambassador, not long after the Queen's coronation, that she was 'dissatisfied and offended' at the Queen's 'only making her one of the Ladies of the Presence whereas she was in the Privy Chamber of the late queen who showed her much favour'.[4] As the heir presumptive under the terms of Henry VIII's will, Lady Katherine had reason to feel slighted, but unfortunately for the teenage royal, the heir by primogeniture was Elizabeth's arch-rival, Mary, Queen of Scots. Elizabeth could not recognise Lady Katherine as her heir without offending the Scottish Queen, who was a powerful player on the European stage at this time, but neither could she change the order of succession to make Queen Mary her heir without undermining her father's will upon which her own right to the throne rested. The result was a succession stalemate that lasted until Elizabeth's dying day. To survive this brutal game of crowns, the Grey sisters had to play a crafty hand, but sadly neither sister quite grasped what was at stake. Both believed they could live ordinary lives, despite being an existential threat to two queens, and both ultimately ruined themselves by clandestine marriages. Lady Katherine secretly married Edward Seymour, Earl of Hertford, in the winter of 1560, and Lady Mary secretly married Thomas Keyes, the Queen's Sergeant Porter, in the summer of 1565. For these offences, as it was treason for an heir to the throne to marry without the consent of the Queen, the Privy Council, and of Parliament, both women found themselves and their husbands behind lock and key. Lady Katherine was imprisoned in the Tower of London, where she later gave birth to two boys deemed illegitimate in law as she could produce no witnesses to her marriage, and Lady Mary at Chequers in Buckinghamshire. Tragically, there was to be no happy ending for either sister. Although Lady Katherine was eventually released from the Tower into the custody of her uncle, Lord John Grey of Pyrgo, along with her youngest son, Thomas, she fell into a deep depression and died a broken woman at only 27 years of age. Lady Mary fared somewhat better, for following the death of her husband she was invited back to court to resume her place as a Chief Lady of Honour, but a year later she fell ill and died, possibly of plague. Margaret Douglas, Lady Lennox, was also in and out of royal favour, for she plotted behind the Queen's back to marry her son, Henry Stuart, Lord Darnley, to her niece, the Queen of Scots, a feat she accomplished but which resulted in her imprisonment in the Tower of London. Upon Darnley's murder she was released by the Queen on compassionate grounds, and for a while she resumed her place as a Chief Lady of Honour, only to be returned to the Tower after plotting a marriage for her youngest son, Charles, to Elizabeth Cavendish, daughter of Bess of Hardwick, Countess of Shrewsbury. Of all her Tudor cousins, it was with Margaret Clifford, Countess of Derby, that the Queen had the best relationship, but this relationship also came to a sad end when Margaret, upon the death of Lady Mary Grey in 1578, became the heir presumptive under the terms of Henry VIII's will. Within months she was accused of treason, her crime allegedly being to discover by the black arts when the Queen would die, and the countess spent the rest of her life in semi-imprisonment, first in the custody of Thomas Seckford and then under close surveillance in her own home at Isleworth,

London. The most successful of the Chief Ladies of Honour were therefore those who did not have a claim to the throne, such as Agnes Howard, Marchioness of Winchester, and Helena Snakenborg, Marchioness of Northampton.

For the magnificent procession through London on the eve of her coronation, the Queen's Ladies of Honour, numbering about forty, were each given sixteen yards of crimson velvet and two yards of cloth of gold or tinsel. Tinsel was very much like cloth of gold, except that it was a lighter fabric as it did not contain as much precious metal, so was more suitable for ladies of frailer health or those in the later stages of pregnancy. These two metallic materials came in a variety of colours and finishes, ranging from 'cloth of gold yellow plain' to 'tinsel purple with work', and as the ladies received an assortment of type between them they probably selected their own cloth based on dynastic colour or personal preference. The Duchess of Somerset, for example, had 'cloth of gold tawny plain', the Countess of Oxford had 'cloth of gold purple with work', the Countess of Sussex had 'cloth of gold russet with knots', the Dowager Countess of Worcester had 'cloth of gold black with work', the Countess of Rutland had 'purple gold tinsel with knots', and the Lady Dacre of the South had 'cloth of gold crimson'. Some of the ladies even had a mix of materials, the Countess of Bedford, for example, having 'cloth of gold black with work' and 'cloth of gold russet with knots', and the Lady Berkeley having 'cloth of gold purple plain' and 'cloth of gold yellow plain'.[5] Sadly, there are no known descriptions of the final outfits, but these glitzy cloths of gold and tinsel were for 'turning up' the wide showy sleeves of the ladies' gowns, whilst the crimson velvet was for the gowns themselves.

Both Lady Lennox and Lady Suffolk accepted the Queen's invitation to serve at her coronation. For the turning up of their sleeves they received 'cloth of gold tawny tinsel wrought with roses', and Lady Lennox, as the Queen's senior cousin of royal blood, served as Chief Lady of Honour. As such, the countess headed the Ladies of Honour, riding behind the palfrey of honour upon a horse draped with crimson velvet, whilst Lady Suffolk followed with the Duchess of Norfolk, the Duchess of Somerset, Lady Katherine Grey and Lady Sidney, all riding in single file upon horses also draped with crimson velvet. Behind them came three chariots of honour, each one adorned with red satin and occupied by four or five Ladies of Honour, and after each chariot came six more ladies riding on draped horses. Behind the Ladies of Honour came the Queen's Ladies, Gentlewomen and Maids of the Privy Chamber, riding upon horses in outfits of crimson velvet, red satin or red damask, depending on their status, and then came the Queen's henchmen and guard.[6] The Maids of Honour, as a group, had no role in this procession. They either rode with the Ladies of Honour or with the women of the Privy Chamber. According to an eyewitness, all the Queen's ladies were so 'exquisitely dressed' and so 'handsome and beautiful' that they presented 'a marvellous sight'.[7]

On the day of the coronation itself, the Queen made her way on foot from Westminster Hall to Westminster Abbey, where the ceremony was to take place, in another grand procession of heralds, gentlemen, peers and statesmen. The peers were clad in their robes and caps of estate, their coronets in their hands, whilst the coronation regalia was carried before the Queen by several nobles. The Earl of

Westmoreland carried the sword of state, the Earl of Arundel carried the sceptre, the Marquess of Winchester carried the orb, and the Duke of Norfolk carried the crown. The Queen was dressed in crimson velvet, the ceremonial parliament robe over her shoulders, and her long train was borne by Lady Lennox with the assistance of the Lord Chamberlain.[8] Over the Queen was a canopy borne by the Barons of the Cinque Ports, and she was flanked by the Earl of Shrewsbury to her right, and by the Earl of Pembroke to her left. After the Queen came the Ladies of Honour, but this time they were restricted to noblewomen only. The ladies walked two by two, peeresses above the rank of viscountess holding their coronets in their hands, and they wore rich robes of scarlet (an expensive red woollen cloth) with a train that they elegantly dragged behind them. The scarlet for these robes was given to the ladies by the Queen, the quantity depending on their rank (viscountesses and above received 12 yards, the rest of the ladies 10), and the robes probably had collars of white fur with 'bars of powders' to denote rank, just as Ladies of Honour had at the coronation of Anne Boleyn, a coronation that her daughter followed closely. Powdering was the technique of attaching the black tails of stouts to white fur to create the 'black spot' effect of ermine, and the highest ranking of the peeresses had the most 'bars of powders', meaning rows of black spots, whilst the lowest ranking had the least. When the ceremony was over, the Queen walked back to Westminster Hall for the celebrations in the same order of procession, except that she now carried the orb and sceptre in her hands and was wearing a dress and mantle of purple velvet, and the escorting nobility were now wearing their coronets on their heads. According to the Venetian Ambassador, the Queen 'returned very cheerfully, with a most smiling countenance for everyone, giving them all a thousand greetings', a demeanour that, in his opinion, 'exceeded the bounds of gravity and decorum'.[9] But this was Gloriana in the making, a queen who shone in the spotlight, a queen whose smile lit up a room, a queen who could laugh and joke and make everyone feel like they mattered, a queen with a gift for oratory, a queen who defied convention but found a home in the hearts of her people, and a queen who left her successors with a hard act to follow.

The Ladies of Honour attended the Queen in like glory at the State Opening of Parliament ten days later. Normally, ladies did not participate in the state procession from the sovereign's residence to Westminster, for ladies had no role in government, but because of Elizabeth's gender, she needed a female, as well as a male, escort. After postponing the opening for two days, due to bad weather and ill health, the Queen finally made the procession on 25 January. Once again she rode in an open litter, the crimson velvet parliament robe over her shoulders, and on her head was 'a cap of beaten gold covered with very fine oriental pearls'. After the Master of the Horse, as before, came the Ladies of Honour, this time all 'on horseback with their footmen dressed in their own fashion', and the entire procession was said to be 'neither more nor less' than the coronation entry into London with 'trumpets, kings-at-arms, heralds, and macebearers'.[10] A similar procession, including Ladies of Honour, took place at every State Opening of Parliament throughout the reign.

Ladies of Honour also attended the Queen on 'days of estate', which were primarily religious festivals like Christmas Day, Epiphany, Easter Day and All Saints Day. On these days the Queen would wear full royal regalia, the colour of her robes depending on the occasion, and she would walk in stately procession from the Privy Chamber, where she resided in a suite of private rooms, to the Chapel Royal for a religious service. Those Ladies of Honour at court would walk behind her, the chief of them carrying her train, whilst her Maids of Honour and Privy Chamber women would follow. The procession would move slowly through the great reception halls of 'the Chamber', including through the Presence Chamber, so that all those present at court could witness the glory and the splendour.

Ladies of Honour also attended the Queen during the Order of the Garter ceremonies. These usually took place at Whitehall or Greenwich, rather than at Windsor, and were a three day affair centred on St George's Day, 23 April. That day began with a morning service for the knights in the Chapel Royal, the Queen's choir of gentlemen and boys singing whilst her organist played upon 'a fine organ mainly of gilt silver with large and small silver pipes', and an hour later there was another service, this time in the presence of the Queen, who would make her way from her Privy Chamber to the Chapel Royal in glorious procession. For the occasion, the Queen wore a garter robe of rich purple velvet, which was lined with white taffeta and 'adorned with costly gems and jewels', and the Chief Lady of Honour, perhaps with assistance, would bear her train. Behind the Chief Lady of Honour came the Ladies of Honour, followed by the rest of the Queen's female entourage, and they were all guarded by the Gentlemen Pensioners carrying their 'small gilt pikes'.[11]

The Queen made a similar procession from her Privy Chamber to the Chapel Royal every Sunday for 'divine service'. In 1598 a German visitor, named Paul Hentzner, witnessed this procession in the Presence Chamber of Greenwich Palace, a chamber he said 'shone with tapestry of gold and silver and silk of different colours', and recorded for posterity what he saw:

> First came gentlemen, barons, earls and Knights of the Garter, all richly dressed and bareheaded. Next came the Chancellor, bearing the seals in a red silk purse, walking between two men, one of whom carried the royal sceptre, the other the sword of state in a red scabbard studded with golden fleurs de lis, the point upwards. Next came the Queen, in the sixty-fifth year of her age we were told, very majestic… That day she was dressed in white silk, bordered with pearls of the size of beans, and over it a mantle of black silk, shot with silver threads. Her train was very long, the end of it born by a marchioness, and instead of a chain she had an oblong collar of gold and jewels. As she went along in all this state and magnificence she spoke very graciously, first to one, then to another… Whoever speaks to her, it is kneeling. Now and then she raises some with her hand. While we were there a Bohemian baron had letters to present to her and she, after pulling off her glove, gave him her right hand to kiss, sparkling with rings and jewels, a mark of particular favour. Wherever she turned her face as she was going along everybody fell down on their knees. The ladies of the court followed next to her,

very handsome and well-shaped, and for the most part dressed in white. She was guarded on each side by the Gentlemen Pensioners, fifty in number, with gilt battle-axes.[12]

The marchioness bearing the Queen's train was either Agnes Howard or Helena Snakenborg, and the 'ladies of the court', of course, were the Ladies of Honour, Maids of Honour, and participating Privy Chamber women.

A number of Ladies of Honour also accompanied the Queen on her annual summer progress, which was a tour of the Home Counties that she made every summer. They also accompanied her on formal and informal visits to various people and places, on hunting expeditions (for almost all noblewomen were skilled horsewomen), and on any state occasion that required their presence. One of the most famous appearances of the Queen's Ladies of Honour was at Tilbury, during the Armada invasion, when the Queen made her famous speech to her troops in the last days of the sea battle. This appearance has been forever immortalised by the poet, Thomas Deloney, in a lengthy ballad:

> Then came the Queen, on prancing steed,
>   attired like an angel bright;
> And eight brave footmen at her feet
>   whose jerkins were most rich in sight.
> Her ladies, likewise of great honour,
>   most sumptuously did wait upon her,
> With pearls and diamonds brave adorned,
>   and in costly cauls of gold:
> Her guards, in scarlet, then rode after,
>   with bows and arrows, stout and bold.
>
> The warlike army then stood still,
>   and drummers left their dubbing sound;
> Because it was our Prince's will
>   to ride about the army round.
> Her ladies she did leave behind her,
>   and her guard which still did mind her,
> The Lord General and Lord Marshal
>   did conduct her to each place.
> The pikes, the colours, and the lances,
>   at her approach fell down apace![13]

That autumn there was a special thanksgiving service at St Paul's Cathedral for the country's miraculous deliverance from the Spanish Armada, and the Queen made a magnificent procession from Somerset House to the cathedral in 'a chariot-throne', drawn by two white horses, that had 'a canopy on the top whereof was made a crown imperial', and a number of pillars 'whereon stood a lion and a dragon, supporters of the arms of England'. The Queen's Ladies of Honour followed, as always after the Master of the Horse, and the Chief Lady of Honour at this event was the Queen's cousin, Agnes Howard.[14]

Like many of the ladies who served the Queen over the years, Agnes Howard is a woman that history has not taken much note of. However, Agnes was one of the Queen's Chief Ladies of Honour for a quarter of a century. Named for her grandmother, Agnes Tilney, Duchess of Norfolk, Elizabeth's chief godmother, Agnes became a marchioness when her husband, William, inherited the marquessate in 1576. Although she and William had a very troubled marriage, and he openly kept a mistress, they had at least four children together: one son, William, who married Lucy Cecil, a granddaughter of William Cecil, Lord Burghley, and who eventually inherited the marquessate, and three daughters, Anne, Catherine and Elizabeth. Because Agnes has escaped the attention of historians for so long, very little is known about her, but she was regularly at court and was probably an honorary Lady of the Privy Chamber from the 1570s onwards. Her will, written in the summer of 1599, two years before her death, reveals a clever, learned, and religious lady with a poetic mind:

> ...calling to my remembrance the ever changing course of all flesh which never remains in one estate, being in the prime but as the summer flowers, and in the declination withered grass, today living, tomorrow dying, and weighing also with myself that the greatest life's happiness is in the happy issue out of this transitory pilgrimage, which is in nothing so much apparent to the world as in the well disposing of those earthly talents which our most excellent God hath lent us in this life ... as touching myself, whose essence is of two principal parts, of a living soul and human flesh subsisting, I do commend my everlasting soul to the everlasting mercy of my redeemer ... that through my settled faith in him, I shall receive by his mercy, not my merit, eternal salvation in the heavenly tabernacle ... and concerning my body, whose matter is dust, and whose mother is earth, I leave the same to the ground, to be interred in his mother's bowels at the Chapel in Basing, close adjoining to my said late honourable husband deceased, with such solemnity and human ceremony as are beseeming my estate without exceeding in pomp or worldly ostentation...

In this will Agnes also affectionately remembered her royal mistress and left her a jewel worth £200:

> I cannot but record my most bounden and loyal duty to my most gracious and dread Sovereign, our most excellent Empress, the Queen's most excellent Majesty, to whom in my most humble and hearty manner I render my most hearty thanks for all Her Highness's most loving and gracious kindnesses at all times (undeserved of me) willingly extended and vouchsafed unto me out of her most high and princely disposition. And in token of my mindfulness of such princely kindnesses I do most humbly beseech her most gracious Majesty to

accept of one jewel to be provided by my executors for Her Highness to the value of two hundred pounds, which although as no other gift of what estimable value soever can any way counterpoise the weight of her princely regard of me, her respected subject, nor is fitting the majesty of her sacred person, yet as the world's owner accepted the widow's mite only, so my hope is Her Grace's accustomed good acceptation of all gifts offered will vouchsafe the acceptation of this my small oblation, joined with my continual prayers, to my last out breathing, to the most sacred, for the long continuance of Her Royal Majesty in all felicity and happiness, Amen.[15]

The longest serving of the Queen's Chief Ladies of Honour was Helena Snakenborg, Marchioness of Northampton, who served in the role for over thirty years. Helena, an exceptional beauty with flaming red hair, came to England in the retinue of Princess Cecilia of Sweden in 1565 and instantly captured the heart of William Parr, Marquess of Northampton, brother of Kateryn Parr, perhaps because she reminded him of his beloved late wife, Elisabeth. Helena, whose native name was Ellin, returned his affection, even though he was a lot older than herself, but unfortunately for the couple William had the status of 'married widow' so they could not marry right away. This was because William was a divorced man, his first marriage to Lady Anne Bourchier having been annulled on the grounds of her adultery. But even though his divorce was recognised in law, remarriage, even in the Protestant Church of England, was tricky while his first wife lived. For this reason, his second marriage to Elisabeth, daughter of George Brooke, Baron Cobham, a man with Boleyn blood in his veins, had always been controversial and was declared unlawful in the reign of Queen Mary. Queen Elizabeth recognised the marriage, and showed great favour to the second marchioness, who during her lifetime often served as Chief Lady of Honour, but even though the Queen was Supreme Governor of the Church of England, authorising a new marriage was difficult. Helena and William thus did not marry until Lady Anne's death in 1571, but Helena stayed in England in the meantime and served the Queen in her Privy Chamber. Sadly, the marriage, when it finally happened, was very short lived, as William died within months, leaving Helena a young widow. She was now known as 'the Lady Marquess', a title she retained for life, and she remained in England serving the Queen. Over the years, she and the Queen became very close, and of all the Chief Ladies of Honour, it was Helena who was most often at the Queen's side, sitting beside her at both public and private events. In 1576, however, their relationship came under strain when Helena wanted to marry one of the Queen's grooms, Thomas Gorges. As fond as the Queen was of Thomas, she did not believe it was appropriate for a marchioness to marry a groom, a man whose status was so below her own, so the Queen was reluctant to give her consent. Helena, fearing the Queen would never give her consent, married Thomas in secret, and for this breach of duty was dismissed from court whilst Thomas was imprisoned in the Tower of London. Eventually, the Queen forgave the couple, welcomed them back to court, and stood as godmother to their first child, a little girl named Elizabeth, but just as the Queen feared, Helena lost a degree of social standing because of the marriage. Although she continued to be known as 'the Lady Marquess', in time her position as one of the Queen's Chief Ladies of Honour became controversial in the cut-throat world of the court. Not only was she a foreigner, but she was not a peeress in her own right, and the husband from whom she had the title of marchioness was long dead. In 1595 Edmund Spenser, the acclaimed poet, felt the need to justify her position as a Chief Lady of Honour in his popular work *Colin Clouts Come Home Again*:

> No less praiseworthy is Mansilia [Helena],
> Best known by bearing up great Cynthia's [Elizabeth's] train:
> That same is she to whom Daphnaida
> Upon her niece's death I did complaine:
> She is the pattern of true womanhead,
> And only mirror of femininity,
> Worthy next after Cynthia to tread,
> As she is next her in nobility.

Daphnaida was an elegy written 'upon the death of the noble and virtuous Douglas Howard', a daughter of Henry Howard, Viscount Howard of Bindon, and Frances Mewtas, a former Maid of Honour. Douglas was married to Helena's nephew, Arthur Gorges, a young man who also happened to be Kat Astley's great nephew as his mother was Winifred Budockshed, the daughter of Kat's sister, Frances. By the time this elegy was written, Queen Elizabeth was celebrated by poets as the virgin goddess of the moon, Cynthia or Diana, as well as an embodiment of the sun. But opinions continued to differ on Helena's pre-eminence and in 1603 Lucy Cecil, Marchioness of Winchester, challenged her for the role of Chief Mourner at the Queen's funeral.[16]

The longest serving Lady of Honour was Anne Morgan, Baroness Hunsdon, Lady Troy's granddaughter. Her father was Sir Thomas Morgan of Arkstone, Herefordshire, another man of Welsh descent, and her mother was Lady Troy's only daughter, Elizabeth Whitney. Only in her teens when she married Henry Carey, who was made Baron Hunsdon just days before the coronation, Anne was still a young woman when Elizabeth became queen. By now, she and Henry were the parents of at least eight children, all but one boys, and their family was still growing. Their only daughter, Katheryn, was probably their eldest child, for she was made a salaried Gentlewoman of the Privy Chamber not long after the coronation, suggesting she was at least 12 years of age at the time. It was not until the winter of 1562 that Katheryn finally had a sister, for three days before Christmas Anne gave birth to her first little girl in years at her London home in Cannon Row. Such was the excitement at court at the news that the Queen herself stood as godmother to the baby girl, along with Margaret Audley, Duchess of Norfolk, and for her new little cousin's name, the Queen chose the unusual one of Philadelphia, meaning 'brotherly love' – a name choice that might pique the interest of those who believe the children of William Carey were really Henry VIII's. Two years later, Anne gave birth to another little girl, her final child, Margaret, who was named for her chief godmother, Lady Lennox.

Although Henry was an unfaithful husband, keeping mistresses and fathering illegitimate children, Anne, like many women of the time, turned a blind eye and played the dutiful wife. At the time of his death, Baron Hunsdon was the Queen's Lord Chamberlain, making Anne the court's Lady Chamberlain, and she was also Keeper of Somerset House in her own right. Anne also served the Queen as a Lady of the Privy Chamber for the entire reign. Indeed, she outlived the Queen and saw not only her three daughters serve in the Privy Chamber but also two granddaughters, Elizabeth and Frauncis Howard. She also saw a third granddaughter, Anne Carey, serve as a Maid of Honour alongside her great granddaughter, Elizabeth Southwell. Baroness Hunsdon seems to have been the only Lady of Honour to serve as such at the Queen's coronation and funeral, and as she walked in procession behind the Queen's coffin in her black mourning livery, no doubt she remembered the young and charismatic queen who had told the cheering Londoners on the eve of her coronation 'be ye well assured I shall stand your good queen' and who had, despite the many challenges of her reign, kept her word.

Chapter Six

Maids of Honour

MAIDS OF HONOUR, like Ladies of Honour, were primarily escorts. Whereas Ladies of Honour were ceremonial escorts, escorting the Queen in public processions and on important state and court occasions, Maids of Honour were personal escorts, escorting the Queen on a daily basis as she moved around her gardens, palaces and parks, or when she made less formal visits to people and places. In the absence of a Lady of Honour, or a Lady of the Privy Chamber, one (or more) of the maids carried the Queen's train or mantle, and in summer they probably had the task of carrying a parasol over the Queen to protect her pale complexion from the tanning power of the sun.

Of all the Queen's female attendants, Maids of Honour are the most famous. This was the case in the Queen's lifetime and has remained so throughout history. The maids, generally six in number, were beautiful and glamourous, confident and charming, and as they spent a lot of time in the Presence Chamber, sitting with the Queen during routine audiences or talking with courtiers, visitors and ambassadors, they were the most visible of the Queen's attendants and the most accessible. The maids also often entertained visitors with masques or ballets which further cast them into the public eye. One of these early entertainments was witnessed by a French visitor, Pierre de Bourdeille, Seigneur de Brantôme, who later recalled it in his memoirs:

> One evening, the Queen gave us all a supper in a grand chamber hung round with tapestry representing the Parable of the Ten Virgins of the Gospels. When the banquet was done, there came in a ballet of her Maids of Honour, whom she had dressed and ordained to represent the same virgins. Some of them had their lamps burning and full of oil, and some of them carried lamps which were empty; but all their lamps were silver, most exquisitely chased and wrought, and the ladies were very beautiful, well mannered, and very well dressed. They came during the ballet and prayed us French to dance with them, and even prevailed on the Queen to dance, which she did with much grace and right royal majesty, for she possessed then no little beauty and elegance.

In the first few days and weeks of her reign, it is likely that Elizabeth was escorted by her Hatfield maids, but by her coronation her first six official Maids of Honour were in place. These were Lady Katherine Grey; Lady Jane Seymour, daughter of the late Lord Protector; Lady Jane Howard, great niece of Lord Howard of Effingham; Mary and Douglas Howard, daughters of Lord Howard of Effingham; and Mary Mansell, daughter of Sir Rhys Mansell, whose brother was married to a granddaughter of Lady Troy's niece, Elizabeth Herbert of Raglan Castle. The two Mary's had previously served as Maids of Honour to Queen Mary but the other four were new recruits. The three titled ladies served as Ladies of Honour in the coronation eve procession, receiving the same sumptuous materials as the Ladies of Honour, as did Mary and Douglas Howard, who rode with the Ladies of Honour even though they were not one themselves. Mary Mansell, on the other hand, who was not a lady or related to the Queen, received sixteen yards of crimson satin for a gown, rather than of velvet, and rode with the women of the Privy Chamber. For the turning up of her sleeves, however, she received the same material as Lady Katherine Grey, which was two yards of 'purple tinsel with work'. The rest of the maids had two yards of cloth of gold in various colours and finishes. Lady Jane Seymour had cloth of gold 'black with work'; Lady Jane Howard, 'purple damask making with work'; Mary Howard, 'green with work'; and Douglas Howard, 'yellow plain'. For the day of the coronation itself, the three titled ladies received ten yards of scarlet for robes whilst the other three received five.[1]

Although it is often said that the Queen's Maids of Honour were young girls, girls as young as 13 or 14, in reality a girl had to be at least 16 years of age (the female age of adulthood) to be a Maid of Honour. There may have been exceptions, of course, especially if a girl was almost 16, but in general a maid was in her late teens or early twenties when she was appointed. Indeed, 'twenty-something' seems to have been the average age of a maid. This can be seen in a snapshot of approximate ages by decade commencement:

    1560: 23, 22, 22, 20, 18, 18
    1570: 32, 25, 21, 20, 18, 18
    1580: 35, 29, 26, 25, 19, 18
    1590: 39, 27, 25, 24, 23, 21
    1600: 25, 22, 22, 21, 20, 16

The Maid of Honour in her late thirties in 1590 was Katheryn Howard, one of the youngest daughters of Lord Howard of Effingham. She was the Queen's second longest serving maid, serving in the role for an impressive twenty years. Very little is known about Katheryn, as she has left a very light historical footprint, but she never married and retired as a maid in 1591, perhaps upon reaching her fortieth birthday. For her many years of dedicated service she received a pension from the Queen amounting to 100 marks a year (about £66) and she was probably made a Gentlewoman of the Privy Chamber upon retirement as she remained at court.[2] Her sister, Mary, was also one of the longest serving maids and by 1570 was the only original Maid of Honour still in service. The following year she married a man named Edward Sutton, Baron Dudley, and for the rest of her life probably served the Queen as a Lady of Honour. The longest serving maid of all was Mary Radclyffe, a cousin of the Queen's, who served in the role for almost a quarter of a century.

As there was huge prestige, and potential political and financial gain in having a daughter serve as a Maid of Honour, the competition for places was fierce. In the reign of Henry VIII, parents or guardians, usually female, would try to butter up the Queen's women with expensive gifts, like jewellery or culinary delicacies, in the hope they would use their influence with the Queen to secure a place for their daughters as a Maid of Honour. One such parent was Honor Grenville, Lady Lisle, the same Lady Lisle who sent Kat's sister a gift. The formidable viscountess was determined to have one of her daughters, Katherine or Anne, appointed as a Maid of Honour to Jane Seymour, and in the hope of achieving this she sent gifts of quail to Lady Rutland for the pregnant queen. Her efforts paid off as her two daughters were summoned to court for an audience with Queen Jane, who wished to see both before choosing one, and Anne, the prettier and the sassier of the sisters, was chosen. This was not the kindest method of recruitment and Queen Elizabeth appears to have done things a little differently. When faced with a choice between two sisters, she would either take them both, as she did with Mary and Dougles, take the eldest first or offer the eldest a position in the Privy Chamber if she did not have the right qualities to be a Maid of Honour. These qualities, in a nutshell, were good looks and a good figure; good posture and a good carriage; good conversational skills; good energy levels; good horse riding skills; and all the usual accomplishments of aristocratic women. If a woman lacked one or more of these qualities, then she was better suited to the Queen's private world where she was less on show.

Sadly, despite the length of the Queen's reign, little survives to tell us what happened after a young woman was chosen to be a Maid of Honour. However, we get a little insight into the process from the letters of Lady Lisle as not much changed over the period. After Anne was 'sworn the Queen's maid', her mother was informed by letter of all the things she would need to serve. These things were primarily clothes, with the Queen being very particular about the kinds of gowns she wanted Anne to wear, but Lady Lisle was also told to provide her daughter with bedding and a gentlewoman to attend her. In return for her service, Anne was to receive bed and board for herself and her servant and a salary of £10 a year. This was not an insignificant amount, for it was two or three times the annual salary of a labourer, but considering that Maids of Honour did not receive livery, except for very special occasions, £10 would barely buy two gowns.[3] However, parents or guardians were more than willing to bear all the charges associated with being a Maid of Honour for the privilege of having a daughter, or close relative, in the Queen's service.

Queen Elizabeth's Maids of Honour also received a salary of £10 a year, rising to £20 by 1600, and the practice of parents and guardians providing gowns and other necessities continued.[4] Black and white gowns were probably requested as standard, perhaps silver too, as the Queen's maids wore silver often, but whether the maids were expected to co-ordinate their appearances so that they always wore gowns of matching colours, or whether they were free to wear gowns in colours of their own choosing, providing they were permitted colours, is unclear. Generally, however, the maids seem to have worn gowns of matching colours, at least on formal occasions, and sometimes the Queen commissioned matching gowns for them, as she did in 1565 during the visit of Princess Cecilia of Sweden, when she ordered six matching gowns of yellow satin for the court wedding of Lady Anne Russell, a Maid of the Privy Chamber, to Ambrose Dudley, by then Earl of Warwick. Sometimes the Queen gifted garments to her Maids of Honour too, but usually on an individual basis, these garments being from her own wardrobe or tailor-made.

Once a Maid of Honour was 'sworn in' she lived permanently at court and had to have special permission from the Queen to leave. The maids lodged together in a dormitory known as the maidens' chamber. In some of the smaller palaces this may have been one room with multiple beds but in the bigger palaces, like Whitehall, at least some of the maids, like Lady Jane Seymour, had their own private closet (small room) within the dormitory. These closets may have been in mezzanine style around a communal space, as might have been the case in Wallingford Castle, or semi-partitioned bays as appears to have been the case in Windsor Castle.[5] Despite its imposing facade, Windsor Castle was not the most comfortable of royal residences, partly because it was not lived in very often, but the Queen was very fond of the castle and embarked on a programme of improvements in the 1580s. As part of these improvements the Queen's maids 'desired to have their chambers ceiled' and 'the partition that is of boards to be made higher' because 'the servants looked over'.[6] The maidens' chamber was probably located near the former queen consort's apartment, rather than near the monarch's, and should not be confused with the coffer chamber, which seems to have been a common room or lounge where the Queen's women, as well as others, socialised. In 1602, for example, the coffer chamber was made ready for a visit to court by an important French embassy, which would not have been the case if it was where the Maids of Honour slept. In 1603, Lady Anne Clifford, who was visiting court with her aunt during the Queen's final illness, was made to 'wait in the coffer chamber'; and in his memoirs, Sir Robert Carey, son of Baroness Hunsdon, tells us that when the Queen was dying he 'left word with one in the coffer chamber' to keep him informed and this 'one' was a man.[7] The coffer chamber was close to the Privy Chamber, according to descriptions and plans of various palaces, and was therefore perfectly located for the Maids of Honour to await the Queen's pleasure, which perhaps they did several times a day. According to a story that emerged in the seventeenth century, the maids could be noisy at night, disturbing those who slept next to the coffer chamber or maidens' chamber:

> The Lord Knollys, in Queen Elizabeth's time, had his lodging at court, where some of the Ladies and Maids of Honour used to frisk and hey about in the next room, to his extreme disquiet at nights, though he had often warned them of it; at last he gets one to bolt their own back door, when they were all in one night at their revels, strips off his shirt, and so with a pair of spectacles on his nose, and Aretino in his hand, comes marching in at a postern door of his own chamber, reading very gravely, full upon the faces of them. Now let the reader judge what a sad spectacle and pitiful fright these poor

creatures endured, for he faced them and often traversed the room in this posture above an hour.[8]

The 'Lord Knollys' of this tale was the Queen's cousin, William Knollys, and the book he was allegedly reading aloud was a work by Pietro Aretino, an Italian author who wrote, amongst other things, about courtesans.

The Queen's Maids of Honour were not always on duty at the same time. When the Queen was taking a walk in her private garden, for example, she was often accompanied by only two maids. The busiest time of day for the maids was probably mealtimes. The Queen had two main meals a day, dinner and supper, and these two meals were officially served in the Presence Chamber with great ceremony. According to Paul Hentzner, who witnessed the ceremony in 1598, after the Queen's table was set by four men, there emerged from the Privy Chamber 'an unmarried lady (we were told she was a countess)' and 'a married one bearing a tasting-knife'. These were the Queen's lady carver and lady taster, favoured noblewomen of the Privy Chamber, who had an important role to play at mealtimes. The lady carver was responsible for carving the Queen's meat when she dined in private (the court's official Carvers did this when she dined in public) and the lady taster was responsible for testing the Queen's food for poison. The lady carver, who at this time was Frauncis Howard, Dowager Countess of Kildare, prostrated herself three times before the Queen's vacant throne and then, 'in most graceful manner', approached the Queen's table where she 'rubbed the plates with bread and salt with as much awe as if the Queen had been present'. When this was done, the Yeomen of the Guard, to the sound of 'twelve trumpets and two kettle-drums', entered the hall bringing in 'a course of twenty-four dishes'. These dishes, 'most of them gilt', were placed upon the Queen's table 'while the lady taster gave to each of the guard a mouthful to eat, of the particular dish he had brought, for fear of poison'. When the ceremony was over 'a number of unmarried ladies' appeared 'who with particular solemnity lifted the meat off the table and conveyed it into the Queen's inner and more private chamber'. These 'unmarried ladies' were probably the Queen's Maids of Honour, perhaps assisted by Maids of the Privy Chamber, and after the Queen had selected the dishes she fancied 'the rest goes to the ladies of the court' who generally dined in the Presence Chamber with favoured courtiers. The Maids of Honour themselves dined in the Great Chamber, along with 'the waiting gentlewomen of great ladies', and had their own table.[9]

Whether the Queen's Maids of Honour had any other duties aside from escorting the Queen, ceremoniously delivering her meals, and entertaining the Queen and her guests, is unclear. An anecdote told by Sir Francis Bacon in the seventeenth century suggests that they may have had light duties in the Privy Chamber, such as assisting the staff in preparing hot snacks for their mistress, but assuming there is truth in the anecdote, the maids referred to might also be the Maids of the Privy Chamber:

Sir Fulke Greville [Gentleman of the Privy Chamber] had much and private access to Queen Elizabeth, which he used honourably and did many men good, yet he would say merrily of himself that he was like Robin Goodfellow, for when the maids spilt the milk pans, or kept any racket, they would lay it upon Robin. So what tales the ladies about the Queen told her, or other bad offices that they did, they would put it upon him.[10]

In charge of the Maids of Honour was the Mother of the Maids. The Mother of the Maids was a woman of mature years who supervised and organised the Maids of Honour. She was always married, or widowed, and was a Gentlewoman of the Privy Chamber. The Mother worked closely with the Queen's senior attendants, for there were schedules to plan, ceremonies to prepare for, clothes and accessories to procure, and entertainments to rehearse. She was paid £20 a year, in addition to the usual perks of service, and she resided at court. Over the course of the Queen's reign at least ten women are known to have served in the role: Anne Morris; Anne Aglionby; Mistress Harvey; Elysabeth Hyde; Agnes Allen; Margaret Battista Castiglione; Elizabeth Jones; Elizabeth Wingfield; Katherine Bromfield; and Mistress Brydges. Unfortunately, not all these women can be identified with certainty, and it is presently unknown when Agnes Allen served as the only reference to her service is her burial entry in a parish register. The identity of Mistress Harvey is a complete mystery, but she is believed to be the Mother of the Maids who caused hysteria by suddenly dropping down dead before the Queen in the Privy Chamber of Greenwich Palace. Believing the unfortunate woman carried some terrible disease, like the plague, 'the Queen took fright' and 'within an hour' had fled the palace 'with a very small company' for 'my Lord of Leicester's house in London'.[11]

As Maids of Honour were, by definition, unmarried, their time in service naturally came to an end when they married. Indeed, for most of the Queen's maids, marriage was the way they retired, and there was, in general, a marriage amongst the maids every two to three years, although sometimes there were several a year. For most of the Queen's reign, scandals involving Maids of Honour were very rare. Between 1558 and 1590 there were only three, literally one per decade. The first, in 1561, was the scandal of Lady Katherine Grey's secret marriage to Lord Hertford. This scandal involved another Maid of Honour too, Lady Jane Seymour, Lord Hertford's sister. The couple claimed that she had procured the priest who had married them, that she was the only one who knew his identity, and that she had been the ceremony's only witness. Elizabeth and her advisors were sceptical, as they found it hard to believe that Lady Jane, 'a woman of singular calling', would 'go abroad out of the house to fetch a priest'. As Lady Jane had recently died of tuberculosis, she could not be called upon to confirm their claims, so it was feared that the couple were making up the story to make respectable their predicament (Lady Katherine was pregnant) or because they were part of a wider plot to take the throne. The result was, of course, years of heartbreak for Lady Katherine, who was permanently imprisoned, which culminated in her tragic death in 1568. It was an unkind and undeserved fate, for Lady Katherine simply wanted to be with the man she loved, but like the Queen of Scots, who was about to be imprisoned herself upon her arrival in England, she had not played the game of crowns as well as Elizabeth and, some might say, Lady Lennox.

However, Lady Katherine would, like the Queen of Scots, have a victory over Elizabeth in death. For while Elizabeth's bloodline died with her, Lady Katherine's, though her eldest son, Edward Seymour, Lord Beauchamp, flowed though the veins of another queen, the longest reigning queen in history, Queen Elizabeth II. The second scandal, seventeen years later, was caused by Martha Howard, the youngest daughter of Lord and Lady Howard of Effingham, who gave birth to an illegitimate child at court in 1578. The father, George Bourchier, fled at the news, fearing for his life, whilst Martha was sent to the Tower of London. George, when apprehended, was also sent there, and George's sister, Lady Susan Bourchier, another Maid of Honour, was dismissed for having helped the couple to meet secretly. For Queen Elizabeth, the scandal was as awkward as it was damaging, given how close she was to the Howards, even though her great uncle had passed away some years before, but when the scandal had blown over, the Queen released the couple from the Tower, permitted them to marry, and helped Martha to restore her shattered reputation by knighting her husband, which gave her the respectable title of Lady Bourchier. The third scandal of a similar nature but even more shocking as it involved adultery, was caused by Anne Vavasour, a new Maid of Honour, who got herself pregnant by Lord Burghley's son-in-law, Edward de Vere, Earl of Oxford, in the early 1580s. Like Martha, Anne was sent to the Tower of London, as was her lover, but unlike Martha, it was harder for Anne to recover her reputation upon release, and although she went go on to make a respectable marriage, she eventually became the mistress of Sir Henry Lee, the Queen's jousting champion.

The 'naughty nineties', as the 1590s might be termed, was when scandals really became a problem. Indeed, the decade saw more scandals than the previous three combined and, disastrously for the Queen, most of them happened at the same time, beginning with the secret marriage of Frances Vavasour, Anne's sister, to Sir Thomas Sherley in 1591. This marriage came as a shock to everyone as Frances, with the Queen's approval, was betrothed to Robert Dudley, the Earl of Leicester's illegitimate son, and Sir Thomas was courting Lady Cobham's widowed daughter, Frances Brooke, Lady Stourton. The outcome was outrage and Robert Cecil, Lady Stourton's brother-in-law and one of the Queen's principal secretaries, informed Sir Thomas's father that his son 'highly hath offended' the Queen who 'graciously hath always furthered, in good sort, any honest and honourable purposes of marriage or preferment to any of hers, when, without scandal and infamy, they have been orderly broken unto her'.[12] As there are no known cases of the Queen withholding her consent from a Maid of Honour, when asked for it, this is surely a fair assessment despite what many history books tell us. Frances was the first Maid of Honour, who was not pregnant, to marry in secret, and only one more maid, who was not pregnant, did so – Maria Tuchet, who, in 1594, married in true Romeo and Juliet style, Thomas Thynne, son of a family at war with her own. As there is no record of the couple ever being punished, it is possible that the marriage was a ploy by Maria's mother, in cahoots with the Queen, to bring the feud, which was making its presence felt at court, to an end. Maria's mother was Lucy Marvyn, Baroness Audley, a daughter of Amy Clarke, Lady Marvyn, who had served the Queen in her Privy Chamber for decades. Lucy was therefore well acquainted with the Queen and probably served as a Lady of Honour from time to time. The story goes that Lady Audley arranged for her daughter and Thomas to meet at an inn one night in the hope that the two teenagers, who had never seen each other before, would fall in love. To her delight, they did, immediately at first sight, so she arranged for them to marry in an upstairs room. Afterwards, Maria went back to court, and Thomas to Oxford, where he was a student, and the marriage was kept secret for a year. When the secret was finally out, it was not the Queen who was furious but Maria's new father-in-law, Sir John Thynne, who vowed that he was going to have the marriage annulled. But, despite a long lawsuit that lasted years, the angry father was unsuccessful in his endeavours and the marriage was declared legal in 1601. Sadly, Maria died ten years later in childbirth, but for a while she and Thomas lived happily at Longleat, the family seat in Wiltshire that Thomas inherited at his father's death, with their young children.

The second scandal of 1591, just a month after Frances Vavasour's secret marriage, was the news that one of the Queen's Maids of Honour had given birth in the maiden's chamber. This maid was Katherine Leigh, a distant cousin of the Queen's, who had been conducting a secret affair with Sir Francis Darcy, a great grandson of Baroness Bryan. At the same time as this scandal broke, it was widely reported that Elizabeth Southwell, a niece of Lady Cobham's, was pregnant by a married man – Thomas Vavasour, Frances's brother – and that Robert Dudley, the Earl of Leicester's illegitimate son, was 'commanded from court for kissing Mistress Cavendish in the Presence', another Maid of Honour.[13] These scandals, all at the same time, were absolutely shocking and one Londoner wrote to a friend that 'the talk in London is all of the Queen's maids that were'.[14] Someone had to take the blame for the deplorable state of things, for the crisis was unprecedented, and that someone was the Mother of the Maids, Elizabeth Jones. The unfortunate lady, who was a granddaughter of Sir John and Lady Shelton, was consequently sent to the Tower of London along with Katherine Leigh and her lover. Just how long she remained there is unknown, but Katherine and Sir Frances were not released until the following summer. Before they were, they were married in the Chapel of St Peter Ad Vincula, and although Katherine went on to have a happy family life with Sir Frances, she never regained the Queen's favour.

Robert Dudley married Elizabeth Cavendish, making respectable that scandal, and Elizabeth Southwell, Lady Cobham's niece, continued as a Maid of Honour, somehow managing to get away with her pregnancy (for she was indeed pregnant, though the Earl of Essex, rather than Thomas Vavasour, was the father) by giving birth away from court and keeping her baby boy a secret, something she appears to have done successfully for some years. However, the Queen eventually found out, and Elizabeth was dismissed from service, but luckily for her it appears as though the Queen did not want to provoke a new scandal so she went unpunished. Frances Vavasour also got off quite lightly with her offence, though her husband spent time in Marshalsea Prison, and she was evidently well thought of by the Queen as she was admitted into her Privy Chamber by the end of the reign. Poor Elizabeth Jones, who shouldered all the blame for the scandals, was also quietly brought back to the Queen's service but never again served as Mother of the Maids.

Elizabeth Wingfield, who took Mistress Jones's place as Mother of the Maids, was successful in restoring order and decorum so it was some years before another scandal broke. That scandal involved another pregnant maid, Elizabeth Vernon, who upon disclosing her condition claimed to be married to Henry Wriothesley, Earl of Southampton. The scandal depressed the Queen, who 'came not to chapel' that Sunday, and Robert Cecil wrote to the earl, who was in France, informing him that the Queen was 'grievously offended' that he had 'married one of her Maids of Honour without her privity [knowledge]' and told him that he must immediately 'repair hither to London', giving no excuses, and to await her pleasure 'without coming to court'.[15] The earl, however, was afraid to return, and a few weeks later another letter was sent to him from Henry Brooke, Baron Cobham, Lady Cobham's son, who was now Lord Warden of the Cinque Ports, reassuring him that 'the Queen's displeasure will not long continue' if he promptly returns.[16] But still the earl stayed away, claiming he lacked the funds to make the journey home, and left his young wife, who was now seven months pregnant, to fret and worry in 'the sweetest and best appointed lodging in the Fleet' where, allegedly, she had been sent.[17] Eventually the earl arrived, just days before Elizabeth gave birth to a little girl, and he was immediately imprisoned in the Fleet. The earl and his new wife were not there long, however, and by 1601 the couple had bigger problems as the earl had been condemned to death for his part in the Essex Rebellion. The Queen lessened his sentence to life imprisonment, keeping him a prisoner in the Tower of London for the rest of her reign, but Elizabeth Vernon may eventually have recovered the Queen's favour as she served as a Lady of Honour at the Queen's funeral in 1603, along with her mother-in-law, Mary Browne, Dowager Countess of Southampton, step-granddaughter of Elyzabeth Fitzgerald.

The last Maid of Honour of the reign to cause a scandal was Mary Fitton, a young woman in her early twenties who fell pregnant after a secret affair with the new Earl of Pembroke, William Herbert. Unfortunately for Mary, the earl refused to marry her, despite pressure from his family and hers, so her reputation was completely ruined. The earl was sent to the Fleet, now the standard place of imprisonment for such offenders, whilst Mary, perhaps due to tender health, was put into the custody of a Lady of the Privy Chamber. When her health took a turn for the worst, perhaps induced by stress, a doctor was called, but sadly the baby she later gave birth to was either born dead or died soon after birth. Like Anne Vavasour before her, Mary never really recovered her reputation, and within months of the scandal had become another man's mistress. After his death, she had an affair with a man named Captain William Polwhele, which resulted in another pregnancy, and her behaviour was so scandalous that her mother wished that 'it had pleased God, when I did bear her, that she and I had been buried, it had saved me from a great deal of sorrow and grief, and her from shame, and such shame as never had Cheshire woman, worse now than ever'.[18] This time Mary married the father, and after his death married again, but her life was difficult and her sad ghost is said to haunt Gawsworth Hall, her childhood home where perhaps she was happiest.

Another Maid of Honour who is said to haunt her childhood home is Margaret Radclyffe, one of only two maids known for certain to have died in service, the other being Lady Jane Seymour. Margaret, a cousin to Mary Radclyffe, was the daughter of Sir John Radclyffe of Ordsall Hall, a moated mansion in Lancashire, and she came to court in the mid-1590s with her twin brother, Alexander, a dashing figure of a soldier who served the Earl of Essex. Like many twins, Margaret and Alexander shared a special bond, and they were absolutely devoted to each other. The Queen, like everyone else at court, was fascinated by the twins, who looked alike, and Margaret, a beautiful, witty and jolly young woman, made such an impression upon the Queen that she made her a Maid of Honour. Margaret was now one of the brightest stars of the court, adored by the Queen and admired by men, and she spent her days in carefree revelry, dancing and laughing and riding with her best friend, Anne Russell, niece of Lady Warwick, upon horses named Bay Compton and Bay Dormer. Courtesy of her brother, who was financially responsible for her as their father was dead, she had every luxury that any maid could dream of, and such beautiful clothes that one day she made a sensation by appearing at court in 'a white satin gown, all embroidered, richly cut upon cloth of silver' that was said to have cost 'one hundred and eighty pounds'.[19] But life was about to take a dark turn for 'the merry maid' that would dim her dazzling star. This began with the death of her younger brother, Captain William Radclyffe, who was killed in the Battle of Blackwater fighting the rebel forces of Hugh O'Neil, Earl of Tyrone, in Ireland. Her twin brother, Alexander, eager to avenge William's death, accompanied the Earl of Essex to Ireland in a military campaign to subdue the Irish earl, but within months he was fatally wounded. When news of his death reached court, the Queen ordered that Margaret should not be told until she herself could tell her. Elizabeth knew that the girl would not take the news well but hoped that hearing it from herself would be of some comfort. But in this the Queen was mistaken. When told of her beloved brother's death, Margaret's heart shattered into a million pieces and she was inconsolable. The Queen allowed her to return home to Ordsall Hall, hoping she would find solace with family, but Margaret found no solace and her health declined. When informed of this, the Queen summoned Margaret back to court, hoping a return to duty would be a helpful distraction, but the Margaret who returned was just a shadow of the Margaret who had left. Gone was the jolly and carefree maid who had captured everyone's heart and in her place was a white skeleton who never smiled and rarely ate. The Queen did everything she could for her favourite maid, summoning the best doctors and doing everything possible to raise her spirits, but Margaret had lost the will to live. Philip Gawdy, whose wife was seemingly in attendance upon the Queen, told his brother in a letter all about the girl's 'tragical death' that November:

> ...ever since the death of Sir Alexander, her brother, [she] hath pined in such strange manner as voluntarily she hath gone about to starve herself and by two days together hath received no sustenance, which meeting with extreme grief hath made an end of her maiden modest days at Richmond upon Saturday last, Her Majesty being present, who commanded her body to be opened and found it all well and sound, saving certain strings striped all over her heart. All the maids ever since have gone in black.[20]

Rowland Whyte, another sometime courtier, also reported the news to Sir Robert Sidney, but gave a rather different account of events:

> Mistress Ratcliffe, the honourable Maid of Honour, died at Mr Kircom's House in Richmond upon Sunday last. She is much lamented.[21]

So, which of these reports is likely to be true? It would seem to be Philip Gawdy's as the inscription on Margaret's monument (now lost) in St Margaret's Church, Westminster Abbey, where her body was laid to rest, recorded that she 'died at Richmond 10 November' and 10 November 1599 was a Saturday. In Tudor times it was not uncommon for bowels or hearts to be buried separately from the body and this appears to have happened in Margaret's case. The parish register of Richmond Church, Surrey, records that her bowels were buried in the chancel there on 12 November, ten days before her funeral proper at Westminster Abbey, a funeral that was a lavish affair paid for by the Queen.[22]

All these scandals and tragedies made the last decade of the Queen's reign a difficult one for her Maids of Honour. However, these last years were not all scandal and grief. There were moments of great joy and celebration too, such as the 'great marriage' of Anne Russell, Margaret's best friend, to Henry Somerset, Baron Herbert, son and heir of Edward Somerset, Earl of Worcester, a descendant of Lady Troy's niece, Elizabeth Herbert of Raglan Castle. This took place in the summer of 1600 and was a magnificent affair that was attended by the Queen herself. A week before the wedding, Anne left court for her mother's house in Blackfriars and was escorted, at the Queen's command, by 'all the maids' and 'all the lords of the court'. Eighteen coaches were needed for the procession and the spectacle was such that 'the like hath not been seen amongst the maids'.[23] The marriage itself, a week later, took place in the Church of St Martin in Ludgate, and after the ceremony had been performed, the wedding party made their way to Blackfriars to greet their guest of honour, the Queen, who was arriving by barge. After a joyous welcome from the bride and groom, the Queen was conveyed in 'a curious chair', that was 'made like half a litter', to the Russell home for the celebratory supper.[24] This procession, although short, was as grand as any other and may have been captured for posterity in a fantastic painting that seems to show the very scene. In what appears to be a 'curious chair', the Queen, in a gorgeous white gown, is seemingly carried aloft whilst the bride, also in a white gown, has pride of place behind her. A closer look at the painting, however, reveals that it is the canopy above the Queen that the gentlemen are carrying and that she is being pushed along on great wheels by one or two footmen clad in red uniforms, a perfect form of transport for a short parade as it saved the hassle of coaches and horses.[25]

After a lavish feast, the wedding guests were entertained by 'a masque of the muses', and the stars of the show were the Queen's remaining five Maids of Honour, two Maids of the Privy Chamber, and the groom's teenage sister, Lady Blanche Somerset. These eight maidens, who represented eight of the muses, wore skirts of cloth of silver, waistcoats of gold and silver silk, mantles of carnation taffeta, and had their loose hair 'curiously knotted and interlaced'. Mary Fitton, perhaps the most confident of the maids, for she was certainly bold enough to 'put off her head tire, and tuck up her clothes, and take a large white cloak, and march as though she had been a man' out of court for secret meetings with her lover, led the masque.[26] The maids danced a 'strange' and 'newly invented' dance, gave a speech in praise of the ninth muse, who was the Queen, and then 'chose eight ladies more to dance the measures'. Mary Fitton, as chief masquer, chose the Queen, but was caught a little off guard when the Queen wanted to know what sentiment she represented. 'Affection', Mary replied. 'Affection', exclaimed the Queen, almost as though she knew that Mary was up to no good, 'affection is false!' Yet the Queen rose and danced, as did her chief companion for the event, the Lady Marquess, Helena Snakenborg.[27]

By the time this wedding took place, the Queen had reigned so long that the maids performing in this 'masque of the muses' were two generations removed from the maids who had first attended upon her at the dawn of her reign. Indeed, Anne Russell's replacement, Elizabeth Southwell, a niece of the Elizabeth Southwell who had caused a scandal, was not only Baroness Hunsdon's granddaughter, but a granddaughter of one of the Queen's very first official maids, Mary Mansell. Sadly, Mary had died very young, possibly giving birth to her only child, Elizabeth's father, Robert. Anne Russell's position had allegedly first been offered to Katherine Bulkeley, a daughter of one of the Queen's favourite ladies, Mary Burgh, Lady Bulkeley, who had been a Maid of Honour herself in her youth. Lady Bulkeley, now a Lady of the Privy Chamber, was supposedly 'most willing' for her daughter to follow in her footsteps, but her husband, Sir Richard Bulkeley of Anglesey, was 'most unwilling'. Undoubtedly the reluctant father was concerned about his daughter's reputation, and thereby his family's, given all the scandals that had befallen the Queen's maids in recent years, so as in the past a compromise was reached and Katherine was admitted into the Privy Chamber instead.[28]

After retiring upon marriage, many of the Queen's Maids of Honour went on to be Ladies of Honour but only a few went on to serve in the Privy Chamber. This is because vacancies in the Privy Chamber were rare and because only the most favoured and trusted of women were given positions in the Queen's inner sanctum. Although Maids of Honour had a very privileged position at court, and may have had some duties in the Privy Chamber, they were not, as many historians have told us, the Queen's 'intimate companions'. Her 'intimate companions' were the women of the Privy Chamber. Of those Maids of Honour who did go on to serve in the Privy Chamber, most were either closely related to the Queen or to the women who had been with her since childhood, such as Mary Burgh, Lady Bulkeley, who was a step-granddaughter of Elyzabeth Fitzgerald; Abygall Heveningham, Lady Digby, who was a granddaughter of Sir John and Lady Shelton; Margaret MacWilliam, Lady Stanhope, who was a daughter of Mary Hill, Lady Cheke; and Katheryn Knyvett who was married to Edward Carey, son of Baroness Hunsdon. The most important promotion from Maid of Honour to the Privy Chamber, however, was that of Mary Radclyffe, the Queen's longest serving maid, who went on to become the most important attendant of the Queen's final years.

Chapter Seven

Of Her Majesty's Privy Chamber

AS THE MOST exclusive zone of the Tudor palace, the Privy Chamber, sometimes called the Privy Lodgings as it was where the Queen lived in a magnificent suite of private rooms, was staffed by her most loved and trusted women. The Privy Chamber was usually on the first floor and included several withdrawing chambers, dining rooms, bedchambers, a study, a private chapel and a private gallery. A gallery was a very long, corridor-type room that could be used by the monarch to exercise in bad weather, and it was lined with fantastical statues and furnished with tables, chairs, portraits and wall hangings. Indeed, all the rooms within the Privy Chamber were majestically furnished with dark oak panelling; plasterwork ceilings; grand fireplaces; wooden or tiled floors; bay windows; glittering tapestries; curtains and cushions of velvet or damask; chandeliers and sconces; chairs, tables, chests and cabinets; and all kinds of wonderful and unique ornaments. In some of her palaces the Queen also had glorious bathrooms, bathrooms that were panelled with mirrors and had running hot water, for it is something of a myth that the Tudors did not bathe as they washed more often than history has given them credit for. The Queen also had a dressing room, called a raying chamber, in which she was kitted out in her glittering gowns and golden crowns, and several rooms for the Removing Wardrobe, which was her personal wardrobe that moved with her from palace to palace. Some palaces, like Whitehall and Windsor, also had a permanent wardrobe known as the Standing Wardrobe. Probably due to the weight of the Queen's clothes, which were often made of heavy fabrics, most of the rooms of the Removing Wardrobe were on the ground floor, and the department was under the care of the Office of Robes, which employed a yeoman, a groom and a page to manage it, and a number of artificers, such as a tailor, embroiderer and shoemaker, to stock it. Almost all these skilled workers were male but the Queen officially appointed at least one woman to the Office of Robes, Dorothy Speckard, who succeeded Alice Montague as silk-woman and was renowned for making delicate garments out of silk.[1]

The Privy Chamber was the Queen's personal and private world in which she could relax away from the unrelenting glare of the spotlight and the unmerciful world of politics. In this haven she could work and study without interruption and she could wear much simpler, more comfortable, gowns and shoes than public appearances demanded. The Queen therefore spent a lot of time in her apartment, sometimes days on end, for as soon as she set foot outside it she was in the public eye and not only had to endure all the pomp and ceremony of her position, such as a fanfare of trumpets whenever she entered or left a room, but all the people clamouring for her attention. However, even in this most private of spaces there were two rooms of public interest: the royal bedchamber and the privy chamber. The royal bedchamber was a grand room where the Queen slept in a magnificent 'bed of state', which was an enormous four poster bed, perhaps eight or nine feet square, that was hung with rich drapes of velvet or silk and topped with a canopy of state. The privy chamber was a prestigious parlour, containing a 'chair of state', that took its name from, and gave its name to, the Privy Chamber as historically it was, and in many ways remained, the principal room in the monarch's apartment. The Queen often held private audiences with foreign diplomats in this parlour, as well as with statesmen or churchmen, and it was usually the first room reached upon entering the Privy Chamber. The parlour was also, in many ways, the Queen's social salon as over the Tudor period it had evolved into the hub of an exclusive club of favoured courtiers, the courtiers being male in the reign of a king and predominantly female in the reign of a queen. To be 'of the Privy Chamber' was to be a member of this exclusive club and the room came alive at night as the Queen's women socialised with their royal mistress there, with each other if she was absent, or enjoyed private entertainments such as dances and dramas. All attempts over the Tudor period to make the parlour completely private had failed, so if the Queen truly wanted privacy then she had to relax in one of her withdrawing rooms.

The way the Privy Chamber was staffed varied from reign to reign. Henry VIII was served in his residential suite by a number of gentlemen and grooms, eighteen and six respectively at his death, who were formally known as Gentlemen and Grooms of the Privy Chamber. The gentlemen were tasked with dressing him, serving him food, and attending to his general needs, whilst the grooms kept his rooms clean and tidy, made the fires, lined the floors with fresh straw, and assisted the gentlemen in their duties.[2] In charge of the Privy Chamber was the Chief Gentleman of the Privy Chamber who, by the end of the King's reign, also served as Groom of the Stool. Although the Groom of the Stool is something of a humorous figure in history, for he may have had the dubious honour of wiping the royal bottom after 'action' on the toilet, he was a very important person at court because he had what so many coveted: the King's ear. In the reign of Queen Mary the Privy Chamber was primarily staffed by women, for the sake of the Queen's honour and modesty, who were known as Ladies and Gentlewomen of the Privy Chamber.

When she became queen, Elizabeth fashioned the Privy Chamber to her own liking. Inspired by the Privy Chamber of her brother, King Edward, who had four principal gentlemen to serve him in his bedchamber, she appointed four of her dearest women to serve her in her bedchamber and named them Ladies and Gentlewomen of the Bedchamber. They were still considered 'of the Privy Chamber', however, and that title often superseded any other. For example, in a patent dated 1563, Blanche Parry, a Gentlewoman of the Bedchamber, was described as a 'Gentlewoman of the Privy Chamber'.[3] Elizabeth also created the novel position of Maids of the Privy Chamber. This innovation was for her Hatfield maids who were amongst the first women appointed to her Privy Chamber. Indeed, the Queen rewarded all the women of 'the Hatfield flock', who had served her faithfully for years, even at risk to themselves during the dangerous decade that had followed Henry VIII's death, with prestigious positions of attendance, most of them within the Privy Chamber. Over thirty women were appointed to the Privy Chamber by the Queen's coronation, some new recruits, and they were assigned one of three employment statuses: honorary, ordinary or extraordinary. Honorary attendants, known as 'Ladies of the Privy Chamber Without Wage', were some of the most prestigious women in court and country. They were generally titled ladies, related to the Queen, or drawn from her circle of friends. They were initially six in number and these six were: Margrett Gamage, Baroness Howard of Effingham, Lady Chamberlain; Elyzabeth Fitzgerald, Baroness Clinton, Lady Admiral; Anne Morgan, Baroness Hunsdon; Margaret Audley, Duchess of Norfolk; Mary Dudley, Lady Sidney, sister of Lord Robert Dudley and wife of Sir Henry Sidney, soon to be Lord President of Wales and Lord Deputy of Ireland; and Anne Rede, Lady Fortescue, who was now known as Lady Parry as Elizabeth had knighted her old servant, Thomas Parry, as soon as she became queen. Thomas was now Comptroller of the Household and John Fortescue, Anne's son, was Keeper of the Great Wardrobe, a position he would hold for the rest of the reign. In terms of duties, honorary attendants were more like companions than servants, but some, like Lady Sidney, are known to have attended upon the Queen, to have sat with her during private audiences, and to have represented her at christenings or funerals.

Extraordinary attendants were essentially reserve attendants. They were summoned to court for important ceremonial events or to serve temporarily in the place of a sick or absent lady or gentlewoman. They did not live permanently at court, and were generally only paid when called to serve, but there were exceptions. For example, at least two women, Bregett Chaworth Carr and Elizabeth Throckmorton, were in continuous attendance and in receipt of a regular wage.[4] Initially, the Queen appointed eleven extraordinary Ladies and Gentlewomen of the Privy Chamber and most of these had served her in her youth. Amongst them were Mary Hill, Lady Cheke; Elizabeth Neville, Mistress Eynns; Anne Poyntz, Mistress Heneage; Joan Berkeley, Lady Poyntz; and Katherine Denys, Lady Buckler. Mary Hill was now married to a man named Henry MacWilliam, future Gentleman Pensioner, but was still known as Lady Cheke (her late husband had been knighted in 1551). She and Elizabeth remained very close and Mary was given the high honour of riding in the magnificent coronation eve procession as one of the Queen's Ladies of Honour. For the occasion she was given the standard livery of sixteen yards of crimson velvet along with two yards of 'cloth of gold yellow plain' for the turning up of her sleeves. Lady Poyntz and Lady Buckler were also given the same honour and the same luxurious fabrics, except that Lady Poyntz had 'cloth of gold yellow with work'.

Ordinary attendants were the Queen's true attendants as they were the ones who took care of her every need around the clock. They received a salary and resided at court, usually in a block of apartments beneath, or close to, the Queen's residential suite. There were three groups of female ordinaries in the Privy Chamber and they were, in hierarchial order: Ladies and Gentlewomen of the Bedchamber, who received a salary of £33 6s 8d (50 marks); Ladies and Gentlewomen of the Privy

Chamber, who received the same wage; and Chamberers, who received a salary of £20 (30 marks) a year. There were also a number of male ordinaries in the Privy Chamber as the women were assisted in their duties by one or two Gentlemen of the Privy Chamber, a Gentleman Usher, and a small number of Grooms of the Privy Chamber. The gentlemen received the same salary as the ladies and gentlewomen whilst the grooms were paid the same as Chamberers.

Regardless of their precise role or salaried status (and both can be difficult to determine) all women of the Privy Chamber were influential figures at court. It was ultimately being 'of the Privy Chamber' that mattered, not role or salary, as every woman admitted into the Privy Chamber was considered in great favour. Therefore all positions in the Privy Chamber were highly sought after and whenever a vacancy arose there were many women desperate to fill it. But, because the Queen and her women were so loyal to each other, and because the Queen was 'never known to desert any for age or other infirmity', salaried vacancies were rare.[5] In fact, vacancies only generally arose when the incumbent died. This makes it very difficult to know just how active some of the Queen's long-serving attendants were in their elderly years as the Queen kept them on her payroll even when they were too old or weak to work. But of course, they were never too old to be her companions, even if they could not do all the things they once had such as dancing or riding.

In the reign of Henry VIII, the staff of the Privy Chamber were expected to be 'loving together, and of good unity and accord, keeping secret all such things as shall be done or said in the Privy Chamber without disclosing any part thereof to any person', and it is likely that this was expected of Queen Elizabeth's staff too.[6] Indeed, this is probably why we have so little information about daily life within the Privy Chamber because the staff kept their silence a little too well!

Because the women of the Privy Chamber had such intimate access to the Queen, more so than Ladies and Maids of Honour, it was vital that the Queen could trust them completely. Therefore there was more pressure on these women to make suitable marriages than there was on Ladies or Maids of Honour. It was absolutely essential that prospective husbands posed no security risk to the Queen, for by marrying one of the Queen's Privy Chamber women a man was effectively gaining access to her inner circle, and because of the influence these women had at court, it was vital that their marriages would not upset the fragile balance of factions. Consequently there were times when the Queen had great reservations about a marriage, and her consent, which was required by court protocol, was not forthcoming. However, these occasions were very rare and there are only four known cases. Claims that the Queen took 'great pleasure in thwarting and interfering with the plans of others for securing' romantic happiness because she 'envied others the love and the domestic enjoyments which ambition forbade her to share' are wholly unsupported. The vast majority of the Queen's women married with her blessing and surviving wardrobe records suggest that she almost always gave her Privy Chamber women a luxurious gown for their wedding. It is also recorded that she spent large sums of money on the 'great marriages with any of her maids or ladies publically in the court'.[7] Only when there were serious grounds for concern did the Queen object and in almost every case she eventually relented.

The first marriage that the Queen objected to, at least according to court rumour, was to the marriage of Katheryn Carey, the eldest daughter of Lord and Lady Hunsdon, with Charles Howard, the son of Lord and Lady Howard of Effingham.[8] Although the Queen held both in high favour, the marriage would unite the Careys and the Howards, the two most powerful branches of the Boleyn family, potentially creating a power block at court. Not only could this upset the balance of factions but could see the Queen isolated. But, whatever her concerns, eventually the Queen gave her consent and the marriage went ahead in the summer of 1563. The next marriage that the Queen objected to was the marriage of Mary Shelton, a young granddaughter of Sir John and Lady Shelton who was serving as a Chamberer, to John Scudamore. John, a new Gentleman Pensioner, was of humble wealth, a widower with several heirs already (so no son he had with Mary would be his heir), and a suspected Catholic. Also, in preliminary negotiations for Mary's hand, John refused to leave any lands to any daughters he had with Mary. The Queen was therefore very reluctant to give her consent and the saga lasted months. Two years later came the drama of Helena Snakenborg's secret marriage to Thomas Gorges and then finally, in 1585, there was a showdown between Charles Howard, now Baron Howard of Effingham and Lord Chamberlain, over his sister's desire to marry Edward Seymour, Earl of Hertford, the man who had supposedly married Lady Katherine Grey and whose sons, although bastards, had a claim to the throne.[9] His sister, Frances, had been a Gentlewoman of the Privy Chamber for sixteen years but for some time had been in a relationship, some say secret marriage, with Lord Hertford. Because of the political awkwardness of the marriage, all concerned were afraid of asking the Queen for her consent, knowing it was likely to be withheld, but finally, wanting to bring the relationship to an honourable conclusion, and believing the match would be a 'great advancement' for his sister, Charles broke the matter to the Queen. As expected, Elizabeth was not best pleased, for she did not like or trust the earl, and allegedly told Charles that he would be better off securing a pension from the earl for his sister rather than a marriage as she doubted the earl was serious. Offended and horrified, as a pension would imply that Frances was, or had been, the earl's mistress, Charles told the Queen that he would not consider Frances his sister if she agreed to such a thing and that 'it touched Her Majesty in honour to have any gentlewoman about her to take a pension of any man in such a manner'. Knowing he was right, and ever conscious of the need for discretion and caution in a dangerous political world, Elizabeth ended the conversation by telling her cousin that he had 'done the office of a good brother' but that she still doubted the earl was serious. The next day, however, she summoned Frances to her and Frances tells us in her own words what happened:

> Presently she told me what my brother had said and asked if I desired to
> have it brought to an end and why. I answered her it hath been a matter
> of affection long between us and, for my part, I would think myself the
> happiest woman in the world if, with her good favour, she would bestow
> me upon him whom my liking is resolved on, for that I knew my Lord
> of Hertford would do nothing to offend her. Many persuasions she used

against marriage ... and how little you would care for me ... how well I was here and how much she cared for me, but, in the end, she said she would not be against my desire. Trust me, sweet lord, the worst is past, and I warrant she will not speak one angry word to you.[10]

So, once again, the Queen gave in, albeit against her better judgement, but the marriage did not take place straight away. Frances had to wait until the summer for the Queen's blessing, perhaps because the Queen feared Frances was pregnant and a scandal would ensue, but when the Queen's blessing finally came Frances joyfully told her betrothed that:

...you may have me now when you will, for the Queen praised you and said with all her heart you should have me.[11]

A few months later, in what was surely a lavish wedding in the Queen's presence at Richmond Palace, Frances married the man she loved. At first, all went well, and the Queen honoured the couple with a very public visit to their home, but in time all the Queen's fears came true as the earl, knowing that the Queen was ageing, made moves to legitimise his sons so they could be restored to the line of succession. For this, he was sent to the Tower of London, and consequently the Queen's relationship with Frances, who was still a salaried attendant, came under great strain. After ten years of marriage, Frances was no less devoted to her husband, and was allegedly so upset with grief and worry over his imprisonment that she went 'stark mad'. In an attempt to comfort Frances, and to reassure her that the earl was in no danger, the Queen sent her a tender note in her own hand:

Good Francke, understanding your disposition to be troubled with sudden impressions, even in matters of little moment, we do not now forget you in your lord's misfortune, and therefore have thought it not amiss, even by our own handwriting ... to assure you of the continuance of our former grace... It is not convenient to acquaint you with all the particular circumstances of his offence ... but (to prevent any misapprehension that this crime is in its nature more pernicious and malicious than an act of lewd and proud contempt against our own direct prohibition), we have vouchsafed to cause a ticket to be shown you by the bearer, which may resolve you from further doubting what it is not...We will use no more severity than is requisite for others' caution in like cases...You will not be one jot the less esteemed for any faults of his... You are therefore to trust to this assurance as the voice of that Prince to whose pure and constant mind you are no stranger, and comfort yourself that you have served one who still wishes your good and cares for the contrary.[12]

The Queen would not see Frances, as she knew her cousin would only plead her husband's case, but she continued to assure the countess of her good will by sending her 'gracious messages' along with 'broths in a morning' and 'meat from her trencher' at mealtimes. But Frances continued to pine away and the Queen, perhaps out of concern for her health, gave into her request to have her husband released from the Tower into the more relaxed custody of the Archbishop of Canterbury. By the following summer, the earl was free, and Frances was reunited with her husband, but the months of stress and worry had taken a terrible toll on Frances's health and she fell into a 'long sickness'. Elizabeth made several visits to the Hertford home, perhaps to comfort and reassure her cousin that all was well and she remained in her favour and affection, but sadly the countess never recovered and died less than two years later at the age of 44. Like many of the Queen's women, she was buried in Westminster Abbey, and upon her monument her husband described her as a lady 'highly renowned for her many virtues, gifts and graces, both of mind and body; greatly favoured by her gracious sovereign; and dearly beloved of her lord'.

Scandals of a romantic nature were very rare amongst women of the Privy Chamber. In fact, it was not until 'the naughty nineties' that there was a pregnancy scandal amongst them – the only one of the reign. This scandal was caused by Elizabeth Throckmorton, a great granddaughter of Baroness Bryan, who found herself pregnant after a secret affair with one of the Queen's great favourites, Sir Walter Raleigh. Sir Walter did the honourable thing and married Elizabeth, who was devoted to him, but did so in secret. When the Queen found out, the couple were sent to the Tower of London for a while, and for some years Lady Raleigh, as Elizabeth was now called, was out of favour, but she may eventually have recovered her position as she is listed as a Lady of the Privy Chamber in the funeral records.

The scandal that has made the most impact in history is the scandal surrounding the marriage of Mary Shelton and John Scudamore. Interestingly, this scandal was not due to Mary's conduct, as might be expected, but to the Queen's. 'The Queen hath used Mary Shelton very ill for her marriage', wrote Maid of Honour, Eleanor Brydges, to Lord or Lady Rutland in the January of 1574, 'she hath dealt liberal both with blows and evil words and hath not yet granted her consent'.[13] By the time the story reached the ears of Mary, Queen of Scots, at least according to a letter purportedly written by the deposed monarch to Queen Elizabeth a decade later, the Queen was guilty of breaking Mary's finger in a fit of rage. This undated letter, written in French, is known as *The Scandal Letter*, and in it Queen Mary lists all the scurrilous things that Bess of Hardwick, Countess of Shrewsbury, has allegedly told her about Elizabeth – i.e. that the Queen is promiscuous but has a physical impairment which prevents her consummating a marriage, that she is extremely tight fisted, that she is so vain that she thinks herself a goddess of heaven, and that she is very cruel to her women. The author of the letter claims that Lady Shrewsbury's daughter, Mary Cavendish, Lady Talbot (who was married to Lady Shrewsbury's stepson, George Talbot, Lord Talbot), who had recently been sworn into the Privy Chamber, had only taken the oath of allegiance 'as a thing done in jest' as she:

> …would not for anything in the world be in your service, near your
> person, seeing that she would be afraid that when you were angry
> you would do to her as you did to her cousin, Scudamore, whose

finger you had broken, making those of the court believe that it was a candlestick which had fallen on it, and that to another, who was serving you at table, you had given a violent blow on the hand with a knife.[14]

The authenticity of this letter has long been a subject of debate amongst historians and a final conclusion has yet to be reached. Even in Victorian times the letter was controversial. Agnes Strickland, for example, argued that the letter 'bears every mark of the grossest forgery' whilst her contemporary, Charles Mitchell, believed there is 'no valid reason for doubting the authenticity'.[15] But regardless of whether the letter is authentic or not, the whole point of it was to expose the Countess of Shrewsbury as a liar and a gossipmonger, so the stories told in it cannot be taken as fact. Clearly there was some kind of altercation between Mary and the Queen over the marriage, an altercation that made a sensation at the time, but the incident appears to have been a rare example of the Queen losing her temper rather than a typical one. For had such angry outbursts from the Queen been routine then we could expect to find more such stories in letters and documents, but even a decade after this incident, this story is the only one that the author of *The Scandal Letter*, whomever he or she was, can reference – except for the story of the Queen giving a 'violent blow' to an unnamed lady at dinner. It is often said that Mary and John married without the Queen's consent, which was the reason for the altercation, but this does not appear to have been the case. The couple appear to have waited for the Queen's consent, albeit impatiently, and that consent seems to have been given by the summer of 1574 as the last reference to 'Mary Shelton' in the records is in the spring of that year when the Queen gifted her a robe of black velvet. Interestingly, this robe, which had belonged to the Queen, had to be 'made wider and longer', revealing that Mary was broader and taller than the Queen. Of course, when it comes to physical abuse, size is irrelevant, but this revelation does much to discredit the notion that the Queen chose to vent her anger on her women because they were smaller and frailer than herself.[16] After her marriage, Mary became known as Mary Scudamore, and she lived to become one of the Queen's most loved and trusted attendants. As to the claims regarding Mary Cavendish, Lady Talbot, a niece of Elyzabeth Cavendish Snow, the Queen's childhood attendant, they are very unlikely to be true. Although Lady Talbot, who became Countess of Shrewsbury in 1590 when her father-in-law died, had Catholic sympathies and became a devout Catholic later in life, she is known to have been highly regarded by the Queen, who is said to have had 'a high opinion' of her, and to have been active in the Queen's service in the 1590s.[17]

The only other potentially credible reference to the Queen striking a woman in her service comes from a letter written by Rowland Whyte to Sir Robert Sidney in 1597. In this letter Whyte writes that 'the Queen hath of late used the fair Mistress Brydges with words and blows of anger'.[18] This 'Mistress Brydges' is not Eleanor Brydges, who had long since died, but her niece, Elizabeth Brydges, a Maid of the Privy Chamber. However, we have already seen that Whyte's reports are not entirely reliable so it would be a mistake to consider them absolute fact. Aside from flippant comments by foreign ambassadors, almost certainly repeating malicious gossip, there are no other known references to the Queen striking her women. There are stories of the Queen 'pinching poor Lady Huntingdon very sorely',[19] Lady Huntingdon being the youngest sister of Robert Dudley, Earl of Leicester, and a Lady of Honour, but these stories come from a misinterpretation of a letter written by her husband, Henry Hastings, Earl of Huntingdon, to her brother, in which he writes:

> At my wife's last being at court to do her duty, as became her, it pleased Her Majesty to give her a privy nip, especially concerning myself, whereby I perceive she hath some jealous conceit of me, and, as I can imagine, of late digested.[20]

The words 'privy nip' do not mean the physical act of 'pinching' but the verbal act of giving a 'private rebuke'. At the time this letter was written, the Queen was very concerned that Lord Huntingdon, who had a claim to her throne, was secretly planning to depose her. But the earl had no such intention and the matter soon blew over. Therefore, whether or not we believe the Queen struck the women in her service depends almost entirely on what we make of these two letters by Eleanor Brydges and Rowland Whyte. As there is room for doubt – both might be repeating court gossip, rather than recounting a scene witnessed, or the similar phrasing 'words and blows' may be a figure of speech – perhaps it is time to give the Queen the benefit of the doubt after centuries of hostile narrative. For to many historians of yesteryear, Elizabeth was 'a woman exceedingly wicked', a 'woman whose avarice and jealousy, whose envious, relentless, and malignant spirit, whose coarse manners and violent temper, render her detestable; whose pedantry and meanness, whose childish vanity and intense selfishness, render her contemptible'. Old history books are full of stories of how the Queen beat her women 'black and blue' and 'cursed, swore, and stamped' at those around her. These history books also tell us that Elizabeth was so vain that she surrounded her palaces with mirrors in her youth, so she could admire her own beauty, but banished them from her sight as she got older 'lest the Queen should behold herself as she was, a lean, haggard, over-dressed old woman'.[21] According to these historians the Queen's women not only secretly despised her but exacted their own kind of revenge:

> … her tire-women, confident in their mistress's prejudice against her mirror, sometimes indulged their own hatred and mirth, and ventured to lay upon the royal nose the carmine which ought to have embellished the cheeks.[22]

Their source for this amusing, yet somewhat absurd claim, was no less an authority than playwright Ben Jonson who, allegedly, told William Drummond of Hawthornden Castle, years after the Queen's death, that 'Queen Elizabeth never saw herself after she became old in a true glass; they painted her, and sometimes would vermilion her nose'.[23] The mirror story (perhaps an inspiration for the fairytale Snow White?)

can also be found in an account of the Queen's death by Elizabeth Southwell, the Maid of Honour who was a great granddaughter of Baroness Hunsdon. Two years after the Queen's death, Mistress Southwell eloped to the Continent with her married lover, Robert Dudley, the Earl of Leicester's illegitimate son, and converted to Catholicism. The couple, who bigamously married in 1606, joined the exiled Catholic community abroad and Elizabeth wrote a damning account of the Queen's final days in a manuscript entitled *A true relation of what succeeded in the sickness and death of Queen Elizabeth.* The content is thought to have been masterminded by Robert Parsons, the Queen's former Catholic foe, who is linked to the most notorious defamatory piece of the period, *Leicester's Commonwealth.* Southwell's account is so macabre, involving bewitched jewellery, hexes, hell fire, walking spirits and exploding corpses, that it defies credibility, yet, like Jonson's comments, her mirror claim has passed into the historical narrative:

> ... in the melancholy of her sickness, she [Elizabeth] desired to see a true looking-glass, which, in twenty years before, she had not seen, but only such a one which of purpose was made to deceive her sight; which glass being brought her, she fell presently exclaiming at all those which had so much commended her, and took it so offensively, that all those which had before flattered her, durst not come in her sight...[24]

According to seventeenth century historian Edmund Bohun, if Queen Elizabeth 'happened by accident to cast her eye upon a true looking glass, she would be strangely transported and offended because it did not still show her what she had been. The courtiers, who knew her humour, if she were to pass through any of the ladies chambers that waited on her, presently conveyed away all the looking glasses and sometimes for haste broke them'.[25] Yet this legend, evidently circulating in the Queen's lifetime or shortly afterwards, is easily discredited by a single entry in the wardrobe accounts of 1600:

> For mending of a looking glass and new covering the same with carnation in grain satin cutwork lined with taffeta, the glass tufted round with carnation silk and silver and strings of carnation ribbon.

Unless we are to believe this mirror needed mending because the Queen had broken it 'in transports of rage', or that it was 'one which of purpose was made to deceive her sight', then it is clear that looking glasses were still very much in use by the Queen as this mirror was delivered, with a number of other items, 'unto the Ladies and Gentlewomen of our Privy Chamber to our use'.[26] These same historians also reveal their prejudice in their descriptions of the Queen as a 'lean, haggard, over-dressed old woman' by the end of her reign, for this was not the opinion of her contemporaries who, in general, believed she looked very well for her age. For example, Paul Hentzner, who saw the Queen up close and personal in 1598, described her as 'fair but wrinkled', the wrinkles disproving the myth that the Queen was so heavily plastered with make-up that her face was lost beneath, and Thomas Platter, a Swiss traveller who visited England in 1599, described the Queen as 'very straight and erect still', 'gorgeously apparelled', 'very youthful still in appearance', and having 'a dignified and regal bearing'. The two travellers also noted, in their fascinating descriptions of the Queen's palaces, the presence of magnificent looking glasses.[27]

More stories of Queen Elizabeth's 'meanness' to her women can be found in a published work entitled *Nugae Antiquae*, which purportedly contains 'original papers in prose and verse' from the Harington Family archive, and in letters published by *The Philobiblon Society* in the 1870s, purportedly from the Knollys family archive. Both publications are highly problematic (see appendices for *Nugae Antiquae*) and aside from these, and the sources already mentioned, there is nothing to support the historic claim that Elizabeth was a 'mean queen'. Quite the contrary, the picture that emerges from a wealth of other sources is of a queen who did care about the women in her service and who was no vainer or stricter than any other queen of the era. But of course, Elizabeth was the only unmarried queen, and the Victorian era, like the era before it, and the one immediately after it, looked very unfavourably upon 'old maids':

A tear for the poor old maids!
I pity their lonely lives,
Not having been blessed to fill
The duties of mothers and wives.

When wives are merry and plump,
Old maids are cross and sere;
We've a smile for the buxom wife,
For the poor old maid a tear!

A wife's a garden of pleasure,
A-blooming after the rain;
A maid's a miser's treasure,
The source of nothing but pain.[28]

'Old maid is,' wrote an old maid fifty years before this poem was published, 'commonly used as a term of reproach: an old maid is an object of general ridicule; and is there not injustice and even cruelty in this? [If] people speak of curiosity, of prudery, of scandal, or of ill-temper, they speak of them as the common attributes of an old maid [yet] I have not found that the faults attributed to old maids are at all more common to them than to others... I have but faintly hinted at the mortifications to which an old maid is exposed; but could I have found heart to do it, I could have related a history which would draw tears from sterner eyes' and a century later Henry Sedgwick, in his *Apology for Old Maids,* wrote that 'married people ... long ago created a legend about celibates, which depicts them as crotchety, graceless, ill-dressed, ill-mannered, ugly, and selfish; and they have taught this legend to so many generations of children that even now little boys look on celibates with disdain'.[29] It is therefore unsurprising that Elizabeth, one of the most famous old maids in history, was considered by past generations to have these characteristics. However, the longevity of service of her senior attendants, not to mention the affection with which they spoke of her, and remembered her, is testimony against this traditional narrative, a narrative that, in many ways, defies reason. 'There are writers', wrote Edward Spencer Beesly in 1900, 'who have made the discovery that Elizabeth was a very poor ruler, selfish and wayward, short sighted, easily duped, fainthearted, rash, miserly, wasteful, and swayed by the pettiest impulses of vanity, spite, and personal inclination. They have not explained, and never will, how it was that a woman with all these disqualifications for government should have ruled England with signal success for forty-four years.'[30]

Ladies and Gentlewomen of the Bedchamber

Over the course of the Tudor period, the importance and prestige of the royal bedchamber grew, and Elizabeth's decision to appoint four principal attendants to serve her there further elevated its status. Indeed, the royal bedchamber was now considered by many to be the most prestigious room in the palace. In charge of the room was the Chief Lady of the Bedchamber, a post seemingly created by the Queen especially for her beloved first cousin, Kathryn Carey, Lady Knollys, one of the four women appointed to the room. Kathryn was the only daughter of Mary Boleyn, sister of Anne Boleyn, and her first husband, Sir William Carey. She was about nine years older than Elizabeth and in her youth had served as a Maid of Honour to Queen Anne of Cleves and Queen Katheryn Howard. Henry Carey, Baron Hunsdon, was her younger brother, and she, like Elizabeth, was a great niece of William Howard of Effingham. Just how much time she and Elizabeth spent together growing up is unknown, but as the two cousins were very close, so much so that Elizabeth was 'heartbroken' when Kathryn left the country in the reign of Queen Mary, it is likely that they saw each other often. Indeed, Lady Knollys was, in many ways, like a big sister to Elizabeth, and Tudor history being the soap saga that it is, there is a very real possibility that she truly was the Queen's sister as her mother is thought to have been one of Henry VIII's mistresses at the time she was born.

Like many sixteenth-century aristocratic girls, Lady Knollys was married in her teens, her husband being Sir Francis Knollys, a son of Baroness Bryan's foster daughter, Lettice Peniston, and by the time Elizabeth succeeded to the throne she was the mother of at least twelve children. According to a recently discovered Latin dictionary, in which the names and birthdates of these children have been recorded, possibly by Sir Francis himself, the eldest son was Henry, a boy with adventure in his veins who eventually became an explorer and died a soldier's death in 1582, and the eldest daughter was Mary who, according to some sources, married a man named Edward Stalker.[31] Lettice, the most famous of the Knollys children, was the second daughter, and Elyzabeth, who lived to become the Queen's favourite of the Knollys sisters, was the fourth daughter. Because of her affection for Lady Knollys, the Queen overlooked her husband's religious zeal, which was of the

Puritan persuasion that she did not like, and honoured Sir Francis with the coveted position of Vice-Chamberlain and made him a Privy Councillor.

Lady Knollys was amongst those who hastily returned to England upon Elizabeth's accession, and in her new role as Chief Lady of the Bedchamber, which made her the Queen's most prestigious attendant in the Privy Chamber, she led, on horseback, all the women of the Privy Chamber in the coronation eve procession. Like the Ladies of Honour, of which she was one, she was given sixteen yards of crimson velvet for the event along with 'two yards of purple gold tinsel with knots'. Totally devoted to her royal cousin, Lady Knollys worked tirelessly in the Queen's service, working, like many of the Queen's women, even when pregnant. Just how many pregnancies she had after Elizabeth became queen is unclear, but she certainly gave birth to a child in 1562, a child named Dudley whose gender is disputed, but sadly this baby died the same year, possibly in an accident as the child was said to have been 'killed'.[32] Surprisingly, working mothers were not unheard of in the sixteenth century, although women were barred from most professions, and as it was not fashionable for aristocratic women to rear their own children, convention dictating that they were brought up by nurses and governesses, it was quite acceptable for the Queen's women to leave their children on their country estates whilst they attended to the Queen at court.

When, in 1568, the Queen of Scots was taken into custody upon arriving in England after failing to recover her throne in Scotland, Lady Knollys's husband was sent up north to be her custodian. Queen Elizabeth knew she could trust Sir Francis, not just because he was family but because his ardent religious beliefs meant that he would never conspire to put a Catholic on the throne. However, little did Lady Knollys realise when she said goodbye to her husband that they would never see each other again. For over the following months, Lady Knollys's health began to fail, and in January 1569, ten years to the day of her cousin's coronation, she died at Hampton Court Palace. The Queen was devastated, for she professed to love no one in the world as much as her cousin, and the court was plunged into mourning. In the eyes of some historians, the Queen is to blame for Lady Knollys's death, partly for keeping Sir Francis up north during his wife's sickness, and partly for treating her cruelly, but much of what we know about Lady Knollys's last months comes from letters published by *The Philobiblon Society* in the late nineteenth century, letters that put the Queen in a bad light. For example, in a letter dated 30 December 1568, Sir Francis allegedly tells his wife that:

> Mr Secretary informed me of your late sickness, wherewith I was the more disquieted because I feared that Her Majesty's ungrateful denial of my coming to the court this Christmas, added to the denial of our suite for Newelme and other misconstruings of me and mine, without any comfort at all to our necessity (saving only shells that have no kernels), had been some provocation of your sickness, whereupon my discontented mind grew to be so much the more full fraught with disquiet, that in my last letter to the Queen's Majesty I was about (after that I had written somewhat plainly to Her

Majesty in her own matters) to have written these words following:
as touching my own particularity, among all my griefs of mind, it is
not the least to understand that my wife is ready to die in discomfort
and in miserable state towards her children, even in Your Majesty's
court. But after I had written thus much in my copy, and that I was
even ready to have written it in the letter self, Mr Secretary's letter
came to me signifying that you were well amended...

And he later continues...

Her Majesty saith she trusts me, and I believe she thinks me not
false. Also Her Majesty saith she loves you, and nature provokes her
thereunto: But what followeth hereof, Her Majesty hath denied us our
suit that might best have relieved us with least charge and burden to
herself, even in this trusty time, and by reason of her trust, she puteth
me to more pains, more careful perils, and more tedious griefs than she
doth any other man... And for the outward love that Her Majesty bears
you, she makes you often weep for unkindness to the great danger of
your health: so that if these be the only fruits of your love and my trust,
happy were we if we were disgraced, I from my trust and you from
your love, that we might retire us by just occasion to lead a country
poor life abased from our courtly countenance: whereunto I thank God
I am ready to prepare myself for my part if you shall like thereof.[33]

Now, this letter may well be genuine, but like all the original letters published by
The Philobiblon Society from this purported collection, letters to and from some of
the most important people of the age, this letter is lost. This may be insignificant,
as documents are sadly lost all the time, but it is highly concerning that all the
letters (except, it seems, those by Eleanor Brydges and Rowland Whyte) that
tell of the Queen's mistreatment of her women are lost. Unless we accept this is
coincidence then a question mark must hang over the authenticity and/or reliability
of these letters. At the time they were published 'the Rt. Hon. Sir William Knollys,
K.C.B.', who allegedly owned the collection, was an important person at the court
of Queen Victoria. He was a celebrated military figure and one of the Queen's
Privy Councillors. It was rather awkward for him, then, in an age that adored Mary,
Queen of Scots, to be descended from a man who was considered her first gaoler.[34]
These published letters do much to redeem Sir Francis' reputation, injecting into
the historical record a convenient narrative, for they reveal how reluctant he was to
be Queen Mary's gaoler, how eager he was to be discharged from the position, and
how sympathetic and kind he was to her. Further, the letters portray Sir Francis and
his wife as two more victims of the 'cruel' Queen Elizabeth.

The other three women appointed to the bedchamber were the Queen's beloved
former governess, Kat Astley, with whom she was joyfully reunited after two
long years of separation; Blanche Parry, who had been at her side through every
ordeal; and Elizabeth Norwich, her dear friend and confidante. Kat was given the

all-important role of Chief Gentlewoman of the Privy Chamber and, like her male predecessors, was also seemingly made Groom of the Stool. This put her in charge of all the Queen's toileting needs and of the close stool itself. This was a box-shaped commode adorned with red or black velvet that had a pewter pan inside and a plush seat of scarlet cloth fringed with gold.[35] It was located in the 'stool room', which was a small room accessed from the bedchamber, but was portable so it could be taken where needed. Because of the size and style of her gowns, it is likely that the Queen needed assistance to use the close stool when fully dressed, so if Kat was not on duty at the time, for the women probably worked on rota, perhaps in shifts of two, then another Lady or Gentlewoman of the Bedchamber would have had to assist her.

Because the Queen depended so much on her Ladies and Gentlewomen of the Bedchamber, not just for physical care but for emotional support, they may have had accommodation within the Privy Chamber, or within the apartment traditionally belonging to the queen consort, rather than within the apartment block assigned to staff. But of course, it was not possible for them to be always at the Queen's side. With the exception of Blanche Parry, who lived only at court and rarely left her mistress, the other women were away for short spells. Just how often they were away is unknown, but the summer months, when the Queen went on progress, was an opportunity for some of her women to spend time with their families on their country estates. For the difficulties in accommodating all the Queen's attendants when she was travelling meant that her staffing numbers, and the size of her court, was reduced.

Presumably, the first task for the Ladies and Gentlewomen of the Bedchamber every morning was to officially wake the Queen. This is likely to have involved some degree of ceremony, such as blowing out the royal mortar (see below), if it was still burning, and/or sending it back to the Presence Chamber. As Elizabeth was famously 'no morning woman', preferring to work late into the night rather than to rise early, she was probably not woken before 8 o'clock on a typical day. Of course, it is difficult to define a 'typical day' for the Queen as she made public appearances, she travelled, she entertained, she held emergency meetings with her advisors, she participated in religious services, she participated in court ceremonies, she went on hunting picnics, she rode on horses, she rode in the royal barge, she held tournaments, she dined in her chambers, she dined in public, she dined in the houses of courtiers, she was up at the crack of dawn some days, burning the midnight oil on others, she was sick, she was in mourning, she was in isolation due to the outbreak of disease, and she moved residence several times a year. However, as she spent most of her life cocooned in the grand chambers of her palaces, escaping them only to walk in her privy garden, which was accessed from her apartment, or to ride or hunt in the palace parks beyond, there would have been a structure to her day, albeit a flexible one. Unless the Queen had an important meeting to attend, or an engagement to keep, she liked to prepare for what was always a demanding day by taking her time in the morning. Rather than dress right away, she liked to relax in a 'robe de chambre', known in English as a loose gown, which was a sumptuous robe of velvet, satin, taffeta or camlet worn by the wealthy in their private chambers. This robe was an acceptable form of outer dress and was far more comfortable than formal attire. It was probably the first item of clothing that the Ladies and Gentlewomen of the Bedchamber procured for the Queen every day, for even on busy days the Queen needed to breakfast before getting formally dressed. If the weather was permitting, the Queen would take a walk in her privy garden after breakfast, usually walking briskly to get the blood pumping, but if it was raining she would read for a while or walk in her privy gallery. The Queen also liked to worship in her private chapel every day, thanking God for his blessings and praying for wisdom and strength in governing.

While the Queen walked, or read, the Ladies and Gentlewomen of the Bedchamber had the opportunity to prepare her wardrobe and to get ready all her accessories, cosmetics and perfumes. At some point in the morning the Queen would wash, perhaps before she breakfasted or after her walk. While the Queen probably had a bath more often than is supposed, especially when residing in those palaces with glorious bathrooms, baths were still very much a luxury in the sixteenth century and daily washing was done with bowls of warm water and linen cloths. The Queen's women of the bedchamber would have prepared these and assisted the Queen with her wash. When it was done, they probably helped the Queen into a clean smock, which was a long linen dress similar to a modern nightdress that was worn by Tudor women under their clothes and for bed. It was not yet common practice to have separate clothes to sleep in, though everyone wore a cap to bed and night-rails were very popular with women. These were capes or gowns made of linen that were worn over smocks and the Queen's were typically 'wrought with black silk'.[36] As the Queen could afford as many smocks as she wanted, she probably wore a clean one for bed, but poor women would be lucky to change their smock twice a week.

The mammoth job of dressing the Queen, perhaps two or three times a day if her schedule demanded it, was probably undertaken by the Ladies and Gentlewomen of the Bedchamber in the Queen's raying chamber, at least when she was not travelling. The raying chamber was a grand chamber, accessed privately from the bedchamber, and was probably stocked with all kinds of accessories from jewellery, furs, hoods, mufflers, hats, gloves, stockings, farthingales, handkerchiefs, shoes, and corsets, to ruffs, bumrolls and wigs in the later years. As the Queen's jewellery was worth a fortune, her extensive collection of rings, necklaces, pearls, bracelets, earrings, broaches and tiaras were kept under lock and key in secure coffers (chests). These wooden coffers were richly lined with velvet or satin and their keys were held in the custody of the Keeper of Her Majesty's Jewels. This was a semi-official position, held by a Lady or Gentlewoman of the Privy Chamber, as records were kept of all the Queen's jewels, even those given to her as gifts, and the Keeper had to personally account for every single item. Opinions differ on just how long it would have taken to dress the Queen. If she was wearing some of the spectacular gowns we see in her portraits, along with make-up and bejewelled wigs, then perhaps the whole process would take up to two hours. If she was wearing simpler gowns, perhaps because she was not appearing in public or because she was going riding, then thirty minutes may have been enough for skilled and experienced fingers to dress her. To go riding, especially in cold or wet weather, the Queen would wear a cloak and a safeguard, which was a type of overskirt, to keep herself warm and to protect her clothes. Of course, being a queen, even these protective garments were luxurious. They were made of velvet, satin, taffeta and perfumed leather, and the Queen had many of them in many different colours.

It is often said that the Queen had a Mistress of the Robes – a senior attendant in charge of her wardrobe – but the Mistress of the Robes did not make her appearance in English history until she was first appointed by Anne of Denmark, wife of King James I, in 1603.[37] The belief that there was a Mistress of the Robes comes from mistranslations in the *Calendar of Spanish State Papers*, published in the nineteenth century, that translate phrases like 'camarera mayor de la Reina' (senior attendant of the Queen) to 'mistress of the robes'. Instead of a Mistress of the Robes, Elizabeth had a Gentleman of the Robes who, for most of her reign, was Thomas Gorges, husband of Helena Snakenborg, and the Gentleman of the Robes came into being in the mid-1560s when the security of the Privy Chamber was tightened. The Privy Council was concerned about the number of people having access to the Queen's Wardrobe so a Gentleman of the Robes was appointed to oversee the department and to take charge of the delivery of the Queen's clothes to her women of the bedchamber. For although the Queen's bedchamber was primarily a female zone, it was not exclusively a female zone. Male servants were needed to move furniture, to carry in coffers, or to bring in fuel for the fire, and as the royal bedchamber, with its 'bed of state', was designed to make an impression upon beholders, just like other areas of the palace, the Queen occasionally invited foreign visitors or diplomats inside.

The Ladies and Gentlewomen of the Bedchamber probably attended upon the Queen off and on all day as they were also 'of the Privy Chamber' and served the Queen throughout her residential suite. They also attended upon the Queen in the state rooms, when needed, and sometimes in public (as in the coronation). The ladies and gentlewomen also helped to take care of the Queen's pets. For it was not just humans who occupied the Privy Chamber but the Queen's small collection of animals. Over the years these ranged from exotic birds to a monkey and a 'muske cat', which was probably a type of ferret, and these animals were either kept in cages or upon chains.[38] The Queen, like several of her women, also had a 'little dog' that went everywhere with her.

The second busiest time of day for the Ladies and Gentlewomen of the Bedchamber was probably when the Queen went to bed. If her schedule permitted it, perhaps the Queen undressed some hours before on quieter days, choosing to relax in one of her many loose gowns, but even on these less demanding days, putting the Queen to bed was still quite a process as the 'ancient ceremony' of 'The Order of All Night' had to be followed. In the Stuart era, the ceremony began at 9 o'clock, when a Gentleman Usher of the Presence Chamber gave word that it was time for 'All Night', but as Queen Elizabeth was more of a night owl than an early bird, in her reign the ceremony may have started later or at no set hour. After announcing that it was time for 'All Night' the usher went with a number of yeomen to the pantry, buttery, spicery and wine-cellar to collect bread, beer, spices and wine for the Queen's overnight use. After twice drinking to the sovereign's health, a ritual that was no doubt enjoyed, the men returned to the Presence Chamber, which was now emptying, and probably gave the victuals to the Grooms of the Privy Chamber to place upon the Queen's cupboard there, a cupboard being a movable piece of furniture that was popular in the Tudor and Stuart era. The men then retired for the night and an Esquire of the Body took over. Of little importance during the day, at least in the reign of a queen, this esquire, who also worked on rota, was invested with extraordinary power at night for he was put in charge of the whole palace, temporarily assuming the combined authority of the Lord Chamberlain and the Lord Steward. This meant that absolutely everyone had to answer to him, even the highest ranking courtiers, and no one or nothing could reach the Queen without his permission. The esquire then put on a cloak and a sword and went into the Privy Chamber to ceremoniously deliver the royal mortar, which was a large and flat candle of virgin wax set afloat in a silver basin, to the royal bedchamber. In the reign of a king, the esquire would wait in the bedchamber until the monarch got into bed and gave the order of 'All Night', but in the reign of a queen, he probably delivered the royal mortar to one of her women of the bedchamber and then waited outside until she gave him the order of 'All Night'. Once the order was given, the esquire locked the main door into the Privy Chamber, went to the Watching Chamber to 'set the watch', which was the Queen's overnight guard, and then returned to the now empty Presence Chamber. To emphasise his temporary sovereignty, the esquire slept on a pallet bed beneath the grand canopy of state, a page boy close by, and providing his services were not needed overnight, he slept until morning. At 8 o'clock he was relieved of duty by a gentleman usher, and then served a beastly feast of a breakfast that included 'a good piece of boiled beef, of fourteen pounds weight, with bread, beer, wine, sometimes a boiled capon, and a piece of veal or mutton'. The royal mortar, meanwhile, was left to burn 'all night' at the Queen's bedside, perhaps as a symbol of sovereign authority.[39]

Over the course of the Queen's reign only ten women are known to have served as a Lady or Gentlewoman of the Bedchamber and for almost thirty years there was little change in the personnel. Until the 1590s only six women had occupied the role: Kathryn Carey, Lady Knollys; Kateryn Astley; Blanche Parry; Elizabeth Norwich, Lady Carew; Francis Newton, Baroness Cobham; and Mary Radclyffe. Of these, Elizabeth Norwich was the longest serving, remaining in the role for thirty-six years. Sadly, by 1594 all the original Ladies and Gentlewomen of the Bedchamber were dead, as was Frances Newton, so the last decade of the sixteenth century saw four new appointments: Katheryn Carey, by then Baroness Howard of Effingham; Elizabeth Brooke, Lady Cecil; Philadelphia Carey, Baroness Scrope; and Elyzabeth Knollys, Lady Leighton. No woman but Lady Knollys is known to have held the position of Chief Lady of the Bedchamber, so the position, created especially for her, may have died with her. However, it is likely that Lady Cobham held the position from the mid-1570s until her death in 1592, then Katheryn Carey, Lady Knollys's niece, until her death in 1603, and finally Philadelphia Carey, Baroness Scrope.

Chamberers

Chamberers are sometimes likened to chambermaids, as they cleaned the Queen's bedchamber and made up her bed, but they were also prestigious attendants who, like Ladies and Gentlewomen of the Bedchamber, came under the umbrella term 'Ladies and Gentlewomen of the Privy Chamber'. Chamberers personally attended upon the Queen and their primary duty appears to have been the Queen's clothes. Aside from assisting in the dressing of the Queen, perhaps even doing most of the dressing themselves under the supervision of a Lady or Gentlewoman of the Bedchamber, they received the Queen's garments from the Gentleman of the Robes, prepared them for wearing, returned garments to the Removing Wardrobe, accepted deliveries of new materials, approved the release of old garments to be given away at the Queen's pleasure, oversaw the shipping of new materials to the Great Wardrobe, received ceremonial gowns for special occasions, and delivered the Queen's dirty laundry to the Mistress Laundress. As they were so busy with the Queen's clothes, and possibly her bedlinen, they were generally lodged near the Removing Wardrobe. Because of the constant coming and going of 'laundresses, tailors, wardrobers and such', for security reasons the Queen was advised by her Privy Council in the early years of her reign to 'give order who shall take the charge of the back doors to your Chamberers' chambers' so that 'the same doors may be duly attended upon, as becommeth, and not to stand open but upon necessity'.[40] The Privy Council was right to be concerned, for despite all the security measures in place, while the Queen was staying at Theobalds in 1587 (Theobalds being the lavish home of Lord Burghley) the lodgings assigned to one of the Queen's ladies, Katheryn Knyvett, Lady Paget, was broken into and plate worth £60 stolen. Chamberers may also have been tasked with warming the Queen's water for washing, warming her bed in cold weather, and with stoking the fires in her bedchamber and raying chamber. They may also have helped to keep other rooms in the Privy Chamber clean and tidy, along with the grooms, for there were no official cleaners. With the Queen only ever staying in a palace for a few weeks at a time, light cleaning was all that was generally needed, as the palace would be extensively 'aired and sweetened' by its permanent staff after the Queen's departure.

Chamberers were seemingly the only women of the Privy Chamber to formally receive livery. Upon their appointment they received a gown of black or russet satin from the Queen, a gown that was trimmed with velvet and lined with sarcenet, and within eighteen months of their appointment a wardrobe warrant was usually issued to the Queen's tailor instructing him to make and deliver a black or russet gown to the new Chamberer annually at Christmas. These gowns complimented in colour the more varied uniform of the Grooms of the Privy Chamber who received every year a fur trimmed robe of black satin, a doublet and coat of black velvet, a coat of marble or russet cloth for winter, and a coat of green cloth for summer.[41] As Chamberers received less pay than Ladies and Gentlewomen of the Privy Chamber, and were often from humbler backgrounds, the Queen regularly gave them gifts of expensive clothes so they would look their best at court. The Queen's first Chamberers were the Hatfield incumbents, Elyzabeth Marbury, Dorothy Broadbelt, and Frances Newton, and they were soon joined by the Queen's dear friend and former servant, Elizabeth Sondes. As Frances Newton and Elizabeth Sondes made wealthy marriages at the beginning of the reign, Frances marrying

William Brooke, Baron Cobham, and Elizabeth marrying Sir Maurice Berkeley, the widower of Kat's former sister-in-law, Kateryn Blount, they did not need to benefit from the Queen's generosity in this respect, but Elyzabeth Marbury and Dorothy Broadbelt remained amongst the poorest of the Queen's attendants. Consequently they received many gifts during their years of service. Elyzabeth Marbury is known to have received a very sumptuous fur trimmed gown of velvet in the royal colour of purple; two gowns of black velvet; several kirtles of black or russet velvet; a petticoat of crimson velvet; a petticoat of crimson cloth of gold; and a 'black fan of feathers with a handle of gold', possibly as a retirement gift. Dorothy Broadbelt is known to have received a gown of black satin with a train; a gown of black velvet; a gown of russet velvet; several kirtles of black or russet velvet or satin; a petticoat of crimson silk; a petticoat of velvet striped with gold; and a petticoat of cloth of silver striped with gold.[42] Dorothy was also given a lavish gown and kirtle by the Queen for her wedding in 1567 to John Abington. This gown was made of black velvet (white had not yet become the bridal colour) and the kirtle was made of murrey velvet and silver lace.[43] Elyzabeth Marbury and Dorothy Broadbelt were also rewarded with very lucrative grants of land. In 1560 Mistress Marbury and her husband, now Sergeant of Her Majesty's Pantry, was given a twenty-one year lease on a rectory and manor in Norfolk, whilst Dorothy Broadbelt was given a forty-one year lease on land and property in Northamptonshire, followed by at least two more grants of land and property in Kent and Lincolnshire.[44] In addition to the general duties of Chamberers, Elyzabeth Marbury and Dorothy Broadbelt also had their own responsibilities. For example, Elyzabeth Marbury was keeper of the Queen's petticoats and coffer of 'sweet waters' (distilled plants used for medicinal or dental purposes) whilst Dorothy Broadbelt was keeper of the Queen's 'pin-pillow of crimson velvet' that was used to hold the many pins needed to dress her. Dorothy was also responsible for looking after the Queen's pet monkey for a time.[45]

As Chamberers primarily worked in the Queen's bedchamber and raying chamber they were considered to be 'of the Bedchamber' as well as 'of the Privy Chamber'. Indeed, their titles were used interchangeably. For example, Elyzabeth Marbury is described as a Chamberer on fee lists, as a Gentlewoman of the Privy Chamber in patents, and as 'one of the gentlewomen of Her Majesty's Bedchamber' in the *Day Book of the Wardrobe of Robes*. Although the position of Chamberer was not the most prestigious, or the best paid, it was highly desirable because of the intimate access it gave to the Queen. In this way, Chamberers were amongst the most important of the Queen's attendants and amongst those most sought after by courtiers and statesmen in their bid to reach the Queen's ear. The prestige and desirability of the position is shown by the fact that the incumbents continued to serve in the role even after becoming titled ladies.

As the Queen's reign progressed, the number of Chamberers increased, but there were never more than six at any given time and, like the rest of the Privy Chamber staff, they worked on rota. Only twelve women are known to have officially held the position over the course of the Queen's reign: Elyzabeth Marbury; Dorothy Broadbelt; Frances Newton, Baroness Cobham; Elizabeth Sondes, Lady Berkeley; Nazareth Newton; Elizabeth Stafford, Lady Drury/Scott; Mary Shelton, Lady

Scudamore; Jane Brussels; Kattrin Paston, Lady Newton; Margaret Vaughan, Lady Hawkins; Lucy Hyde; and Anne Vavasour (not the Maid of Honour of the same name). Of these, the longest serving were Mary Shelton and Elizabeth Stafford, both serving in the role for over thirty years. However, at least two more women probably served as Chamberers: Sara Snow and Bregett Chaworth Carr. Sara Snow was the daughter of the Queen's childhood attendant, Elyzabeth Cavendish Snow, who was made an extraordinary Gentlewoman of the Privy Chamber at the Queen's accession. Little is known about Sara, but in 1566 she received 'twelve yards of russet satin' and 'two yards of black velvet' for a gown, and in 1567 'twelve yards of black satin' and 'two yards of velvet' for the same, suggesting she was a Chamberer as these were their livery gowns. Although Chamberers were usually given fourteen yards of satin and three yards of velvet, Sara may have been very young, perhaps only 12 or 13 years of age, as the material was 'delivered to her mother' in 1566 who signed for it in the *Day Book of the Wardrobe of Robes*. Sadly, Sara seems to have died within a year or two of her appointment, as an official livery warrant was never issued for her, and she does not appear on any surviving fee lists or in her mother's will of 1584. Bregett Chaworth Carr began her long court career about a year after her first cousin, Kattrin Paston, began hers. Both women had Boleyn blood, as they were descended from Sir Geoffrey Boleyn, the Queen's great, great grandfather, and Kattrin was also the step-niece of Elyzabeth Fitzgerald who undoubtedly played a part in securing for her the position in 1577. Bregett was in her thirties when she entered the Queen's service and appears to have been an extraordinary Gentlewoman of the Privy Chamber for most of her career, serving regularly as a Chamberer alongside her cousin, until she was seemingly officially appointed to the position in 1601. Like the other Chamberers, Bregett received a number of gifts from the Queen, including kirtles and petticoats, a loose gown of black taffeta that had 'buttons and hoops of silver and gold', and for her wedding to William Carr that probably took place during the twelve days of Christmas in 1584, she received a gown of 'carnation cloth of silver' that was trimmed with murrey satin, adorned with laces of gold and silver, and edged with sable fur.[46]

Ladies and Gentlewomen of the Privy Chamber

Ladies and Gentlewomen of the Privy Chamber attended upon the Queen throughout her Privy Chamber but were principally based in her prestigious parlour of the same name. Their first duty of the day was probably serving the Queen's breakfast. In the reign of Henry VIII, this was delivered by the staff of the privy kitchen, which was a special kitchen to prepare and cook the monarch's food, to the door of the Privy Chamber where it was received by an usher or a groom and taken to the privy chamber. When there, the dishes were placed on the King's cupboard and guarded until the Gentlemen of the Privy Chamber arrived to serve the food to the King. A similar ritual was probably observed in Elizabeth's reign with the ladies or gentlewomen taking the dishes from her privy chamber to whichever room the Queen chose to have her breakfast in. This may have been her bedchamber, or even the privy chamber itself, but was probably one of her dining rooms. This way her breakfast would be all laid out when she arrived, and her women ready to serve, and she could eat in a more private setting. According to tradition, the Queen shared this breakfast, which included ten loaves, a joint of beef, and gallons of ale, with the women of her Privy Chamber who were on duty.[47]

Later in the day, when the Queen had the first of her two formal meals, those ladies and gentlewomen on duty probably received her many dishes from her maids and then laid them out on the Queen's table. Officially, the Queen chose which dishes to keep and which to send back to the Presence Chamber, but in reality her ladies and gentlewomen, knowing her preferences, probably chose for her. When she was young, Elizabeth often invited foreign ambassadors and diplomats to dine with her, but as she got older she preferred to 'dine and sup alone with few attendance'. One of those in attendance was surely the lady carver, who was responsible for carving the Queen's meat, and another was possibly a lady cupbearer, who would have been responsible for pouring the Queen's wine and, perhaps, for bringing in the grace cup at the end of the meal. The grace cup, sometimes called a great mazer, was a cup of wine that was commonly handed around a table in Tudor times after the diners had said grace, for even when the Queen was officially 'dining alone' she was probably joined by those 'few' women on duty. In addition to serving the Queen at table, the Ladies and Gentlewomen of the Privy Chamber took care of any luxury foods gifted or delivered to her, such as olives and oranges, and prepared sweet snacks for their mistress, such as jellies and confectionary, and warm, spicy drinks.[48]

Between them, the Queen's Ladies and Gentlewomen of the Privy Chamber were on duty all day and all night. As well as attending upon the Queen at mealtimes, they attended upon her in her privy chamber, whether she was relaxing there or entertaining, and in any other room on an as needed basis. When the ladies and gentlewomen were not needed, they probably awaited the Queen's pleasure in her privy chamber, as their counterparts had done in the reign of Henry VIII. At night, one of the women had the privilege of being 'the Queen's bedfellow'. This meant sleeping in the royal bedchamber with the Queen upon a pallet bed and being ready to attend her if needed. This pallet bed may have been assembled by the grooms every night, for pallet beds were designed to fit under greater beds, but for convenience it may have been left assembled in a corner of the room. Of course, when the bedchamber door was locked, and the Queen and her bedfellow were alone, they may have slept together in her huge four poster bed, especially on cold winter nights, so they could talk more intimately. For the first few years of the Queen's reign, when she was young and lively, her sleeping companions were her bedfellows of old, Dorothy Broadbelt, the Chamberer, and her Hatfield maids.

The Hatfield maids, too important to the Queen to be relegated to the Presence Chamber as Maids of Honour, soon lost their novel title of Maids of the Privy Chamber as two of the maids, Isabella Markham and Margaret Willoughby, married not long after the Queen's coronation. Elizabeth Clyffe, Kateryn Parr's former attendant, was seemingly never given the title, perhaps because she was older than the other girls. Instead she was made a Gentlewoman of the Privy Chamber along with Anne Morris, Mother of the Maids. In these early weeks of the reign, the Hatfield Maids were joined by two new recruits, Lettice Knollys, Lady Knollys's daughter, and Anne Wingfield, possibly Lady Knollys's niece.[49] For the coronation eve procession, the six Maids of the Privy Chamber (Isabella Markham, Margaret Willoughby, Bridget Skipwith, Elyzabeth St Loe, Lettice Knollys and Anne Wingfield) were given fifteen yards of crimson satin with two yards of 'purple gold tinsel with knots' for the turning up of their sleeves whilst Mistress Clyffe and Mistress Morris were given fifteen yards of crimson satin and two yards of 'tinsel purple with work'.[50]

The first ordinary Lady of the Privy Chamber was the woman who would become the Queen's principal bedfellow, Dorothee Stafford, Lady Stafford. Dorothee, who was about seven years older than the Queen, was her step-aunt, of sorts, as she was the widow of Mary Boleyn's second husband, Sir William Stafford. She was also related to the Queen as she was a granddaughter of Margaret Pole, Lady Salisbury, Queen Mary's beloved governess. Unlike her grandmother, who was a devout Catholic, Dorothee was of the Protestant faith, and during the reign of Queen Mary had lived in exile abroad. Indeed, she took Elizabeth Sondes under her wing after the girl left England, and it was probably from Mistress Sondes and Lady Stafford that John Foxe acquired much of his information for his *Book of Martyrs*.[51] While in exile, Dorothee's husband died, leaving her a young widow with five or six small children, but she stayed on the Continent and was still there when Elizabeth became queen. Getting back to England in winter, especially with children, was not easy, so it was some weeks, if not months, before Dorothee arrived at court, but by the summer she was in the Queen's service.

Lady Stafford was, by all accounts, a gentle and quiet soul, and she quickly became one of the Queen's most loved ladies. As Lady Stafford never remarried after her husband's death, even though she was relatively young, she was perfectly placed to be the Queen's main bedfellow, and this she had become by the late 1560s after Dorothy Broadbelt married. With Lady Stafford, the Queen could talk about things that she could not easily do with some of her other attendants, for even some of those of 'the Hatfield flock' had not proved to be entirely trustworthy.[52] It is likely that Lady Stafford was amongst those women who breakfasted with the Queen, for the Queen's bedfellows surely had this privilege, and Lady Stafford was often the Queen's companion of choice when dining with guests. The Queen also enjoyed riding with Lady Stafford, who could match her speed and vigour, but was shaken in 1576 when Lady Stafford fell from her horse and broke her leg. This meant that Lady Stafford could not work for weeks so the Queen was without her principal bedfellow. Consequently, Mary Scudamore, the Queen's second favourite bedfellow by then, was recalled to court by the Lord Chamberlain, Robert Radclyffe, Earl of Sussex, who told her in a letter that 'until you come Her Majesty shall not in the night have for the most part so good rest as she will take after your coming'.[53] Lady Stafford made a full recovery from her fall, and was soon back in post, but there was more drama in early 1587 when her son, William, was accused of conspiring with the French Ambassador to kill Elizabeth and put Mary, Queen of Scots, on the throne. William allegedly had a plan to 'blow up' the Queen in her bed by placing 'barrels of gunpowder inside his mother's apartment', which was underneath the Queen's. When the French Ambassador pointed out to him that he could not accomplish this without killing his mother, 'as she and the Queen both sleep in the same room', William declared that he would stab the Queen to death instead.[54] When told of the conspiracy, Lady Stafford was devastated. Not only was she horrified at the thought of her son killing her beloved mistress, but she was afraid what his treachery meant for her own position at court, for that of her daughter, and for her eldest son's position as English Ambassador in France. The Queen too was distressed at the news. Although she was in daily danger from conspiracies, to the extent that 'she could scarcely stir out of her chamber with assurance of safety', it was rare for the conspirators to be so closely connected to her inner circle, and she told Sir Edward Stafford, Lady Stafford's ambassador son, that the plot was all the more 'grievous to ourself in respect of your mother, whose sorrow, being so near as she is unto us, cannot but add some affliction to ours'.[55] But as sorrowful as Lady Stafford and the Queen were, there was no avoiding the fact that the Stafford family was now tainted by treason, so while the conspiracy was being investigated the Queen had no choice but to send Lady Stafford and her daughter from court. As they left, the Queen was surely as upset as both women, not just for their departure but because she was losing, in Lady Stafford, one of her dearest confidantes at the very moment that she was facing tremendous pressure to execute the Queen of Scots. Indeed, many historians theorise that William Stafford was 'an agent provocateur' secretly working on behalf of Sir Francis Walsingham, the Queen's famous spymaster, who wanted to push the Queen to sign Mary Stuart's death warrant by making her believe she was not even safe within her apartment. It is telling, perhaps, that William was never charged with treason, despite his direct involvement in the plot, although he did spend some months in the Tower of London. When a respectable amount of time had passed, Lady Stafford and her daughter returned to court and resumed their positions. For Lady Stafford, being the Queen's principal bedfellow was a great privilege, and undoubtedly her hours of unrivalled access to the Queen were envied, but being the Queen's bedfellow was not the easiest of jobs as Elizabeth was a very poor sleeper, especially in times of stress. 'The Queen did not sleep all night', King Philip of Spain was once told by his ambassador, 'and constantly woke Lady Stafford who sleeps in the same room'.[56]

Over the course of the Queen's reign, only sixteen women are known to have served as an ordinary Lady or Gentlewoman of the Privy Chamber: Bridget Skipwith, who married a man named Brian Cave in 1565; Isabella Markham, who married the poet John Harington in 1559; Margaret Willoughby, who married the Queen's cousin, Thomas Arundel, in 1559; Elizabeth Clyffe, who sadly died within months of the coronation; Elyzabeth St Loe, who also died early in the reign; Anne Wingfield, whose identity is uncertain; Lettice Knollys, who married Walter Devereux, future Earl of Essex, in 1560, and later, in secret, Robert Dudley, Earl of Leicester; Dorothee Stafford, Lady Stafford; Katheryn Carey, Baroness Howard of Effingham and later Countess of Nottingham; sisters Amy and Elizabeth Shelton, daughters of Sir John and Lady Shelton; Elyzabeth Knollys, Lady Leighton; Frances Howard, Countess of Hertford; Dorothy Edmonds, Lady Edmonds, a probable relation; Catherine Knyvett, Baroness Howard of Walden, another relation with close connections to Blanche Parry; and Audrey Shelton, Lady Walsingham, a great granddaughter of Sir John and Lady Shelton.

Maids of the Privy Chamber

In the early years of the Queen's reign, a new group of Privy Chamber attendants emerged that are best described as Maids of the Privy Chamber. Whether they were actually known by this title is unclear, as the only attendants known to have been described as such are the former Hatfield maids, and the two new recruits, who were known by this title for the first few months of the Queen's reign, but the title is a useful one to distinguish this new group of attendants from the Ladies and Gentlewomen of the Privy Chamber, who were their superiors, and from the Maids of Honour, who were in a different role. These Maids of the Privy Chamber came into being in the early 1560s when a small number of teenage girls were admitted into the Privy Chamber. These girls, typically the daughters, or close relations, of favourite attendants and courtiers, were often only 12 or 13 years of age. The Queen was therefore in a position of *loco parentis* over them, especially if their mothers were not at court, and the Queen took this responsibility seriously, as can be seen in a letter she wrote to Lady Sidney, and to her husband, inviting their 13-year-old daughter, Mary, into her service in 1575:

> ... if you shall think good to ... send her unto us ... assure yourself
> that we will have a special care of her, not doubting but, as you are
> well persuaded of our favour towards yourself, so will we make
> further demonstration thereof in her, if you will send her unto us.[57]

Because of their tender age, these girls needed schooling, so it is reasonable to conclude that they were taught by the Queen's own tutors, perhaps under the supervision of one of the Queen's ladies or gentlewomen. For those girls eager to learn, like Mary, this would have been a great privilege as the Queen's tutors were some of the cleverest minds of the time. The girls would also have had music lessons, dancing lessons, riding lessons, needlework lessons, and every other lesson necessary for them to grow up into accomplished young women.

In terms of duties, the maids, who were essentially trainee attendants, probably assisted the Ladies and Gentlewomen of the Privy Chamber in their tasks rather than having specific ones of their own. They may also have assisted the Maids of Honour at mealtimes and filled in for a sick or absent Maid of Honour occasionally. Indeed, it can sometimes be very difficult to determine whether a young girl served as a Maid of the Privy Chamber or as a Maid of Honour. The best guides in this respect are the surviving New Year's gift rolls as they generally list the Maids of Honour by name. Also adding to the confusion is the probability that the Maids of the Privy Chamber received the same wage as Maids of Honour (£10 a year, rising to £20 by 1600) and shared the maidens' chamber with them. This is hinted at in a letter by Rowland Whyte to Sir Robert Sidney in which he says that 'Mistress Brydges' and 'Mistress Russell', two Maids of the Privy Chamber in the 1590s, were 'put out of the coffer chamber' for three nights after sneaking out of the palace to watch the Earl of Essex, and others, 'playing at ballon', and were forced to lodge in Lady Stafford's house in London (Whyte probably means the maidens' chamber rather than the coffer chamber).[58]

The first of these new Maids of the Privy Chamber was possibly Lady Frances Radclyffe, a paternal half-sister of the Queen's cousin, Robert Radclyffe, Earl of Sussex, future Lord Chamberlain. In the autumn of 1561 the Queen invited Lady Frances to court as a Maid of Honour, the invitation being sent to her brother via Sir William Cecil: 'The Queen's Majesty willeth me to signify to Your Lordship,' wrote Cecil, 'her contentation to have my lady, your sister, in her court as one of her Maids of Honour, if Your Lordship will give order therein'.[59] There was no reason for the earl to object (indeed, the kind nobleman was probably delighted at the prospect of having his sister as a Maid of Honour) but Lady Frances never became a Maid of Honour so it must have been she herself who objected. Perhaps she was of a quiet, private disposition, unwilling to parade herself before the court, and her objection may have given the Queen, or Kat Astley, the idea of inviting her to be a Maid of the Privy Chamber instead, for as a Maid of the Privy Chamber she would be in a more private, companionship role. Lady Frances was certainly at court from that autumn onwards, for she famously caught the eye of Shane O'Neil, Earl of Tyrone, when he arrived at court on Twelfth Night, 1562, to make peace with the Queen. Lady Frances, then, may have been the reason that the novel position of Maid of the Privy Chamber made a return and came to be an alternative debutante serving position for young aristocratic girls.

The first Maid of the Privy Chamber who can be identified for certain is Lady Anne Russell. Lady Anne, the eldest daughter of Francis Russell, Earl of Bedford, is thought to have come to court with her mother, Margaret St John, Countess of Bedford, when she was 12 or 13 years of age. Perhaps recruited in 1562 to keep Lady Frances company, who was not much older, the young girl suffered a personal tragedy that summer when her mother, who was not at court at the time, died of smallpox. The deadly disease was rife that year and two months later caused chaos at court when the Queen herself was infected. Just who she caught the disease from is unknown, as the Queen met all kinds of people from all kinds of places every day, but she fell so seriously ill that for some days she was at death's door. The Queen obviously survived, and reputedly escaped disfiguring pox pits, but Sybil Penn, King Edward's nurse who may have nursed her, lost her life to the disease whilst Lady Sidney, who was in attendance, lost her looks. From the time of her mother's death, the Queen became, in many ways, a second mother to Lady Anne, and the two developed a close bond that would last for the rest of their lives. In the autumn of 1565, when she was about 16 years of age, Lady Anne married, in a lavish wedding at Whitehall Palace, the twice widowed Ambrose Dudley, Earl of Warwick. The Queen very much approved of the marriage and spent a lot of money preparing the court for the wedding and on having matching gowns of yellow satin made for her Maids of Honour. She also gave Lady Anne an expensive gown of 'purple cloth of tissue' for her wedding dress, tissue being a rich silk fabric woven with threads of real gold or silver. On the day, Lady Anne was escorted from her chamber to the Chapel Royal, where she was to be married, by a procession of courtiers, her gown's train carried by Lady Knollys's 6-year-old daughter, Kathryn, with the Queen's Maids of Honour following. After the ceremony, there was a grand feast in the Council Chamber, which had been hung with glittering tapestries for the occasion, and then began a three day jousting tournament. Lady Anne was now the Countess of Warwick, and as the Countess of Warwick she became a Lady of Honour, but more importantly she became an honorary Lady of the Privy Chamber, and for the next four decades was one of the Queen's most influential attendants.

Lady Anne's place as a Maid of the Privy Chamber was filled by Swedish beauty, Helena Snakenborg, whilst she waited to marry the Marquess of Northampton, and for a while she may have been the only Maid of the Privy Chamber as Lady Frances, who did not return Shane O'Neil's affection, married Sir Thomas Mildmay in 1566. The next maid known to join the Privy Chamber was Anne Knollys, another of Lady Knollys's daughters, whom the Queen took under her wing following her mother's death in 1569 when Anne was just 13 years of age. Although Anne only served for two and a half years, as she married a young man named Thomas West in the winter of 1571, during those years she was showered with gifts by the Queen. These gifts included a gown of blue and orange taffeta adorned with gold and silver lace; a gown of white camlet; a gown of black frizado (woollen cloth); two gowns of crimson satin; a gown of black silk; a gown of black taffeta; a gown of carnation satin; a furred loose gown of purple camlet; a loose gown of black satin; a kirtle of white taffeta; a kirtle of yellow velvet; a kirtle of purple satin; three farthingales; two crimson petticoats; several cloaks and hats of crimson satin or taffeta; more than a dozen pairs of stockings and leather shoes, and two pairs of velvet slippers.[60]

From the 1570s onwards, the new position really came into its own, and it was common for there to be at least two or three Maids of the Privy Chamber at the same time. Mary Sidney, for example, served alongside Elizabeth Howard, daughter of Katheryn and Charles Howard of Effingham, and Mary Hopton, daughter of Sir Owen Hopton, Lieutenant of the Tower of London. All these girls received gifts of clothing from the Queen. Mary Sidney received several gowns, including a gown of green velvet from the Queen's own wardrobe and a brand new gown of murrey damask; Elizabeth Howard received a gown of crimson taffeta, several gowns of black velvet, a kirtle or forepart of black taffeta, several petticoats, and two black hats; and Mary Hopton received a train gown of crimson velvet, possibly for her marriage to William Brydges, future Baron Chandos, along with a kirtle 'of cloth of silver striped with purple silk'. Mary Sidney also received a gown from the Queen made of blue cloth of silver edged with orange satin, along with a forepart of purple velvet 'set with turquoise, garnet and pearl', for her wedding to Henry Herbert, Earl of Pembroke, in the spring of 1577.[61] Once again, the wedding took place in the Chapel Royal of Whitehall Palace, in the presence of the Queen, and although it was not quite on the scale of the wedding of her uncle and aunt, Lord and Lady Warwick, it was still a magnificent affair. As the Countess of Pembroke, Mary retired from the Privy Chamber, but for the rest of the reign served as a Lady of Honour.

In addition to giving her Maids of the Privy Chamber gifts of clothing on an individual basis, the Queen sometimes gave the maids matching gowns and accessories. Amongst those who benefited from matching gowns were Dorothy and Penelope Devereux, the young daughters of Lettice Knollys and Walter Devereux, Earl of Essex, who served in the late 1570s. The two sisters received matching gowns 'of flesh colour satin', evidently a peachy sort of colour, with sleeves of 'white satin', and the gowns were lavishly adorned with laces and spangles of silver and gold, silver 'Spanish' buttons, and yards of ribbon. The Devereux sisters were unfortunate in that their time of service clashed with their mother's falling out of favour over her secret marriage to Robert Dudley, Earl of Leicester. The Queen famously never forgave 'the she-wolf' for the marriage, and for the rest of her reign Lettice was unwelcome at court. However, Lettice was not entirely innocent in the feud as she often provoked Elizabeth's anger by having herself magnificently attended, as though she was a queen herself, and by travelling in great style. In short, there was a love-hate relationship between the two cousins, a relationship that was rather unique, and it may have been due to a clash of personality as well as their rivalry for the Earl of Leicester's affections. Indeed, the Queen may have preferred her 'sweet Robin' to marry her other cousin, Douglas Howard, one of her first Maids of Honour, with whom the earl had fathered his illegitimate son, if the earl was to marry someone other than herself. For when the Queen found out about the earl's marriage to Lettice, she allegedly wanted to know from Douglas 'whether there were a contract between her and the Earl of Leicester, which if there were, then she would make him make up her honour with a marriage or rot in the Tower', but Douglas could only say that 'she had trusted the said earl too much to have anything to show to constrain him to marry her'. By now Douglas was married to Edward Stafford, Lady Stafford's son, who told this story many years later, with the claim that the Queen had promised to 'better his estate' in compensation for losing Douglas.[62] Whether or not any of this is true, is one of history's mysteries, but Douglas certainly remained in favour, despite her affair with Lord Leicester, as is evident from the New Year's gift rolls, for Douglas participated in the gift exchange for the rest of the Queen's reign whereas Lettice did not. Penelope and Dorothy were not unduly impacted by their mother's fall, for they remained in service for some years, but they never ranked amongst the Queen's favourite attendants and both made disastrous marriages: Penelope to Robert Rich, Baron Rich, an arranged marriage that was very unhappy, and Dorothy to John Perrot, a marriage that was conducted in secret and saw Dorothy out of favour for some years.

Other maids known to have received matching gowns are: Elizabeth Howard and her sister, Frauncis, who received matching gowns of 'carnation and black velvet'; Philadelphia and Margaret Carey, the daughters of Baroness Hunsdon, who received gowns of 'purple cloth of silver' along with Elizabeth and Frauncis Howard; and Lady Bridget Manners and Lady Elizabeth de Vere, a granddaughter of Lord Burghley, who received matching gowns of 'murrey cloth of silver' and matching gowns of 'green velvet'. The Queen also sometimes gave sisters matching gowns even if one was a Maid of Honour. For example, Lady Stafford's granddaughters, Elizabeth and Frances Drury, daughters of Elizabeth Stafford, received matching gowns of 'haircolour velvet' and of 'watchet velvet' (a shade of blue) even though Frances was a Maid of Honour; Elizabeth and Anne Russell (the Maid of Honour who later married Lord Herbert) also received matching gowns of 'haircolour velvet'; and Ladies Elizabeth and Katherine Somerset, the latter a Maid of Honour, received matching gowns of tawny velvet with Lady Elizabeth de Vere, and matching 'high bodied gowns of velvet' with Lady Elizabeth Clinton, a step-granddaughter of Elyzabeth Fitzgerald.[63]

Although the position of Maid of the Privy Chamber is particularly hard to document, much is known about the career of one of the Queen's favourite maids, Lady Bridget Manners, thanks to the survival of the Rutland papers.[64] Lady Bridget was the eldest daughter of John Manners, Earl of Rutland, who died in 1588, and his wife, Elizabeth Charleton, the Dowager Countess. After her father's death, Bridget, who was about 13 years of age, was placed in the care of her step-grandmother, and possible godmother, Bridget Hussey, Dowager Countess of Rutland and Bedford. Lady Bedford, a step-mother of Lady Warwick, was of the opinion that she could secure a place for Bridget in the Queen's service, but Bridget's mother did not think that the time was right. 'I hope this will not as yet fall so', she wrote to her servant, Thomas Screvener, 'for Bridget has no acquaintance in that place and is therefore most unfit for it'. The widowed countess may also have had concerns about Bridget's accomplishments as she had previously told Lady Bedford that 'her education has been barren hitherto, nor has she attained to anything except to play a little on the lute, which now, by her late discontinuance, she has almost forgotten'. Bridget also had a tendency to stoop which concerned her mother. Lady Bedford appears to have respected Lady Rutland's wishes, as Bridget was not at that time presented to the Queen, but a year later Lady Rutland was given the surprising news that the Queen had taken her daughter into service. 'I did not expect the favour', she wrote to Lady Bedford, 'because it pleased the Queen so lately to receive Lady Elizabeth [de] Vere. But as it is the Queen's pleasure I hope she [Bridget] will behave herself as shall be pleasing'. Struggling financially since her husband's death, Lady Rutland added:

> I send £200 towards furnishing her for the place, which is all I can afford now. I hope those that are wise will remember the estate of a fatherless maid and that you will give her your advice as to what is most needful for her, because I myself am altogether inexperienced in the fashions of the court.

Upon taking up her position, Bridget was given written words of advice from her great uncle, John Manners:

> Understanding of her excellent Majesty's great and special favour towards you in accepting of you to her service, and that of Her Majesty's Privy Chamber, I must needs let you know that it is to the exceeding great comfort of all your friends that wish your behaviour

to be such as may be to Her Majesty's best liking. Whereunto (for that in nature I am bound to love and honour you) I am bold to give you these advices. First, and above all things, that you forget not to use daily prayers to the almighty God to endue you with His grace; then that you apply yourself wholly to the service of Her Majesty with all meekness, love and obedience; wherein you must be diligent, secret and faithful. To your elders and superiors, of reverent behaviour; to your equals and fellow servants, civil and courteous; to your inferiors you must show all favour and gentleness. Generally that you be no meddler in the causes of others. That you use much silence, for that becometh maids, especially of your calling. That your speech and endeavours ever tend to the good of all and to the hurt of none. Thus in brief, Madam, have you these rules which, if you have grace to follow, you shall find the benefit, and your friends shall rejoice of your well doing.

Bridget did her family and friends proud for she was an immediate success at court. The Queen took to her instantly and the other Ladies and Gentlewomen of the Privy Chamber rallied around to make her feel welcome. It was therefore not long before Lady Rutland was hearing about her daughter's triumph. 'The exceeding good, modest and honourable behaviour and carriage of my Lady Bridget, your daughter', wrote Sir Thomas Heneage, by then Vice-Chamberlain, 'with her careful and diligent attendance of Her Majesty, so contenting to Her Highness, and so commendable in this place where she lives, where vices will hardly receive visards and virtues will most shine, that Her Majesty acknowledgeth she hath cause to thank you for her, and you may take comfort of so virtuous a daughter, of whose being here and attendance, Her Majesty hath bidden me to tell Your Ladyship that you shall have no cause to repent'. The countess received similar news from Bridget's gentlewoman attendant, Mary Harding:

> I assure Your Ladyship that she is very well thought of, as well of Her Majesty as also especially of the Lady Dorothee Stafford, who she findeth more like a mother than a stranger, and so doth she of Mistress Radclyffe also; and great kindness is showed her also by the Lady Talbot and divers others, but surely well liked of all, and endeavoureth herself to be thankful and to follow the courtly order in all points.

As to Lady Bridget's stooping, Mary reassured her that 'it is very little or none at all, and if I discern it, I will be ready to put her in mind to forbear the same, as it pleaseth you to command'. With Christmas around the corner, Lady Rutland was advised that her daughter was likely to receive 'divers New Year's gifts' and would need to 'reward the bringers thereof as the manner and order is'. Consequently the countess, who was clearly proud of her daughter, even if she did not say so, sent Bridget 'money against Christmas'. Also, in gratitude for their care of her daughter, the countess gave gifts of money at New Year to Lady Stafford, to Mary Radclyffe, to Lady Talbot and to Mary Scudamore.

Three years later, Bridget had risen so high in the Queen's favour that she was made lady carver. 'She is in very great favour with Her Majesty', Mary Harding told Lady Rutland, 'and is employed with the nearest service about her for she carves at all times and is no way at commandment but by Her Majesty'. Bridget's health had improved in the Queen's service too, perhaps due to good food and exercise, and she 'never looked better in all her life'. The young lady carver, then, looked set for a glittering career at court – but there was a problem. Lady Bridget did not want a glittering career at court. Like most of the young women in the Queen's service, she dreamed of getting married and having children, and by 1594 she was fed up with court life. The young girl had always found 'the late watchings and sittings up' tedious, suggesting that she was on duty, perhaps awaiting the Queen's commands, well into the night, and for the last couple of years she had been on the lookout for a husband so she would not have to 'stay too long' at court. In the summer of 1594, Lady Rutland, whose health was failing, received a letter from Mary Harding telling her that 'if Your Ladyship did know how weary my lady were of the court, and what little gain there is gotten in this time, Her Majesty's favourable countenance excepted, which my lady hath, your honour would willingly be contented with a meaner [poorer] fortune to help her from hence'. This 'meaner fortune' was a proposed 'match' for Bridget with Philip Wharton, Baron Wharton, a man about two decades Bridget's senior who was a widower with several young children. According to Mary, Bridget was of the opinion that 'she should live a happier life with him than with the greatest lord here'. The rich Earls of Bedford and Southampton, Bridget had no interest in, 'for they be so young and fantastical' that 'she doubteth their carriage of themselves' and 'would choose my Lord Wharton before them'. This is interesting as it shows that Bridget was not only a good judge of character, for the Earl of Southampton did indeed get into trouble, but it also shows that young noblewomen like Bridget, who all too often ended up married to men much older than themselves, were not always attracted to the young men of the court, preferring those they deemed older and wiser. Mary hoped that Lady Rutland would help bring the match 'to pass' and suggested that the best way was for Bridget 'to fain the measles so she might have leave for a month'. Then, when she was home, 'you might sue to get the Queen's favour' which Mary believed 'would be easily granted when she were so far from her'. The countess, who had a plan of her own for her daughter's marriage, was eager to get Bridget from court, but endeavoured to do so properly rather than through faking sickness. She therefore wrote to Mary Radclyffe, who was in charge of the Queen's women by then, with the following request:

> I much long to see my daughter, Bridget, after five years absence, especially owing to my danger through sickness and weakness of body. I entreat you therefore to ask the Queen to allow my daughter to visit me.

The countess also wrote to her cousin, Kattrin Paston, Lady Newton, who was still a Chamberer, in the hope she would use her influence with the Queen to secure leave for Bridget. Leave was granted, perhaps with less difficulty than anticipated, and Bridget soon left court for Belvoir Castle, her family home in Leicestershire. However, it was not to marry Lord Wharton that Lady Rutland had helped bring Bridget from court. No, the countess had an entirely different husband in mind for her daughter – Robert Tyrwhit, a young man who had just become her ward. Robert, a great great nephew of Sir Robert and Lady Tyrwhit, the Queen's custodian and governess of long ago, was not of great wealth or status, and he was far from the older man that Bridget preferred, but the countess had the means to make the marriage happen, and so she did. Indeed, the young couple, who found each other pleasing, were married then and there at Belvoir Castle during Bridget's leave of absence. As the Queen's consent had not been obtained, this was a breach of duty on Bridget's part and an offence against the Queen on Robert's. Consequently, when word of the marriage reached the Queen's ear she was 'highly offended'. Lady Rutland, who was told by her servant that the Queen's anger was 'principally against Your Ladyship', claimed that the marriage was done without her knowledge or consent, but her servant told her that the Queen could not 'be persuaded to believe that Your Honour could be ignorant' of 'the marriage of your own daughter, in your own house, and by your own chaplain'. Nor did the Queen believe that 'Lady Bridget would have adventured so great a breach of duty as to have done this, her last and greatest act, without Your Honour's acquaintance and consent first had thereto'. But as much as the Queen was offended with Lady Rutland, it was Bridget, and her young husband, who had committed the offence, so it was they who had to be punished. 'The gentleman is like to be imprisoned', Lady Rutland was told by the Lord Chamberlain of the time, Henry Carey, Baron Hunsdon, 'and my Lady Bridget must also be committed, only Her Majesty vouchsafeth this grace that she shall not be sent to a prison but committed forthwith to custody of some lady'. This lady turned out to be the girl's former guardian, Lady Bedford, who took custody of her for several weeks, whilst Bridget's husband was imprisoned in the Tower or Fleet. By the autumn, however, both prisoners were set at liberty. Robert, a kind and sensitive soul, had fallen ill from all the upset and stress, and this, along with petitions to the Queen by his family and friends, had successfully moved her to pity. Also, the Queen did not want to imprison them too long, just long enough to deter others from disrespecting her authority, for she still believed that Lady Rutland was the chief offender, and Lady Rutland was told so by the Lord Chamberlain: 'though my Lady Bridget hath taken the fault upon herself, to excuse your fault, yet Her Majesty is well assured that my Lady Bridget would never have married without your consent and special commandment so she thinks Your Ladyship more fault worthy than they'.

And so ended, on a sad note, Bridget's time in the Privy Chamber. However, the Queen continued to think fondly of Bridget, who had served her so well for five years, and the following May, perhaps upon a visit to court following the death of her mother, the Queen gave Bridget a jewel from her own collection. Bridget also

1. King Henry VIII, Elizabeth's father. All the women appointed to care for Elizabeth in her youth were appointed by the King, usually upon recommendation.

2. Anne Boleyn, Elizabeth's mother. As queen, Elizabeth preferred to be served by her maternal relations.

3. Kateryn Astley, Elizabeth's governess and Chief Gentlewoman of the Privy Chamber.

4. Blanche Parry, childhood attendant, Chief Gentlewoman of the Privy Chamber, Keeper of Her Majesty's Jewels, and longest serving attendant in continuous service.

5. Mary Hill, Lady Cheke, childhood companion, Lady of the Privy Chamber, and longest serving attendant in intermittent service.

6. Elyzabeth Fitzgerald, Countess of Lincoln, Elizabeth's cousin, childhood companion, and a long-serving Lady of the Privy Chamber and Lady of Honour.

7. Kathryn Carey, Lady Knollys, daughter of Mary Boleyn, Anne Boleyn's sister. She was Chief Lady of the Bedchamber until her death in 1569 and a Lady of Honour.

8. Mary Shelton, Lady Scudamore, longest serving Chamberer. She was a granddaughter of Anne Boleyn, Lady Shelton, who presided over Elizabeth's household as a child.

9. Elizabeth Throckmorton, Gentlewoman of the Privy Chamber. She was Baroness Bryan's great granddaughter and caused a scandal by secretly marrying Sir Walter Raleigh.

10. Sir Walter Raleigh, Elizabeth's great favourite, was Kateryn Astley's nephew.

11. Katheryn Carey, Countess of Nottingham, granddaughter of Mary Boleyn and great granddaughter of Lady Troy. She entered the Queen's service as a child and served her, in many roles, for forty-four years.

12. Margaret Vaughan, Lady Hawkins, recruited by Blanche Parry to serve in the royal bedchamber.

Above: **13.** Elizabeth attends a Maid of Honour's wedding in 1600.

Right: **14.** Helena Snakenborg, Marchioness of Northampton, longest serving Chief Lady of Honour, as Chief Mourner at the Queen's funeral.

The Lady Marchiones of Northampton Principall mourner asisted by the Lord Buckherst Lord Thresorer & the Erle of Nottingham Lord Admirall.

Her Trayne Asisted by two Countesses. & Sr John Stanhop vicechamberlaine.

15. Ladies of Honour at the Queen's funeral.

16. Ladies and Maids of Honour at the Queen's funeral.

17. Signatures of long-serving women. Privy Chamber: Astley, Parry, Radclyffe, Fitzgerald, Kathryn Carey, Norwich, K. Knyvett, E. Stafford, Marbury, D. Stafford, Morgan, F. Newton, E. Knollys, Katheryn Carey, Frances Howard, Snakenborg, Gamage, M. Shelton, Paston, Brussels, Chaworth, Burgh, Heveningham, E. Snow, Abington, Frauncis Howard, Hill. Maids of Honour: M. Howard, K. Howard.

18. Kateryn Astley's resting place, Savoy Chapel, Westminster.

19. Blanche Parry's tomb, St Faith's Church, Bacton.

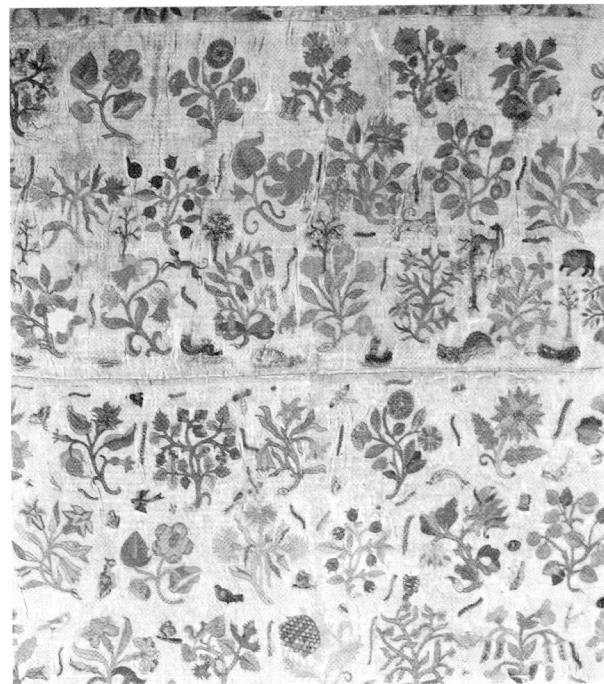

Above: **20.** Blanche Parry's Window, St Eata's Church, Atcham.

Right: **21.** Bacton Altar Cloth, possibly sent by Elizabeth to Bacton, now all that survives of her dresses.

22. Tomb of Elizabeth Norwich, Lady Carew, in Exeter Cathedral. Lady Carew served Elizabeth for half a century and was the longest serving Lady of the Bedchamber.

23. Memorial to Elizabeth Stafford, Lady Drury/Scott, in St Mary's Church, Nettlestead. Elizabeth was a Chamberer for over thirty years.

Right: **24.** Lady Bridget Manners on the tomb of her parents in Bottesford Church, Leicestershire. Lady Bridget, a Maid of the Privy Chamber, is one of only two women known to have served as lady carver.

Below: **25.** Memorial to Bregett Chaworth Carr, St Andrew's Church, Ufford. Bregett served in the Privy Chamber for a quarter of a century.

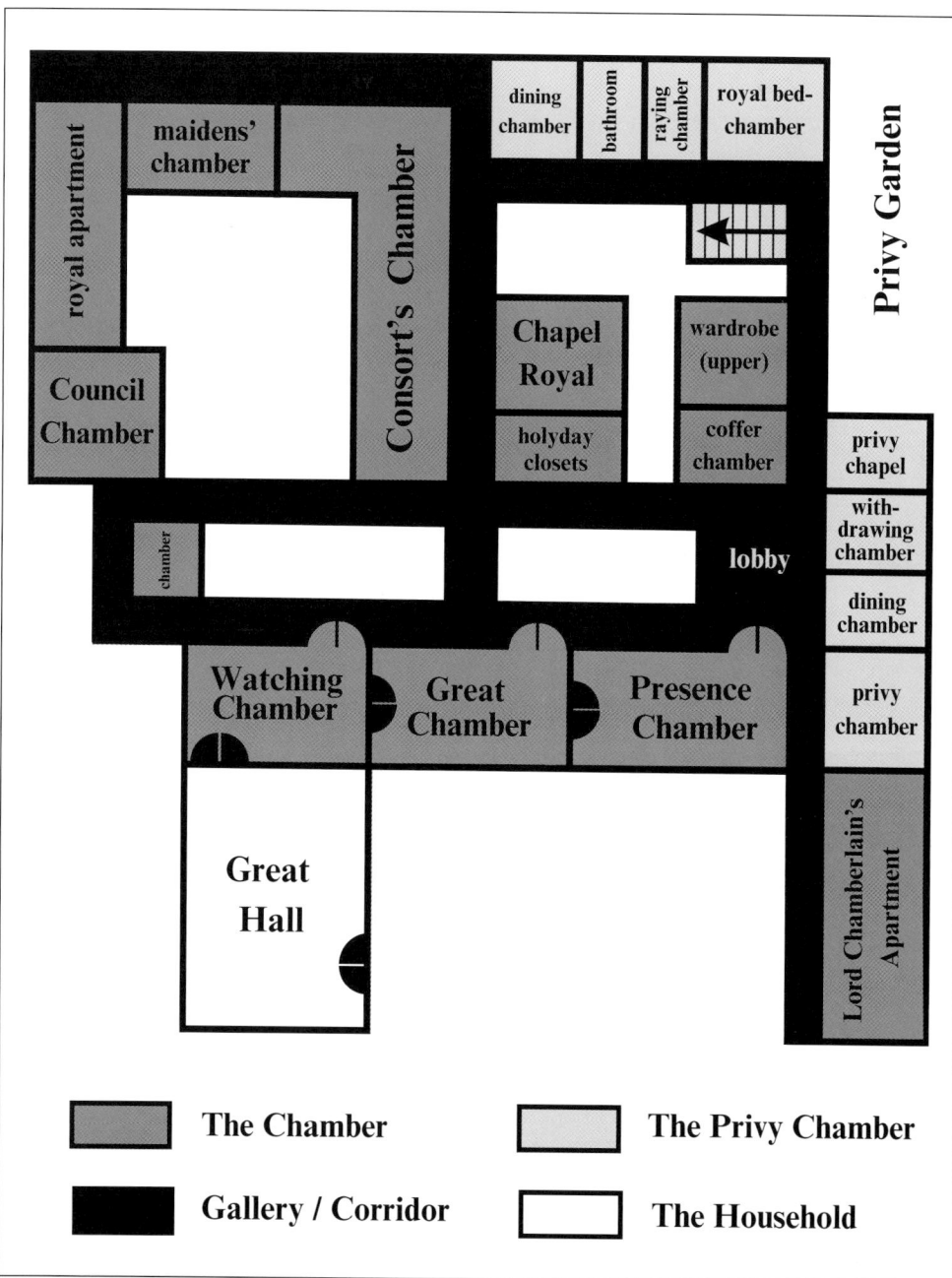

26. Typical layout of the *Domus Magnificencie* in a Tudor Palace based on plans and descriptions of several palaces (not to scale).

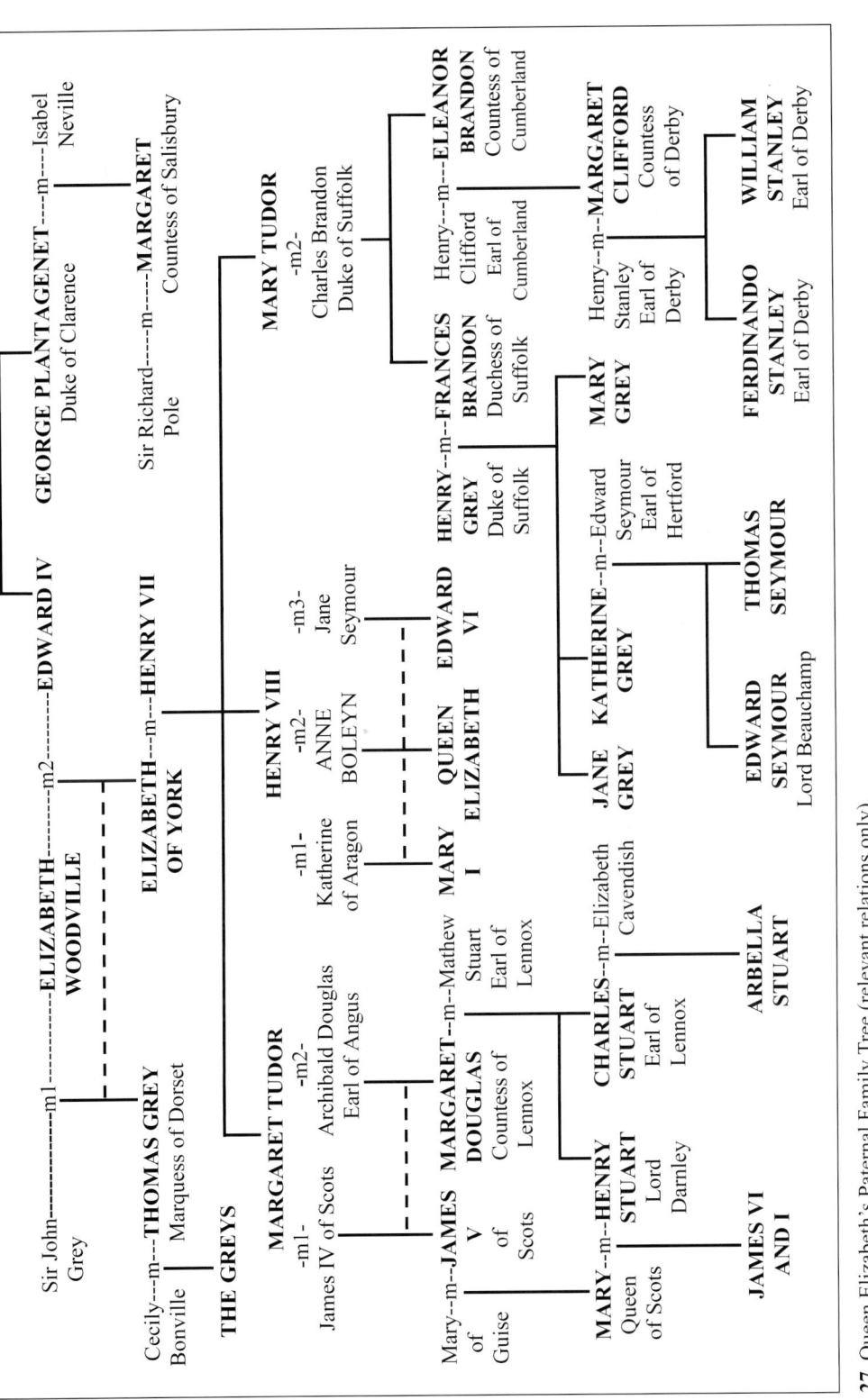

27. Queen Elizabeth's Paternal Family Tree (relevant relations only).

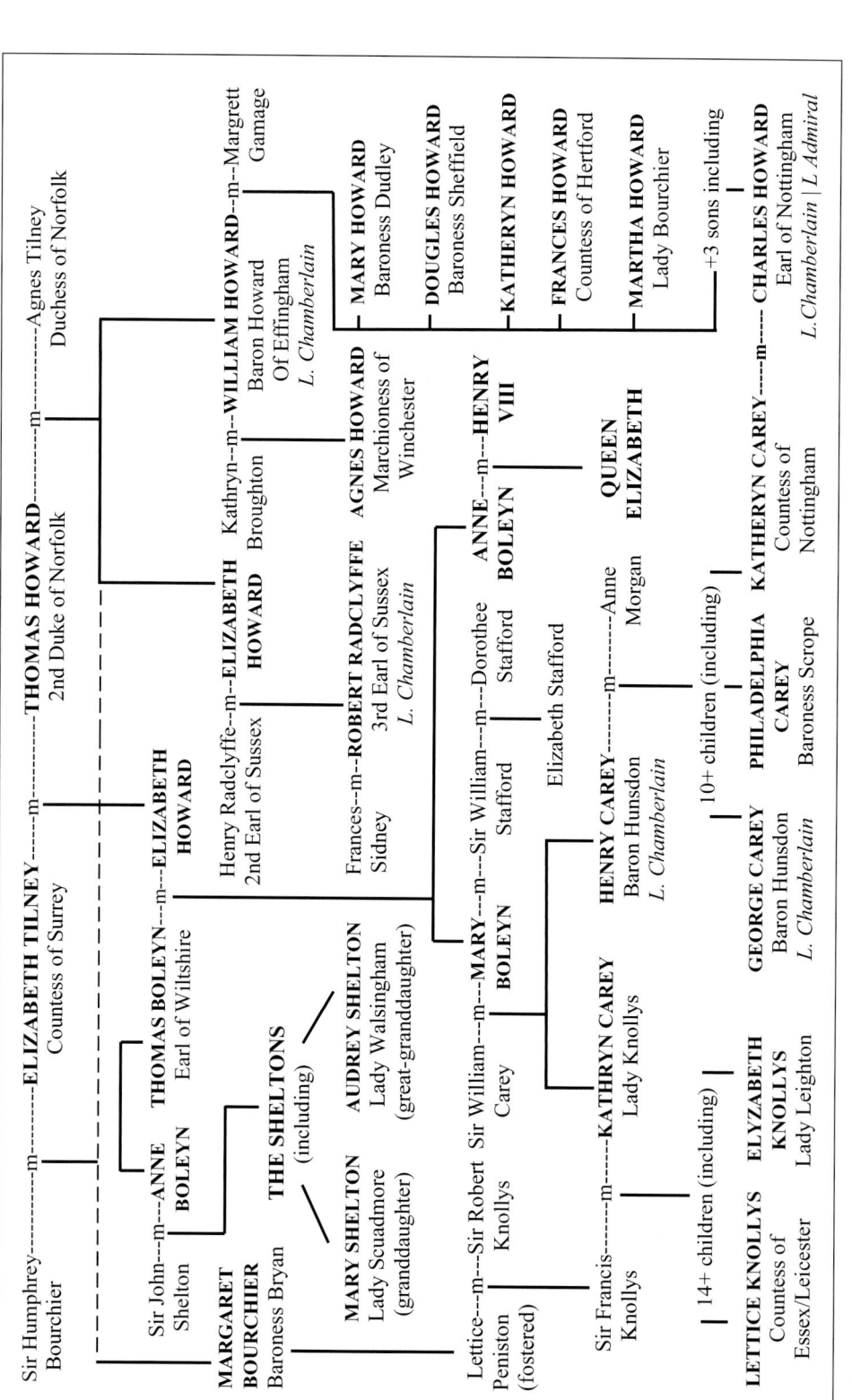

28. Queen Elizabeth's Maternal Family Tree (relevant relations only).

continued to serve the Queen from time to time as a Lady of Honour. With her husband, Bridget had four children, three sons and a daughter, but sadly her life with the family she had always dreamed of was short as she died, just a year after the Queen, in 1604. On a memorial in the church where Bridget was laid to rest, her heartbroken husband described her as 'of speech affable, of countenance amiable, nothing proud of her place and fortunes, and using her grace rather to benefit others than herself'.

Only twenty-five girls are presently known to have served as a Maid of the Privy Chamber for certain, but there were surely more. Of these, the two longest serving were Frauncis Howard and Elizabeth Brydges. Both girls served for a decade, although not at the same time, and Elizabeth was still in service when the Queen died, serving alongside Lady Susan de Vere and Lady Anne Herbert. Lady Anne was the daughter of Mary Sidney, Countess of Pembroke, and is the last known Maid of the Privy Chamber to have been appointed. Her brother, William, was the young Earl of Pembroke who had impregnated Mary Fitton and refused to marry her, but William's behaviour had in no way impacted the Queen's regard for his mother and sister. At the time of their serving, Lady Anne and Lady Susan could not have known that in the near future they would be sisters-in-law, as in 1604 Lady Susan married Philip Herbert, Lady Anne's younger brother. Both ladies were the third generation in their maternal line to serve the Queen, for Lady Susan's mother, Anne Cecil, Countess of Oxford, had served as a Maid of the Privy Chamber in her youth, whilst her grandmother, Mildred Cooke, Baroness Burghley, had served as a 'lady of the household' and later as a Lady of Honour.

As the Maids of the Privy Chamber were in a very privileged position, and most of them knew it, scandals amongst them were very rare. Aside from Lady Bridget, only two maids are known to have married in secret: Lady Dorothy Devereux, who secretly married Sir John Perrot in 1583, and Elizabeth Drury, who eloped with Lord Burghley's grandson and namesake, William Cecil, in 1593. Both women eventually recovered the Queen's favour, Lady Dorothy becoming a Lady of Honour upon her second marriage to Henry Percy, Earl of Northumberland, in 1594, and Elizabeth Drury becoming a Gentlewoman of the Privy Chamber. Only two maids are known to have died unmarried: Elizabeth Russell, who died of a mysterious illness in 1600, and Lady Anne Herbert, who died of a long illness in 1606. The rest of the maids either married during the Queen's lifetime, with her consent, or in the reign of her successor. At least nine of the maids went on to be Ladies or Gentlewomen of the Privy Chamber, showing how well the recruitment process worked, and two of these, Elizabeth Brooke, Lady Cecil, and Philadelphia Carey, Baroness Scrope, went on to be Ladies of the Bedchamber. About two thirds of the maids went on to be Ladies of Honour, and two of these, Helena Snakenborg, Marchioness of Northampton, and Lucy Cecil, Marchioness of Winchester, became Chief Ladies of Honour.

Chapter Eight

Chief Gentlewomen

IN OVERALL CHARGE of the Privy Chamber and all the Queen's female staff, whether of the Privy Chamber or not, was the Chief Gentlewoman of the Privy Chamber. Over the course of the Queen's reign there were three: Kateryn Astley (1558–1565), Blanche Parry (1565–1590), and Mary Radclyffe (1590–1603). The Chief Gentlewoman answered only to the Queen and to the Lord Chamberlain and her professional responsibilities were extensive. These responsibilities included organising and supervising all the Queen's ladies, gentlewomen and maids; liaising with the Mother of the Maids; organising and supervising the gentlemen and grooms; assisting in the recruitment of new attendants; consulting with all household departments to ensure that the Queen's domestic needs were met (i.e. linen, furniture, laundry, lighting and heating); maintaining order and routine in the Queen's chambers; creating a quiet, peaceful and relaxing environment for the Queen to live in; ensuring that the Queen's personal belongings and New Year's gifts were properly taken care of; attending upon the Queen's person; briefing the Queen daily about her schedule; assisting and advising the Queen on suitable attire for public events; co-ordinating the outfits of all her ladies, gentlewomen and maids for these events; safeguarding the Queen's honour; safekeeping any money in the Queen's possession or any gifted to her; overseeing the Queen's move from one residence to another; attending upon the Queen in public when required; and accompanying the Queen on her travels. The Chief Gentlewoman was also responsible for keeping and organising the Queen's personal papers, such as private correspondence, and was expected to provide administrative assistance when needed, such as writing a letter on the Queen's behalf. For the first thirty years of the Queen's reign the Chief Gentlewoman of the Privy Chamber seems also to have held the position of Groom of the Stool.

Because the Chief Gentlewoman was indispensable to the Queen, and was a woman the Queen had a very close bond with, the position required living permanently at court in accommodation close to, or within, the Privy Chamber. The position did not come with an additional salary, as might be expected, for Kat and Blanche received the standard salary of a Lady or Gentlewoman of the Privy Chamber, £33 6s 8d, but the Chief Gentlewoman was rewarded in other ways, not least by having the prestige of being the Chief Gentlewoman of the Privy Chamber.

Kateryn Champernon Astley (Part Two)

The decade following the death of Henry VIII had been a very difficult one for Kat. Not only had she been imprisoned three times, first in the Tower of London, then in the custody of Sir Roger Cholmley, then in the Fleet, but she had lost her beloved sister, Lady Denny, who had died in 1553. Kat was one of those who witnessed her sister's will and may have been at her side when she passed away.[1] Sadly, Lady Denny's death left her many children orphaned and Kat's own difficulties meant that she could be of little help to them. In these years Kat also had to endure a long absence from her husband, John, not only because she was in Sir Roger Cholmley's custody for over a year, but because John had probably fled the country following her arrest. He was back in England the following year, when Kat had returned to Elizabeth's service, for he resumed his fledgling career as a politician by sitting in the Parliament of 1555 as the Member for St Albans. When Kat was imprisoned for the third time in 1556, John may have left the country again, perhaps for the rest of the reign, but Kat remained in England following her release from the Fleet in October of that year. With her uncle, George Carew, Archdeacon of Exeter, she was named executor of the will of a man named John Pollard in 1557, but nothing more is known of her until Elizabeth's triumphant accession in the November of 1558.[2]

As soon as Kat was reunited with Elizabeth, a reunion that was surely heartfelt and joyful, she was taken back into service and given the most important, though not the most prestigious, position of all the Queen's women: that of Chief Gentlewoman of the Privy Chamber. For Kat, this was a new beginning, a chance to wipe the slate clean, and for the first time she began to sign herself as 'Kateryn Asteley' rather than 'Kateryn Aschyly', this being a new name for a new era, a way to distance herself from the disgrace and shame that 'never will out of my heart'. The years of heartache, stress and worry, however, had taken its toll on Kat's health and she may have been somewhat frail when she first arrived at Hatfield. Tudor winters were unkind too, and perhaps on account of the weather, Kat was not listed amongst the women taking part in the coronation eve procession through London. Perhaps this was a clerical oversight, as she was given livery for the occasion (fifteen yards of crimson velvet, a yard less than Ladies of Honour, and two yards of 'purple tinsel with work') but she, along with a few other women who received livery but were not listed as participants in the procession, may have travelled ahead of the Queen to receive her at Westminster Palace at the procession's end.

Kat's husband, whether in exile or in England, also survived Mary's reign and was honoured by the new queen. He was made the Privy Chamber's only gentleman (a man named Drew Drury was appointed the only usher) whilst his brother, Thomas, was made a groom. In addition, John was given the prestigious and lucrative position of Master of the Jewel House. This put him in charge of the crown jewels, which were kept then as now in the Tower of London, and of all the palace jewel houses where treasures in regular use were stored. The role was perfect for John, as one of his duties was to work closely with the Chief Gentlewoman and the Keeper of Her Majesty's Jewels to ensure that the Queen had all the jewellery, plates and treasures she needed. For when the Queen wanted to entertain in magnificence, or to make an extra special impression upon guests, jewels and plates were summoned from the various jewel houses. In this role, John was to have an annual salary of £50, in addition to his wage of £33 6s 8d as a Gentleman of the Privy Chamber, and the post came with the perk of a free private apartment in every royal palace. This Kat and John had anyway, on account of their positions in the Privy Chamber, but between them the couple were now earning well over £100 a year, an income greater than they had ever known.

Kat's uncle, George Carew, who may have taken her under his wing following her release from the Fleet, was also rewarded with the prestigious position of Dean of the Chapel Royal. This put him in charge of the Chapel Royal, which included choosing its staff, and gave him an officiating role in important religious services. Indeed, it may have been him, instead of Bishop Owen Oglethorpe (who anointed and crowned the new queen), who celebrated the Mass during Elizabeth's coronation.[3] In 1559, George was made Dean of Christ Church, Oxford; in 1560 he was made Dean and Canon of Windsor, meaning he was in charge of the canons of St George's Chapel in Windsor Castle; and in 1571 he was made Dean of Exeter. Another of Kat's uncles, Sir Gawain Carew, George's younger brother, also benefited from his niece's closeness to the Queen as he was made Master of the Queen's Henchmen.

The first few months of Elizabeth's reign were gloriously giddy for 'the Hatfield flock' as they took up their prestigious positions at court and attended upon their mistress amidst all the magnificence of majesty, but by the summer of 1559 Kat was beginning to worry about the new queen. Elizabeth was spending her days riding, her nights dancing, and was spending far too much time with her married Master of the Horse, Lord Robert Dudley. The power and freedom of her new position had gone to her head and Kat was terrified that Elizabeth was heading for disaster. Tongues were wagging and foreign dignitaries, who had an especial interest in the Queen's virtue as she was now the most sought after bride in Europe, were becoming concerned. Baron Casper Breuner, Spanish Ambassador, wrote home that:

> I have made most diligent inquiries into the calumnies that are current about the Queen, not only abroad but also here in England, but have not been able to learn anything definite. I believe that if anyone could have obtained intelligence thereon it must have been I. For I have employed as my agent a certain Francois Borth who is on very friendly terms with all the Ladies of the Bedchamber and all other persons who have been about the Queen and have brought her up since her childhood. They all swear by all that is holy that Her Majesty has most certainly never been forgetful of her honour. And yet it is not without significance that Her Majesty's Master of the Horse, My Lord Robert, is preferred by the Queen above all others, and that Her Majesty shows her liking for him more markedly than is consistent with her reputation and dignity.

His boast about intelligence was seemingly correct as he reported to his masters an apparent confrontation that took place between Kat and the Queen over her behaviour:

Her most intimate Lady of the Bedchamber, Catharine Ashley, some days ago fell at Her Majesty's feet and, on being questioned, implored her in God's name to marry and put an end to all these disreputable rumours, telling Her Majesty that her behaviour towards the said Master of the Horse occasioned much evil-speaking, for she showed herself so affectionate to him that Her Majesty's honour and dignity would be sullied, and her subjects would, in time, become discontented. Her Majesty would thus be the cause of much bloodshed in this realm, for which she would have to give account to God, and by which she would merit the eternal curse of her subjects. Rather than that this should happen she would have strangled Her Majesty in the cradle.

To this, the Queen replied that she well knew that these were the outpourings of a good heart, and true fidelity, and that she was quite willing to marry in order to console her and all her subjects. But she [Kat] should reflect that she [Elizabeth], till now, had had no wish to change her state, and that such a marriage must be well weighed. Thereupon the said lady again entreated her, for the love of God, where she had so many and worthy offers of marriage to resolve upon one, lest God, to punish her, call her away from this world before her time.

Her Majesty rejoined that she hoped that God, who had freed her from the violence of her enemies, and suffered her to rise to her exalted dignity, would continue to preserve her and the realm and would dispose, according to His Divine Will, whether she were alive or dead. But as regards the question that they in their talk coupled her with her Master of the Horse, she hoped that she had given no one just cause to associate her with her equerry, or any other man in the world, and she hoped that they never would truthfully be able to do so. But in this world she had had so much sorrow and tribulation and so little joy. If she showed herself gracious towards her Master of the Horse, he had deserved it for his honourable nature and dealings. She had also never understood how any single person could be displeased, seeing that she was always surrounded by her Ladies of the Bedchamber and Maids of Honour, who at all times could see whether there was anything dishonourable between her and her Master of the Horse. If she had ever had the will, or had found pleasure in such a dishonourable life, from which may God preserve her, she did not know of anyone who could forbid her, but she trusted in God that nobody would ever live to see her so commit herself.[4]

Just who had repeated this private conversation to the Spanish Ambassador is a mystery, but clearly there was a mole within the Privy Chamber. Certainly the women of the bedchamber would not have betrayed the Queen's confidence, so the tale-teller had to be another member of staff or one of the Queen's Maids of Honour. Although it is, perhaps, unfair to speculate without évidence, it is possible that the ambassador's source was either Lady Katherine Grey or one of her supporters, like Margaret Willoughby, who were on friendly terms with the Spanish. Kat's words – words that no one else would have dared to speak – seem to have had an impact on Elizabeth, as she reined in her behaviour, but she continued to spend an inappropriate amount of time with Lord Robert Dudley, and the disaster Kat feared came to pass when his young wife, Amy, was found dead at the bottom of a staircase in suspicious circumstances the following year. The ensuing scandal was explosive, and shook Elizabeth's throne to the core, for it was said everywhere that Lord Robert had murdered his wife so he could marry the Queen. Kat and Elizabeth once again came to blows, for John, allegedly, was banished from court for offending the Queen, but eventually the scandal, and the quarrel, blew over and John was forgiven.

Although Kat could not persuade Elizabeth to marry, there were plenty of marriages amongst the Queen's women in these early years of her reign, and two of them were personally significant for Kat. These were the marriages of Frances Newton, her cousin, and Elizabeth Norwich. Frances married William Brooke, Baron Cobham, in a lavish court wedding, one of the first of the reign, and became a Lady of Honour in addition to her position as Chamberer. Elizabeth Norwich married the same year, which was 1560, and her choice of husband was surely a source of great amusement in the Privy Chamber as he was Kat's uncle, the new Master of the Queen's Henchmen, Sir Gawain Carew. This means that Mistress Norwich, who had always been Kat's subservient, was suddenly her aunt! Sadly, nothing is known about the wedding, which suggests it was a private affair, but for the occasion the bride was given a gorgeous gown of purple velvet from the Queen that had sleeves of cloth of gold.[5] These marriages heightened the sense of 'family' within the Privy Chamber for they connected all the Queen's senior attendants to each other. Now Kat could call Elizabeth Norwich family, as well as the Howards of Effingham, whose daughters were her sister's nieces, and the Careys, who were (at least officially) her kindred. Blanche too was related to the Careys, as well as being a distant relative of the Queen's, and Lady Knollys was related to the Careys and to the Howards.

It is sometimes said that Kat was Mother of the Maids for a while but this is unlikely as Anne Morris and Anne Aglionby consecutively held the position in these years. Kat may have schooled the younger Maids of Honour, however, given that she was an experienced governess, and she was given charge of Aura Soltana, a former Tartar slave who was presented to Queen Elizabeth by Anthony Jenkinson, an explorer associated with the Muscovy Company who had acquired the girl on his travels. Slavery was not practised in England at this time, for slaves, upon setting foot on English soil, were considered as 'free of condition as their masters' with 'all note of servile bondage utterly removed from them', so Aura, who was perhaps only 13 or 14 years of age, was not taken in by the Queen as a slave.[6] Instead, she was made one of the Queen's attending gentlewomen (previously, and perhaps still, known as 'gentlewomen of the household'). Kat took charge of the girl's welfare and procured, at the Queen's expense, everything she needed to live, including a generous wardrobe of expensive clothes and shoes. The former governess may also have helped Aura to improve her English, if she could speak some, or to learn it if she could not. Kat may also have had the task, along with her uncle and royal chaplains, of converting Aura to Christianity ahead of her christening in the summer of 1561. The Queen is thought to have been her godmother and, as was customary, Aura was given a new Christian name during the ceremony, Ippolyta (Hippolyta), a name meaning 'Queen of the Amazons', and from then on was known as either 'Mistress Ippolyta', signifying her status as a gentlewoman, or 'Ippolyta the Tartarian'. As with so many of the women who served the Queen, little is known about her subsequent life, but she received annual livery from the Queen, being one of the few women to do so, regularly exchanged New Year's gifts with the Queen, is thought to have inspired a fashion trend for shoes of Spanish leather, and was described by the Queen as her 'dear and well beloved woman'. Sadly, Ippolyta died in the winter of 1575/76, for she was described as 'late' on the New Year's gift roll of 1576, but her cause of death, and marital status at the time, is presently unknown.

Kat, always a heart speaker rather than a head thinker, had landed herself in trouble many times over the years, and even now, in the winter of her life, she could not resist meddling in Elizabeth's romantic affairs. Still concerned about the Queen's relationship with Lord Robert Dudley, Kat, along with Dorothy Broadbelt, dearly wished to see her marry the new King of Sweden, Erik XIV. The King was the same age as Elizabeth, was considered handsome with his youthful golden looks, was learned and artistic, and, most importantly, was a Protestant. For some time the young monarch had been pursuing Elizabeth, for he too was unmarried, and in the summer of 1562, when it looked like Elizabeth might marry Lord Robert, Kat and Dorothy wrote to Nicolas Guildenstern, former Swedish Ambassador, urging the King to make his much talked about visit to England as they were sure he would be welcome. The letter was intercepted by William Cecil, who had spies everywhere, and before long Kat and Dorothy were in deep trouble. 'Of late there have been committed to the Tower of London some that were formerly high in favour with the Queen', wrote an Italian diplomat, 'among them being Mistress Ashley who had such influence with the Queen that she seemed, as it were, patroness of all England', and Mistress Dorothy 'who was so intimate with Her Majesty that oftentimes she slept in the same bed with her'.[7] This was an exaggeration, as neither Kat nor Dorothy were sent to the Tower of London, but Kat's former servant, James Goldberne, was, along with a man named John Keyle, both accused of interfering in matters of state. Another report of the fallout is more realistic, as according to it Kat was 'commanded to keep her chamber' whilst Dorothy was 'committed to the custody' of William Cecil, but even if this report is also an exaggeration, the two women were certainly out of favour for a while – at least officially.[8] Some historians are of the opinion that Kat and Dorothy wrote to

Guildenstern on the Queen's command. Whatever the truth, by the autumn, both women were back at their posts and as high in the Queen's favour as ever.

By now, Kat and John had been given additional positions by the Queen. Jointly they were Keepers of St James's Palace, and in his own right John was Steward of Enfield Manor, Master Forester of Enfield Chase, and Bailiff of St James's Fair. He was also still serving as a member of parliament from time to time. However, by the summer of 1565, Kat's health had taken a turn for the worst and she was very ill. Perhaps she had been deteriorating for some time as changes had been made in the bedchamber which suggest that Lady Cobham was taking over some of her duties. These changes seem to have happened in 1564 when Lady Cobham's younger sister, Nazareth, seemingly replaced her as Chamberer whilst she herself became a Lady of the Bedchamber. It is well known that Elizabeth saw sons, stepsons or nephews as natural successors to her male favourites, hoping to find the same qualities and loyalties in them, and she seems to have followed the same practise with her female staff. In this way, Lady Cobham was Kat's natural successor, being her cousin, as Kat did not have a daughter and none of her nieces were in the Queen's service. It is likely that Lady Cobham eventually became Chief Lady of the Bedchamber, for even though her salary remained that of a Chamberer, she is clearly listed as a Lady of the Bedchamber in fee lists and she heads the lists. The reason for the stagnant salary was probably a practical one: Lady Cobham simply did not need a raise due to her husband's wealth.

Even in Kat's lifetime Lady Cobham had risen so high in the Queen's favour that her gift of two gilt salt cellars from the Queen at New Year 1565 weighed more, at 66 ounces, than the gifts of all other female attendants, with the exception of Lady Knollys, Chief Lady of the Bedchamber, whose gift of two gilt pots weighed 80 ounces, and of Chief Ladies of Honour, Margaret Douglas, Lady Lennox, and Elisabeth Brooke, Marchioness of Northampton, who received gifts weighing 76 and 70 ounces respectively. Kat herself received the next weightiest gift, receiving a collection of gilt goods weighing 39 ounces, a weight greater than the gifts given to Lord Hunsdon, the Duchess of Suffolk, the Duchess of Somerset, and all countesses and baronesses, showing just how much Elizabeth valued her beloved governess. Elizabeth Norwich, now Lady Carew, also received one of the weightiest gifts at 35 ounces, as did Lady Parry at 32 ounces, and Lady Stafford at 29 ounces. The Lady Admiral, Elyzabeth Fitzgerald, had a gilt bowl weighing 27 ounces and the Lady Chamberlain, Margrett Gamage, had one weighing 23. Blanche Parry, Dorothy Broadbelt, Elyzabeth Marbury, and the rest of the Queen's gentlewomen, received somewhat less, Blanche receiving a gilt bowl of approximately 17 ounces, Dorothy a salt cellar of about the same, and Elyzabeth Marbury a cup of about 13 ounces.[9] Although still on the payroll, Elizabeth Sondes does not appear to have been an active attendant after her marriage, perhaps preferring domestic life to court life, so she rarely participated in the New Year's Gift Exchange after 1562.

Sadly, Kat did not recover from her illness and died, probably at Whitehall Palace, on the 18 July 1565. Elizabeth was in the middle of a palace move at the time, so was not with Kat when she passed away, but had visited her the day before and probably believed she would recover. When news of Kat's death came, then, it was a devastating blow to Elizabeth and she cancelled all her engagements for several days. This led to the usual stream of comments from foreign diplomats who reported the news far and wide. 'Some few days ago a lady of the name of Ashley died here', wrote one of these ambassadors. 'The Queen visited her before her death, for she it was who had the upbringing of the Queen, [and her] decease grieved the Queen so much that she commanded me not to appear until the 22 of July'.[10] A similar report was sent to the King of Spain with a comment, in cipher, saying 'what a heretic she was!'.[11]

A heretic, indeed, Kat may have been in the eyes of Catholic Europe, but given the profound influence she had on Elizabeth, perhaps shaping her attitudes and values more than any other person, it is unlikely she was as fervently Protestant as her sister, Lady Denny, who had belonged to the circle of religious reformists around Kateryn Parr. Nevertheless, Kat was not a woman who loved worldly pomp, preferring the simple and the practical, and she was seemingly buried on the same day that she died in the Savoy Chapel, Westminster. Elizabeth did not attend funerals, always sending a representative, but as Kat's burial was clearly a small, private affair in a royal chapel, the Queen may have secretly attended with Blanche Parry, Lady Cobham or Lady Carew. This chapel still exists but was gutted by fire in the nineteenth century and the historic interior was lost. Therefore, if Kat was given a tomb or a monument there is now no trace of it.[12]

With Kat's death, Elizabeth lost one of the few people in the world who truly loved her. The Queen felt this loss deeply and her life was surely never quite the same again. And, to add to her grief, Kat's husband, John, whose marriage to Kat may have been difficult for some years, took a new wife within weeks of her death. Although he kept his court positions, and remained in favour, he never again held quite as much sway as he had in Kat's lifetime, and despite his many years of loyal service, he was never knighted, perhaps because a part of Elizabeth never forgave him for replacing so soon in his heart her irreplaceable Kat. But Kat's death was not the end of the Champernon story. Her brother, Arthur, who had been knighted in 1549, was a courtier, naval commander and pirate who successfully raided a Spanish treasure fleet in 1568, and from the 1570s onwards a young nephew of Kat's, who shared her dark looks, rose rapidly in the Queen's favour to become one of the most famous men of the age – Sir Walter Raleigh.

Blanche Parry

After Kat's death, Blanche, who had been at Elizabeth's side even longer, took over as Chief Gentlewoman of the Privy Chamber. Blanche was not much younger than Kat, as she was born between 1507 and 1508 in Hertfordshire's Golden Valley, but life had been kinder to her and she was blessed with a stronger constitution. Blanche was also a shrewder soul than Kat and consequently survived the reigns of Henry VIII, Edward VI and Mary I without once getting into trouble – not an easy feat.

Blanche grew up in a predominantly Welsh speaking household in the Welsh Marches and was the daughter of Harri ap Miles and his wife Alice Milborne, Lady

Troy's sister. Strictly speaking her full name was Blanche ferch Harri, meaning 'Blanche Harri's daughter', as her family still practised the Welsh custom, called patronymics, of giving children their father's first name as a surname prefixed by ap for a boy (meaning son of) and ferch for a girl (meaning daughter of). However, because the Welsh word 'ferch' is much harder to pronounce than 'ap' it seems that Blanche used the masculine prefix instead of the feminine when she began to move in English circles, calling herself Blanche ap Harri which became Blanche Parry, the name by which she is known. Blanche was raised, with a number of siblings, in the family home of Newcourt Manor, a medieval mansion in Bacton built by her great grandfather, Harri ap Gruffudd, who was nicknamed Harri Ddu (Harri the black) by his contemporaries on account of his dark looks and his love of black clothing. Blanche's father, like his father and grandfather before him, was an influential man locally, serving as Sheriff of Herefordshire three times, and for many years he was Steward of Dore Abbey, a Cistercian monastery nearby. Through his mother, Joan Stradling, Harri was a third cousin (once removed) of Henry VII, as they shared descent from John of Gaunt and Kathryn Swynford, and he was also related to the Herbert family of Raglan Castle.

Blanche is thought to have had a happy childhood, spending her earliest years playing in Newcourt's extensive grounds, riding on ponies in the fresh country air, listening to Welsh bards sing or recite Welsh poems and dancing by candlelight to harps. On cold winter nights, before crackling fires, it is easy to imagine Blanche and her siblings listening to magical and mystical Welsh stories about princes and castles and wizards and fairies. All her life Blanche had an interest in the occult and it is likely that her interest was sparked in these formative years. Of course, life was not all playing, dancing, stories and music for Blanche. The children of country gentlemen, including girls, were expected to learn how to read and to write, so Blanche and her siblings would have been schooled. Their first teacher was probably their mother, Alice, an Englishwoman who had made some waves by marrying into a Welsh family, and she would have taught them their alphabet and other basic skills such as numbers and counting. As they got older, the children were probably tutored by their father's chaplain, Sir John ap Harri, and then when the boys went to Dore Abbey to complete their education, Blanche and her sisters may have gone to Aconbury Convent, a religious house near Hereford where local gentlemen often sent their daughters. Here, under the guidance of the prioress, Isabella Gardiner, who was a skilled herbalist, the Herefordshire girls learnt a little Latin, perfected their housekeeping and needlework skills, studied and prayed, participated in religious ceremonies, and practised chastity, modesty and obedience, the essential female virtues of the day.[13]

If Blanche was amongst the local girls who lived and studied at Aconbury convent, it may have been the nuns who inspired in her an appreciation of the single life. Before the Reformation, celibacy was a respected alternative to marriage for women, and empowered them in an otherwise male dominated world, for being single meant they did not have to answer to a husband, who was considered their lord and master, or spend years of their life childbearing. Marriage and family were still the ideal for most women, but for women like Blanche, who did not want to marry but to maintain their independence as much as was possible for a woman in this period, the closure of the convents that came with the suppression of religious houses in the late 1530s considerably narrowed their options. For not all monks and nuns led cloistered lives. Many were very active in the community, bestowing poor relief, nursing the sick, giving refuge, working the land and educating children. Blanche may have considered becoming a nun herself, but her father's death in 1522, when she was about 14 years of age, took her life in another direction, a direction that ultimately led to Princess Elizabeth's nursery.

Probably recommended for a position in the nursery by her aunt, and likely godmother, Lady Troy, who is thought to have taken her in after her father's death, Blanche worked her way up from rocker or nursemaid to become one of Elizabeth's principal gentlewomen attendants. She was probably with Elizabeth in the Tower of London, was probably with her at Woodstock Manor, and was probably in charge of her female staff during the last years of Queen Mary's reign. Blanche may also have been with Elizabeth when she received the history changing news that she was queen.

Upon Elizabeth's accession Blanche was made a Gentlewoman of the Bedchamber and Keeper of Her Majesty's Jewels. The latter was a position of immense trust as the Keeper was in charge of all the Queen's personal jewellery, which was worth a fortune, and all her personal belongings that were adorned with jewels, such as expensive furs and velvet bound books. In this role Blanche worked closely with John Astley, to procure and return jewels on an as needed basis, and with the royal librarians to request and return books for the Queen's use from the great royal libraries at Richmond and Whitehall Palace. Blanche was also responsible for processing all the jewellery gifted to the Queen at New Year, as well as many gifts adorned with jewels, which involved sending some to the various jewel houses and keeping others for the Queen's use.

Following Kat's death in the summer of 1565, Blanche was promoted to Chief Gentlewoman of the Privy Chamber and she remained in the role for a quarter of a century. At the same time, she is likely to have taken over from Kat as Groom of the Stool. Hardworking and loyal, Blanche also continued as Keeper of Her Majesty's Jewels and she juggled all roles successfully for some years. It was not until Blanche was in her sixties that she began to reduce her workload. In 1571 she retired as Keeper of Her Majesty's Jewels and the role went to Katheryn Carey, soon to be Baroness Howard of Effingham, her first cousin twice removed. Blanche retained some responsibility for the Queen's jewels, however, and might be described as the Keeper's assistant. In the early 1580s, during preparations for the visit of the Queen's most successful suitor, Francis, Duke of Anjou, Blanche, along with Mary Scudamore, made an emergency dash by barge one night from Richmond Palace, where the Queen was residing, to Whitehall Palace to fetch certain jewels. In her role as Gentlewoman of the Bedchamber, Blanche also often assisted the Chamberers in receiving deliveries of fabrics for the Queen's wardrobe.

Blanche and Mary Scudamore, along with Anne Russell, Countess of Warwick, were once described by Blanche's great nephew, Rowland Vaughan, the grandson of her brother, Milo, as 'a trinity of ladies able to work miracles'. According to him, whilst 'none of these near and dear ladies' dared meddle 'in matters of commonwealth' they 'would steal opportunity to serve some friends turns'.[14] Indeed, Blanche was amongst the most respected and sought after of the Queen's women, not just because of her influence but because of her approachability. For although Blanche was a formidable lady with a commanding presence, she was also kind and fair and, like most of the Queen's women, knew how to have a good time. By her own admission she was not as careful with her money as she should have been and was very partial to gambling in the Privy Chamber with the Queen and her favourites.

By the mid-1580s Blanche's health was starting to decline and at some point in these years she began to lose her eyesight, perhaps due to cataracts. In 1587 she relinquished all responsibility for the Queen's jewels but remained Chief Gentlewoman of the Privy Chamber. Although Mary Radclyffe took over most of her duties, Blanche was still in overall charge of the Queen's women, and for her entire tenure as Chief Gentlewoman there were no sexual scandals amongst the Maids of the Privy Chamber and very few amongst Maids of Honour. Unlike Kat, who got into trouble even as Chief Gentlewoman, Blanche never did, making her one of the Queen's few long-serving attendants to avoid this calamity. Unfortunately for Lady Cobham, she had been forced to leave the Queen's service for several years in the 1570s due to treasonous activities by an in-law, a situation regrettable to both her and the Queen as Frances's personal loyalty was never in question, and in addition to having to leave court briefly over her son William's alleged treason, Lady Stafford was once rumoured to have been sent from court for 'slandering ladies'. The rumour was probably false, however, as it seems out of character for Lady Stafford who, according to her son, was 'loved by all' and 'never hurted any'.[15] Mary Hill, Lady Cheke, was also the subject of gossip from time to time and in the 1590s fell out with Frances Cooke, daughter of Lord John Grey of Pyrgo, over which of them should have precedence at court.

Of all her siblings, Blanche seems to have had the closest relationship with her sister, Elizabeth, who married into a branch of the influential Vaughan family of Wales to which she and Blanche were related. Very little is known about Elizabeth, but she was the mother of at least one son, John Vaughan, and Blanche is known to have adored her nephew. Sadly, he died in 1577, but the following year Blanche secured for his daughter, Frances Vaughan, one of the vacancies amongst the Maids of Honour caused by the dismissal of Martha Howard and Lady Susan Bourchier. Like most of the Queen's maids, Frances retired to get married after a couple of years in service, but she continued to visit court and from 1584 onwards, when her husband became Baron Burgh, she served the Queen as a Lady of Honour. Frances's place as a Maid of Honour was taken by her niece, Anne Vavasour, but unfortunately Anne was not a success in the role due to her affair with the married Earl of Oxford. For Blanche, Anne's conduct must have been disappointing, for Anne was one of the few women connected to herself that she was able to bring into the Queen's service, but the young woman's behaviour in no way reflected badly on Blanche as Anne was also connected to the Queen through her mother, Margaret Knyvett, who was the Queen's second cousin through the Howard line.

One of the most successful recruitments made by Blanche from her family circle was that of Margaret Vaughan to the post of Chamberer in 1589. Margaret, a cousin to Rowland Vaughan, was the daughter of Charles Vaughan of Hergest and his second wife, Margaret. As it was difficult for Blanche to bring her own relatives into the Queen's circle, given that women of the Queen's blood had to take precedence, it helped in securing a position for Margaret that she was also connected to Mary Scudamore as her great aunt was John Scudamore's grandmother. The fact that Margaret made her debut as a Chamberer, which would give her intimate access to the Queen, shows just how much confidence and trust Blanche had in the girl, and in turn just how much confidence and trust the Queen had in Blanche. Margaret was in her late teens or early twenties at the time of her appointment and had probably spent much of her childhood at Hergest Court, a moated medieval manor house near Kington, Herefordshire, that had been in her family for generations. This house is now famous as the haunting ground of 'Black Vaughan and his black bloodhound', Black Vaughan being a great, great grandfather of Margaret's who was killed in the Wars of the Roses, and the legend is said by some to have inspired Sir Arthur Conan Doyle's classic Sherlock Holmes tale *The Hound of the Baskervilles*. In about 1592 Margaret married, with the Queen's blessing, Sir John Hawkins, a man much older than herself who has acquired an infamous reputation because of his involvement in the transatlantic slave trade. The marriage was very short lived, however, for Sir John died in 1595 on a voyage to Puerto Rico. Margaret, now known as Lady Hawkins, never remarried and continued to serve the Queen as a Chamberer for the rest of the reign, at least on a part time basis. In 1601 she was the lady entrusted with the safe keeping of disgraced Maid of Honour, Mary Fitton, and in 1603 she participated in the Queen's funeral as a Lady of the Privy Chamber. Like most of the Queen's women, Margaret was learned and accomplished, and although she herself was a wealthy woman, she cared deeply about the education of the poor. In her will of 1619, drawn up a couple of years before her death, she left hundreds of pounds out of the proceeds of her estate for a 'free school' to be established in Kington for 'the instructing of youths and children in literature and good education'.[16] This school was duly founded after her death and was named Lady Hawkins' School in her honour. Remarkably, this school still exists in Kington today, although the location has changed, and is now a state comprehensive school teaching children aged 11–16 years. In this way, Lady Hawkins, one of the most overlooked of the Queen's ladies, is one of the few to have left a lasting legacy.

Although Queen Elizabeth never gave a woman a title in her own right, she sometimes made it clear that a certain woman was to be treated as though she had a title. Blanche, and probably Kat before her, was one of these women. At court, Blanche had the status of a baroness, a status she had held from at least the time of becoming Chief Gentlewoman of the Privy Chamber. For example, in 1569, when the Queen gifted two sable furs each to Anne Morgan, Elyzabeth Fitzgerald, Margrett Gamage and Frances Newton, all baronesses, Blanche was gifted the same. Therefore, when Blanche died in the February of 1590, at the age of 82, the Queen instructed that she was to be buried 'as a baroness'. Consequently,

Blanche was given a lavish funeral, paid for by the Queen, in St Margaret's Church, Westminster Abbey, where she was laid to rest near her beloved nephew, John Vaughan. The chief mourner was her great niece, Frances Vaughan, Baroness Burgh, and a few years after her death a grand monument, with a kneeling effigy of Blanche, was put up in the church.

St Margaret's Church was not Blanche's initial choice of burial place, however. Initially she wanted to be buried in the Parish Church of Bacton, where she grew up, and in the 1570s she commissioned a magnificent tomb there for herself. This tomb, although not in its original location, still exists and depicts a statue of Blanche kneeling besides a statue of the Queen, who wears full royal regalia, with a much smaller statue of the Queen's beloved 'little dog' sleeping on a cushion next to her. This 'little dog' clearly meant a lot to Blanche too and the tomb touchingly depicts a 'family' as well as a queen and her longest serving attendant. This tomb, prepared with such care, is seemingly empty, but in St Eata's Church, Ascham, near Shrewsbury, there is a stained glass window, believed to date from the sixteenth century, that commemorates Blanche and tells us that she was 'entombed at Westminster, her bowels at Bacton in the county of Herefordshire'. This window is said to have been originally in Bacton Church but moved to its present location in the early nineteenth century by a descendant of Blanche's family whose husband was the vicar of St Eata's Church. The truth of this claim, and the history of the window, are presently unknown, but it is entirely possible that Blanche, like Margaret Radclyffe, and others of the period, had her bowels or heart buried separately to her body. It may have been for the burial service that the Queen sent the now famous altar cloth to Bacton. This richly embroidered cloth, of royal fabric, is thought to have come from one of the Queen's magnificent dresses and, as such, is all that remains from the Queen's vast collection of gowns. Upon her tomb in Bacton, Blanche has left us an account of her life, making her the only one of the Queen's women to tell us about her life of service. This account, in poetic form, is therefore worth quoting (in modern English for easier reading):

I, Parry's daughter Blanche of Newcourt born
That trained was in Prince's court with gorgeous wights [people]
Where fleeting honour sounds with blast of horn
Each of account to place of world's delights,
Am lodged here within this stony tomb.
My harbinger is paid I owe of due.
My friends of speech herein do find me dumb,
The which in vain they do so greatly rue,
For so much as it is the end of all
This worldly route of state what so they be,
The which unto the rest hereafter shall
Assemble thus each wight in his degree.
I lived always as handmaid to a queen,
In chamber chief my time did overpass,
Uncareful of my wealth there was I seen

Whilst I abode the running of my glass,
Not doubting want whilst that my mistress lived
In womans state whose cradle saw I rocked,
Her servant then as when she her crown achieved
And so remained till Death my door had knocked.
Preferring still the causes of each wight,
As far as I dared move Her Grace's ear,
For to reward deserts by course of right
As needs recite of service done each where.
So that my time I thus did pass away,
A maid in court and never no man's wife.
Sworn of Queen Elizabeth's bedchamber always,
With Maiden Queen a maid did end my life.[17]

In her will, overseen by her kinsman, Lord Burghley, Blanche left the Queen, 'my sovereign lady and mistress', her 'best diamond', and amongst her many other bequests were gifts to Lady Cobham and to Lady Stafford, the two women of the Privy Chamber she was closest to and had worked longest with. Blanche also left Lady Cobham's daughter, Elizabeth Brooke, 'a table with two rock rubies in it'.[18] Surprisingly, she left nothing to her Carey cousins, Baroness Hunsdon and Katheryn Carey, or to Elizabeth Norwich, Lady Carew, but perhaps she had already given these mementos.

Blanche's passing, although not unexpected given her age, left a huge void in the Queen's life. Blanche was one of the few people with whom she could be herself and with whom she had a deep and special bond. After Kat's death, it was Blanche who became her mother figure, and in the lonely years to come she would miss her reassuring and loving presence.

Mary Radclyffe

Mary Radclyffe, who took over Blanche's duties as Chief Gentlewoman of the Privy Chamber, had been in the Queen's service since her teens. According to tradition, Mary was gifted to the Queen at New Year, 1562, by her father, Sir Humphrey Radclyffe, who hoped to see her become a Maid of Honour, but in reality Mary was already a maid by that Christmas, probably having been suggested for the role by her cousin, Robert Radclyffe, Earl of Sussex, in place of his sister, Lady Frances, who seemingly declined the Queen's invitation to be a maid. Nothing is yet known of Mary's childhood but she was of noble blood as her father was a younger son of the first Earl of Sussex, and her paternal grandmother, Elizabeth Stafford, was the daughter of Henry Stafford, Duke of Buckingham, and his wife, Katherine Woodville, maternal aunt of Elizabeth of York. This made Mary a third cousin to the Queen and a second cousin to Lady Stafford. Mary's mother, Isabella Harvey, was from humbler stock, being the daughter of Edmund Harvey, a London merchant, but even on the maternal side Mary had notable relations as her maternal great grandfather was Sir Roger Wentworth of Codham Hall, Essex. On the maternal side, Mary also had a connection to Kat Astley as her mother was a first cousin of Anne Harvey, wife of Kat's uncle, George Carew.

According to nineteenth century writer, Edward Walford, who wrote a chapter about Mary's parents in his book *Chapters from Family Chests*, the couple had quite a romantic meeting, a meeting that is vividly brought to life by Violet Wilson in her book *Queen Elizabeth's Maids of Honour*:

> One day, during the reign of King Henry VIII, the Earl of Sussex with his son, Humphrey, and a party of friends rode out of London to take part in a tournament. As the gay cavalcade passed through the little village of Kensington, people hurried to the windows to catch a glimpse of the gorgeously caparisoned riders and horses. One girl, Isabella Harvey, who with her father happened to be visiting some friends, leaned out so far in her eagerness to see all there was to see that she dropped her glove just as Sir Humphrey Radcliffe rode by. Gloves being costly luxuries, and chivalry the pursuit of every true knight, Sir Humphrey dipped his lance, impaled the glove, and returned it to its owner, who blushed as she thanked him for his courtesy. The Earl and his companions rode on, but Isabella's beauty had cast such a spell upon Sir Humphrey that he contrived to leave his companions and returned in all haste to Kensington.
>
> Edmund Harvey and his daughter were about to set off for London, and as the road thence bore an evil reputation for robbery, generally accompanied with violence, the merchant readily acquiesced in the knight's suggestion that he should bear them company. Sir Humphrey represented himself as a squire in service with the Earl of Sussex, and so agreeable did he make himself that when they reached Edmund Harvey's house in Cheapside he received an invitation to come in to supper.
>
> The friendship between Isabella and Sir Humphrey soon ripened into love, nor did her father raise any objection when asked to give his consent to their marriage. Isabella Harvey came to her husband a richly dowered bride, but they had been married some time before she learned the fact that her husband was the son, not the servant, of Robert, Earl of Sussex, Lord High Chamberlain of England.[19]

Just how much truth is in this story remains to be discovered, but Mary's parents almost certainly married for love and eventually made their home in Elstow, Bedfordshire. Sir Humphrey was made a Gentleman Pensioner by Henry VIII, a mark of royal favour, and due to his flexible religious views he also did well in the reigns of King Edward and Queen Mary, becoming Lieutenant of the Gentleman Pensioners in 1553. He found favour at the court of Queen Elizabeth too and Mary's mother, Isabella, served the Queen as a 'lady of the household', and then as a Lady of Honour, for thirty five years.

Given that Maids of Honour were rarely younger than 16, Mary must have been about that age when she was sworn into the role. Pretty and witty, Mary soon had admirers amongst the gallant young men of the court, but although she enjoyed a brief flirtation with one love struck suitor, none of them could win her heart. Like her mistress, Mary loved the single life, and unlike Lady Bridget Manners, who constantly dreamed of retiring, Mary loved court life and was a natural courtier. In time, through her longevity of service, she became a friend to the Queen, as well as an attendant, and by the late 1560s she had seemingly been admitted into the Privy Chamber as she had responsibility for 'making' the Queen's 'habiliments' (decorative headpieces of silk, satin or lace). This either means that Mary made the habiliments herself from the luxurious fabrics regularly delivered to her, or that she took charge of delivering the materials to a tailor or seamstress. The same is true of Lady Carew who regularly received material for hoods. In recompense for her service, Mary was receiving a stipend of £40 a year by 1569, an extraordinary sum that probably reflects her unique status as both a Maid of Honour and a Gentlewoman of the Privy Chamber.[20]

Probably the longest serving Maid of Honour of the Tudor era, Mary finally retired from the role in about 1585. From them on she served in the Privy Chamber only, probably becoming a Gentlewoman of the Bedchamber upon her retirement so she could perform Blanche Parry's duties, but is not named on official fee lists because of the stipend she was already receiving. As a Maid of Honour, Mary had always been given a gift from the Queen at New Year, her first gift in 1562 being a silver gilt cup with a cover, but now she began participating in the New Year's Gift Exchange in her own right. By 1588 she was already listed second on the gift roll after Blanche Parry, signifying her importance, and following Blanche's death she topped the list of gentlewomen. In general, Mary received a gift from the Queen weighing 18 ounces, a weight greater than most gentlewomen received, and in return she gave the Queen gifts like ruffs, muffs, jewels and kirtles. It is likely that Mary exchanged gifts with many other courtiers at New Year too in additional to receiving gifts from thankful parents like Lady Rutland.

In 1587, Mary formally took over from Katheryn Carey, Baroness Howard of Effingham, as Keeper of Her Majesty's Jewels. From then on, Mary had charge of most of the Queen's personal jewellery and her jewel adorned books and furs. In her first year as Keeper, Mary took charge of more than twenty jewelled gifts given to the Queen at New Year, gifts ranging from 'a bodkin of gold with a fair flower of gold hanging at it, fully garnished with diamonds, having a naked man therein', given by Robert Devereux, Earl of Essex, to a 'jewel of gold with a hand out of clouds garnished with opals' given by a Master Chidley. Another gift was 'a bodkin of silver and gilt with a pendant of a salamander of mother of pearls' and this gift, perhaps as a token of appreciation for her new Keeper, the Queen gave to Mary.[21] For the rest of the reign, Mary took charge of most of the jewels given to the Queen at New Year, whilst Mary Scudamore, who had been taking charge of New Year's gifts since the 1560s, took charge of clothing items like ruffs and kirtles.

Mary became, in every practical sense, Chief Gentlewoman of the Privy Chamber following Blanche's death, but it is unclear whether she ever had the title. The position of Groom of the Stool went to Katheryn Carey, who probably became Chief Lady of the Bedchamber two years later following Lady Cobham's death, beginning a long-standing tradition of the Chief Lady of the Bedchamber also being Groom of the Stool. However, whether or not Mary had the title of Chief Gentlewoman, she was doing the job, so deserves to be considered the Queen's third and final Chief Gentlewoman of the Privy Chamber. A happily single woman like Blanche, and totally devoted to the Queen, Mary was perfect for the job as she had no family commitments and no household of her own to manage. She lived permanently at court, just like Kat and Blanche had done, and had lodgings within the Privy Chamber itself. Of course, Mary's relationship with the Queen was rather different to what Kat's and Blanche's had been. Whereas Kat and Blanche had been mother figures to the Queen, the Queen was, in some ways, a mother figure to Mary, although Mary was lucky enough to have her own mother at court for most of her career. Mary also had a harder task of managing the Privy Chamber than her predecessors as her time in charge coincided with a much darker time in the Queen's life and reign. The golden age that was dawning during Kat's tenure, and in full splendour during Blanche's, was gradually fading away due to the Queen's ageing, the ongoing war with Spain, and a series of bad harvests. Mary herself was not as experienced in managing the Queen's staff as Kat and Blanche had been, for she had never before been in charge, and was seemingly a much softer touch than Blanche who had kept order and discipline amongst the Queen's women until the very end. Indeed, within months of Blanche's death, several Maids of Honour were engaging in illicit love affairs, resulting in the sordid scandals of 1591. The Queen's own authority was also declining as she aged, for the young courtiers around her, ever looking to the future, were increasingly aware of her mortality and the reality that soon another royal sun would be shining over their world. This made them more likely to flaunt the rules, perhaps, to have secret affairs, and to be 'disquiet at nights'.

After a horrible end to 1591, the year 1592 was one of mixed fortune for the Queen's women. For three of them, Mary Scudamore, Kattrin Paston, and Dorothy Edmonds, the year was a good one as their husbands were knighted by the Queen during her summer progress. These knighthoods gave Mary, Kattrin and Dorothy the courtesy title of 'Lady', and it was probably more for their sake, in appreciation of their long service, that the Queen conferred the knighthoods upon their husbands. This was much easier than bestowing titles on women *suo jure* which, coming from a female sovereign, may have upset the patriarchal world that the Queen ruled over and had to survive within. The joys of the summer, however, turned into a sad and anxious autumn. Lady Cobham died at her home, Cobham Hall, leaving another huge void in the Queen's life, and London was gripped by an outbreak of plague. For Mary Radclyffe, the following weeks and months were hectic as the Queen was forced to enter a period of semi-isolation and had to move residence several times to escape the dreaded disease. During this time, access to court was restricted to 'ordinary' staff only and none of them were permitted to go into London without permission. Christmas saw a brief respite from the disease, with cases falling, but the Queen was back in semi-isolation by the spring of 1593 due to an insurgence of the disease. There was no summer progress that year and things were not much better by the autumn. Indeed, although the Queen had retreated to Windsor Castle, well away from London, the plague reached there and the Queen had to move again, this time to Hampton Court Palace where she remained for the rest of the epidemic.

Another change in the 1590s that made managing the Privy Chamber harder for Mary was the change in personnel. One by one the old stalwarts of 'the Hatfield flock', like Lady Cobham, who had been at the Queen's side for decades, supporting and encouraging her and helping to make her reign great, were passing away. By 1594 not a single original appointee to the bedchamber was still alive and the Queen had also outlived almost all the original appointees to the Privy Chamber. Elyzabeth Fitzgerald, Countess of Lincoln since the Queen bestowed an earldom on her husband in 1572, had died at her home in 1590; Anne Poyntz, Lady Heneage, had died in 1593; Elizabeth Norwich, Lady Carew, in 1594; and in the preceding years Margrett Gamage, Lady Howard of Effingham, had died, along with Dorothy Broadbelt, Elyzabeth Marbury, Bridget Skipwith, Isabella Markham and Elizabeth Sondes. Of the old time ordinaries still in service, like Lady Stafford, Mary Scudamore, and Katheryn Carey, they were all ageing themselves and not always able to serve. Therefore, Mary had to work alongside a number of new appointees to the Privy Chamber, like Elizabeth Brooke, Lady Cecil, and Philadelphia Carey, Baroness Scrope, who were learning the ropes themselves.

Philadelphia Carey was, of course, Baroness Hunsdon's second daughter born amidst great joy in the winter of 1562. In her late teens she had served as a Maid of the Privy Chamber, alongside her youngest sister, Margaret, and after her marriage to Thomas Scrope, future Baron Scrope, in 1583, she was an extraordinary member of the Privy Chamber until she joined the Queen's full time staff as a Lady of the Bedchamber in the early 1590s. With her husband, Philadelphia had one son, Emmanuel, who was about 8 or 9 years of age at the time of her promotion to the bedchamber. She and the Queen were very close, although Philadelphia's older sister, Katheryn, was the favourite, and in her final years the Queen depended much on Philadelphia to fill the void in her life created by the deaths, and absences, of so many other loved attendants.

Elizabeth Brooke, Lady Cecil, was the eldest daughter of Lady Cobham, and had become a Lady of the Bedchamber in 1591 when her mother's health was failing. Frances Brooke, Lady Stourton, who had been courted by Sir Thomas Sherley, was Elizabeth's twin sister, but as the younger twin, with another sister, Margaret, at home, she had never been as favoured by the Queen. From a very young age, Elizabeth had attended court with her mother, and as a little girl had once been gifted an angel of gold adorned with gemstones by the Queen at New Year, a very rare honour. In her teens, Elizabeth, like Philadelphia, became a Maid of the Privy Chamber, and after a brief period of retirement following her marriage to Lord Burghley's son, Robert Cecil, she was appointed to the bedchamber. The Queen thought the world of Elizabeth, and had hoped to make her a mainstay of support in her old age, but sadly the dark cloud of death that had fallen over the court since the turn of the decade continued to cast a shadow over the Queen's women and in 1597 Elizabeth died giving birth to her third child. The Queen was devastated, the Cecils too, and Elizabeth's father, Lord Cobham, now the court's Lord Chamberlain, was so heartbroken that he died himself less than two months later.

Lady Cecil's place in the bedchamber was taken by Elyzabeth Knollys, Lady Leighton, the Queen's favourite of Lady Knollys's daughters, who had been an ordinary Lady of the Privy Chamber for over thirty years. Like many of the Queen's cousins, she had been admitted into the Privy Chamber in her teens, and in 1578, in her late twenties, she had married Sir Thomas Leighton, Governor of Guernsey. It is likely that Elyzabeth lived partially in Guernsey with her husband, perhaps during the summer months when the weather was better for travel, but Sir Thomas did not live there permanently as he was also a politician and soldier as well as a courtier. With her husband, Elyzabeth had at least three children, two daughters and a son, and by 1600 was a grandmother. Elyzabeth adored the Queen, who had been like a mother to her since the death of her own mother, but according to court rumour fell out with the Queen briefly in 1597 when her suit for Eltham Parks was unsuccessful. According to Rowland Whyte:

> My Lady Leighton hath been a long suitor for Eltham Parks but can have no grant made unto her of them; she is determined (as I hear) if the Queen give them any other to leave the court; and here is already a whole dozen of ladies that would succeed her in the Bedchamber; but it is thought that either my Lady Hoby [Margaret Carey], my Lady Burgh [Frances Vaughan], or my Lady Thomas Howard [Catherine Knyvett] shall have it.[22]

Elyzabeth did not retire, although she is said to have left for Guernsey for a while, so how much truth is in this story is anyone's guess.

After Lady Cecil's death came several more. In 1598 the Queen's 'good Francke', Frances Howard, Countess of Hertford, died, and in 1599 Elizabeth Stafford, the Queen's long-serving Chamberer, and the much loved daughter of Lady Stafford, passed away, as did Katheryn Howard, the Queen's cousin and second longest serving Maid of Honour, and Margaret Radclyffe, the tragic Maid of Honour who starved herself to death after losing her twin brother. The new century, which held promise of better times, brought with it no relief. Elizabeth Russell, one of the Queen's Maids of the Privy Chamber, died of a sudden sickness in the summer of 1600; the Mother of the Maids, Elizabeth Wingfield, also died that year; and in quick succession the Queen lost two more Howard sisters – Mary, Baroness Dudley, one of her original Maids of Honour who also died in 1600, and Agnes, Marchioness of Winchester, who died the following year. 1601 was also the year that the Queen's former great favourite, Robert Devereux, Earl of Essex, a grandson of Lady Knollys, was executed for raising a rebellion in London against the Queen's advisors. Unlike her father, who beheaded former favourites left, right and centre, Elizabeth found it torture to have to sign the death warrant of someone she had known and loved. Consequently, Essex was only the second nobleman of the reign to be executed at the Tower of London, the first being Thomas Howard, Duke of Norfolk, who was executed for treason on Tower Hill in 1572. Four other men were also put to death for their part in the rebellion, including Sir Christopher Blount, the third husband of the Queen's estranged cousin, Lettice Knollys, who was executed at Tower Hill. Lettice was, of course, the Earl of Essex's mother, so the unfortunate countess lost both her husband and her only surviving son all at once.

Following the earl's execution, the Queen fell into a depression from which she never really recovered. The earl, an important figure at court for so long, was associated with so many of her courtiers and women that his execution shattered their world and things were never quite the same again. Mary Radclyffe herself, however, was a ray of sunshine in these dark times. Always upbeat and positive, with a jolly heart, she has been called the 'Merry Guardian'.[23] However, it would be a mistake to think of her as a pushover. To have been given so much responsibility by the Queen she clearly possessed all the qualities needed to manage the Privy Chamber, and was so quick witted that she allegedly once 'told a lord, whose conversation and discourse she did not like, that his wit was like a custard, nothing good in it but the sop, and when that was eaten you might throw away the rest'.[24]

By the winter of 1602, Elizabeth had been on the throne for forty-four years. She was 69 years of age and had lived longer, and reigned longer, than any monarch for over two centuries. Most of the people she ruled could not remember a time without her, and whilst those around her, who attended upon her every day, were aware of her human frailty, to the people at large she was still Gloriana. Up until the end, Elizabeth did everything she could to present herself as an ever youthful, ever strong figure, for the sake of her country, but by the spring of 1603 she was exhausted. For so many years she had tried to keep so many people happy, had jumped through hoops to satisfy both sides of a political or religious divide, striving for the impossible and sometimes being forced to do the incomprehensible, and she had tried to balance the factions at court, to navigate the endless wars of Europe, to find allies and beat enemies, to address all the problems at home, to establish peace in the realm, to keep order and discipline, and to set the country on the path to prosperity, and to do all these things while retaining the love and support of her people. For nothing mattered more to Elizabeth than the love of her people. 'I desire not to live longer than my life and reign shall be for your good', she had told Parliament in her Golden Speech of 1601, and by the spring of 1603 she had concluded that her life and reign was no longer for their good.[25] All the difficulties in the country had seen public affection for the Queen cool, although most people still loved and respected her, and the execution of the Earl of Essex had damaged her reputation as he was very popular. The early weeks of 1603 had also seen a desire amongst some of the Queen's advisors to imprison Arbella Stuart, a great great granddaughter of Henry VII and a possible heir, in the belief that she posed a threat to the Queen. If Arbella was imprisoned, it would be the Mary, Queen of Scots saga all over again and Elizabeth could not face it. Besides, she had always liked Arbella and is said to have hinted, in the past, that she would not object to Arbella succeeding her.[26]

On top of all these difficulties, by February 1603 the Queen's beloved cousin, Katheryn Carey, was dying. Katheryn had been ailing for some time, perhaps due to a long term illness, and her sister, Philadelphia, was probably performing most of her duties. By now, Katheryn, who had been known as 'Lady Howard' for decades, was the Countess of Nottingham as her husband, Charles, had been made Earl of Nottingham in 1597. The country owed him a debt for his part, as Lord Admiral, in the defeat of the Spanish Armada in 1588, and the Queen may have been spurred to honour him with an earldom over regret of not bestowing one upon his father-in-law, Henry Carey, Baron Hunsdon, her cousin, who had died the previous year. By now, Katheryn and Charles, the power couple of the court, had been married for almost forty years and were parents and grandparents. Of their five children, three were daughters, and at least two, Elizabeth and Frauncis, served the Queen in their youth. Their third daughter, Margaret, may have served for a time, but she married very young and proved to be mentally unstable. The cause of her affliction was, according to her father, inconsolable grief for the loss of her only child, 'which her nature and weak spirit could not resist', and the harm done to her by her father-in-law, Sir Walter Leveson, who was accused of poisoning her with 'a cup of wine boiled with cantharides'.[27] Her husband, Sir Richard Leveson, ended up living with disgraced Maid of Honour, Mary Fitton, with whom he had a daughter, but the naval officer was still well thought of by the Howard family because of his wife's condition. In these last years of the reign, Katheryn's daughter, Frauncis, now Dowager Countess of Kildare and wife of Henry Brooke, Baron Cobham, Lady Cobham's son, was serving the Queen as lady carver, whilst Elizabeth, now Lady Southwell, was serving as a Lady of Honour. Lady Southwell's daughter too was in service, for her daughter was the Elizabeth Southwell who eloped to the Continent with the Earl of Leicester's illegitimate son in the next reign. By all accounts, the Christmas of 1602 was a good one at court, with everyone in high spirits, but within weeks the mood had completely changed. By the end of February, Katheryn was on her deathbed, and when it came, the news of her passing so grieved the Queen that her depression became fatal. Perhaps Katheryn's death was one death too many, for the two women were very close, but there may be more to the story. According to legend, as Katheryn lay on her deathbed she confessed to the Queen that she had intercepted a ring sent to her by the Earl of Essex from the Tower of London, a ring that the Queen had once given him as a promise of help should he ever be in trouble. Persuaded to keep the ring by the earl's enemies, who wanted him dead, she had not given it to the Queen, but had let the Queen believe that the earl was unrepentant. Consumed by remorse, Katheryn is said to have begged the Queen for forgiveness, but the Queen, broken by the confession, is said to have told her 'God may forgive you but I never can'.

Whatever the truth of the legend, the Queen's decline after Katheryn's death was rapid. For hours she would lie on her cushions, uninterested in anything, lost in her own world, eating little, sleeping less, and in no time at all she became deathly weak. To make matters worse, the coronation ring, which she had proudly worn on her finger for over forty-four years, and which she saw as a symbol of her marriage to her people, had to be sawn off due to swelling in her hands. For Mary Radclyffe, and for all the Queen's devoted women, this sudden and unexpected decline in the Queen's health was heartbreaking. There was nothing anyone could do or say to lift the Queen's spirits, and, by the end of March, it had become apparent that the Queen was not going to live. 'There was no hope of her recovery', wrote Sir Robert Carey, brother of Philadelphia Carey who was now acting Chief Lady of the Bedchamber, 'because she refused all remedies'. The Queen had clearly lost the will to live and by the morning of 23 March she had also lost the use of her voice. The end was clearly near and Sir Robert, who was present, tells us in his memoirs of the Queen's final hours:

> About six at night she made signs for the Archbishop [of Canterbury] and her Chaplains to come to her; at which time I went in with them, and sat upon my knees, full of tears to see that heavy sight. Her Majesty lay upon her back, with one hand in the bed, and the other without. The Bishop kneeled down by her, and examined her first of her faith, and she so punctually answered all his several questions, by lifting up her eyes and holding up her hand, as it was a comfort to all the beholders. Then the good man told her plainly what she was, and what she was to come to, and though she had been long a great queen here upon earth, yet shortly she was to yield an account of her stewardship to the King of Kings. After this he began to pray and ... after he had continued long in prayer, till the old man's knees were weary, he blessed her, and meant to rise and leave her. The Queen made a sign with her hand. My sister, Scrope, knowing her meaning, told the Bishop the Queen desired he should pray still... By this time it grew late, and everyone departed, all but her women that attended her. This that I heard with my ears, and did see with my eyes, I thought it my duty to set down, and to affirm it for a truth, upon the faith of a Christian, because I know there have been many false lies reported of the end and death of that good lady.[28]

In the early hours of the following morning, between one and two of the clock, the Queen died in the company of her women. Philadelphia was almost certainly one of those present at this sad, but historic, moment, and it is likely that Mary Radclyffe was too. When Sir Robert received word that the Queen was dead, he rushed from his lodgings to the coffer chamber, where he found 'all the ladies weeping bitterly'. The grief and sorrow that the Queen's women felt for her passing was genuine and heartfelt and they were her first mourners.

For Mary Radclyffe, the Queen's death was life-changing, but for the moment she still had duties to perform for her dead mistress. Two days after the Queen's death, her body, enclosed in a coffin draped with black velvet, was taken by water from Richmond Palace, where she died, to the Palace of Whitehall. Mary, as Chief Gentlewoman of the Privy Chamber, would have assisted in the preparations, working with the Lord Chamberlain and other officials to co-ordinate the move, and to ensure that everyone was appropriately dressed for the escorting procession. This procession took place at night, when it was dark, and the Queen's coffin was solemnly conveyed along the Thames with a 'multitude of torches burning'. Accompanying the coffin in the royal barge was 'a great company of ladies', principally the Queen's Ladies of Honour, and the Queen's Privy Councillors. Behind them, in more barges, came the Gentlemen Pensioners and various household officials. Whether Mary and other Ladies and Gentlewomen of the Privy Chamber were in the royal barge with the Ladies of Honour is unknown, but if they were not then some of them would have been waiting at Whitehall Palace to receive the Queen at the procession's end. When there, the Queen's coffin was placed in her withdrawing chamber and 'watched', meaning attended, by several ladies and lords. Four weeks later, the Queen's coffin was brought out of the withdrawing chamber and placed in the prestigious parlour that was the privy chamber beneath a cloth of state. The following day, the Queen's body was taken to the Presence Chamber, and from there conveyed to the Chapel Royal where it remained until the funeral.

Even when the Queen was in her grave, Mary's duties had not ended. Still Keeper of Her Majesty's Jewels, Mary remained in charge of the Queen's personal collection of jewellery for some time. In the May of 1603, she and Catherine Knyvett, Baroness Howard, were given the task of sorting through the Queen's hundreds of jewels, including those upon clothes or furs, and of gathering them together in an orderly fashion for assessment. It was not until the August of that year that Mary, after many years of dedicated service, was finally discharged from her post and dismissed as an attendant by the new queen, Queen Anne

Very little is known about the rest of Mary's life. She seems to have lived in London, for St Martin's in the Field is where she was living when she made her final will in 1617, and a wealthy woman in her own right, she lived comfortably with at least two servants to attend her. Unable to write by the time she made her will, Mary signed it with her mark, and was clearly on her deathbed as she talked about her life in the past tense. To her principal servant, Anne Lotham, she left 'twenty pounds in money', an annuity of £6, and 'my little cup I used to drink broth in', and to Elizabeth Lee, her second servant, she left 'ten pounds in money', an annuity of £4, and 'my little silver salt and a silver spoon that useth to stand upon my cupboard'. The executor of her will was her nephew, Sir Henry Cheke, grandson of Mary Hill, Lady Cheke, whose son had married Mary's sister, and in her will Mary described herself as 'sometimes one of the gentlewomen of Her Late Majesty's honourable Privy Chamber'. Amongst her many bequests and requests was one for 'a comely and convenient monument in stone' to be 'set up in or near such place where I shall be buried' showing 'both the race and birth whereof I am descended and also the room and place wherein I lived and served under her late said Majesty'.[29] Mary was clearly very proud of having served Queen Elizabeth, especially as a Gentlewoman of the Privy Chamber, and wanted posterity to remember. Sadly, the place where Mary died, and was buried, is unknown. There is no record of her burial in the Church of St Martin's in the Field or in the Church of St Mary and St Helena in Elstow. However, her wish for a monument seems to have been carried out as Edward Walford, who wrote about her parents, refers to this monument in his book, a monument which told us that Mary was a 'Maiden of Honour and Gentlewoman of the Privy Chamber' to Queen Elizabeth and served her 'honourably, virtuously and faithfully for 40 years'.[30] Regrettably, Walford does not tell us where this monument was, but perhaps it was in Elstow, where her parents have a memorial, and was lost during the restoration of the church in the late nineteenth century.

Funeral

ON 28 APRIL 1603, Queen Elizabeth, who had reigned for forty-four years and four months, made her final public procession. The occasion was her funeral, and 'the city of Westminster was surcharged with multitudes of all sorts of people in their streets, houses, windows, leads, and gutters' all hoping to catch a glimpse of the funeral cortege as the Queen's coffin was solemnly carried upon a black chariot drawn by four horses from the Palace of Whitehall, where she had lain in state for a month, to Westminster Abbey where she was to be laid to rest.[1] The Queen's coffin, which was covered with purple velvet, was topped with a lifelike effigy of the Queen clad in her red parliament robes with the orb and sceptre in her hands. Before the royal hearse walked 260 poor women, all dressed in black with 'linen kerchiefs over their heads', and after them came a legion of men, including the male staff of the Queen's household, four trumpeters, standard bearers, two equerries leading 'two great horses' draped in black, the gentlemen and children of the chapel singing 'a mournful tune', aldermen of London, statesmen, churchmen, foreign dignitaries, noblemen, and the Gentlemen Pensioners, whose battle-axes were 'covered with black and the heads of them carried downwards'. Behind the hearse, after the Master of the Horse, Edward Somerset, Earl of Worcester, came, as always, the Queen's Ladies of Honour. Numbering about sixty, they were all wearing liveries of black mourning robes with hoods and veils, and fronting them, in a robe with a train so long that it needed to be supported by two countesses and the Vice-Chamberlain, Sir John Stanhope, Lady Cheke's son-in-law, was the Chief Mourner, Helena Snakenborg, Marchioness of Northampton. Although Lucy Cecil, Marchioness of Winchester, had challenged Helena for the role, placing the Earl Marshal's office, which was responsible for organising the funeral, in a dilemma as they were not sure which of 'our very good ladies, the Lady Marquess of Northampton and the Lady Marquess of Winchester' should have precedence, the matter was finally settled in favour of Helena after the office consulted 'the roll of the creation of the said Marquess of Northampton' and found that the marquessate was older, by a whisker, than that of Winchester.[2] The ruling evidently caused offence, however, as Lady Winchester did not attend the funeral.

After the Chief Mourner and the Ladies of Honour came the Queen's Maids of Honour, unusually numbering seven, and after them came the Ladies and Gentlewomen of the Privy Chamber. All these ladies, gentlewomen and maids were in black mourning livery too, the quantity of black cloth they had received depending on their status, and for the occasion there was, just as there had been at the coronation, some juggling of positions. The young Maids of the Privy Chamber served as either Ladies of Honour or Maids of Honour for the event, and some of the Ladies and Gentlewomen of the Privy Chamber served as Ladies of Honour. After the Queen's women came the Yeomen of the Guard, led by the Captain of the Guard, Kat Astley's nephew, Sir Walter Raleigh.

Amongst all the women who walked in this sombre procession were the Queen's close cousins, Philadelphia Carey, Baroness Scrope; Elyzabeth Knollys, Lady Leighton; Margaret Carey, Lady Hoby; Elizabeth Howard, Lady Southwell; and Frauncis Howard, Countess of Kildare. There were also a number of women who had been dear to the Queen over the years, such as Mary Sidney, Countess of Pembroke, and Lady Bridget Manners, and those who had served her loyally for decades, such as Dorothee Stafford, Lady Stafford; Anne Russell, Countess of Warwick; Mary Radclyffe; Mary Shelton, Lady Scudamore; and those very rare women who had also served at the Queen's coronation. Indeed, those women were so rare that there were only five: Anne Morgan, Baroness Hunsdon; Dougles Howard, Baroness Sheffield; Lettice Knollys, Countess of Leicester; Elizabeth Huggins, formerly a 'gentlewoman of the household' now one of 'the Queen's women'; and Mary Hill, Lady Cheke, who had served the Queen intermittently for over sixty years.

As the Queen's ladies, gentlewomen and maids escorted their mistress one final time to her grave, the people of London, and those from beyond who had travelled there for the event, said goodbye to a queen who would go down in history as one of the greatest monarchs to have ever lived. As they did, there was, according to John Stow, who witnessed the scene, 'such a general sighing, groaning, and weeping as the like hath not been seen or known in the memory of man; neither doth any history mention any people, time, or state, to make like lamentation for the death of their sovereign'.[3]

In years to come, Elizabeth's reign would be remembered as a golden age, not because it was perfect, but because the age over which she had ruled was better than most that had been before and most that were to come. The Stuart sun that now rose over a new nation – the nation of Great Britain that had been born at Elizabeth's death, a union of crowns that she undoubtedly hoped would bring peace and security to a divided isle and spare her successors the soul destroying struggles that she had faced with her rival, Mary, Queen of Scots – never shined as bright as the light from her glorious sun. For those devoted women who had served the Queen for the best years of their lives, the sun had set on their world too, for without their dazzling mistress to attend, their lives were dark and empty, devoid of all purpose, and by the Christmas of 1604, Lady Stafford, Lady Warwick, and Lady Scudamore were all dead. By the following summer, Elyzabeth Knollys, Lady Leighton, had also passed away, and in a letter to Robert Cecil shortly before her death she told him that:

> ...my dull spirits have been long time oppressed by cross occasions, from whence have proceeded a long and tedious time of sickness and weakness, among which the loss of my dear and excellent mistress

was not the least, for I confess that though I will be a loyal and sound hearted subject to His Majesty, yet shall I never have razed out of my heart the worthy memory of my gracious Queen, so that it rejoiced me much to find that out of Your Lordship's noble and thankful disposition you hold her still in fresh memory.[4]

A few of the Queen's younger attendants impressed their new mistress, Queen Anne, such as Catherine Knyvett, Baroness Howard, who was made Keeper of Her Majesty's Jewels, and Audrey Shelton, Lady Walsingham, who became the first Mistress of the Robes in English history, but the new queen had little time for Elizabeth's old ladies. To her they were relics of the past, living mementos of a dead age, and her eyes were firmly on the future.

Anne Morgan, Baroness Hunsdon, lived on until 1607, survived by only one of her daughters, Philadelphia, who lived into the reign of King Charles I; Mary Hill, Lady Cheke, lived on until 1616, her daughter, Margaret, Lady Stanhope, until 1640; Lettice Knollys, Countess of Leicester until 1634; and Helena Snakenborg, Marchioness of Northampton, who rarely attended court after the Queen's demise as she had 'completely given up life at the place', lived on until 1635. For those young women who had attended the Queen in the winter of her life, many lived on through the devastation of the Civil War, and some beyond that. The last of the Queen's women known to die is Frances Brockett, Baroness North, a young Lady of Honour in the 1600s who lived on through the Restoration of the Monarchy in 1660, the Great Plague of 1665, and the Great Fire of London in 1666, finally departing this mortal world in the year 1677, more than two centuries after Elizabeth's Lady Mistress, Margaret Bourchier, Baroness Bryan, was born.

Further Reading

THE FOLLOWING IS a very selective list of books, articles, theses and online resources chosen for their relevancy and/or exceptional scholarship. See *Notes and References* for more works consulted in the writing of this book.

Books

Arnold, Janet, *Lost From Her Majesties Back*, (1980).

Arnold, Janet, *Queen Elizabeth's Wardrobe Unlocked*, (1988).

Borman, Tracey, *Elizabeth's Women*, (2009).

Doran, Susan, *Elizabeth I's Circle*, (2015).

Emerson, Kathy Lynn, *A Who's Who of Tudor Women*, (2020).

Evans, Victoria Sylvia, *Ladies in Waiting: Women Who Served at the Tudor Court*, (2014).

Heywood, Maria, *Dress at the Court of King Henry VIII*, (2007).

Kinney, A., Lawson, J., *Titled Elizabethans: A Directory of Elizabethan Court, State, and Church Officers 1558–1603*, (2014).

Lawson, Jane A., *The Elizabethan New Year's Gift Exchanges 1559–1603*, (2013).

Loades, David, *The Tudor Court*, (1986).

Mumby, Frank Arthur, *The Girlhood of Queen Elizabeth: A Narrative in Contemporary Letters*, (1909).

Richardson, Ruth Elizabeth, *Mistress Blanche: Revised Edition with New Findings*, (2018).

Soberton, Sylvia Barbara, *Ladies in Waiting: Women Who Served Anne Boleyn*, (2023).

Somerset, Anne, *Ladies in Waiting: From the Tudors to the Present Day*, (1984).

Starkey, David, *Elizabeth*, (2000).

Starkey, David *et al.*, *The Tudor Court*, (1987).

Tallis, Nicola, *Young Elizabeth*, (2024).

Whitelock, Anna, *Elizabeth's Bedfellows: An Intimate History of the Queen's Court*, (2013).

Wilson, Violet, *Queen Elizabeth's Maids of Honour*, (1922).

Articles

Harris, Oliver, 'A Lady of the Bedchamber to Elizabeth I: Elizabeth, Lady Carew', *Friends of Exeter Cathedral Eighty-Fourth Annual Report*, (2014).

Harris, Oliver, 'Generations of Adam: The Monument of Sir Gawen Carew in Exeter Cathedral', *Church Monuments*, Volume XXIX, (2014).

Lawson, Jane A., 'Rainbow for a Reign: The Colours of a Queen's Wardrobe', *Costume*, Volume 41, (June, 2007).

Lawson, Jane, A., 'Always on Duty: Personnel of Elizabeth's Pre-Accession Household', (Conference Paper, 2015, available via researchgate.net).

Varlow, Sally, 'Sir Francis Knollys's Latin Dictionary: New Evidence for Katherine Carey', in *Historical Research*, Volume 80, Issue 209, 2007.

Unpublished Theses

Bowles, Carole De Witte, *Women of the Tudor Court 1501–1568,* (MA, Portland State University, 1989).

Goldsmith, Joan Barbara Greenbaum, *All the Queen's Women: The Changing Place and Perception of Aristocratic Women in Elizabethan England 1558–1620,* (Ph.D, Northwestern University, 1987).

Howey, Catherine Louise, *Busy Bodies: Women, Power and Politics at the Court of Queen Elizabeth I 1558–1603,* (Ph.D, The State University of New Jersey, 2007).

Hocking, Joanne Lee, *Aristocratic Women at the Late Elizabethan Court: Politics, Patronage and Power,* (Ph.D, University of Adelaide, 2015).

Merton, Charlotte, *Ladies, Gentlewomen and Maids of the Privy Chamber 1553–1603: The Women Who Served Queen Mary and Queen Elizabeth,* (Ph.D, University of Cambridge, 1991).

Online Resources

Colthorpe, Marion E., *Elizabethan Court Day by Day,* (folgerpedia.folger.edu).

Leed, Drea, *Elizabethan Costuming Page,* (elizabethancostume.net).

Also Useful

academia.edu (for academic articles).

britishhistory.net (primary and secondary resources).

nationalarchives.gov.uk (court records, wills etc).

bl.uk (The British Library).

Notes and References

Abbreviations

CIPM	Calendar of Inquisitions Post Mortem.
CPR	Calendar of Patent Rolls.
CP	Cecil Papers (Hatfield House).
CSP	Calendar of State Papers.
DBWR	Day Book of the Wardrobe of Robes (TNA, C 115/91).
HEPE	Strangford, Viscount, (ed.), *Household Expenses of the Princess Elizabeth,* (1853).
IPM	Inquisition Post Mortem.
LPH8	Letters and Papers, Foreign and Domestic, Henry VIII.
OLEH	Ellis, Henry, *Original Letters Illustrative of English History.*
RP	Rutland Papers (Belvoir Castle).
ECDBD	Colthorpe, Marion E., *Elizabethan Court Day by Day* (folgerpedia. folger.edu).
Haynes	Haynes, Samuel, *A Collection of State Papers* 1540–1572, (1740).
Merton	Merton, Charlotte, *Ladies, Gentlewomen and Maids of the Privy Chamber 1553–1603: The Women Who Served Queen Mary and Queen Elizabeth,* (Ph.D, University of Cambridge, 1991).
Mumby	Mumby, Frank A., *The Girlhood of Queen Elizabeth,* (1909).
Nichols	Nichols, John, *The Progresses and Public Processions of Queen Elizabeth,* (1823).
NYGE	Lawson, Jane A., *The Elizabethan New Year's Gift Exchanges 1559–1603,* (2013).
Ordinances	Society of Antiquaries, London, *A Collection of Ordinances and Regulations for the Government of the Royal Household,* (1790).
Richardson	Richardson, Ruth Elizabeth, *Mistress Blanche: Revised Edition with New Findings,* (2018).
TNA	The National Archives.

Prologue

1. CSP Spanish, 1531–1533, Vol.4, Pt.2, No.1124.
2. For why Margaret Finch was probably the Countess of Kent who bore the train see her entry in the *Index of Women*.
3. This is likely as godparents, rather than parents, usually chose a child's name, which is why Henry VIII askes Cranmer in Shakespeare's *Henry VIII* 'what is her name?' (Henry VIII, Act 5, Scene5.)
4. Nichols, Vol.1, pp.1–2; LPH8, Vol.6, No.1111.

Chapter One: Lady Mistress

1. Ordinances, pp.126–7.
2. CSP Domestic, 1534, No.1668; Schroder, Timothy, *A Marvel to Behold: Gold and Silver at the Court of Henry VIII*, (2020), pp.186–188.
3. For types of livery see Hayward, Maria, *Dress at the Court of Henry VIII*, (2007).
4. Lady Darcy was granted a tun of red wine for life by Edward IV in 1480, confirmed by Henry VII in 1488. Lady Denton and Baroness Bryan were granted a tun of Gascon wine in 1510 and 1519 respectively. The modern equivalent of a Tudor tun of wine is approximately 1266 standard bottles of wine (750 ml). CPR, 1476–1485, p.241; Campbell, William, *Materials for a History of the Reign of Henry VII*, (1873), p.370; LPH8, Vol.1, No.519, No.58; LPH8, Vol.3, No.361.
5. LPH8, Vol.2, No.3802.
6. TNA, E 404/74/1/100.
7. LPH8, Vol.11, No.203; OLEH, Vol.2, Series 2, p.79.
8. Murphy, Beverley Anne, *Bastard Prince: Henry VIII's Lost Son*, (2002), p.35.
9. HEPE, p.35; Richardson, p.76.
10. LPH8, Vol.7, No.214.
11. LPH8, Vol.7, No.1172.
12. Richardson, W. C., *The Report of the Royal Commission of 1552*, (1974), p.23.
13. CSP Spanish, 1536–1538, Vol.5, Pt.2, No.13.
14. CSP Spanish, 1536–1538, Vol.5, Pt.2, No.55.
15. LPH8, Vol.11, No.203; OLEH, Vol.2, Series 2, pp.78–82.
16. LPH8, Vol.11, No.860.
17. LPH8, Vol.14 Pt.2, No.9.
18. Ibid.
19. Funeral records of Henry VIII, TNA, LC 2/2. Francis was married to Lady Ormond by the summer of 1548 but Philippa may still have been alive in early 1547.
20. Nichols, John Gough, *Literary Remains of King Edward the Sixth*, (1857), p.xxxii.

Chapter Two: Governesses

1. I.e. LPH8, Vol.3, No.896; LPH8, Vol.4, No.1577; LPH8, Vol.6, No.1009.
2. Madden, Frederic, *Privy Purse Expenses of the Princess Mary*, (1831), pp.xli–xlii.
3. TNA, LC 2/2, folio 48.v; TNA, SP 10/6/16 (CSP Domestic 1547–1580, Vol.1, p.13).
4. For the original Welsh poem see Lake, Cynfael A., (ed.) *Gwaith Lewys Morgannwg I*, (2004), pp.139–140. For a literal translation of the entire poem see Richardson, pp.40–41. Versified translation by myself.
5. *Calendar of the Carew Manuscripts (Lamberth Palace)*, 1575–1583, Vol.2, No.501.
6. Sybil Penn's annuity: LPH8, Vol.14, Pt.1, No.1354. Sidney letter: LPH8, Vol.13, Pt.2, No.524.
7. Boyle, Frederick, 'The Oldest of Horticultural Societies', *The Living Age*, (31 July 1909), p.300.
8. Richardson, p.4.
9. CP (Calendar, Vol.11, pp.133–4).
10. LPH8, Vol.12, Pt.2, No.911.
11. Letter CXXX in Wood, Mary Anne Everett, *Letters of Royal and Illustrious Ladies*, Vol.2, 1846, p.318 (note: in a facsimile of Lady Kildare's signature her name is spelled 'Elyzabeth').
12. Anne is probably the 'Anne Morgan' listed in attendance on Princess Mary (LPH8, Vol.10, No.1187 – the dating of the document is unreliable).
13. Richardson, p.45.
14. Richardson, W. C., op.cit., p.23; HEPE, p.41.
15. Lake, Cynfael A., op.cit, p.139.
16. Although her identity has been disputed, my own research, in addition to the wealth of evidence presented by Rosemary Griggs in her article *Who Was Kat Ashley?* (rosemarygriggs.co.uk/blog/21/) confirms that Kat was the eldest daughter of Sir Philip Champernon. See, for example, Sir Philip's IPM (TNA, WARD 7/2/77, Champernoun) which says in Latin 'Katherine Champernon, the eldest daughter of the aforesaid Philip' (discovery made by Griggs). For more evidence see Note 20.
17. IPM (1508) of Sir John Champernon: 'the said Philip and Katharine were married in his (John's) lifetime' and 'have occupied the premises (Manor of Aston Rowant) since long before his death'; CIPM, Henry VII, Vol.3, No. 437.
18. Kat's mother was born c.1485. The marriage settlement of Sir Edmund Carew and Kateryn Huddesfield (Kat's maternal grandparents) was dated 1479 and her uncle, William, was born in 1483. Although her grandmother's age was given as '21 and more' in the IPM of Sir William Huddesfield in 1500 this is clearly a mistake and should be '31 and more'. Kat's father was born c.1484 as his age was given as 24 in 1508.
19. The names of the last nuns are not known.

20. Kateryn Ashley/Astley, Joan/Jane Gamage, Katherine/Catherine Gilbert Raleigh, and Joan/Johan Denny were all definitely the daughters of Sir Philip Champernon. This is supported in a series of contemporary documents: LPH8, Vol.13, Pt.1, No. 384, 47; CP 150/85 (Haynes, p.100); Siddons, Michael Powell, *Visitations by the Heralds in Wales*, (1996), p.63; Sidney/Gamage Pedigree, De L'Isle MS U1500 F13; Latham, Agnes, Youings, Joyce, *The Letters of Sir Walter Ralegh*, (1999), p.224–225; TNA, PRO 11/27/504; TNA, PROB 11/31/41. To help avoid the historic confusion between the six known daughters of Sir Philip Champernon it is useful to name them as Kateryn (Ashley/Astley), Joan (Gamage), Frances (Budockside), Elizabeth (Cole), Catherine (Gilbert, Raleigh) and Joanne (Denny).
21. TNA, SP 1/107 F.131.
22. Kat's grandmother, Lady Carew, was a maternal half-sister to William Carey's grandmother, Alice Fulford Carey.
23. Vasoli, Sandra, *Anne Boleyn's Letter From the Tower*, (2015).
24. LPH8, Vol.14 Pt.1, No.1145.
25. Haynes, p.98.
26. Adams, Simon, *Leicester and the Court*, (2002), p.139.
27. As published in 1557 in *Songes and Sonnettes written by the right honorable Lorde Henry Haward late Earle of Surrey and other,* (Oxford Text Archive). This poem is difficult to date but 1541–3 is more convincing than some of the earlier dates given.
28. LPH8, Vol.16, 1389.
29. Hooker, John, Maclean, John (ed.), *The Life and Times of Sir Peter Carew*, (1857), p.34.
30. Sir Philip's Will: TNA, PROB 11/31/41.
31. Giles, J. A., *The Whole Works of Roger Ascham*, Vol.1, Pt.1, pp.85–87.
32. Haynes, p.95.
33. Ibid., pp.95–99.
34. Ibid., p.100.
35. CP 150/85 (Haynes, pp.99–101).
36. Haynes, p.70.
37. Ibid., p.88.
38. Ibid., p.102.
39. TNA, SP 10/6/16 (CSP Domestic 1547–1580, Vpl.1, p.13).
40. TNA, SP 10/6/22 (printed in Marcus, Leah S., *et al.*, *Elizabeth I: Collected Works*, (2000), pp.29–30).
41. For the charges against Seymour see: St Maur, H., *Annals of the Seymours*, (1902), p.452.
42. Letter CLXV, OLEH, Vol.2, Series 1.
43. Haynes, p.107.
44. Taylor, Rupert, *The East Sussex Village Book*, (1986), pp.24–25.
45. Haynes, pp.103–4.
46. Ibid., p.101.
47. Ibid., p.108.

48. Ibid., p.109.

49. Ibid., p.108.

50. Mumby, pp.55–57.

51. Ibid., p.70.

52. Nichols, Vol.1, p.xxxvii. For more information on the girdle book see: Tait, Hugh, 'The Girdle Prayer-Book or Tablett' in *Jewellery Studies,* Vol.2, (1985).

53. Lady Scudamore's father-in-law, William Scudamore, was the sister of Jane Scudamore, mother of Lady Littleton. Lady Hawkins was the great granddaughter of Watkin Vaughan and Sybil Baskerville, as was Lady Littleton.

54. Ashby Pedigree: Fletcher, W. G. D., *Leicestershire Pedigrees and Royal Descents,* (1887), p.15. Rev. George Ashby was the son of Edmund Ashby (son of George Ashby, born 1656) who married Judith Lock in 1720.

55. *Semper Eadem* means 'Always the Same' or 'Be Always One'. Some historians believe *Semper Eadem* was a motto first used by Anne Boleyn.

Chapter Three: The Hatfield Flock

1. Hasler, P. W., *The House of Commons 1558–1603,* (1981), A–C, p.428.

2. HEPE, p.33–34.

3. TNA, LC 2/2, folio 48.v. Elizabeth Sondes was probably a chamberer as this was her position post-accession.

4. TNA, SP 10/6/16 (CSP Domestic 1547–1580, V.1, p.13). Sir Robert says in this letter that 'Mestrys Norwege' was Elizabeth's bedfellow 'after she came to the ....' and the illegible word (for his handwriting is very hard to read) may be choyrt (court) for that is where Elizabeth went after Chelsea.

5. Harris, Oliver, 'Generations of Adam: The Monument of Sir Gawen Carew in Exeter Cathedral', in *Church Monuments,* Vol. XXIX, (2014); Harris, Oliver, 'A Lady of the Bedchamber to Elizabeth I: Elizabeth, Lady Carew' in *Friends of Exeter Cathedral Eighty-Fourth Annual Report,* (2014), pp. 28–31, available at academia.edu; Metcalfe, Walter C., (ed.), *The Visitations of Northamptonshire made in 1564 and 1618–19,* (1887), p.120; Brown, O. F., *The Tyrells of England,* (1982), p.243; Nichols, John, *The History and Antiquities of the County of Leicester,* (1795), Vol.2 Pt.2, p.519.

6. *A Descriptive Catalogue of Ancient Deeds in the Public Record Office,* (1906), Vol.5, p.513; *List of Proceedings in the Court of Requests,* Vol.1, (1963), p.161.

7. Maddison, A. R., *Lincolnshire Pedigrees,* (1904), pp.1019–1020.

8. Coverdale New Testament (British Library C.45 a.13). For authorship of the poem see Hughey, Ruth, *John Harington of Stepney,* (1971), p.85, p.256.

9. Walpole, Horace, (ed.), *A Journey into England by Paul Hentzner in the year 1598,* (1757), p.24; TNA, SP 10/6/22.

10. While Foxe's account of *The Miraculous Preservation of the Lady Elizabeth* contains some inaccuracies, it was published during the Queen's lifetime in a book considered so important that a copy was placed next to the Bible in

every cathedral in the land. Foxe's account, therefore, must have met with the Queen's approval and is as close to an official version of the truth as we will get.

11. Mumby, pp.137, 150, 178.
12. Ibid., pp.141, 150, 165, 169, 180.
13. Borman, Tracy, *Anne Boleyn and Elizabeth I*, (2023).
14. Mumby, pp.137, 140, 141. Bridget Southwell's role in Elizabeth's life is unclear. According to her brother, Sir Thomas Copley, a Catholic exile, she had served the Queen for 'near forty years' by 1583, which would mean she had entered her service in the 1540s, but he provides no more information. According to some history books she was one of the Queen's Latin tutors. It is reasonable to conclude, then, that she may have been appointed to teach Elizabeth at Woodstock. Levin, Carole, *et al.*, *A Biographical Encyclopedia of Early Modern Englishwomen*, (2016), p.180; Hasler, P. W., op.cit., pp.650–651.
15. Bedingfield Papers, British Library, Add MS 34563.
16. Mumby, p.143.
17. Bedingfield Papers, op.cit.
18. Mumby, p.137.
19. Acts of the Privy Council, 1554–1556, Vol.5, p.129.
20. Account book of George Medley in *Report on the Manuscripts of Lord Middleton, Preserved at Wollaton Hall, Nottinghamshire,* (1911), p.409.
21. CSP Venice, 1555–1558, Vol.6, Pt.1, No.505.
22. Foxe says these events happened at 'Lamheyre' which may be the Manor of Lemar, Wheathampstead, which has a confused history so could have belonged to Elizabeth for a time (she may have been staying there while Hatfield Palace was aired and sweetened).
23. CSP Venice, 1555–1556, Vol.6, Pt.1, No.510.
24. Ibid., N.514.
25. Account book of George Medley, op.cit., p.412.
26. Blanche Whitney seemingly disappears from history in the mid–1550s. Ethelreda Harington is another possibility if in service (see *Nugae Antiquae: A Problem Source*).
27. CSP Venice, 1555–1556, No.775. This quarrel probably caused Elizabeth's departure but there may have been another outbreak of smallpox amongst her staff.

Chapter Four: Stars in the Presence of the Sun

1. Baker, Richard, Sir, *A Chronicle of the Kings of England*, (1679), p.400.
2. Some portraits with the sun in splendour on the Queen's gown are: *The Armada Portrait* (Woburn Abbey); *Allegory of the Tudor Succession c.*1590 (Yale Center for British Art); *Elizabeth I* by School of Nicholas Hilliard *c.*1590 (Jesus College, Oxford University); *Elizabeth I with a Miniature Sieve*

(Charlecote Park); two portraits of Elizabeth I by unknown artists (Christ Church, University of Oxford); and *Elizabeth I* by Marcus Gheeraerts *c.*1597, (Trinity College, Cambridge).

3. Walpole, Horace, (ed.), op.cit, p.83.
4. Joan may have died by 1558 as Robert was married to a Katherine by 1570 (TNA, PROB 11/56/3). This Robert was definitely Joan's husband as the Sidney/Gamage pedigree confirms it (De L'Isle MS U1500 F13).
5. CSP Spanish, 1554–1558, Vol.13, No.435.
6. Harrison, William, 'The Descriptions of England', in *Holinshed's Chronicles of England, Scotland and Ireland*, Vol.1., (1807), p.331.
7. There is no mention of 'ladies of the household' in the Funeral Records (TNA, LC2/2/4).
8. TNA, LC 5/49.
9. Coronation Records (TNA, LC2/4/3).
10. Wardrobe Records; Lawson, Jane A., 'Rainbow for a Reign', in *Costume*, V.41, June 2007.
11. For more information on Christmas at court see my article 'Gloriana's Christmas' in *All Things Tudor Magazine*, Issue 4, 2022. For why Twelfth Night was 6 January not 5, see my article 'When Was Twelfth Night?' ibid.
12. NYGE.
13. Harrison, William, op.cit., pp.311–12.
14. 'William Latymer, "A brief treatise or cronickille of the moste vertuous Ladye Anne Bulleyne late Quene of Englande", with a preface addressed to Queen Elizabeth', Oxford, Bodleian Libraries, MS. Don. c. 42, fols. 21–23.
15. There are several versions of Queen Elizabeth's Golden Speech and they all differ from each other; Marcus, Leah S., *et al.*, *Elizabeth I Collected Works*, (2000).
16. Osborne, Francis, *Historical Memoires on the Reigns of Queen Elizabeth and King James*, (1658), pp.40–41.
17. Ogborne, Elizabeth, *The History of Essex*, (1814), p.114.

Chapter Five: Ladies of Honour

1. This is the outfit worn in *The Coronation Portrait*. It was not new as it was originally Queen Mary's.
2. Froude, James, *The Reign of Elizabeth*, Vol.1, (1912), p.270.
3. *Queen Elizabeth's Entertainment at Mitcham*, Yale Elizabethan Club, (1953).
4. CSP Simancas, 1558–1567, Vol.1, No.21.
5. Coronation Records (TNA, LC2/4/3).
6. TNA, LC5/32.
7. CSP Venice, 1558–1580, Vol.7, No.10.
8. According to official records, but Margaret Audley, Duchess of Norfolk, may have done the honours at the last minute (ibid.).
9. Ibid.

10. Ibid., No.15.
11. Klarwill, Victor Von, *Queen Elizabeth and Some Foreigners* (1928), p.378.
12. Walpole, Horace, (ed.), op.cit., pp.31–2.
13. Deloney, Thomas, 'The Queen's visiting of the Camp at Tilbury, with her entertainment there', (1588), in Pollard, A. F., *Tudor Tracts 1532–1588*, (1903), pp.495–6.
14. Stow, John, *A Summarie of the Chronicles of England*, (1590), p.754.
15. TNA, 11/98/494.
16. Bradford, Charles Angell, *Helena, Marchioness of Northampton*, (1936), pp.176–177.

Chapter Six: Maids of Honour

1. Coronation Records (TNA, LC2/4/3).
2. Women at Court, ECDBD.
3. LPH8, Vol.12 Pt.2, Nos.808, 923, 711, 626.
4. Women at Court, ECDBD.
5. CP 238/3; there is mention of a 'pair of stairs' in the maidens' chamber of Wallingford Castle (1568, ECDBD). The castle was not in good shape by Elizabeth's reign but repairs were made for a visit in 1568.
6. Stoughton, John, *Notice of Windsor in Olden Times*, (1844), p.140.
7. Boyle, John, Earl of Orrey, (ed.), *Memoirs of the Life of Robert Carey*, (1759), pp.144–145. The Memoirs were purportedly published 'from an original manuscript' in the editor's possession but unfortunately this manuscript is lost. The coffer chamber is written as 'cofferer's chamber'.
8. Nicolas L'Estrange, 'Merry Passages and Jests', (1655) quoted in Thoms, William J., *Anecdotes and Traditions Illustrative of Early English History and Literature*, (1889), pp.70–71.
9. Walpole, Horace, (ed.), op.cit., pp.51–53; Fisher, F. J. (ed.), *The State of England Anno Dom. 1600 by Thomas Wilson*, Camden Miscellany, Vol. XVI, (1936).
10. Bacon, Francis, 'Apothegms', (1625), reprinted in Ellis, Robert Leslie *et al.*, *The Works of Francis Bacon*, V.XIII, (1864), p.377.
11. 1573, ECDBD.
12. CSP Domestic, 1591–4, Vol.3, p.105.
13. CP 20/89; CP 20/65.
14. CP 20/89.
15. CSP Domestic, 1598–1601, Nos.50, 47.
16. CP 64/39.
17. 1598, ECDBD.
18. Newdigate-Newdegate, A. E. G., *Gossip from a Muniment-Room: Being Passages in the Lives of Anne and Mary Fitton 1574–1618*, (1897), p.76.
19. This was surely an exaggeration. Collins, Arthur, *Letters and Memorials of State, Vol.2*, (1746), p.48.

20. Jeayes, Isaac Herbert, *Letters of Philip Gawdy*, (1906), p.103.
21. Collins, Arthur, op.cit., p.141.
22. Smith, J. C. C., *The Parish Registers of Richmond*, Vol.1, (1903), 12 November 1599, p.166. The entry mistakenly gives her name as Elizabeth.
23. Collins, Arthur, op.cit., p.201.
24. Ibid., p.203.
25. Strong, Roy, *The Cult of Elizabeth*, (1999).
26. Newdigate-Newdegate, A. E. G., op.cit., p.36.
27. According to Whyte. Collins, Arthur, op.cit., p.203.
28. Ibid., p.195.

Chapter Seven: Of Her Majesty's Privy Chamber

1. Funeral Records (TNA, LC2/2/4).
2. Eltham Ordinances of 1526 in *A Collection of Ordinances and Regulations for the Government of the Royal Household made in Divers Reigns*, (1790).
3. CPR, Elizabeth, Vol.2, p.533.
4. They were probably extraordinaries as they were not named in fee lists.
5. Osborne, Francis, op. cit., p.40.
6. Eltham Ordinances, op.cit.
7. Abbott, Jacob, *Queen Elizabeth*, (1904), p.193; Fisher, F. J. (ed.), op.cit.
8. 1563, ECDBD.
9. 'Charles Lord Howarde Baron of Effingham our Lord Chamberlayne' (Wardrobe Warrant, 16 August 1584, TNA, LC 5/49).
10. *Calendar of the Manuscripts of the Marquis of Bath*, Vol 4, p.158.
11. Ibid., p.160.
12. CSP Domestic, 1595–1597, p.121–122.
13. Rutland, Vol.1, p.107.
14. The French letter, with an English translation, can be found in *The Century of Queens* by an anonymous author, (1872), pp.90–97.
15. Strickland, Agnes, *Lives of the Queens of England*, Vol.7, (1844), p.49; Mitchell, Charles, *Expert Witness*, (1923), p.173.
16. Wardrobe Warrant, 14 April 1574, transcript at elizabethancostume.net.
17. Talbot Papers, MSS 3192–3206, f.10, Lambeth Palace Library.
18. Collins, Arthur, op.cit., p.38.
19. Jameson, Anna, *Memoirs of Celebrated Female Sovereigns*, (1831), p.320.
20. Bell, Henry Nugent, *The Huntingdon Peerage*, (1820), p.64.
21. Jameson, Anna, op.cit., p.284; Campbell, Hugh, *The Case of Mary Queen of Scots*, (1825), p.287; Wilson, *Queen Elizabeth's Maids of Honour*, (1922), p.199.
22. Jameson, Anna, op.cit., pp.319–20; Strickland, Agnes, *The Queens of England*, (1854), p.278.
23. Sidney, Philip, (ed.), *Conversations of Ben Jonson with William Drummond*, (1900), p.37.
24. Steinmetz, Andrew, *History of the Jesuits*, (1848), p.126.

25. Bohun, Edmund, *The Character of Queen Elizabeth*, (1693) p.302.
26. Wardrobe Warrant, 8 April 1600, TNA, LC 5/37 f.195, transcript at elizabethancostume.net.
27. Walpole, Horace, (ed.), op. cit., p.48; Williams, Clare, (ed.), *Thomas Platter's Travels in England 1599*, (1937), p.192. For an overview of the make-up myth see Steven Veerapen's online article 'Elizabeth I: The Myth of the Makeup' at www.stevenveerapen.com/elizabeth-i-the-myth-of-the-makeup.
28. Howell, James, *A Tale of the Sea: Sonnets, and Other Poems*, (1873), p.181.
29. *The Calcutta Journal of Politics and General Literature*, 22 June 1822, Vol.3, Issue 149.
30. Beesly, Edward Spencer, *Queen Elizabeth*, (1900), p.239.
31. Varlow, Sally, 'Sir Francis Knollys's Latin Dictionary: New Evidence for Katherine Carey', in *Historical Research*, Vol.80, Issue 209, (2007).
32. Dunn, Wendy J., *Henry VIII's True Daughter: Catherine Carey, a Tudor Life*, (2023).
33. 'Papers Relating to Mary, Queen of Scots, Communicated by Gen. Sir W. Knollys', *Miscellanies of the Philobiblon Society*, Vol.14, (1872–6), pp.60–67.
34. There was a question hanging over the legitimacy of his paternal line.
35. Wardrobe Warrant, 20 October 1562, TNA, LC 5/3, transcript at elizabethancostume.net.
36. I.e. Wardrobe Warrant, 4 April 1588, TNA, LC 5/36, transcript at elizabethancostume.net.
37. Merton, p.247.
38. Merton, p.96; Richardson, p.61.
39. Based upon *The Order of All Night* as described by Ferdinando Marsham, Esquire of the Body to King Charles I and King Charles II. See Pegge, Samuel and Nichols, John, *Curialia*, (1782), pp.19–23 (p.36 for a description of the royal mortar).
40. Haynes, p.368.
41. Wardrobe Warrants, TNA, LC 5/49.
42. DBWR.
43. Arnold, Janet, *Queen Elizabeth's Wardrobe Unlock'd*, (1988), p.102.
44. CPR, Elizabeth, Vols.1, 3, 5.
45. Merton, p.66, pp.82, 96.
46. DBWR.
47. Eltham Ordinances, op.cit.; Merton, p.18.
48. Walpole, Horace, (ed.), op.cit, p.53; Merton, p.80.
49. I agree with Wendy J. Dunn (op.cit) that Lady Knollys is more likely to have taken her older children, like Lettice, with her into exile than her younger ones. Anne Wingfield is usually identified as a daughter of Sir Anthony Wingfield and Elizabeth de Vere but she may have been a daughter of Joan Knollys, Lady Knollys's sister-in-law, who was married to Sir Charles Wingfield of Kimbolton Castle and is known to have had a daughter named Anne.
50. Elizabeth Clyffe is listed as a 'Maid of the Privy Chamber' in coronation records, and Anne Wingfield as a 'Lady of the Privy Chamber Without Wage', but these are probably clerical errors.

51. David Starkey is also of this opinion. Starkey, David, *Elizabeth*, (2000).
52. Margaret Willoughby, for example, assisted Lady Mary Grey in her secret marriage.
53. TNA, C 115/101/7543.
54. CSP Simancas, 1587–1603, Vol.4, No.15.
55. CSP Foreign, Vol.21, Pt.1, 1586–88.
56. CSP Simancas, 1580–1586, Vol.3, p.274.
57. Bourne, H. R. Fox, *A Memoir of Sir Philip Sidney*, (1862), p.110.
58. Collins, Arthur, op.cit., p.38.
59. Wright, Thomas, *Queen Elizabeth and Her Times*, (1838), Vol.1, p.80.
60. DBWR; various wardrobe warrants (see elizabethancostume.net).
61. DBWR (16 April 1577); Wardrobe Warrant (27 September 1577).
62. Warner, George F., *The Voyage of Robert Dudley*, (1899), p.xlv.
63. Various wardrobe warrants (elizabethancostume.net).
64. Rutland, Vol.1.

Chapter Eight: Chief Gentlewomen

1. Lady Denny's original will survives (TNA, PROB 10/26). Kat signed herself 'Kateryn Aschyly'.
2. Griggs, Rosemary, op.cit.; TNA, PROB 11/43/234.
3. It is presently unclear what Carew's role was in the coronation as reports differ.
4. Klarwill, Victor Von, op.cit., pp.113–114.
5. Howey, Catherine Louise, 'Busy Bodies: Women, Power and Politics at the Court of Queen Elizabeth I 1558–1603', (Ph.D, The State University of New Jersey, 2007), p.99.
6. Harrison, William, op.cit, p.275.
7. CSP Rome 1558–1571, No.190, p.105.
8. 1562, ECDBD.
9. NYGE.
10. Von Klarvill, Victor, op.cit., p.247.
11. CSP Simancas, 1558–1567, Vol.1, No.310.
12. Her place of burial is recorded in the parish register of St Mary le Strand (Savoy Chapel). This 'Katherine Ashley' was definitely Kat as five months later Bridget Skipwith married Brian Cave in the same chapel.
13. For more information on Blanche's early life see Richardson.
14. Wood, Ellen Beatrice, *Rowland Vaughan: His Book*, (1897), p.57.
15. Lady Stafford's monument (Westminster Abbey) put up by her son, Edward.
16. Will of Lady Hawkins, TNA, PROB 11/137/11.
17. The present inscription reads 'hedd chamber' but this is probably a mistake made during the monument's restoration. Ruth Elizabeth Richardson argues that this monument is primary evidence that Queen Elizabeth lived and died a virgin (Richardson, p.vii) and I agree with her conclusion. Blanche is not only asserting Elizabeth's virginity by referring to her as 'a maiden queen'

but is telling us that she is in a position to know as she was 'sworn of Queen Elizabeth's bedchamber *always*'.

18. Will of Blanche Parry, TNA, PROB 11/75/180.
19. Wilson, Violet, op. cit, pp.37–38.
20. Nichols, Vol.1, pp.269–70.
21. British Library Add MS 8159.
22. *Report on the Manuscripts of Lord De l'Isle and Dudley Preserved at Penshurst Place*, Vol.2., p.271.
23. Wilson, Violet, op.cit., p.190.
24. L'Estrange, Nicholas, *et al.*, *Anecdotes and Traditions Illustrative of English History*, (1839), p.8.
25. There are several versions of the Golden Speech. See Marcus, Leah S., *et al.*, *Elizabeth I Collected Works* (2000).
26. Costello, Louisa Stuart, *Memoirs of Eminent Englishwomen*, Vol.1, (1844), p.200.
27. CP 111/149.
28. Boyle, John, Earl of Orrey, op. cit., pp.141–144.
29. Will of Mary Radclyffe, TNA, PROB 11/132/128.
30. Walford, Edward, op. cit., p.265.

Epilogue: Funeral

1. Stow, John, *Annales or a General Chronicle of England*, (1631), p.815.
2. Bradford, Charles Angell, op.cit., pp.177.
3. Stow, John, *Annales,* op.cit., p.815.
4. CP 114/78.

Illustrations

1. Portrait of Henry VIII. Wellcome Collection, licence CC By 4.0.

2. Anne Boleyn (cropped, enhanced). Austrian National Library, Europeana, public domain.

3. Kateryn Astley. Private collection, reproduced with kind permission of Lord Hastings.

4. Blanche Parry, old photo of a lost portrait (cropped). BethANZ via Wikimedia Commons.

5. Mary Hill, Lady Cheke. Private collection, reproduced with kind permission of the Hon. Edward Tollemache.

6. Elyzabeth Fitzgerald, Countess of Lincoln. Reproduced with kind permission of Agecroft Hall and Gardens, Richmond, VA.

7. Portrait believed to be of Kathryn Carey, Lady Knollys. Yale Center for British Art, public domain.

8. Portrait believed to be of Mary Shelton, Lady Scudamore. Yale Center for British Art, public domain.

9. Elizabeth Throckmorton, Lady Raleigh. Private collection, alamy.com.

10. Sir Walter Raleigh. Stipple engraving by W. Holl. Wellcome Collection, public domain.

11. Katheryn Carey, Countess of Nottingham (cropped). Heritage Image Partnership Ltd, alamy.com.

12. Margaret Vaughan, Lady Hawkins. Reproduced with kind permission of Lady Hawkins' School.

13. The Procession Picture of Queen Elizabeth I. Yale Center for British Art, public domain.

14, 15, 16. Funeral Procession. Engraving by J. Basire after a drawing by William Camden, 1791. Wellcome Collection, public domain.

17. Signature collage by Heather Shanette. Signatures taken from *Day Book of the Wardrobe of Robes* (TNA, C 115/91). Signatures reproduced with permission.

18. Savoy Chapel (cropped). © John Salmon, geograph.org.uk.

19. Blanche Parry's monument, St Faith's Church (cropped). © Fabian Musto, geograph.org.uk.

20. Window, St Eata's Church (cropped). © Michael Day, flickr.com.

21. Bacton Altar Cloth (cropped). © Philip Pankhurst, geograph.org.uk.

22. Lady Carew's tomb, Exeter Cathedral. © Oliver D. Harris.

23. Memorial to Elizabeth Stafford, Lady Drury/Scott, St Mary's Church (cropped). © Julian P. Guffogg, geograph.org.uk.

24. Lady Bridget Manners, Bottesford Church, Leicestershire. © J. Hannan-Briggs, geography.org.uk.

25. Memorial to Bregett Chaworth Carr, St Andrew's Church, Ufford. © Richard Croft, geograph.org.uk.

26. Layout of a Tudor Palace. © Heather Shanette.

27. Queen Elizabeth's Paternal Family Tree. © Heather Shanette.

28. Queen Elizabeth's Maternal Family Tree. © Heather Shanette.

Glossary

bed of state: the monarch's bed, typically a grand four poster bed with curtains and a canopy of state. Paul Hentzner, a visitor to England in 1598, described the Queen's bed at Whitehall Palace as 'ingeniously composed of woods of different colours, with quilts of silk, velvet, gold, silver, and embroidery', and revealed that at Windsor Castle 'the royal beds of Henry VII and his Queen, of Edward VI, of Henry VIII and of Anne Boleyn' were on display in a chamber, 'all of them eleven feet square and covered with quilts shining with gold and silver', but tells us that Queen Elizabeth's bed, 'with curious coverings of embroidery', was 'not quite so long or large as the others'.

caffa: a silk fabric blended with wool or another material.

camlet: an expensive fabric made of silk, wool, mohair, camel or chamois hair and was also known as chamlet or chamblet.

canopy/cloth of state: generally consisted of a tester (luxurious fabric embroidered with the monarch's coat of arms) and a ceeler (canopy) that hung behind and over a monarch's throne, chair, or bed.

chair of state: a ceremonial or formal chair used by a monarch complete with a cloth of state.

Chamber, The: the 'upstairs' of a Tudor palace known in Latin as *Domus Magnificencie*. This was where the monarch lived, worked, worshipped and entertained in a maze of private and state rooms. The private area of the Chamber was known as the Privy Chamber. The state rooms were the Great Chamber, the Guard or Watching Chamber, and the Presence Chamber. Also within the Chamber was the Council Chamber and the Chapel Royal. The Chamber was overseen by the Lord Chamberlain. A monarch's consort traditionally had his/her own Chamber. In Elizabeth's reign this was probably occupied by favourite attendants and courtiers.

Chamberers [*court position*]: women who attended upon the Queen in her Privy Chamber. They were based in the Queen's bedchamber and their main duty appears to have been dressing the Queen and taking care of her clothes. They also performed chambermaid duties and possibly helped the Grooms of the Privy Chamber to keep the other rooms of the Privy Chamber clean and tidy. Chamberers wore gowns of black or russet satin, which they received as livery once a year, and their typical annual salary was £20. The position was a desirable one, as it gave intimate access to the Queen, and was held by ladies as well as gentlewomen. Chamberers were considered 'of the Privy Chamber' and sometimes 'of the Bedchamber'.

chamberers [*general*]: chambermaids in great households.

Chapel Royal: a glorious chapel within the Chamber where the monarch worshipped with courtiers. The monarch had his/her own room within the chapel, known as a holyday closet, that overlooked the chapel below. There was also a holyday closet for the consort.

Chief Gentlewoman of the Privy Chamber: the most important position in the Privy Chamber. The Chief Gentlewoman was in charge of the Privy Chamber, of all its staff, and had overall charge of all the Queen's women (whether of the Privy Chamber or not). She also personally attended upon the Queen and managed her daily schedule.

Chief Lady of the Bedchamber: the most prestigious position in the Privy Chamber. This position was seemingly created in 1558/9 for Queen Elizabeth's first cousin, Kathryn Carey, Lady Knollys. The Chief Lady of the Bedchamber was in charge of the royal bedchamber and was the Queen's principal attendant there. She was assisted in her duties by the Groom of the Stool and the Ladies and Gentlewomen of the Bedchamber.

Chief Lady of Honour: highest ranking or closest in blood to the Queen of the Ladies of Honour present at any given event. The Chief Lady of Honour fronted the other ladies, had the honour of bearing the Queen's train (often with assistance) in processions, and sat with the Queen in public.

cloth of gold: an expensive metallic fabric containing real gold. It came in various colours and finishes.

coffer chamber: a room within the Chamber, close to the Privy Chamber, where the Queen's women, and other favoured courtiers, socialised. It was perfectly situated for Ladies and Maids of Honour, who did not have right of access to the Privy Chamber, to await the Queen's pleasure in.

Council Chamber: a sizeable room in the Chamber where the Privy Council met. The Council Chamber of Whitehall Palace was so large and grand that Lord and Lady Warwick's wedding reception was held in it.

damask: a patterned silk fabric but could also be made of wool or linen.

Esquires/Knights of the Body: historically these were body servants who dressed the monarch but by the reign of Henry VIII their duties had been taken over by the Gentlemen of the Privy Chamber. By the reign of Queen Elizabeth they were based in the Presence Chamber and their main importance was at night. At night one of the esquires would be invested with the combined authority of the Lord Chamberlain and the Lord Steward, following an ancient ceremony known as 'The Order of All Night', and he would take charge of the entire court until morning.

gentlewomen of the household: gentlewomen who served the Queen but were not 'of the Privy Chamber'. The exact nature of their role is presently unclear but they probably assisted the women of the Privy Chamber by performing more menial tasks. By 1603 they were known as 'the Queen's women'.

Gentlemen of the Privy Chamber: gentlemen who attended upon a monarch in the Privy Chamber. There were few in the reign of a queen. They were paid £33 6s 8d a year and received livery.

Gentlemen Pensioners: 50 courtiers who served as the monarch's ceremonial bodyguard. They famously carried gilt battle-axes. In charge of them was the Captain of the Gentlemen Pensioners.

Great Chamber: first state room within the Chamber. In some palaces it was combined with the Watching Chamber to form the Great Watching Chamber. It was a grand reception hall where important courtiers congregated and where the Lord Chamberlain, Lord Steward, Master of the Horse and Maids of Honour dined.

Great Hall: a glorious hall that bridged the 'upstairs' and 'downstairs' areas of a Tudor palace. Courtiers who did not have right of access to the Chamber congregated here and workers dined here twice a day. The Great Hall was often the monarch's choice of venue for plays and masques.

Groom of the Stool: in the reign of Henry VIII the Groom of the Stool was in charge of the royal bedchamber and of the King's close stool (commode). Famously he assisted the King on the toilet (though he may have handed the King a cloth rather than wiping the royal bottom). The position was held by the Chief Gentleman of the Privy Chamber. In the reign of Elizabeth, the Chief Lady of the Bedchamber was in charge of the royal bedchamber, but for the first three decades of the Queen's reign the position of Groom of the Stool was seemingly held by the Chief Gentlewoman of the Privy Chamber. For the last decade the Chief Lady of the Bedchamber assumed the role, beginning a long-standing tradition. Perhaps for the sake of decorum the title was never feminised.

Grooms of the Privy Chamber: men who served in the Privy Chamber. They assisted the gentlemen and were responsible for keeping the rooms clean and tidy, making fires, and lining the floors with fresh straw. They received livery and were paid £20 a year.

grosgrain: a ribbed fabric made of silk and wool.

Gentleman Usher of the Privy Chamber: a gentleman or knight who controlled access to the Privy Chamber. He was paid £33 6s 8d a year and received livery.

Household, The: the 'downstairs' of a Tudor palace known in Latin as *Domus Providencie*. It was staffed exclusively by men and included the kitchens, cellar, laundry, chaundry, scullery, wood yard and gardens (see *Stars in the Presence of the Sun*).

Keeper of the Privy Purse: responsible for managing the monarch's private income.

Ladies and Gentlewomen of the Bedchamber: ladies and gentlewomen who attended upon the Queen in her bedchamber. The position was created in 1558/9 when Queen Elizabeth, inspired by the staffing structure of her brother's reign, appointed four principal attendants to serve her in her bedchamber. Ladies and Gentlewomen of the Bedchamber topped the hierarchy of female attendants in the Privy Chamber and were also considered 'of the Privy Chamber'. Typical salary £33 6s 8d a year.

Ladies and Gentlewomen of the Privy Chamber: ladies and gentlewomen who attended upon the Queen in her Privy Chamber. Salaried attendants were known as 'ordinaries' and reserve attendants were known as 'extraordinaries'. There were also honorary attendants who were known as 'Ladies of the Privy Chamber Without Wage'. Typical salary of ordinaries was £33 6s 8d a year. Ladies and Gentlewomen of the Bedchamber, Chamberers, and Maids of the Privy Chamber also fell under the umbrella term 'Ladies and Gentlewomen of the Privy Chamber'.

Ladies of Honour: peeresses, dames (wives of knights), titled daughters of nobles. These were ceremonial escorts who escorted the Queen on state occasions, in public processions, and in court ceremonies. They also sometimes accompanied the Queen on her travels. Their number ranged from dozens to just a few depending on the event.

Lady Admiral: courtesy title given to the Lord High Admiral's wife.

lady carver: carved the Queen's meat in private and ceremoniously accepted the Queen's meals in the Presence Chamber when the Queen was not dining there. The position was an honorary one bestowed (as needed or for a certain period of time) upon a favoured noblewoman of the Privy Chamber. Only the names of two lady carvers are known, both serving in the 1590s: Lady Bridget Manners and Frauncis Howard, Countess of Kildare. The court's official Carvers (there was more than one) carved when the Queen dined in public.

Lady Chamberlain: courtesy title given to the Lord Chamberlain's wife.

Lord Chamberlain: presided over the Chamber and was the most important of three officials in charge of the royal court. He was assisted by the Vice-Chamberlain.

lady cupbearer: it is presently unclear whether the Queen had a lady cupbearer, as did her successor, Queen Anne, but if she did then the lady cupbearer's duty was to pour the Queen wine at mealtimes and, possibly, to bring in the grace cup at the end of dinner. The role, if it existed, was honorary and was probably reserved for noblewomen.

Lady Governess: by the reign of Henry VIII she presided over the household of a prince or princess or was responsible for the 'governance' and 'education' of royal children once they left the care of their Lady Mistress. There could be several Lady Governesses at the same time.

Lady Mistress: presided over the royal nursery and was known as 'Lady Mistress of the King's Nursery' or 'Lady Mistress to the Prince/Princess' (if only one child in the nursery). By the reign of Henry VIII she looked after children in early childhood only (0–6 years) and her 'office and fee' had seemingly become a lifelong honour meaning there could be no other official Lady Mistress during her lifetime.

lady taster: responsible for 'tasting' the Queen's food for poison. She did not taste the food herself but gave every yeoman who brought in a dish for the Queen a mouthful of the dish he had brought. The role was honorary, like that of lady carver and lady cupbearer, and was probably reserved for noblewomen.

Lord High Admiral: official in charge of the royal navy and maritime affairs.

Lord Steward: presided over the Household and was the second most important of three officials in charge of the royal court.

Laundress of the Board: a laundress responsible for the Queen's table cloths. She received livery and a salary.

ladies of the household: court ladies who served the Queen but were not 'of the Privy Chamber'. They existed in 1558 but were gone by 1603, probably having been absorbed into the Ladies of Honour very early in the reign.

Mistress Laundress: the Queen's personal laundress. She received livery and a salary of about £4 a year.

Maids of the Privy Chamber: junior/trainee attendants of the Privy Chamber. They were usually the teenage daughters of favoured attendants and courtiers, some as young as 12 or 13. They may have received the same wage as Maids of

Honour and may have slept in the maidens' chamber with them. The position was first created in 1558/9 for the Queen's Hatfield maids but was abandoned in 1559 when the maids started to marry. The position was seemingly revived (and revised) in the early 1560s as an alternative debutante position to Maids of Honour for young aristocratic girls. Whether these girls were actually known as 'Maids of the Privy Chamber' is uncertain but the title is a useful one to describe them.

Maids of Honour: unmarried girls and women who were primarily the Queen's personal escort. They generally numbered six and they escorted the Queen around her palaces, gardens and parks, and accompanied her wherever she went. The maids also entertained the Queen, and sometimes visitors to court, with dances and masques; had a role to play at mealtimes; and may have had some duties in the Privy Chamber. Contrary to myth, the maids were at least 16 years of age upon recruitment and 'twenty-something' seems to have been the average age of a maid. The maids slept together in the maidens' chamber and received a salary of £10 rising to £20 by the end of the reign. They were supervised by the Mother of the Maids.

Mother of the Maids: supervised and organised the Maids of Honour (and possibly had some responsibility for the young Maids of the Privy Chamber). She was usually a Gentlewoman of the Privy Chamber and her salary was £20 a year.

maidens' chamber, the: a dormitory where the Maids of Honour, and possibly the young Maids of the Privy Chamber, slept. In smaller palaces this may have been one single room with multiple beds but in larger palaces some of the maids had their own private closet or partitioned bay within the dormitory (see *Maids of Honour*). The maidens' chamber was probably close to, or within, the apartment traditionally occupied by the queen consort.

Master of the Horse: presided over the royal stables and was responsible for all the horses used for travel, ceremony and sport. He was the third most important of three officials in charge of the royal court. Usually rode before Ladies of Honour in processions.

murrey: a reddish purple colour.

Order of All Night, The: a court ceremony that officially put the monarch to bed. It was led by an Esquire of the Body who, wearing a cloak and sword, carried the royal mortar to the royal bedchamber. When the monarch gave the order of 'All Night' the esquire was placed in charge of the entire court until morning.

parasol: described in the Queen's wardrobe records as a 'canopy of crimson caffa damask to carry over one, striped with lace of Venice gold and silver, the handle mother-of-pearl', parasols were increasing in popularity over the course of the sixteenth century. They were often a grand canopy supported by two poles and Queen Elizabeth stands under one of these, which is held up by her women, in a painting entitled *Elizabeth I and the Three Goddesses* by Isaac Oliver *c.*1588 (National Portrait Gallery).

passamayne: a type of bobbin lace (made by braiding and twisting lengths of thread wound on bobbins of bone, ivory or wood).

Presence Chamber: third and most important state room within the Chamber. Also known as 'the throne room', it was a magnificent hall where the monarch formally held court. Seated upon a throne topped with a canopy of state the monarch would receive visitors to court, hold audiences, watch entertainments and socialise with courtiers. The monarch's two official meals a day were served in the Presence Chamber with great ceremony. Amongst those based in the Presence Chamber were the Gentlemen Pensioners and the Esquires of the Body.

Privy Chamber *(capitalised)*: [apartment] privy (private) area of the Chamber where the monarch resided in a magnificent suite of rooms. This apartment contained several withdrawing chambers, dining rooms, bedchambers, a study, a privy chapel, a gallery, sometimes a bathroom, and most importantly the royal bedchamber and the privy chamber [parlour]. The Privy Chamber was also known as the Privy Lodgings.

privy chamber *(uncapitalised)*: [parlour] a prestigious parlour, containing a 'chair of state', within the Privy Chamber where the monarch relaxed, held private audiences, socialised with favourite courtiers, and enjoyed private entertainments. By the reign of Queen Elizabeth the privy chamber had evolved into the hub of an exclusive club of courtiers (predominantly female in the reign of a queen) who were 'of the Privy Chamber'. This parlour gave its name to, and took its name from, the Privy Chamber, as historically it was the principal, if not the only, room in the Privy Lodgings.

privy kitchen: a private kitchen to prepare and cook food for the monarch. It was separate to the court's other kitchens that prepared and cooked food for workers and courtiers. Henry VIII liked to have his privy kitchen close to his apartment. Queen Elizabeth, who did not share his appetite and was sensitive to 'heat and noise', preferred to have hers further away.

privy chapel: a private chapel in the Privy Chamber where the monarch could worship and pray alone or with favoured attendants.

privy garden: this was a private garden for the monarch's use and was accessed, usually by stairs, from the Privy Chamber.

puke: a woollen cloth of reddish or greenish brown.

Queen's colours: white, green, red, black. In Tudor times the servants of aristocrats wore uniforms or badges in their master's or mistress's colours (determined by dynastic tradition or personal preference). The colours of the Tudor monarchs were white and green and Elizabeth's personal colours were red and black (her yeomen pre-accession wore red and black coats).

royal bedchamber: this was a grand room in the Privy Chamber where the monarch slept on a 'bed of state'.

royal mortar: a large and flat candle of virgin wax set afloat in a silver basin. It was delivered to the royal bedchamber every night in a ceremony called 'The Order of All Night'.

sarcenet: a soft and thin silk fabric mainly used for lining garments.

scarlet: an expensive red woollen cloth.

taffeta: a soft and smooth silk fabric.

tawny: a brownish orange colour.

tinsel: very similar to cloth of gold except that it was lighter as it did not contain as much precious metal.

Vice-Chamberlain: assisted the Lord Chamberlain in managing the Chamber.

Watching Chamber: second state room within the Chamber where Yeomen of the Guard controlled access to the Presence Chamber. It was sometimes combined with the Great Chamber to form the Great Watching Chamber.

Yeomen of the Guard: the monarch's official bodyguard, sometimes 100 or more in number. They wore red coats adorned with the Queen's badge (Tudor rose with crown) and they guarded the Queen and the passages of her palaces. Some yeomen held more than one position, and the wives of some yeomen served the Queen. The Watching Chamber was their main base.

APPENDICES

Nugae Antiquae:
A Problem Source

THE BOOK *Nugae Antiquae*, first published in two volumes between 1769 and 1775, purportedly contains transcripts of 'original papers in prose and verse' from the Harington family archive. The Haringtons were a prominent family in the Elizabethan age as one of the Queen's favourite attendants, Isabella Markham, married into the family and her son, John, became something of a favourite with the Queen who was his godmother. *Nugae Antiquae* proved to be a popular publication and was enlarged into three volumes. For generations it has been a primary source of information for historians, not least because it contains many interesting and amusing anecdotes, but unfortunately, when it comes to material about the Queen's women, the book is a problem source.

It is from a single letter, printed within the second volume of 1775, that two very popular stories about Queen Elizabeth and her women are taken. The letter is purportedly from John Harington to his cousin, Robert Markham, and is dated 1606. The two stories are best told directly from the letter:

> (**Story 1**) [The Queen] did oft ask the ladies around her chamber if they loved to think of marriage. And the wise ones did conceal well their liking hereto as knowing the Queen's judgement in this matter. Sir Mathew Arundel's fair cousin, not knowing so deeply as her fellows, was asked one day hereof, and simply said she had thought much about marriage, if her father did consent to the man she loved. 'You seem honest, i'faith,' said the Queen, 'I will sue for you to your father.' The damsel was not displeased hereat and, when Sir Robert came to court, the Queen asked him hereon, and pressed his consenting, if the match was discreet. Sir Robert, much astonished at this news, said he never heard his daughter had liking to any man, and wanted to gain knowledge of her affection, but would give free consent to what was most pleasing to Her Highness will and advice. 'Then l will do the rest;' saith the Queen. The lady was called in, and the Queen told her her father had given his free consent. 'Then,' replied the lady, 'I shall be happy, and please Your Grace.' 'So thou shalt, but not to be a fool

and marry. I have his consent given to me, and I vow thou shalt never get it into thy possession: so, go to thy business. I see thou art a bold one, to own thy foolishness so readily.'[1]

(**Story 2**) She [Elizabeth] did love rich clothing, but often chid those that bought more finery than became their state. It happened that Lady M. Howard was possessed of a rich border, powdered with gold and pearl, and a velvet suite belonging thereto, which moved many to envy; nor did it please the Queen who thought it exceeded her own. One day the Queen did send privately, and got the lady's rich vesture, which she put on herself, and came forth the chamber among the ladies. The kirtle and border was far too short for Her Majesty's height and she asked everyone how they liked her new-fancied suit? At length, she asked the owner herself, if it was not made too short and ill-becoming? – which the poor lady did presently consent to. 'Why then, if it become not me, as being too short, I am minded it shall never become thee, as being too fine, so it fitteth neither well.' This sharp rebuke abashed the lady and she never adorned her herewith any more. I believe the vestment was laid up till after the Queen's death.[2]

The Queen's problems with a 'Lady Mary Howard' are also told in another letter, allegedly written to Harington by a man named William Fenton and published in the first volume of 1769:

I have not seen Her Highness, save twice, since Easter last, both of which times she spoke vehemently and with great wrath of her servant, the Lady Mary Howard, forasmuch as she had refused to bear her mantle at the hour Her Highness is wonted to air in the garden, and on small rebuke did vent such unseemly answer as did breed much choler in her mistress. Again, on other occasion, she was not ready to carry the cup of grace during the dinner in the Privy Chamber, nor was she attending at the hour of Her Majesty's going to prayer. All which doth now so disquiet Her Highness, that she swore she would no more show her any countenance, but out with all such ungracious flouting wenches; because, forsooth, she hath much favour and marks of love from the young earl, which is not so pleasing to the Queen, who doth still much exhort all her women to remain in virgin state as much as may be. I adventured to say, as far as discretion did go, in defence of our friend, and did urge much in behalf of youth and enticing love, which did often abate of right measures in fair ladies; and moreover related whatever might please the Queen, touching the confession of her great kindness to her sister Jane before her marriage; all which did nothing soothe Her Highness's anger, saying, 'I have made her my servant, and she will now make herself my mistress; but in good faith, William, she shall not, and so tell her'. In short, pity doth move me to save this lady, and would beg such suit to the Queen from you and your friends, as may win her favour to spare her on future amendment. If you could speak to Mr. Bellot, to urge the Lord Treasurer on this matter, it might be to good purpose, when a better time doth offer to move the Queen than I had, for words then were to no avail, though as discreetly brought as I was able. It might not be amiss to talk to this poor young lady to be more dutiful, and not absent at meals or prayers, to bear Her Highness's mantle and other furniture, even more than all the rest of the servants, to make ample amends by future diligence; and always to go first in the morning to Her Highness's chamber, forasmuch as such kindness will much prevail to turn away all former displeasure. She must not entertain my lord the earl in any conversation but shun his company and, moreover, be less careful in attiring her own person, for this seemeth as done more to win the earl than her mistress's good will. [3]

There are numerous problems with these anecdotes. First, Lady M. Howard and Lady Mary Howard cannot be the same lady as the Fenton letter is dated 1597 whereas Sir John tells his cousin that the incident involving Lady M. Howard 'fell out when I was a boy', i.e. thirty years earlier. Identifying the ladies is also problematic. There is no record of a Lady Mary Howard having served the Queen in the last decade of her reign or of her alleged sister Lady Jane Howard. Lady M. Howard of the dress incident could be Margrett Gamage, Baroness Howard of Effingham, the Queen's great aunt, or her daughter, Mary Howard, a Maid of Honour, but Mary was not a titled lady and the Queen was very close to both women. Indeed, rather than jealously wanting to deprive Mary of beautiful clothes, the Queen gave her cousin at least two luxurious velvet gowns, one in the royal colour of purple and the other in black. The Queen's women were also exempt from the sumptuary laws for the very reason that they could 'dress in more finery than became their state'. Regarding Lady Jane Howard, the only woman of that name known to have served the Queen did so at the beginning of the reign, not at the end, and she was not Mary's sister but her cousin. There is also no record of a young girl surnamed Arundel having ever served the Queen. The only Arundel known to have served was Margaret Willoughby, Lady Arundel, wife of Sir Thomas Arundel himself. The 'Sir Robert' of the anecdote is sometimes identified as Sir Robert Arundel of Trerice, a distant relative of Sir Thomas's, but there is no record of any daughter of his having served the Queen. There are also things said in the Fenton letter that stretch credulity. For example, it is hard to believe that Fenton would need Harington's intervention to save Lady Mary Howard, or that he would want to bother someone as important, busy, and by then infirm as Lord Burghley on the matter, especially as his daughter-in-law had just died, for if the lady was a Howard she would have the whole Howard clan at court pleading her case.

William Fenton also makes the claim that:

[The Queen] doth not now bear with such composed spirit as she was wont, but since the Irish affairs seemeth more froward than commonly she used to bear herself toward her women, nor doth she hold them in discourse with such familiar matter, but often chides for small neglects, in such wise as to make these fair maids often cry and bewail in piteous sort, as I am told by my sister, Elizabeth.[4]

This letter has done much to feed the myth that 'Queen Elizabeth of England used to beat her Maids of Honour so that they cried piteously'[5] but how much should we credit this letter? Is it genuine? Is the letter by John Harington genuine? William Fenton has yet to be identified and there is no record of an Elizabeth Fenton serving the Queen (although she may have been married, so known by another name, or may have retired prior to the Queen's funeral). Just because a book is published claiming to contain 'original papers' does not mean that it actually does. There are many reasons why a publication may contain fictional or semi-fictional content, for instance to make a publication more interesting; to increase sales and thereby profit; to further a certain political, religious or social agenda; or to redeem or ruin a reputation. The only way of knowing for sure that published transcripts are genuine is to locate the originals and make a comparison. If the originals are lost then this is impossible and a historian must consequently make a value judgement regarding the authenticity of the alleged transcripts. Unfortunately, the history of the *Nugae Antiquae* itself does not inspire confidence in its reliability. This is because the first two volumes were allegedly compiled by a teenage boy, Henry Harington, who was only 14 years old in 1769. Despite recognising the historical value of the 'original papers', the boy supposedly gave the manuscripts to the printer and allowed over eighty folios to be destroyed.[6] Amongst those manuscripts lost are seemingly these letters by Harington and Fenton. However, the editor of the 1769 edition tells us that some of the letters were not transcribed from originals at all but from 'very obscure and ill-written copies'. The editor also asks the reader to 'excuse any erroneous dates or names which may occur from the transcriber's mistaking obscure characters in the MSS, or if he finds any pieces which may be inserted in some old scarce publications, unknown to the editor'. Further, the editor tells us that 'the original spelling in some of these letters is not preserved' due to the 'great difficulty' in transcribing from these 'obscure and ill-written copies' and 'to save time'. A red flag, perhaps, regarding the authenticity of the Harington anecdotes is a poem published in later editions of *Nugae Antiquae* entitled *The Praise of Eight Ladies of Queen Elizabeth's Court.* Two of these ladies are surnamed 'Howard' and 'Arundel':

Howard is not haughty,
But of such smiling cheer,
That would allure each gentle heart,
His love to hold full dear.

Arundel is ancient
In these her tender years,

In heart, in voice, in talk, in deed,
A matron's wit appears.[7]

However, the women named in the poem (Howard, Arundel, Dacre, Baynam, Dormer, Mansell, Cooke, and Brydges) were not attendant upon Queen Elizabeth but upon her predecessor, Queen Mary. Amongst Queen Mary's maids at the close of her reign were: Mary Howard, Cecilia Arundel, Magdelene Dacre, Mary Mansell, Margaret Cooke and Jane Dormer. Cecilia Arundel is of particular interest as she was 'Sir Mathew Arundel's fair cousin', as their fathers were brothers, but she did not go on to serve Queen Elizabeth as she was a devout Catholic. So, the inevitable conclusion is that *if* someone was going to make up stories (even Harington himself), forge historical letters, or make fictional additions to authentic letters, then using the names of two women included in a poem thought to be about 'eight ladies of Queen Elizabeth's court' would be a very good place to start.

Other letters in the *Nugae Antiquae* that are relevant to the Queen's women also have a confused chronology. The most important are those concerning Isabella Markham, John Harington's mother, and Ethelreda Harington, his father's first wife. Based on a letter, purportedly written from the Tower of London by John's father, also named John Harington, to Stephen Gardiner, Bishop of Winchester, it is assumed that Ethelreda, along with Isabella, was in the service of Queen Elizabeth pre-accession and that she was one of the 'three gentlewomen' attendant upon her during her imprisonment in the Tower in 1554. In this letter, also amongst the lost, John's father says 'my wife is her [Elizabeth's] servant'.[8] If this letter is indeed genuine, then Ethelreda certainly was in the service of Princess Elizabeth as she, not Isabella, was married to John's father at the time. However, there is considerable room for doubt over the authenticity of the letter. It is clear that the compilers of the various volumes of *Nugae Antiquae* were under the impression that Isabella, not Ethelreda, was married to John's father at the time, as they have dated love poems to her from John's father to 1549, a decade before the couple were actually married and when John's father was still married to Ethelreda. The traditional narrative goes that John's father, regardless of being married, had fallen in love with Isabella when he was first imprisoned in the Tower in 1549, as her father was Lieutenant of the Tower and she may have been living there with him before entering the princess's service, but this is in conflict with another statement in *Nugae Antiquae* by John's father that says 'I first thought her [Isabella] fair as she stood at the princess's window in goodly attire and talked to divers in the courtyard'.[9] The dating of poems to 1549 is obviously a mistake and the late 1550s would be a more accurate date when John's father was a widower and Isabella was in the princess's service. Besides this printed letter from John's father to Stephen Gardiner there is nothing to suggest that Ethelreda was in the princess's service.

Nugae Antiquae (1769) also makes the bold claim that Ethelreda was an illegitimate daughter of Henry VIII. This claim is made in a letter purportedly written by John Harington to William Cecil, Lord Burghley, in 1595, in which he says 'my father ... had his [the King's] goodly Esther to wife' and in a supporting note the editor says 'This Esther was a natural daughter of the King's'.[10] This claim is again made in another letter, dated sixty years later, from a John Leslie to a James Harington:

> The great King Henry VIII matched his darling daughter to John Harington, and, though a bastard, dowered her with the rich lands of Baths priory, and Queen Elizabeth affected these faithful servants so much, as to become godmother to their son, and made him a knight for his wit and his valour.[11]

Again, Isabella and Ethelreda have been confused, for it was Isabella, not Ethelreda, who was John's mother, and Isabella who was in the princess's service. Also, Ethelreda's name was not Esther. Her name is sometimes given as Audrey but Audrey was a shortened form of Ethelreda that was common in the sixteenth century. Esther or Hester was Ethelreda's daughter, John Harington's half-sister, and she is thought to have lived into the seventeenth century. It is true that Henry VIII bestowed the lands of Bath's Priory upon Ethelreda, the grant being made to her and her reputed father, John Malte, the King's tailor, in 1546, just before John Malte died, but this does not prove that the King was her father. Although the grant was unusual, Henry could be generous to those he liked, and John Malte had served him well for many years. Because of this claim in *Nugae Antiquae*, the question of whether Ethelreda was the King's illegitimate daughter will forever be asked, but in his will of 1546 John Malte described Ethelreda, who was not yet 15 years of age, as 'my bastard daughter begotten upon the body of Joanne (Johane) Dyngley' and this, in a document made 'in the name of God, Amen', is probably the truth.[12]

There are more historical inaccuracies in another letter, also seemingly lost, by John Harington to Prince Henry, son of King James I. In this letter Harington tells the prince that his mother, Isabella, was amongst the women separated from Princess Elizabeth when she was imprisoned in the Tower and 'obliged to dwell with Mr Topcliffe as an heretic'.[13] This 'Mr Topcliffe' is clearly meant to be Richard Topcliffe, the infamous state torturer, but he was not in royal service in 1554 as he was still a very young man. However, Harington makes this claim in his *Brief View of the State of the Church of England*, first published in 1653 (and a work to which this letter refers) so it is not a claim new to *Nugae Antiquae*. Indeed, in this work, Harington says Isabella was glad to lodge with Topcliffe because 'her father dared not take her into his house'. In a postscript to this letter to Prince Henry, Harington tells the prince that he is sending him a picture of Princess Elizabeth, a picture 'printed from a copper, graved by a most skilful artist, and given by her, as a token of her affection, to my mother', informing him that it is 'of rare workmanship, as it is cut in metal, which few did then ever attempt to do'. The editor of the first edition claims to still have this copper plate, from which a picture of 'Lady Elizabeth' has been printed at the beginning of the book, and informs readers that the plate was given by the princess 'to her attendant, Isabella Harington, soon after her enlargement from the Tower, 1554'. But of course, Elizabeth did not gain her freedom for another year, as she was kept a prisoner in Woodstock, and unless Isabella was one of the gentlewomen in attendance upon her there (it is a possibility) then there would not have been an opportunity for Elizabeth to give her the plate until late 1555 when she was back at Hatfield. The print of the princess purportedly made from this plate also suggests a costume more consistent with the 1580s than the 1550s.

There are, then, tremendous problems with *Nugae Antiquae* as a historical source, which is unfortunate as it has had a profound influence on the historiography of Queen Elizabeth's reign. The problems are also frustrating because it is incredibly difficult, if not impossible, to discern what is true in the publication and what is not. Some letters by Harington survive, and the poems written by his father are undoubtedly authentic, so the resource is impossible to discredit completely but also impossible to credit completely. A historian, therefore, needs to use this resource with great caution and, for all these reasons, *Nugae Antiquae* has not been used as a source for this book, and Ethelreda Harington has not been listed as one of the Queen's gentlewomen attendants. However, a poem by John Harington (senior) in praise of six maids attending Elizabeth at Hatfield, either before her accession or immediately upon it, is worth quoting in full.[14] The identity of the first maid, surnamed Grey, remains something of a mystery, but popular candidates include Honora Grey, daughter of William Grey, Baron Grey de Wilton, who married Kat Astley's nephew Henry Denny; a young daughter, sometimes named Anne, of Lord John Grey of Pyrgo; and Lady Katherine Grey. Of these, a young daughter of Lord John Grey of Pyrgo is most convincing in context, for John had the courtesy title of 'Lord' as the son of a Marquess, which the line 'the falcon's courtesy kind' might be alluding to, but if she was indeed in Elizabeth's service then she had died by the coronation.

> The great Diana chaste,
> In forest late I met,
> Who did command in haste
> To Hatfield for to get;
> And to you six a row,
> Her pleasure to declare,
> Thus meaning to bestow
> On each a gift most rare.
>
> First doth she give to *Grey*,
> The falcon's courtesy kind,
> Her lord for to obey,
> With most obedient mind;
> Fraught with such virtues rare,
> His love aye [ever] to renew,
> With Thisbe to compare
> Or Pyramus most true.
>
> To worthy *Willoughby*,
> As eagle in her flight,
> So shall her piercing eye

Both wound and heal each wight
That shall upon her gaze,
And soon perceive, I see,
A Laura in her face,
And not a Willoughby.

To *Markham's* modest mind,
That phoenix bird most rare,
So have the gods assigned
With Griselde to compare.
Oh, happy twice is he
Whom Jove shall do the grace,
To link in unity,
Such beauty to embrace.

To *Norwich*, good and grave,
Such sapient ears we send,
As prudent serpents have,
That charmer to defend;
With knowledge in foresight
Of such things yet to come,
As had Cassandra bright,
Who told of Troy the doom.

For *St Loe*, doth she say,
So stable shall she stand,
As rock within the sea
Or huge hill on the land.
Die rather with the mace
From Hercules' stout hand,
Than once her truth disgrace,
If she therein do stand.

If *Skipwith* should escape
Without her gift most rare,
Diana would me hate,
And fill my life with care.
Since in her temple chaste,
Full high upon the wall,
Her bow there hangeth fast,
Unbroke and ever shall.

Thus have I showed you all,
This gracious Goddess' will,
Who hath decreed you shall
As her own imps live still;
Long in such favour'd sort,

Whereof Dame Fame shall blow
Such trump of true report
As through the Earth shall go.

References

1. *Nugae Antiquae*, 1775, pp.218–9.
2. Ibid., pp.219–220.
3. *Nugae Antiquae*, 1769, pp.75–6.
4. Ibid, p.77.
5. For example: *The Youth's Companion*, 1 October 1874, Vol.47, p.320.
6. MacKinnon, M. H. M, 'The Arundel Harington Manuscript', *University of Toronto Quarterly*, Vol.32, No.1, October 1962, p.81.
7. Park, Thomas (ed.), *Nugae Antiquae*, Vol.2, 1804, p.393.
8. *Nugae Antiquae*, 1769, p.63.
9. Ibid., p.129.
10. Ibid., pp.132–3.
11. Ibid., p.83.
12. Will of John Malte, TNA, PROB 11/31/525.
13. *Nugae Antiquae,* 1769, p.61.
14. Jessica Carey-Bunning suggests that the poem was written at Elizabeth's accession (or soon after): www.tudortreasures.net/new-research-a-poem-on-elizabeth-is-ladies. Until her first six official Maids of Honour were appointed, which would not have been immediately, Elizabeth's existing Hatfield maids would have escorted her.

Women Who Served
1533–1603

THIS SECTION LISTS all the women presently known to have served Elizabeth over the course of her life and reign, the positions they served in, and their length of service. Also listed are all the women known to have served at Elizabeth's coronation and funeral. As most noblewomen served as Ladies of Honour from time to time, only those Ladies of Honour who served at the coronation and funeral have been listed.

For brief biographical details on each woman see the *Index of Women,* which lists every woman by surname (not title). Most women are listed under their maiden name, or the name they were known by when entering the Queen's service, but if they married during their time in service and are listed under their married name then this name is shown within []

The information in this section (and in the *Index of Women*) should be considered guide material only as there is still much research needed on the Queen's ladies, gentlewomen and maids.

The lists in this section have been compiled from a number of sources. The main secondary sources are those given in the *Further Reading* section. The main primary sources are the following:

Princess Elizabeth (1533–1558)

- Staff Lists in the State Papers (LP Henry VIII, Vol.10, No.1187). Note: These two staff lists are both dated 1536 in the state papers but this is too early. The first dates from about 1538 as Lady Troy heads the list followed by 'Mrs. Chambrum, Lady Garet, Eliz. Candysche, Mary Norice'. The second list is harder to date but is no earlier than 1539 and no later than 1543 as 'Kateryne Chambernowne' heads the list followed by 'Elizabethe Garret, Mary Hyll, Blanche ap Harrye' (Elizabethe Garret is Elyzabeth Fitzgerald).
- Funeral Records Henry VIII (TNA, LC 2/2).
- Strangford, Viscount, (ed.), *Household Accounts of the Princess Elizabeth 1551–52,* (1853).

Queen Elizabeth (1558–1603)

- Coronation Records (TNA, LC2/4/3).
- Privy Chamber Staff Lists:
  1559 (British Library, Lansdowne MS 3 No. 88 fols.191–2).
  1580 (British Library, Lansdowne MS 29 No.68 fol.161).
  1589 (British Library, Lansdowne MS 59 No.22 fol.43).
- Funeral Records (TNA, LC2/2/4).
- Calendar of Patent Rolls: Elizabeth I (Published Series).
- Day Book of the Wardrobe of Robes (TNA, C 115/91). For a transcript see: Arnold, Janet, *Lost From Her Majesties Back*, (1980).
- Wardrobe Records (many available at elizabethancostume.net)

Abbreviations

D: Duchess of
M: Marchioness of
C: Countess of
V: Viscountess of
B: Baroness of
L: Lady

ast: assistant
d: died
ds: dismissed
c: circa
f: from
m: married
n: new
r: retired

(–): dates unknown

CHRISTENING
10 September 1533

CHIEF GODMOTHER
(D. Norfolk) Agnes Tilney

GODMOTHERS
(M. Dorset) Margaret Wotton
(M. Exeter) Gertrude Blount (Confirmation)

TRAIN BEARER
(C. Kent) Margaret Finch

CHRISOM BEARER
Lady Mary Howard

CHILDHOOD
1533–1549

LADY MISTRESS
(B. Bryan) Margaret Bourchier (1533–1537)

WET NURSE
Agnes Pendred (to *c.*1535)

NURSEMAIDS/ROCKERS
Blanche Parry (possibly) (f.1533)
3+ more

DRY NURSE
Unknown. Possibly Elyzabeth Cavendish [Snow].

GOVERNESS (of Household)
Anne Boleyn, Lady Shelton (possibly) (1536–1537)

GOVERNESSES (of Elizabeth)
(L. Troy) Blanche Milborne (1537–*c.*1539)
Kateryn Champernon Astley (f.*c.*1539–1549)
(L. Tyrwhit) Elizabeth Oxenbridge (1549)

LADIES AND GENTLEWOMEN
(L. Troy) Blanche Milborne (*c.*1533–1537 possibly, *c.*1544–*c.*1547)
Kateryn Champernon [Astley] (1536–*c.*1539)
(L. Gerald) Lady Elyzabeth Grey (by *c.*1538 to *c.*1539)
Elyzabeth Cavendish [Snow] (by *c.*1538–*c.*1539)
Mary Norris (by *c.*1538–*c.*1539)

Blanche Parry (f.*c.*1539)
Elyzabeth Fitzgerald (officially f.*c.*1539–*c.*1543)
Mary Hill (*c.*1540–*c.*1547)
Blanche Whitney (by 1547)

MAIDS
Elizabeth Norwich (by 1547)
Elizabeth Neville [Eynns] (by 1547)
Elizabeth Clyffe (f.*c.*1549)
Bridget Skipwith [Cave] (f.*c.*1549)

CHAMBERERS
Alice Huntercombe (by *c.*1538 to before 1547)
Jane Broadbelt (by *c.*1538 to *c.*1549)
Mistress Poore (possibly) (by 1547)

LAUNDRESS
Joanne Hilton (f.*c.*1533 probably)

THE HATFIELD FLOCK
1550–1558

CHIEF GENTLEWOMAN
Kateryn Champernon Astley (*c.*1550–1554, 1555–1556)
Blanche Parry (f.1556 probably)

GOVERNESS
Widowed Gentlewoman (1556)

GENTLEWOMEN
Blanche Parry (to 1556)
Blanche Whitney (d.*c.*1556)
Elizabeth Norwich (f.1556 possibly)

MAIDS
Elizabeth Neville [Eynns] (m.1550s)
Elizabeth Norwich (to 1554, f.1555)
Elizabeth Clyffe (to 1554, f.1555)
Bridget Skipwith [Cave] (to 1554, f.1555)
Isabella Markham [Harington] (*c.*1550–1554, f.1555)
Anne Poyntz (*c.*1550–*c.*1554)
Elyzabeth St Loe (*c.*1550–1554, f.1555)
Margaret Willoughby (f.1555)

CHAMBERERS
Dorothy Broadbelt [Abington] (*c.*1550–1554, f.1555)
Elyzabeth Marbury (by 1554, f.1554)
Elizabeth Sondes (by 1554 to 1554)
Frances Newton (f.*c.*1555)

LAUNDRESS
Joanne Hilton

TOWER OF LONDON (17 March to 19 May 1554)
WOODSTOCK (May 1554 to April 1555)

ELIZABETH'S THREE WOMEN

1. Elizabeth Sondes – Tower (ds), Woodstock (ds.1554)
   Elyzabeth Marbury – Woodstock (f.1554)
2. Blanche Parry (likely) – Tower and Woodstock
3. Blanche Whitney (possibly) – Tower and Woodstock

QUEEN MARY'S THREE WOMEN SENT TO SERVE ELIZABETH

1. (L. Grey) Anne Jerningham (probably) – Tower and Woodstock (r.1554?)
2. Mary Thomeo – Woodstock (and possibly the Tower)
3. Dorothy Broughton – Woodstock (and possibly the Tower) (r.1554)
   Margaret Morton – Woodstock (f.1554)

OTHERS
Mistress Coldburn – Tower
Bridget Southwell – possibly tutored Elizabeth in Latin at Woodstock

QUEEN
1558–1603

CHIEF GENTLEWOMAN OF THE PRIVY CHAMBER
Kateryn Champernon Astley (1558–1565)
Blanche Parry (1565–1590)
Mary Radclyffe (acting) (1590–1603)

KEEPER OF HER MAJESTY'S JEWELS
Blanche Parry (1558–1571, ast. 1571–1587)
(B. Howard/C. Nottingham) Katheryn Carey (1571–1587, ast. 1587–1603)
Mary Radclyffe (1587–1603)

CHIEF LADY OF THE BEDCHAMBER
(L. Knollys) Kathryn Carey (1559–1569)
(B. Cobham) Frances Newton (possibly) (1574–1592)
(B. Howard/C. Nottingham) Katheryn Carey (possibly) (c.1592–1603)
(B. Scrope) Philadelphia Carey (acting) (1603)

GROOM OF THE STOOL
Kateryn Champernon Astley (1558–1565)
Blanche Parry (probably) (1565–1590)
(B. Howard/C. Nottingham) Katheryn Carey (1590–1603)
(B. Scrope) Philadelphia Carey (probably) (1603)

LADIES AND GENTLEWOMEN OF THE BEDCHAMBER
Kateryn Champernon Astley (1558–1565)
Blanche Parry (1558–1590)
(L. Carew) Elizabeth Norwich (1558–1594)
(B. Cobham) Frances Newton (c.1564–1571, 1574–1592)
Mary Radclyffe (c.1585–1603)
(B. Howard/C. Nottingham) Katheryn Carey (c.1590–1603)
(L. Cecil) Elizabeth Brooke (1591–1597)
(B. Scrope) Philadelphia Carey (c.1592–1603)
(L. Leighton) Elyzabeth Knollys (1597–1603)

CHAMBERERS
Dorothy Broadbelt Abington (1558–1577)
Elyzabeth Marbury (1558–c.1580)
(B. Cobham) Frances Newton (1558–c.1564)
(L. Berkeley) Elizabeth Sondes (c.1560–1585)
Nazareth Newton (1564–1573)
Sara Snow (possibly) (c.1566–c.1567)
(L. Drury/Scott) Elizabeth Stafford (1568–1599)
(L. Scudamore) Mary Shelton (c.1570–1603)
Jane Brussels Heneage (1577–c.1596)
(L. Newton) Kattrin Paston (1577–1603)
(L. Hawkins) Margaret Vaughan (1589–1603)
Lucy Hyde (c.1593–1603)
Bregett Chaworth Carr (1601–1603)
Anne Vavasour (1601–1603)

Liveries: 14 yards of black or russet satin for gowns, 3 yards of velvet to trim the gowns, and 6 yards of sarcenet to line the gowns.

LADIES AND GENTLEWOMEN OF THE PRIVY CHAMBER (ORDINARY)
(L. Arundel) Margaret Willoughby (1558–1584)
Bridget Skipwith Cave (1558–1588)

Elizabeth Clyffe (1558–1559)
Isabella Markham Harington (1558–1579)
Lettice Knollys (1558–1560)
Elyzabeth St Loe (1558–*c.*1566)
Anne Wingfield (1558–*c.*1571)
(B. Howard) Katheryn Carey (1559–*c.*1590)
(L. Stafford) Dorothee Stafford (1559–1603)
Elizabeth Shelton (*c.*1561–*c.*1568)
Amy Shelton (*c.*1561–1579)
(L. Leighton) Elyzabeth Knollys (1566–1597)
(C. Hertford) Frances Howard (1569–1598)
(L. Edmonds) Dorothy Edmonds (1569–1603)
(B. Howard of Walden) Catherine Knyvett (probably) (1599–1603)
(L. Walsingham) Audrey Shelton (1601–1603)

LADIES OF THE PRIVY CHAMBER (HONORARY)
(D. Norfolk) Margaret Audley (1558–1564)
(B. Clinton/C. Lincoln) Elyzabeth Fitzgerald (1558–1590)
(B. Howard of Effingham) Margrett Gamage (1558–1581)
(B. Hunsdon) Anne Morgan (1558–1603)
(L. Parry) Anne Rede (1558–*c.*1566)
(L. Sidney) Lady Mary Dudley (1558–1562)
(C. Sussex) Frances Sidney (likely) (*c.*1559–1589)
(M. Northampton) Elisabeth Brooke (possibly) (*c.*1559–1565)
(C. Bedford) Margaret St John (possibly) (*c.*1560–1562)
(C. Pembroke) Katherine Talbot (possibly) (1563–1575)
(C. Warwick) Lady Anne Russell (1565–1603)
(B. Paget) Katheryn Knyvett (*c.*1569–1603)
(M. Northampton) Helena Snakenborg (1571–1603)
(M. Winchester) Agnes Howard (possibly) (1576–1601)
(C. Ormond) Elizabeth Sheffield (*c.*1582–1600)
(C. Huntingdon) Lady Katherine Dudley (possibly) (1595–1603)
(C. Kildare) Frauncis Howard (*c.*1597–1603)

LADIES AND GENTLEWOMEN OF THE PRIVY CHAMBER
(EXTRAORDINARY)
(L. Buckler) Katheryn Denys (1558–*c.*1575)
(L. Cheke) Mary Hill (1558–1603)
(L. Clarke) Catherine Le Strange (1558–*c.*1559)
(L. Poyntz) Joan Berkeley (1558–*c.*1564)
(L. Heneage) Anne Poyntz (1558–1593)
(L. Edmonds) Dorothy Edmonds (1558–1569)
Elizabeth Neville Eynns (1558–1585)
(L. Marvyn) Amy Clarke (1558–1581)
Dorothy Quadring (1558–*c.*1576)
Mary Seymour (1558–*c.*1560)
Elyzabeth Cavendish Snow (1558–1587)

Levina Teerlinc (possibly) (*c.*1559–1576)
(L. St Loe) Elizabeth Hardwick (*c.*1560–1568)
(L. York) Anne Smith (possibly) (*c.*1560–1575)
Margaret Battista Castiglione (*c.*1561–1603)
(L. Sidney) Lady Mary Dudley (1562–1586)
Elizabeth Wingfield (*c.*1562–1600)
Mary Radclyffe (*c.*1567–1585)
(L. Digby) Abygall Heveningham (1571–1603)
(L. West/B. De La Warr) Anne Knollys (probably) (1571–1603)
Elizabeth Nott (*c.*1574–1587)
(B. Hunsdon) Elizabeth Spencer (*c.*1574–1603)
(B. Willoughby) Mary de Vere (possibly) (*c.*1574–1603)
(L. Bulkeley) Mary Burgh (1577–1603)
Bregett Chaworth Carr (*c.*1577–1601)
Margery Killigrew (*c.*1580–1603)
(L. Gerald) Kathryn Knollys (*c.*1580–1603)
Eleanor Brydges Gifford (1581–*c.*1585)
Lady Anne Askew (*c.*1582–1585)
(L. Hoby) Margaret Carey (*c.*1582–1603)
(L. Talbot/C. Shrewsbury) Mary Cavendish (*c.*1582–1603)
(B. Scrope) Philadelphia Carey (1583–*c.*1592)
Elizabeth Throckmorton (*c.*1584–1592)
(L. Walsingham) Audrey Shelton (probably) (*c.*1587–1601)
(L. Stanhope) Margaret MacWilliam (1589–1603)
(L. Talbot/C. Shrewsbury) Mary Cavendish (by 1590–1603)
Katheryn Howard (possibly) (1591–1599)
(L. Long) Katherine Thynne (probably) (1593–1603)
(L. Egerton) Elizabeth Wolley (*c.*1595–1600)
(L. Guildford) Elizabeth Somerset (1596–1603)
Elizabeth Norton Rainsford (*c.*1597–1603)
Rebecca Seckford (*c.*1597–1603)
Catherine Bulkeley (1600–1603)
Lady White (1601–1603)

LADIES AND GENTLEWOMEN OF THE PRIVY CHAMBER BY 1603
(UNCLEAR STATUS)
(L. Brouncker) Alice Parker
(L. Carey) Mary Hyde
(L. Carey) Elizabeth Trevanion
(L. Cavendish) Catherine Ogle
(L. Cecil) Elizabeth Drury
(L. Fortescue) Alice Smith
(L. Hatton) Elizabeth Cecil
(L. Howard) Frances Gouldwell (the widow)
(L. Knyvett) Elizabeth Knyvett
Lady Mainwaring

(L. Raleigh) Elizabeth Throckmorton
(L. Sherley) Frances Vavasour
(L. Waller) Margaret Lennard
Mistress Brooke
Elizabeth Jones
Frances Lucy
Mistress Otemore
Mistress Saville
Elizabeth Gorges Smith
Anne Stanhope

MAIDS OF THE PRIVY CHAMBER
Lady Frances Radclyffe (possibly) (c. 1561–1566)
Lady Anne Russell (c. 1561–1565)
Helena Snakenborg (1566–1571)
Anne Knollys (1569–1571)
Anne Cecil (c. 1570–1571)
Mary Hopton (c. 1574–1576)
Mary Sidney (1575–1577)
Elizabeth Howard (c. 1576–1583)
Frauncis Howard (c. 1578–1589)
Lady Penelope Devereux (c. 1579–1581)
Lady Dorothy Devereux (c. 1579–1583)
Philadelphia Carey (c. 1581–1583)
Margaret Carey (c. 1581–1582)
Elizabeth Brooke (c. 1582–1589)
Lucy Cecil (c. 1586)
Lady Elizabeth de Vere (c. 1589–1595)
Lady Bridget Manners [Tyrwhit] (1589–1594)
Elizabeth Drury (c. 1592–1593)
Elizabeth Brydges (1593–1603)
Lady Elizabeth Somerset (1594–1596)
Elizabeth Russell (1594–1600)
Lady Elizabeth Clinton (c. 1596–1597)
Catherine Darcy (c. 1596–c. 1601)
Lady Elizabeth Talbot (c. 1600–c. 1601)
Lady Susan de Vere (c. 1601–1603)
Lady Anne Herbert (c. 1602–1603)

CHIEF LADIES OF HONOUR
(C. Lennox) Lady Margaret Douglas (intermittently 1559–1578)
(D. Suffolk) Lady Frances Brandon (1558–1559)
(D. Suffolk) Katherine Willoughby (probably) (1559–1580)
Lady Katherine Grey (1559–1561)
Lady Mary Grey (1562–1565, 1577–1578)

(C. Derby) Lady Margaret Clifford (c.1559–1579)
(D. Norfolk) Margaret Audley (1558–1564)
(D. Somerset) Anne Stanhope (probably) (1558–1587)
(M. Northampton) Elisabeth Brooke (c.1559–1565)
(M. Northampton) Helena Snakenborg (1571–1603)
(M. Winchester) Winifred Brydges (probably) (1572–1586)
(M. Winchester) Agnes Howard (1576–1601)
(M. Winchester) Lucy Cecil (1598–1603)

LADIES OF HONOUR
Duchesses
Marchionesses
Countesses
Viscountesses
Baronesses
Dames (knight's wives)
Titled Ladies (daughters of nobles)

LADY CHAMBERLAIN (Lord Chamberlain's wife)
(B. Howard of Effingham) Margrett Gamage (1558–1572)
(C. Sussex) Frances Sidney (1572–1583)
(B. Howard of Effingham) Katheryn Carey (1583–1585)
(B. Hunsdon) Anne Morgan (1585–1596)
(B. Hunsdon) Elizabeth Spencer (1597–1603)

VICE–CHAMBERLAIN'S WIFE
(L. Knollys) Kathryn Carey (1559–1569)
(L. Heneage) Anne Poyntz (1587–1593)
(C. Southampton) Mary Browne (1594–1595)
(L. Stanhope) Margaret MacWilliam (1601–1603)

LADY ADMIRAL (Lord High Admiral's wife)
(B. Clinton/C. Lincoln) Elyzabeth Fitzgerald (1558–1585)
(B. Howard/C. Nottingham) Katheryn Carey (1585–1603)

MAIDS OF HONOUR
1558–1569
Lady Katherine Grey (ds.1561)
Lady Jane Howard (r.c.1561)
Lady Jane Seymour (d.1561)
Mary Howard
Dougles Howard (m.1560)
Mary Mansell (m.1562)
Katheryn Knyvett (n.c.1560, m.1567)
Frances Mewtas (n.1561, r.1565)

Mary Radclyffe (n.*c.*1561)
Anne Windsor (n.*c.*1561, m.*c.*1568)
Katheryn Cooke (n.*c.*1563, m.1565)
Dorothy Brooke (n.*c.*1565, m.1568)
Katherine Brydges (n.*c.*1565, r.*c.*1566)
Abygall Heveningham (n.1567)
Lady Susan Bourchier (n.*c.*1568)
Lady Elizabeth Hastings (n.*c.*1568)
Isabell Holcroft (n.*c.*1569)

1570–1579
Mary Howard (m.1571)
Mary Radclyffe
Abygall Heveningham (m.1571)
Lady Susan Bourchier (ds.1578)
Lady Elizabeth Hastings (m.1571)
Isabell Holcroft (m.1573)
Katheryn Howard (n.*c.*1571)
Eleanor Brydges [Gifford] (n.1571)
Elizabeth Fitzgerald (n.*c.*1571)
Mary Burgh (n.1573, m.1577)
Martha Howard (n.1577, ds.1578)
Frances Vaughan (n.*c.*1578)
Lady Margaret Garrett (possibly) (n.*c.*1579)

1580–1589
Mary Radclyffe (r.1585)
Katheryn Howard
Eleanor Brydges [Gifford] (m.1581)
Elizabeth Fitzgerald (to 1584)
Frances Vaughan (m.1580)
Lady Margaret Garrett (possibly) (r or d.*c.*1580)
Margaret Macwilliam (n.*c.*1580, m.1589)
Anne Vavasour (n.1580, ds.1581)
Elizabeth Trentham (n.1581)
Margaret Edgecombe (n.1581, m.1586)
Anne Hopton (n.1584, m.1589)
Grace Ansley (n.1585, m.1587)
Elizabeth Cavendish (n.*c.*1586)
Elizabeth Southwell (n.*c.*1587)
Cecilia MacWilliam (n.1589)
Katherine Leigh (n.1589)

1590–1599
Katheryn Howard (r.1591)
Elizabeth Trentham (m.1591)

Elizabeth Cavendish (m.*c*.1591)
Elizabeth Southwell (ds.1595)
Cecilia MacWilliam (m.*c*.1590)
Katherine Leigh (ds.1591)
Christian Ansley (n.1591, m.1596)
Frances Drury (n.*c*.1591, m.1596)
Katherine Thynne (n.1591, m.1593)
Frances Vavasour (n.*c*.1591, ds.1591)
Margaret Radclyffe (n.*c*.1592, d.1599)
Maria Tuchet (n.*c*.1592, r.1595)
Elizabeth Vernon (n.*c*.1593, ds.1598)
Lady Katherine Somerset (n.1594, m.1596)
Anne Russell (n.1595)
Mary Fitton (n.1596)
Cordell Ansley (n.1597)
Anne Carey (n.1597)
Lady Dorothy Hastings (n.1598)
Lettice Fitzgerald (n, m, 1598)

1600–1603
Anne Russell (m.1600)
Lady Dorothy Hastings
Cordell Ansley
Anne Carey (m.1601)
Mary Fitton (ds.1601)
Elizabeth Southwell (n.1600)
Mary Neville (n.1601)
Gresham Thynne (n.*c*.1601)
Margaret Wharton (n.1602)

MOTHER OF THE MAIDS
(Also of the Privy Chamber)
Anne Morris (1558–*c*.1561)
Anne Aglionby (*c*.1561–*c*.1569)
Mistress Harvey (*c*.1569–1573)
Elysabeth Hyde (1573–*c*.1581)
Margaret Battista Castiglione (*c*.1581–1588)
Agnes Allen (–)
Elizabeth Jones (1588–1591)
Elizabeth Wingfield (1591–1593, 1597–1600)
Katherine Bromfield (1593–1597)
Mistress Brydges (1601–1603)

QUEEN'S WOMEN (GENTLEWOMEN OF THE HOUSEHOLD)
(In addition to those listed in coronation and funeral records)
Lucy Penn Barley (possibly) (1558–1603)

Elizabeth Smallpage Randall (1560s)
Joan West (*c.*1562–*c.*1577)
Ippolyta (*c.*1560–*c.*1576)
Lucretia de Conti (*c.*1563–1577)
Alice Seckford (*c.*1563–*c.*1582)
Catherine Cruxson (*c.*1574–1586)
Margaret Lichfield (*c.*1574–*c.*1582)
Joanne Allen (*c.*1575–*c.*1589)
Elizabeth Dale (*c.*1576–*c.*1590)
Mistress Harman (*c.*1576–*c.*1580)
Eleanor Giulio Borgarucci (*c.*1577–*c.*1581)
Catherine Cromer (*c.*1580–1602)
Lucy Morgan (*c.*1580–*c.*1590)
Cecilia Bone (*c.*1583–*c.*1594)
Frances Lyfeld *c.*1583–*c.*1590
Helen Seckford (*c.*1583–*c.*1593)
Kathryn West (*c.*1584–*c.*1591)
Lucy Alley Blount (*c.*1597–1603)

MISTRESS LAUNDRESS
Joanne Hilton (1558–*c.*1560)
Elyzabeth Smythson (*c.*1560–1575)
Anne Twist (1575-1603)

Livery: 3 yards of puke for a gown, 3 yards of black velvet to trim the gown,
7 yards of grosgrain for lining the gown, and 7 yards of tawny camlet for a kirtle.

WOMEN WHO SERVED AT THE CORONATION
14–15 January 1559

CHIEF LADY OF HONOUR
(C. Lennox) Lady Margaret Douglas

LADIES OF HONOUR
(D. Suffolk) Lady Frances Brandon
(D. Norfolk) Margaret Audley
(D. Somerset) Anne Stanhope
(C. Bath) Margaret Donnington
(C. Bedford) Margaret St John
(C. Huntingdon) Katherine Pole
(C. Northumberland) Lady Anne Somerset*
(C. Ormond) Elizabeth Berkeley

* Probably did not attend.

(C. Oxford) Margery Golding
(C. Pembroke) Lady Anne Talbot
(C. Rutland) Lady Margaret Neville
(C. Sussex) Frances Sidney
(C. Worcester) Elizabeth Browne
(C. Worcester) Christiana North
(V. Montagu) Magdalen Dacre
(B. Audley) Lady Elizabeth Grey
(B. Abergavenny) Lady Frances Manners
(B. Berkeley) Lady Catherine Howard
(B. Burgh) Catherine Clinton (Coronation Day)
(B. Darcy) Lady Elizabeth de Vere (Coronation Day)
(B. Chandos) Dorothy Bray
(B. Clinton) Elyzabeth Fitzgerald
(B. Dacre of the South) Anne Sackville
(B. Howard of Effingham) Margrett Gamage
(B. Hunsdon) Anne Morgan
(B. Latimer) Lady Lucy Somerset
(B. Lumley) Lady Jane Fitzalan
(B. Morley) Lady Elizabeth Stanley
(B. Mountjoy) Catherine Leigh
(B. Talbot) Lady Gertrude Manners
(B. Tailboys) Margaret Skipwith
(B. Tailboys) Elizabeth Tailboys
(B. Windsor) Lady Katherine de Vere
(L. Buckler) Katheryn Denys (Coronation Eve)
(L. Cawarden) (Lady?) Elizabeth Cawarden (Coronation Day)
(L. Cheke) Mary Hill (Coronation Eve)
(L. Grey) Mary Browne
(L. Knollys) Kathryn Carey (Coronation Eve)
(L. Parry) Anne Rede (Coronation Eve)
(L. Poyntz) Joan Berkeley (Coronation Eve)
(L. Sidney) Lady Mary Dudley
Lady Katherine Grey
Lady Jane Howard
Lady Jane Seymour

(riding with on Coronation Eve)
Mary Howard (Maid of Honour)
Dougles Howard (Maid of Honour)

Liveries:
Coronation Eve: 16 yards of crimson velvet (for gowns); 2 yards of cloth of gold or tinsel (for sleeves).
Coronation Day: 10-12 yards of scarlet for robes.

WOMEN OF THE PRIVY CHAMBER (Coronation Eve)

BEDCHAMBER
Kateryn Champernon Astley
Blanche Parry
Elizabeth Norwich

Liveries:
15 yards of crimson velvet (for gowns); 2 yards of cloth of gold or tinsel (for sleeves).

GENTLEWOMEN
Elizabeth Clyffe
Anne Morris (Mother of the Maids)

(riding with)
Mary Mansell (Maid of Honour)

Liveries:
15 yards of crimson satin (for gowns); 2 yards of purple tinsel with work (for sleeves).

MAIDS OF THE PRIVY CHAMBER
Bridget Skipwith [Cave]
Isabella Markham [Harington]
Lettice Knollys
Elizabeth St Loe
Margaret Willoughby
Anne Wingfield

Liveries:
15 yards of crimson satin (for gowns); 2 yards of purple gold tinsel with knots (for sleeves).

CHAMBERERS
Dorothy Broadbelt [Abington]
Elyzabeth Marbury
Frances Newton

Liveries:
15 yards of crimson damask (for gowns); 2 yards of crimson velvet (for sleeves).

WOMEN OF THE PRIVY CHAMBER (Coronation Day)
(L. Buckler) Katheryn Denys
(L: Cheke) Mary Hill
(L: Clarke) Catherine Le Strange
(L. Knollys) Kathryn Carey

(L: Parry) Anne Rede
(L: Poyntz) Joan Berkeley
Dorothy Broadbelt [Abington]
Kateryn Champernon Astley
Bridget Skipwith [Cave]
Elizabeth Clyffe
Dorothy Edmonds
Elizabeth Neville Eynns
Isabella Markham [Harington]
Anne Poyntz Heneage
Lettice Knollys
Elyzabeth Marbury
Amy Marvyn
Anne Morris (Mother of the Maids)
Frances Newton
Elizabeth Norwich
Blanche Parry
Dorothy Quadring
Mary Seymour
Elyzabeth Cavendish Snow
Elyzabeth St Loe
Margaret Willoughby
Anne Wingfield

Liveries: 5-7 yards of scarlet for robes.

MAIDS OF HONOUR
Lady Katherine Grey
Lady Jane Howard
Lady Jane Seymour
Mary Howard
Dougles Howard
Mary Mansell

Liveries:
5-10 yards of scarlet for robes.

LADIES OF THE HOUSEHOLD
(Coronation Day)
(L. Arnold) Margaret Isham
(L. Bacon) Anne Cooke
(L. Benger) Agnes Seycolle
(L. Berkeley) Kateryn Blount
(L. Cecil) Mildred Cooke
(L. Darcy) Mary Carew

(L. Fitzwilliam) Jane Roberts
(L. Heveningham) Mary Shelton
(L. Hopton) Anne Itchingham
(L. Knyvett) Anne Pickering
(L. Palmer) Jane Windebank
(L. Radclyffe) Isabella Harvey
(L. Throckmorton) Anne Carew
(L. Warner) Elizabeth Brooke

Liveries: 7 yards of scarlet for robes.

GENTLEWOMEN OF THE HOUSEHOLD
(Coronation Day)
Dorothy Curzon
Anne Denys
Anne Grey
Elizabeth Huggins
Mistress Norris
Sybil Penn
Mistress Robinson
Elizabeth Smallpage
Mistress Wayneman
Mistress Weston
Mistress Winter
Mary Yetsweirt

Liveries: 5 yards of scarlet for robes.

LAUNDRESSES
(Coronation Day)
Joanne Hilton (Mistress Laundress)
Elyzabeth Smythson (Laundress of the Board)

Liveries: their usual.

WOMEN WHO SERVED AT THE FUNERAL
28 April 1603

CHIEF MOURNER
(M. Northampton) Helena Snakenborg

Livery: 24 yards of black cloth for a mourning robe; mourning headwear.

LADIES OF HONOUR
(C. Clanricarde) Frances Walsingham
(C. Cumberland) Lady Margaret Russell
(C. Derby) Alice Spencer
(C. Derby) Lady Elizabeth de Vere
(C. Leicester) Lettice Knollys
(C. Huntingdon) Lady Katherine Dudley
(C. Kent) Susan Bertie
(C. Kildare) Frauncis Howard
(C. Hertford) Frances Pranell
(C. Northumberland) Lady Dorothy Devereux
(C. Oxford) Elizabeth Trentham
(C. Pembroke) Mary Sidney
(C. Rutland) Elizabeth Sidney
(C. Shrewsbury) Mary Cavendish
(C. Southampton) Mary Browne
(C. Southampton) Elizabeth Vernon
(C. Sussex) Bridget Morrison
(C. Warwick) Lady Anne Russell
(C. Worcester) Lady Elizabeth Hastings
(B. Berkeley) Jane Stanhope
(B. Buckhurst) Cecily Baker
(B. Burgh) Frances Vaughan
(B. Chandos) Lady Frances Clinton
(B. Compton) Anne Spencer
(B. De La Warr) Anne Knollys
(B. Hastings) Sarah Harington
(B. Howard of Walden) Catherine Knyvett
(B. Howard of Effingham) Ann St John
(B. Hunsdon) Anne Morgan
(B. Hunsdon) Elizabeth Spencer
(B. Lumley) Elizabeth Darcy
(B. Norris) Lady Bridget de Vere
(B. North) Frances Brockett
(B. Paget) Katheryn Knyvett
(B. Rich) Lady Penelope Devereux
(B. Russell) Elizabeth Cooke
(B. St John of Bletso) Elizabeth Chamber
(B. St John of Bletso) Katherine Dormer
(B. Sandys) Christian Ansley
(B. Scrope) Philadelphia Carey
(B. Sheffield) Dougles Howard
(B. Sturton) Frances Brooke
(B. Wentworth) Anne Hopton
(B. Willoughby) Lady Mary de Vere

(L. Glemham) Anne Sackville
(L. Gorges) Lady Elizabeth Clinton
(L. Guildford) Lady Elizabeth Somerset
(L. Southwell) Elizabeth Howard
(L. Stafford) Dorothee Stafford
Lady Frances Egerton
Lady Dorothy Hastings
Lady Anne Herbert
Lady Adeline Neville
Lady Katherine Somerset
Lady Alethea Talbot
Lady Elizabeth Talbot
Lady Mary Talbot
Lady Bridget Manners Tyrwhit
Lady Susan de Vere

Liveries: 14-16 yards of black cloth for mourning robes; mourning headwear.

MAIDS OF HONOUR
Cordell Ansley
Elizabeth Brydges
Mary Neville
Gresham Thynne
Elizabeth Southwell
Margaret Wharton
[Mary?] Zouche

Liveries: 7 yards of black cloth for mourning robes; mourning headwear.

LADIES AND GENTLEWOMEN OF THE PRIVY CHAMBER
(L. Brouncker) Alice Parker
(L. Bulkeley) Mary Burgh
(L. Carey) Mary Hyde
(L. Cavendish) Catherine Ogle
(L. Carey) Elizabeth Trevanion
(L. Cecil) Elizabeth Drury
(L. Cheke) Mary Hill
(L. Digby) Abygall Heveningham
(L. Edmonds) Dorothy Edmonds
(L. Fortescue) Alice Smith
(L. Gerald) Kathryn Knollys
(L. Hatton) Elizabeth Cecil
(L. Hawkins) Margaret Vaughan
(L. Hoby) Margaret Carey
(L. Howard) Frances Gouldwell [the widow]

(L. Knyvett) Elizabeth Knyvett
(L. Leighton) Elyzabeth Knollys
Lady Mainwaring
(L. Newton) Kattrin Paston
(L. Raleigh) Elizabeth Throckmorton
(L. Scudamore) Mary Shelton
(L. Sherley) Frances Vavasour
(L. Stanhope) Margaret Macwilliam
(L. Waller) Margaret Lennard
(L. Walsingham) Audrey Shelton
Lady White
Mistress Brooke
Catherine Bulkeley
Mistress Brydges (Mother of the Maids)
Bregett Chaworth Carr
Margaret Battista Castiglione
Lucy Hyde
Elizabeth Jones
Margery Killigrew
Frances Lucy
Mistress Otemore
Mary Radclyffe
Elizabeth Norton Rainsford
Mistress Saville
Elizabeth Gorges Smith
Anne Stanhope
Anne Vavasour

Liveries: 7-9 yards of black cloth for mourning robes; mourning headwear.

THE QUEEN'S WOMEN
Mistress Bowyer
Thomasine Dethick
Ursula Drake
Mistress Fuller
Bridget Gawdy
Lucy Griffin
Elizabeth Huggins
Ursley Hummings
Susan Pemberton
Margaret Poole
Mary Powell
Rebecca Seckford
[Elizabeth] Skinner
Mistress Sterne

Mistress Thomazine (Queen's dwarf)
Margaret Trevor
Elizabeth Wake

Liveries: 7 yards of black cloth for mourning robes; mourning headwear.

MISTRESS LAUNDRESS
Anne Twist

Livery: 7 yards of black cloth for a mourning robe; mourning headwear.

STARCHWOMAN
Elizabeth Greene

Livery: 7 yards of black cloth for a mourning robe; mourning headwear.

SERVANTS
Mistress Askam
Mistress Fortescue (the widow)
Mistress Russell
Mistress Sheffield
Mistress Wye

Livery: 5 yards of black cloth for mourning robes; mourning headwear.

OTHERS
Elinor Cobham (Laundress of the Board)
Dorothy Speckard (silkwoman)
Katherine Oglefield
Joan Kaye (milkwife)

Liveries: 4 yards of black cloth for mourning robes; mourning headwear.

Index of Women

WOMEN ARE LISTED by their surnames, not titles, and maiden names are generally used. Titles acquired after leaving the Queen's service, or after her death, are shown within []. Burial place of principal attendants given where known.

Additional Abbreviations

LOB/GOB: Lady/Gentlewoman of the Bedchamber
CHA: Chamberer
LPC/GPC: Lady/Gentlewoman of the Privy Chamber (ordinary)
MPC: Maid of the Privy Chamber
LPCH: Lady of the Privy Chamber (honorary)
LPCE/GPCE: Lady/Gentlewoman of the Privy Chamber (extraordinary)
LPCU/GPCU: Lady/Gentlewoman of the Privy Chamber (unclear status)
KHMJ: Keeper of Her Majesty's Jewels
MOH: Maid of Honour
MOM: Mother of the Maids
LOH: Lady of Honour
LOTH/GOTH: Lady/Gentlewoman of the household (Coronation List)
QW: Queen's Woman (previously known as GOTH)
(B): Buried
(H) Husband
(P) Parents
SM: Stepmother
NB: Note
NYGR: New Year's Gift Roll
af: after
ex: executed
k: knighted
*: listed in the index.

Abington, Dorothy (Dorythe) Broadbelt (c.1533–1577): CHA c.1550–1554, 1555–1558, 1558–1577. (P) Jane Broadbelt* (likely). (H) (m.1567) John Abington.

Aglionby, Anne (–): MOM c.1561–c.1569. (H) Hugh Aglionby (d.c.1554). (NB) Anne was once governess to Kateryn Parr's daughter. She may be one and the same as Agnes Allen*.

Allen, Agnes (d.1589): MOM (–). (NB) Her service is known only from a burial entry in the parish register of St Michael's Church, Cornhill, London: (29 July 1589) 'Agnes Allen, wife of Thomas Allen, merch[ant], mother to the maydes of honnor to Queen Elsabeth'. They may have married 1 December 1575 in the same church as there is an entry for 'Thomas Allyn and Agnes Hylle' (perhaps her previous surname/maiden name). It is possible that she is one and the same as Anne Aglionby* (if Anne married a Hill between 1569 and 1575).

Allen, Joanne (Johane) (d.af.1589): GOTH/QW c.1575–c.1589. (P) Edward Woodgate of Kent. (H) Thomas Allen.

Ansley, Christian, Baroness Sandys (c.1570–d.1605): MOH 1591–1596, LOH Funeral. (P) Brian Ansley and Audrey Tyrrell. (H) (m.1596) William Sandys, 3rd Baron Sandys (d.1623).

Ansley, Cordell, [Baroness Hervey] (c.1575–d.1636): MOH 1597–1603. (P) Brian Ansley and Audrey Tyrrell. (H) (m.1607) Sir William Hervey (f.1620) 1st Baron Hervey (d.1642).

Ansley, Grace, [Lady Wildgoose] (c.1565–1644): MOH 1585–1587. (P) Brian Ansley and Audrey Tyrrell. (H) (m.1587) Sir John Wildgoose.

Askam, Mistress (–): Servant by 1603.

Askew, Lady Anne (c.1542–1585): LPCE c.1582–1585. (P) Edward Clinton, 1st Earl of Lincoln and Ursula Stourton; (SM) Elyzabeth Fitzgerald*. (H) William Askew (d.1585).

Astley, Kateryn Champernon (c.1503–1565): Gentlewoman 1536–c.1539, Governess from c.1539 (probably) to 1549, Chief Gentlewoman c.1550–1554 and 1555–1556, Chief GPC 1558–1565, GOB 1558–1565, Coronation. (P) Sir Philip Champernon and Kateryn Carew. (H) (m.c.1546) John Astley (d.1596), Gentleman of the Privy Chamber, Master of the Jewel House. (B) 18 July 1565, Savoy Chapel, Westminster. (NB) Kat may have been acting governess between c.1539 and 1544 if Blanche Milborne, Lady Troy*, remained Elizabeth's official Lady Governess. Although the spelling of Kat's surname varied by family member, Kat and her sister-in-law, Kateryn Blount*, consistently used the spelling 'Champernon' rather than 'Champernowne' or 'Champernoun'.

Audley, Margaret, Duchess of Norfolk (c.1540–1564): LPCH 1558–1564, Chief LOH 1558–1564, LOH Coronation. (P) Thomas Audley, 1st Baron Audley of Walden and Lady Elizabeth Grey*. (H) Lord Henry Dudley (d.1557); (m.1558) Thomas Howard, 4th Duke of Norfolk (ex.1572). (B) Church of St John the Baptist, Norwich.

Baker, Cicely, Baroness Buckhurst, [Countess of Dorset] (c.1535–1615): LOH Funeral. (P) Sir John Baker and Elizabeth Dinley. (H) Thomas Sackville, 1st Baron Buckhurst, (f.1604) 1st Earl of Dorset (d.1608).

Barley, Lucy Penn (–): GOTH/QW 1558–1603 (possibly). (P) Edmund Chevall. (H) John Penn; Henry Barley. (NB) Reputedly a daughter-in-law of Sybil Penn*.

Berkeley, Elizabeth, Countess of Ormond (c.1533–1582): LOH Coronation. (P) Thomas Berkeley, 6th Baron Berkeley and Anne Savage. (H) Thomas Butler, 10th Earl of Ormond (d.1614).

Berkeley, Joan, Lady Poyntz, Lady Dyer (c.1518–c.1564): LPCE 1558–c.1564, LOH Coronation Eve. (P) Thomas Berkeley, 5th Baron Berkeley and Eleanor Constable. (H) Sir Nicholas Poyntz (d.1557); Sir Thomas Dyer (d.1565).

Bertie, Susan, Countess of Kent (1554–af.1602): LOH Funeral. (P) Richard Bertie and Katherine Willoughby, 12th Baroness Willoughby de Eresby and Duchess of Suffolk*. (H) (m.c.1570) Reginald Grey (f.1572) 5th Earl of Kent (d.1573); Sir John Wingfield (d.1596).

Blount, Gertrude, Marchioness of Exeter (c.1499–1558): Godmother (Confirmation). (P) William Blount, 4th Baron of Mountjoy and Elisabeth Saye. (H) Henry Courtenay, 1st Marquess of Exeter (ex.1538).

Blount, Kateryn, Lady Berkeley (c.1518–1560): LOTH Coronation. (P) William Blount, 4th Baron of Mountjoy and Inez de Venegas. (H) John Champernon (d.1541); Sir Maurice Berkeley (d.1581).

Blount, Lucy Alley (d.1612): GOTH/QW c.1597–1603. (P) Thomas and Anne Twist*. (H) Verney Alley; John Blount.

Boleyn, Anne, Lady Shelton (1475–1556): Governess of Elizabeth's household 1536–1537 (possibly). (P) Sir William Boleyn and Lady Margaret Butler. (H) Sir John Shelton (d.1539). (NB) Lady Shelton was Lady Governess to Princess Mary 1533–1536.

Bone, Cecilia (–): Starchwoman c.1583–c.1594. (H) Guillam Bone.

Borgarucci, Eleanor Giulio, (d.c.1581): GOTH/QW c.1577–c.1581. (H) Cooper; Giulio Borgarucci, physician of the royal household. (NB) Known as Mistress Giulio.

Bourchier, Margaret, Baroness Bryan (suo jure) (c.1468–c.1552): Lady Mistress 1533–1537. (P) Sir Humphrey Bourchier and Elizabeth Tilney. (H) (m.c.1478) John Sandys (possibly); Sir Thomas Bryan (d.1517); (m.c.1519) David Zouche. (B) St Giles Church, Cheddington, Bedfordshire.

Bourchier, Lady Susan (c.1549–c.1609): MOH c.1568–1578. (P) John Bourchier, 2nd Earl of Bath and Margaret Donnington*. (NB) Dismissed following her brother's secret affair with Martha Howard*.

Bowyer, Mistress (–): QW by 1603. Perhaps a wife or daughter of Simon Bowyer, Gentleman of the Black Rod (d.1606).

Brandon, Lady Frances, Duchess of Suffolk (1517–1559): LOH Coronation, Chief LOH 1558–1559. (P) Charles Brandon, 1st Duke of Suffolk and Mary Tudor, Queen Dowager of France. (H) (m.1553) Henry Grey, 3rd Marquess of Dorset (ex.1554); (m.1555) Adrian Stokes (d.1585).

Bray, Dorothy, Baroness Chandos (c.1530–1605): LOH Coronation. (P) Edmund Bray, 1st Baron Bray and Jane Halliwell. (H) (c.1548) Edmund Brydges, 2nd Baron Chandos (d.1573); (m.1578) William Knollys (k.1586) (d.1632).

Broadbelt, Jane (–): CHA by 1539 to c.1549.

Brockett, Frances, Baroness North (1583–1677): LOH Funeral. (P) Sir John Brockett and Elizabeth Moore. (H) (m.1600) Dudley North, 3rd Baron North (d.1665).

Bromfield, Katherine (Elizabeth in some sources) (d.1597): MOM 1593–1597. (P) Bartholomew Fromonds and Elizabeth Mynds. (H) William Bromfield (d.1582).

Brooke, Dorothy, [Lady Parry] (d.1624): MOH c.1565–1568. (P) Possibly Sir David Brooke of Bristol and his first wife Catherine Brydges as her father is said to have been a 'Brooke of Bristol' (Nichols, John, *Progresses of King James I*, Vol.1, p.253). (H) (m.1568) Thomas Parry (k.c.1597) (d.1616). (NB) After the death of her parents Dorothy may have been placed in the care of her first cousin, Edmund Brydges, 2nd Baron Chandos, explaining why she became a MOH at about the same time as his daughter, Katheryn Brydges*. It has always been assumed that Sir David died without issue (he certainly died without male issue) but he may have had one or more daughters.

Brooke, Elisabeth, Marchioness of Northampton (1526–1565): Chief LOH c.1559–1565, LPCH c.1559–1565 (possibly). (P) George Brooke, 9th Baron Cobham and Anne Bray. (H) William Parr, 1st Marquess of Northampton, (d.1571) but their marriage was controversial as his first wife, Lady Anne Bourchier (d.1571), was still alive.

Brooke, Mistress (–): GPCU by 1603. She is probably Elizabeth Burgh (*c*.1580–*c*.1619), daughter of Frances Vaughan* and wife since 1599 of George Brooke (son of Frances Newton*).

Brooke, Elizabeth, Lady Cecil (1562–1597): MPC *c*.1582–1589, LOB 1591–1597. (P) William Brooke, 10th Baron Cobham and Frances Newton*. (H) (m.1589) Robert Cecil (k.1591) (d.1612).

Brooke, Elizabeth, Lady Warner (1503–1560): LOTH 1559–1560. (P) Thomas Brooke, 8th Baron Cobham and Dorothy Heydon. (H) Sir Thomas Wyatt (d.1542); Sir Edward Warner (d.1565), Lieutenant of the Tower of London.

Brooke, Frances, Baroness Stourton (1562–*c*.1620): LOH Funeral. (P) William Brooke, 10th Baron Cobham and Frances Newton*. (H) (m.1580) John Stourton, 9th Baron Stourton (d.1588); (m.1592) Sir Edward Moore (d.1623).

Broughton, Dorothy (–): One of Queen Mary's GPC chosen to attend Elizabeth at Woodstock (and possibly the Tower) until recalled to be MOM.

Browne, Elizabeth, Countess of Worcester (d.1565): LOH Coronation. (P) Sir Anthony Browne and Lucy Neville. (H) (m.*c*.1526) Henry Somerset, 2nd Earl of Worcester (d.1549).

Browne, Mary, Countess of Southampton (1552–1607): Vice-Chamberlain's wife 1594–1595, LOH Funeral. (P) Anthony Browne, 1st Viscount Montagu and Lady Jane Radclyffe. (H) (m.1566) Henry Wriothesley, 2nd Earl of Southampton (d.1581); (m.1594) Sir Thomas Heneage (k.1577) (d.1595) widower of Anne Poyntz*; (m.*c*.1599) Sir William Harvey (d.1642).

Browne, Mary, Lady Grey of Pyrgo (*c*.1527–*c*.1617): LOH Coronation. (P) Sir Anthony Browne and Alice Gage; SM: Elyzabeth Fitzgerald. (H) Lord John Grey of Pyrgo (d.1564); (m.*c*.1572) Henry Capel (d.1588).

Brydges, Katherine, [Baroness Sandys] (*c*.1550–1596): MOH *c*.1565–*c*.1566. (P) Edmund Brydges, 2nd Baron Chandos and Dorothy Bray*. (H) (m.1573) William Sandys, 3rd Baron Sandys (d.1623).

Brydges, Mistress (–): MOM 1601–1603. Possibly Katherine Brydges, daughter of Henry Fortescue and Elizabeth Stafford. If so she was the wife of Anthony Brydges, brother of Edmund Brydges, 2nd Baron Chandos.

Brydges, Winifred, Marchioness of Winchester (*c*.1515–1586): Chief LOH 1572–1586 (probably). (P) Sir John Brydges and Agnes Ayolffe. (H) Sir Richard Sackville (d.1566); (m.*c*.1568) John Paulet (f.1572) 2nd Marquess of Winchester (d.1576).

Brydges, Elizabeth (1578–1617): MPC 1593–1603, MOH at Queen's Funeral. (P) Giles Brydges, 3rd Baron Chandos and Lady Frances Clinton*. (H) (m.1603) Sir John Kennedy (later learned he was already married).

Bulkeley, Catherine, [Lady Sandys] (c.1575–1634): GPCE 1600–1603. (P) Sir Richard Bulkeley and Mary Burgh*. (H) (m.1604) Sir Edwin Sandys (d.1629).

Burgh, Mary, Lady Bulkeley (c.1555–af.1603): MOH c.1573–1577, LPCE 1577–1603. (P) William Burgh, Lord Burgh and Catherine Clinton. (H) (m.1577) Sir Richard Bulkeley (d.1621). (NB) Mary's marriage date is sometimes given as 18 February 1576 but she was still a MOH in 1577. (See NYGR) so the given date must be old style.

Carew, Anne, Lady Throckmorton (1519–1586): LOTH 1559. (P) Sir Nicholas Carew and Elizabeth Bryan. (H) (m.c.1540) Sir Nicholas Throckmorton (d.1571); Adrian Stokes (d.1585).

Carew, Mary, Lady Darcy (c.1519–1559): LOTH 1559. (P) Sir Nicholas Carew and Elizabeth Bryan. (H) Sir Arthur Darcy (d.1561).

Carey, Anne, [Lady Lovell] (1580–1622): MOH 1597–1601. (P) Sir John Carey, (f.1603) 3rd Baron Hunsdon, and Mary Hyde. (H) (m.1601) Sir Francis Lovell (d.1624).

Carey, Kathryn, Lady Knollys (c.1524–1569): Chief LOB 1559–1569, LOH Coronation Eve, Vice-Chamberlain's wife 1559–1569. (P) Sir William Carey (but rumoured to be King Henry VIII) and Mary Boleyn. (H) (m.1540) Sir Francis Knollys (d.1596), Vice-Chamberlain 1559–1570s, Treasurer of the Household 1570–1596. (B) St Edmund's Chapel, Westminster Abbey, London.

Carey, Katheryn, Baroness Howard of Effingham, Countess of Nottingham (c.1547–1603): GPC 1559–1572, LPC 1572–c.1590, LOB c.1590–1603, KHMJ 1571–1587, Assistant KHMJ 1587–1603, Lady Chamberlain 1583–1585, Lady Admiral 1585–1603. (P) Henry Carey, 1st Baron Hunsdon and Anne Morgan*. (H) (m.1563) Charles Howard (k.1572) (f.1573) 2nd Baron Howard of Effingham, (f.1597) 1st Earl of Nottingham, Lord Chamberlain 1583–1585, Lord Admiral 1585–1619. (B) All Saint's Church, Chelsea, London.

Carey, Margaret, Lady Hoby (1564–1605): MPC c.1581–1582, LPCE 1582–1603 (probably). (P) Henry Carey, 1st Baron Hunsdon and Anne Morgan*. (H) (m.1582) Edward Hoby (d.1617) who was knighted the day after the wedding. (B) All Saints Church, Bisham, Berkshire.

Carey, Philadelphia, Lady Scrope, Baroness Scrope (1562–1627): MPC c.1581–1583, LPCE 1583–1592, LOB c.1592–1603, Chief LOB (acting) 1603, LOH Funeral. (P) Henry Carey, 1st Baron Hunsdon and Anne Morgan*. (H) (m.1583)

Thomas Scrope (k.1585) (f.1592) 10th Baron Scrope (d.1609). (B) St Dunstan Church, Hunsdon, Hertfordshire.

Carr, Bregett Chaworth, [Lady Carr] (*c.*1542–1621): GPCE *c.*1577–1601, CHA (unofficially *c.*1577–*c.*1601) *c.*1601–1603. (P) Sir John Chaworth and Mary Paston. (H) (m.*c.*1584) William Carr. (NB) Bregett probably became an 'ordinary' GPC on 18 June 1601 (this may have been a daughter but she is not thought to have had any children). (B) St Andrew's Church, Ulford, Northamptonshire.

Castiglione, Margaret Battista (d.1622): GPCE *c.*1561–1603 (probably), MOM *c.*1581–1588. (P) Bartholomew Compagni. (H) Lazarus Allen; Giovanni (John) Battista Castiglione (d.1598), Italian Tutor, Groom of the Privy Chamber. (B) St Mary the Virgin Church, Speen, Berkshire.

Cave, Bridget Skipwith (*c.*1532–1588): Maid *c.*1549–1554 and 1555–1558, GPC 1558–1588. (P) Sir William Skipwith (d.1586) and Alice Dymoke. (H) (m. 11 December 1565 Savoy Chapel, Westminster) Brian Cave (d.1592). (NB) Although her identity has been disputed, her mother's will affirms it, for Alice left Bridget jewellery and '£10 lawful money of England to be delivered to her at the day of her marriage' or 'twenty pounds' if her sister, Elizabeth, died before either of them were married (TNA PROB 11/33/176).

Cavendish, Elizabeth (*c.*1567–*c.*1595): MOH *c.*1586–*c.*1591. (P) Traditionally identified as William Cavendish and Mary Wentworth (of Boleyn descent) but now identified as Margaret, a daughter of Richard Cavendish of Hornsey. However she is named as Elizabeth in the NYGR of 1588 giving some weight to the traditional identification. (H) (m.*c.*1591) Robert Dudley, illegitimate son of Robert Dudley, 1st Earl of Leicester, and Douglas Howard*.

Cavendish, Mary, Lady Talbot, Countess of Shrewsbury (*c.*1556–1632): LPCE *c.*1582–1603, LOH Funeral. (P) Sir William Cavendish and Elizabeth Hardwick*. (H) (m.1568) Gilbert Talbot, (f.1582) Lord Talbot, (f.1590) 7th Earl of Shrewsbury. (B) Sheffield Cathedral, England.

Cawarden, (Lady?) Elizabeth (d.1560): LOH Coronation Day. (H) Sir Thomas Cawarden (d.1559). NB: As she was (seemingly) a LOH on Coronation Day she may have been the daughter of a peer (she received 10 yards of scarlet, the same quantity as baronesses and ladies. The wives of knights received 7).

Cecil, Anne, Countess of Oxford (1556–1588): MPC *c.*1570–1571. (P) William Cecil, 1st Baron Burghley and Mildred Cooke*. (H) (m.1571) Edward de Vere, Earl of Oxford (d.1604).

Cecil, Elizabeth, Lady Hatton (*c.*1578–1646): LPCU by 1603. (P) Sir Thomas Cecil (later) 1st Earl of Exeter and Dorothy Neville. (H) (m.*c.*1596) Sir William Newton alias Hatton (d.1597); (m.1598) Sir Edward Coke (d.1634).

Cecil, Lucy, Marchioness of Winchester (1568–1614): MPC *c.*1586, Chief LOH 1598–1603. (P) Sir Thomas Cecil (later) 1st Earl of Exeter and Dorothy Neville. (H) (m.1586) William Paulet, Lord St John, (f.1598) Marquess of Winchester (d.1629). (B) St John the Baptist's Chapel, Westminster Abbey.

Chamber, Elizabeth, Baroness St John of Bletso (*c.*1515–1603): LOH Funeral. (P) Geoffrey Chamber and Alice Burgh. (H) Sir William Stonor (d.1551); Reginald Conyers (d.1560); Edward Griffin (d.1569); (m.*c.*1572) Oliver St John, 1st Baron John of Bletso (d.1582).

Clarke, Amy, Lady Marvyn (d.1581): GPCE 1558–1574, LPCE 1574–1581. (P) Valentine Clark and Elizabeth Brydges. (H) Edmund Horne; Sir James Marvyn (k.1574) (d.1611). (NB) Her daughter, Lucy Marvyn, Baroness Audley, (d.*c.*1600) was probably a LOH.

Clifford, Lady Margaret, Baroness Strange, Countess of Derby (1540–1596): Chief LOH *c.*1559–1579. (P) Henry Clifford, 2nd Earl of Cumberland and Lady Eleanor Brandon. (H) Henry Stanley, 12th Baron Strange, (f.1572) 4th Earl of Derby (d.1593). (B) St Edmund's Chapel, Westminster Abbey.

Clinton, Catherine, Baroness Burgh (*c.*1536–1621): LOH Coronation. (P) Edward Clinton, 1st Earl of Lincoln and Elizabeth Blount; (SM) Elyzabeth Fitzgerald*. (H) William Burgh, 2nd Baron Burgh (d.1584).

Clinton, Lady Elizabeth, Lady Gorges (*c.*1580–1659): MPC *c.*1596–1597 (probably), LOH Funeral. (P) Henry Clinton, 2nd Earl of Lincoln and Lady Catherine Hastings. (H) Sir Arthur Gorges (d.1625).

Clinton, Lady Frances, Baroness Chandos (c.1550–1623): LOH Funeral. (P) Edward Clinton, 1st Earl of Lincoln and Ursula Stourton; (SM) Elyzabeth Fitzgerald*. (H) (m.*c.*1574) Gyles Brydges, 3rd Baron Chandos (d.1594). (NB) Lady Frances is probably the Baroness Chandos who attended the Queen's funeral (there were two more living).

Clyffe, Elizabeth (d.1559): Maid *c.*1549–1554, 1555–1558, GPC 1558–1559. (P) Probably Robert Clyffe, Clerk of the Cheque to Edward VI.

Cobham, Elinor (–): Laundress of the Board by 1603. Unidentified.

Coldburn, Mistress (–): Attended Elizabeth at the Tower (1554). Unidentified. May have been one of 'the Hatfield flock'.

Cooke, Anne, Lady Bacon (*c.*1527–1610): LOTH 1559. (P) Sir Anthony Cooke and Anne Fitzwilliam. (H) (m.1533) Sir Nicholas Bacon, Lord Keeper of the Great Seal 1558–1572 (d.1579).

Cooke, Elizabeth, Baroness Russell (1528–1609): LOH Funeral. (P) Sir Anthony Cooke and Anne Fitzwilliam. (H) (m.1558) Thomas Hoby (k.1566) (d.1566); (m.1574) John Russell, 3rd Baron Russell (d.1584).

Cooke, Katheryn (c.1542–1583): MOH c.1563–1565. (P) Sir Anthony Cooke and Anne Fitzwilliam. (H) (m.1565) Henry Killigrew (k.1591) (d.1603).

Cooke, Mildred, Lady Cecil, Baroness Burghley (1526–1589): LOTH 1559. (P) Sir Anthony Cooke and Anne Fitzwilliam. (H) Sir William Cecil (f.1571) Baron Burghley (d.1598).

Cromer, Catherine (d.1602): GOTH/QW c.1580–1602. (H) William Cromer MP.

Cruxson, Catherine (d.1586): GOTH/QW c.1574–1586. (H) Simon Cruxson.

Curzon, Dorothy (–): GOTH 1559. (P) Thomas Curzon of Croxall and Elizabeth Lygon. (H) (said to be) John Mynne. (NB) Dorothy originally served Anne of Cleves who asked Elizabeth in her will to take Dorothy, a 'poor maid', into her service.

Dacre, Magdalen, Viscountess Montagu (1538–1608): LOH Coronation. (P) William Dacre, 3rd Baron Dacre and Elizabeth Talbot. (H) Anthony Browne, 1st Viscount Montagu (d.1592).

Dale, Elizabeth (d.c.1590): GOTH/QW c.1576–c.1590. (P) Lawrence Scherer. (H) Valentine Dale (d.1589), Ambassador, Master of Requests.

Dane, Margaret (c.1521–1579): GOTH/QW c.1561–1579 (possibly). (P) Edmund Kempe and Bridget Styles. (H) William Kemp.

Darcy, Catherine (c.1580–1646): MPC c.1596–c.1601. (P) Edward Darcy (k.1603) and Elizabeth Astley. (H) (m.c.1601) William West of Firbeck.

Darcy, Elizabeth, Baroness Lumley (c.1566–1616): LOH Funeral. (P) John Darcy, 2nd Baron Chiche and Frances Rich. (H) John Lumley, 1st Baron Lumley (d.1609).

De Conti, Lucretia (Lucretia the Italian) (d.1577): GOTH/QW c.1563–1577. (H) Antonio Pagano; Anthony Conti (d.1579), court musician. (NB) Believed to have been an entertainer or dancer. The Queen was godmother to her daughter, Elizabeth, born in 1574. When Lucretia's husband died in 1579 the Queen gave an annuity of £15 each to the couple's orphaned daughters (Elizabeth and Lucretia de Conti).

De Vere, Lady Elizabeth, Baroness Darcy of Chiche (c.1512–1564): LOH Coronation Day. (P) John de Vere, 15th Earl of Oxford and Elizabeth Trussell. (H) Thomas Darcy, 1st Baron Darcy of Chiche (d.1558).

De Vere, Lady Bridget, Baroness Norris, [Countess of Berkshire] (1584–1631): LOH Funeral. (P) Edward de Vere, 17th Earl of Oxford and Anne Cecil*. (H) (m.1599) Francis Norris (f.1601) 2nd Baron Norris of Rycote, (f.1621) 1st Earl of Berkshire (d.1622).

De Vere, Lady Elizabeth, Countess of Derby (1575–1627): MPC *c.*1589–1595, LOH Funeral. (P) Edward de Vere, 17th Earl of Oxford and Anne Cecil*. (H) (m.1595) William Stanley, 6th Earl of Derby (d.1642).

De Vere, Lady Katherine, Baroness Windsor (1540–1600): LOH Coronation. (P) John de Vere, 16th Earl of Oxford and Dorothy Neville. (H) Edward Windsor, 3rd Baron Windsor (d.1575).

De Vere, Lady Mary, Baroness Willoughby de Eresby (*c.*1554–1624): LPCE *c.*1574–1603, LOH Funeral. (P) John de Vere, 16th Earl of Oxford and Margery Golding*. (H) (m.1578) Peregine Bertie (f.1580) 13th Baron Willoughby de Eresby (d.1601); (m.*c.*1605) Sir Eustace Hart (d.1634).

De Vere, Lady Susan, [Countess of Montgomery] (1587–1629): MPC *c.*1601–1603, LOH Funeral. (P) Edward de Vere, 17th Earl of Oxford and Anne Cecil*. (H) (m.1604) Philip Herbert (f.1605) Earl of Montgomery, (f.1630) 4th Earl of Pembroke (d.1650).

Denys, Anne (–): GOTH 1559. (P) Sir John St John of Bletso. (H) Richard Denys (d.1593).

Denys, Katheryn, Lady Buckler (*c.*1518–*c.*1582): LPCE 1558–*c.*1575, LOH Coronation Eve. (P) Sir William Denys and Anne Berkeley. (H) Edward Tame (d.1521); Sir William Buckler (d.1554), Chamberlain of Princess Elizabeth's Household; Roger Lygon (d.1584). (B) St Mary's Church, Fairfold, Gloucestershire.

Dethick, Thomasine QW by 1603. (P) possibly the daughter of Robert Young. (H) probably the wife of William Dethick (d.1612).

Devereux, Lady Penelope, Baroness Rich, [Countess of Devonshire] (1563–1607): MPC *c.*1579–*c.*1581, LOH Funeral. (P) Walter Devereux, 1st Earl of Essex and Lettice Knollys*. (H) (m.1581) Robert Rich, 3rd Baron Rich (f.1618) 1st Earl of Warwick (d.1619) but they divorced in 1605; (m.1605) Charles Blount, 1st Earl of Devonshire (d.1606).

Devereux, Lady Dorothy, Countess of Northumberland (*c.*1564–1619): MPC *c.*1579–1583, LOH Funeral. (P) Walter Devereux, 1st Earl of Essex and Lettice Knollys*. (H) (m.1583) Sir Thomas Perrot (d.1594); (m.1594) Henry Percy, 9th Earl of Northumberland (d.1632).

Donnington, Margaret, Countess of Bath (c.1509–1561): LOH Coronation. (P) John Donnington and Elizabeth Pye. (H) (m.c.1523) Sir Thomas Kitson (d.1540); (m.c.1541) Sir Richard Long (d.1546); (m.1548) John Bourchier, 2nd Earl of Bath (d.1561).

Dormer, Katherine, Baroness St John of Bletso (d.c.1615): LOH Funeral. (P) Sir William Dormer and Dorothy Catesby. (H) (m.c.1575) John St John, 2nd Baron St John of Bletso (d.1596).

Douglas, Lady Margaret, Countess of Lennox (1515–1578): Chief LOH intermittently 1559–1578. (P) Archibald Douglas, 6th Earl of Angus and Margaret Tudor, Queen of Scots. (H) (m.1544) Mathew Stuart, 4th Earl of Lennox (d.1571). (B) Chapel of Henry VII, Westminster Abbey.

Drake, Ursula (–): QW by 1603. (P) Probably Sir William Stafford and Dorothee Stafford*. (H) (m.c.1574) Richard Drake (d.1603), first cousin of Sir Francis Drake.

Drury, Elizabeth, Lady Cecil, [Countess of Exeter] (1579–1659): MPC c.1592–1593, LPCU by 1603. (P) Sir William Drury and Elizabeth Stafford*. (H) (m.1593 in secret) William Cecil (k.1603) (f.1605) 3rd Baron Burghley, (f.1623) 2nd Earl of Exeter. (NB) Elizabeth is likely the 'Lady Cecil' listed as a member of the Privy Chamber in 1603 as her husband was knighted by King James before the funeral records were completed.

Drury, Frances, [Lady Bobbing, Lady Wray] (1576–1642): MOH c.1591–1596. (P) Sir William Drury and Elizabeth Stafford*. (H) (m.1596) Sir Nicholas Clifford of Bobbing (d.1599); (m.1600) Sir William Wray (d.1617).

Dudley, Lady Katherine, Countess of Huntingdon (c.1537–1620): LPCH 1595–1603 (possibly), LOH Funeral. (P) John Dudley, 1st Duke of Northumberland and Jane Guildford. (H) Henry Hastings, 3rd Earl of Huntingdon (d.1595).

Dudley, Lady Mary, Lady Sidney (c.1530–1586): LPCH 1558–1562, LPCE 1562–1586 (probably), LOH Coronation. (P) John Dudley, 1st Duke of Northumberland and Jane Guildford. (H) Sir Henry Sidney (d.1586). (B) St John the Baptist Church, Penshurst, Kent.

Edgecombe, Margaret, [Lady Denny] (1560–1648): MOH 1581–c.1586. (P) Peter Edgecombe MP and Margaret Luttrell. (H) (m.1586) Edward Denny (k.1588) (d.1600).

Edmonds, Dorothy, Lady Edmonds (1545–1615): GPCE 1558–1569, GPC 1569–1592, LPC 1592–1603. (P) Christopher Lidcott and Katherine Cheyne. (H)

Sir Christopher Edmonds (k.1592) (d.1596). (B) Christ Church Greyfriars, London (destroyed in the Great Fire of London).

Egerton, Lady Frances, [Countess of Bridgewater] (1583–1636): LOH Funeral. (P) Ferdinando Stanley, 5th Earl of Derby and Alice Spencer*. (H) (m.*c.*1601) John Egerton (f.1617) 1st Earl of Bridgewater (d.1649).

Eynns, Elizabeth Neville (*c.*1527–1585): Maid by 1547 to 1550s, GPCE 1558–1585. (P) Sir Edward Neville and Eleanor Windsor. (H) (m.1550s) Thomas Eynns (d.1578).

Finch, Margaret, Countess of Kent (d.*c.*1540): Train bearer at christening. (P) James Finch of London. (H) Oliver Curteys; John Dawes of London; Richard Grey, 3rd Earl of Kent (d.1524). (NB) Margaret is probably 'the Countess of Kent' who carried the train as there was no official Earl of Kent after the death of her husband until the title was restored to his nephew, Reginald Grey, in 1572.

Fitton, Mary (1578–1641): MOH 1596–1601. (P) Sir Edward Fitton and Alice Holcroft. (H) Captain William Polwhele (d.1610); John Lougher (d.1636).

Fitzalan, Lady Jane, Baroness Lumley (1537–1578): LOH Coronation. (P) Henry Fitzalan, 19th Earl of Arundel and Katherine Grey. (H) John Lumley, 1st Baron Lumley (d.1609).

Fitzgerald (Garrett), Elizabeth (*c.*1554–af.1583): MOH *c.*1571–1584. (P) Edward Fitzgerald and Anne Leigh. (NB) Sometimes mistaken for her sister, Lettice Fitzgerald, wife of Sir Ambrose Coppinger. Elizabeth died or retired in 1584.

Fitzgerald, Elyzabeth, Baroness Clinton, Countess of Lincoln (*c.*1527–1590): childhood companion *c.*1534–*c.*1539, gentlewoman *c.*1539–*c.*1543, LPCH 1558–1590, LOH Coronation, Lady Admiral 1558–1585. (P) Gerald Fitzgerald, 9th Earl of Kildare and Lady Elyzabeth Grey*. (H) (m.*c.*1544) Sir Anthony Browne (d.1548); (m.1552) Edward Clinton, 9th Baron Clinton, (f.1572) 1st Earl of Lincoln (d.1585), Lord Admiral 1558–1585. (B) St George's Chapel, Windsor Castle. (NB) It is often said that Elyzabeth was in the service of Princess Mary but the evidence suggests she was raised with Princess Elizabeth and remained with her until she became a MOH to Kateryn Parr. Evidence: Fair Geraldine poem, CSP Spanish, 1554–1558, Vol.13, No.435 (childhood companion); LPH8, Vol.14 Pt.1, No.1145 and Vol.10, No.1187 (gentlewoman attendant from *c.*1539); Michael Drayton's expanded *Heroical Epistles* (1598) which says Geraldine was 'one of the honourable maids to Queen Katherine Dowager' (i.e. Parr). As Lady Browne, Elyzabeth continued to attend upon Kateryn Parr (TNA, LC 2/2).

Fitzgerald, Lettice, [Lady Digby] (*c.*1580–1658): MOH 1598. (P) Gerald Fitzgerald, Lord Gerald and Kathryn Knollys*. (H) (m.1598) Robert Digby (k.1599) (d.1618).

Fortescue, Mistress 'the widow' (–): Servant by 1603. Unidentified.

Fuller, Mistress (–): QW by 1603. Unidentified.

Gamage, Margrett, Baroness Howard of Effingham (1515–1581): LPCH 1558–1581, Lady Chamberlain 1558–1572, LOH Coronation. (P) Sir Thomas Gamage and Margaret St. John. (H) (m.1535) William Howard, 1st Baron Howard of Effingham (d.1573), Lord Chamberlain 1558–1572. (B) Church of St Mary Magdalene, Reigate, Surrey.

Garrett, Lady Margaret (–): MOH c.1579–c.1580 (possibly). (P) Perhaps Gerald Fitzgerald, 11th Earl of Kildare and Mabel Browne.

Gawdy, Bridget (–): QW by 1603. (NB) Probably 'Bidd', the wife of Philip Gawdy, MP and letter writer. If so she was the daughter of Bartholomew Strangman and Mary Crain.

Gifford, Eleanor Brydges (c.1555–c.1585): MOH c.1571–1581, GPCE 1581–c.1585. (P) Edmund Brydges, 2nd Baron Chandos and Dorothy Bray*. (H) (m.1581) George Gifford (d.1613).

Golding, Margery, Countess of Oxford (c.1526–1568): LOH Coronation. (P) Sir John Golding and Elizabeth Tonge. (H) (m.1548) John de Vere, 16th Earl of Oxford (d.1562); (m.c.1563) Sir Charles Tyrrell, Gentleman Pensioner (d.1570).

Gouldwell, Frances, Lady Howard (c.1540–1616): LPCU by 1603. (P) William Gouldwell and Elizabeth Cheney. (H) Sir William Howard (d.1600).

Greene, Elizabeth (–): Starchwoman c.1594–1603. (P) Guillam and Elizabeth Bone.* (H) Francis Greene.

Grey, Lady Elizabeth, Baroness Audley of Walden (c.1510–1564): LOH Coronation. (P) Thomas Grey, 2nd Marquess of Dorset; Margaret Wotton*. (H) George Norton; Thomas Audley, Baron Audley of Walden (d.1544).

Grey, Lady Elyzabeth, Countess of Kildare, Lady Gerald (c.1497–af.1548): Attending by 1538, retired c.1539. (P) Thomas Grey, 1st Marquess of Dorset and Cecilly Bonville. (H) (m.c.1520) Gerald Fitzgerald, 9th Earl of Kildare (d.1534). (NB) Became Lady Gerald following the forfeiture of the earldom of Kildare in 1536.

Grey, Lady Katherine, [Countess of Hertford] (1540–1568): MOH 1558–1561, LOH Coronation, Chief LOH 1559–1561. (P) Henry Grey, 3rd Duke of Suffolk and Lady Frances Brandon*. (H) (m.1560) Edward Seymour, 1st Earl of Hertford (d.1621). (B) Originally in Cockfield Chapel, Suffolk, then Salisbury Cathedral, Wiltshire.

Grey, Lady Mary (*c.*1545–1578): Chief LOH 1562–1565, 1577–1578. (P) Henry Grey, 3rd Duke of Suffolk and Lady Frances Brandon*. (H) (m.1565) Thomas Keyes (d.1571), Sergeant Porter. (B) St Edmund's Chapel, Westminster Abbey.

Grey, Anne: GOTH 1559. (H) Thomas Grey. (NB) Anne received a 31-year lease of lands 'for her service' on 1 July 1559 (CPR, Elizabeth, Vol.1, p.113).

Griffin, Lucy (–): QW by 1603. (P) Reginald Conyers and Elizabeth Chamber*. (H) (m.*c.*1569) Edward Griffin.

Hardwick, Elizabeth, Lady St Loe, [Countess of Shrewsbury] (*c.*1527–1608): LPCE *c.*1560–1568. (P) John Hardwick and Elizabeth Leche. (H) Robert Barlow (d.1544); Sir William Cavendish (d.1557); William St Loe (d.1565); (m.1568) George Talbot, 6th Earl of Shrewsbury (d.1590).

Harington, Isabella (Elizabeth) Markham (1527–1579): Maid *c.*1550–1554, 1555–1558, GPC 1558–1579. (P) Sir John Markham and Anne Strelley. (H) (m.1559) John Harington (d.1582). (B) St Gregory's by St Paul's Church, London (destroyed in the Great Fire of London).

Harington, Sarah, Baroness Hastings, [Baroness Zouche] (1565–1629): LOH Funeral. (P) Sir James Harington and Lucy Sidney. (H) (m.1585) John Hastings, Baron Hastings (d.1595); Sir George Kingsmill (d.1606); Edward Zouche, 11th Baron Zouche (d.1625); Sir Thomas Edmondes.

Harman, Mistress (–): GOTH/QW *c.*1576–*c.*1580. Unidentified. Possibly the wife (or other relation) of James Harman, Keeper of the Standing Wardrobe at Westminster.

Harvey, Isabella, Lady Radclyffe (d.1594): LOTH 1559. (P) Edmund Harvey and Margaret Wentworth. (H) Hill; Sir Humphrey Radclyffe (d.1566).

Harvey, Mistress (–): MOM *c.*1569–1573. Unidentified. (NB) Said to have died suddenly before the Queen at Greenwich Palace in November 1573.

Hastings, Lady Dorothy, [Lady Stewart] (1579–*c.*1621): MOH 1598–1603, LOH Funeral. (P) George Hastings, 4th Earl of Huntingdon and Dorothy Port. (H) (m.1606) Sir James Stewart (d.1609); Robert Dillon (f.1641) 2nd Earl of Roscommon (d.1642).

Hastings, Lady Elizabeth, Countess of Worcester (*c.*1550–1621): MOH *c.*1568–1571, LOH Funeral. (P) Francis Hastings, 2nd Earl of Huntingdon and Katherine Pole*. (H) (m.1571) Edward Somerset (f.1589) 4th Earl of Worcester, (d.1628).

214

Heneage, Jane Brussels (c.1543–1596): CHA 1577–c.1596. (P) Francis and Barbara Hawk of Flanders. (H) Brussels; (m.1589) William Heneage.

Herbert, Lady Anne (1583–c.1606): MPC c.1602–1603, LOH Funeral. (P) Henry Herbert, 2nd Earl of Pembroke and Mary Sidney*.

Heveningham, Abygall, Lady Digby (c.1552–1611): MOH 1567–1571, GPCE 1571–1586, LPCE 1586–1603. (P) Probably Sir Anthony Heveningham and Mary Shelton*. (H) (m.1571) George Digby (k.1586) (d.1587); (m.1588) Edward Cordell (d.1590); (m.1591) Ralph Bowes (d.1598).

Hill, Mary, Lady Cheke (c.1530–1616): Gentlewoman c.1540–c.1547, LPCE 1558–1603, LOH Coronation Eve. (P) Richard Hill and Elizabeth Isley. (H) (m.1547) Sir John Cheke (d.1557); (m.1558) Henry MacWilliam (d.1586). (B) Church of St Martin's in the Fields, Westminster (since rebuilt).

Hilton, Joanne (–): Laundress c.1533–1558, Mistress Laundress 1558–c.1560. (P) Unknown. (NB) She is probably one and the same as 'Agnes Hylton' and 'Anne Hilton' in the staff lists of c.1538 and c.1542. 'Anes Bylliarde' listed on the NYGR of 1559, the wife of Lewis Billiard, royal crossbow maker, is not likely to be 'Agnes Hylton' as Lewis married a woman named Aves (Avis) Amis in 1540 in St Laurence Pountney (she is also named Avis on NYGR 1557).

Holcroft, Isabel, Countess of Rutland (c.1552–1606): MOH c.1569–1573. (P) Sir Thomas Holcroft and Juliana Jennings. (H) (m.1573) Edward Manners, 3rd Earl of Rutland (d.1587). (NB) The Countess of Rutland who served at the Queen's funeral was probably Elizabeth Sidney* but may have been Isabel.

Hopton, Anne, Baroness Wentworth (c.1561–1625): MOH 1584–1589, LOH Funeral. (P) Sir Owen Hopton and Anne Itchingham*. (H) (m.1589) Henry Wentworth, 3rd Baron Wentworth (d.1593); (m.1595) William Pope (f.1628) 1st Earl of Downe (d.1631).

Hopton, Mary, [Baroness Chandos] (d.1624): MPC c.1574–1576. (P) Sir Owen Hopton and Anne Itchingham*. (H) (m.1576) William Brydges (f.1594) Baron Chandos (d.1602).

Howard, Agnes, Marchioness of Winchester (c.1533–1601): Chief LOH 1576–1601, LPCH 1576–1601 (possibly). (P) William Howard, 1st Baron Howard of Effingham and Kathryn Broughton. (H) William Paulet (f.1576) 3rd Marquess of Winchester (d.1598). (B) St Mary's Church, Old Basing, Hampshire.

Howard, Lady Catherine, Baroness Berkeley (1538–1596): LOH Coronation. (P) Henry Howard, Earl of Surrey and Lady Frances de Vere. (H) (m.1554) Henry Berkeley, 7th Baron Berkeley (d.1613).

Howard, Dougles, Baroness Sheffield (c.1542–1608): MOH 1558–1560, LOH Funeral. (P) William Howard, 1st Baron Howard of Effingham and Margrett Gamage*. (H) (m.1560) John Sheffield, 2nd Baron Sheffield (d.1568); (m.1579) Sir Edward Stafford (d.1605). (NB) Although 'Douglas' is the standard modern spelling of Lady Sheffield's name she signed herself 'Dougles Sheffelde' in the *Day Book of the Wardrobe of Robes*.

Howard, Elizabeth, Lady Southwell, [Countess of Carrick] (c.1564–1646): MPC c.1576–1583, LOH Funeral. (P) Charles Howard, 2nd Baron Howard of Effingham, 1st Earl of Nottingham and Katheryn Carey*. (H) (m.1583) Robert Southwell (k.1585) (d.1598); (m.1604) Sir James Stewart (f.1628) 1st Earl of Carrick, (d.c.1645).

Howard, Frances, Countess of Hertford (c.1554–1598): GPC 1569–1585, LPC 1585–1598. (P) William Howard, 1st Baron Howard of Effingham and Margrett Gamage*. (H) (m.1585) Edward Seymour, Earl of Hertford (d.1621). (B) St Benedict's Chapel, Westminster Abbey.

Howard, Frauncis, Countess of Kildare (c.1566–1628): MPC c.1578–1589, LPCH c.1597–1603, LOH Funeral. (P) Charles Howard, 2nd Baron Howard of Effingham, 1st Earl of Nottingham and Katheryn Carey*. (H) (m.1589) Henry Fitzgerald, 12th Earl of Kildare (d.1597); (m.1601) Henry Brooke, 11th Baron Cobham (d.1618). (B) Westminster Abbey.

Howard, Lady Jane, [Countess of Westmoreland] (1542–1593): MOH 1558–c.1561, LOH Coronation. (P) Henry Howard, Earl of Surrey and Lady Frances de Vere. (H) (m.c.1563) Charles Neville, 6th Earl of Westmoreland (d.1601), co-leader of the Northern Rebellion (1569).

Howard, Katheryn (c.1551–1599): MOH c.1571–1591, GPCE 1591–1599 (possibly). (P) William Howard, 1st Baron Howard of Effingham and Margrett Gamage*.

Howard, Lady Mary (c.1519–1557): Chrisom Bearer at Christening. (P) Thomas Howard, 3rd Duke of Norfolk and Lady Elizabeth Stafford. (H) (m.1533) Henry Fitzroy (d.1536).

Howard, Martha, [Lady Bourchier] (c.1555–1598): MOH 1577–1578. (P) William Howard, 1st Baron Howard of Effingham and Margrett Gamage*. (H) (m.1578) George Bourchier (k.1579).

Howard, Mary, [Baroness Dudley] (c.1538–1600): MOH 1558–1571. (P) William Howard, 1st Baron Howard of Effingham and Margrett Gamage*. (H) (m.1571) Edward Sutton, 4th Baron Dudley (d.1586); (m.c.1587) Richard Mompresson (d.1627).

Huggins, Elizabeth (d.af.1603): GOTH/QW 1559–1603. (H) William Huggins (d.1588), Keeper of the Gardens at Hampton Court.

Hummings, Ursley (–): QW by 1603. Unidentified.

Huntercombe, Alice (–): CHA by 1539 to before 1547.

Hyde, Elysabeth (–): MOM 1573–*c*.1581. (P) Shipman. (H) William Hyde.

Hyde, Lucy, [Lady Osborne] (d.af.1604): CHA 1593–1603. (P) William Hyde and Elysabeth Hyde*. (H) (m.1603) Sir Robert Osborne.

Hyde, Mary, Lady Carey, [Baroness Hunsdon] (*c*.1554–1627): LPCU by 1603. (P) Sir Leonard Hyde; Ann Boteler. (H) Richard Peyton; (m.1576) John Carey (k.1598) (f.1603) 3rd Baron Hunsdon (d.1617). (NB) Mary is probably the second 'Lady Carey' listed in the funeral records and the 'Carew' listed as a member of the Privy Chamber.

Ippolyta (the Tartarian) (d.*c*.1576): GOTH/QW *c*.1560–*c*.1576. (NB) Believed to be Aura Soltana, a former slave.

Isham, Margaret, Lady Arnold (–): LOTH 1559. (P) John Isham of Braunston. (H) Sir Nicholas Arnold (d.*c*.1580).

Itchingham, Anne, Lady Hopton (*c*.1525–1599): LOTH 1559. (P) Sir Edward Itchingham and Anne Everard. (H) Sir Owen Hopton, Lieutenant of the Tower of London *c*.1570–1590 (d.1595).

Jerningham, Anne, Lady Grey (*c*.1504–*c*.1555): Probably the Lady Grey appointed by Queen Mary to attend to Elizabeth at the Tower and briefly at Woodstock. (P) Sir Edward Jerningham and Margaret Bedingfield. (H) Lord Edward Grey (d.1517); Henry Barley (d.1529); Sir Robert Drury (d.1535); Sir Edmund Walsingham (1550).

Jones, Elizabeth (d.1608): MOM 1588–1591, GPCU by 1603. (P) Thomas Woodhouse and Margaret Shelton. (H) Thomas Jones. (NB) She is most likely the Mistress Jones listed as 'of the Privy Chamber' in the Funeral records.

Kaye, Joan (–): 'milkwife' by 1603. Unidentified.

Killigrew, Margery, [Lady Killigrew] (*c*.1543–1625): GPCE *c*.1580–1603. (P) Thomas Saunders and Elizabeth Wolman. (H) (m.1580) William Killigrew (1574–1603) (k.1603) Groom of the Privy Chamber.

Knollys, Anne, Lady West, Baroness De La Warr (1555–1608): MPC 1569–1571, LPCE 1571–1603 (probably), LOH funeral. (P) Sir Francis Knollys and Kathryn Carey*. (H) (m.1571) Thomas West (k.1587) (f.1595) Baron De La Warr (d.1602).

Knollys, Elyzabeth, Lady Leighton (1549–1605): GPC 1566–1579, LPC 1579–1597, LOB 1597–1603. (P) Sir Francis Knollys and Kathryn Carey*. (H) (m.1579) Thomas Leighton (k.1579) (d.c.1611).

Knollys, Kathryn, Lady Gerald (1559–c.1630): LPCE c.1580–1603. (P) Sir Francis Knollys and Kathryn Carey*. (H) (m.1578) Gerald Fitzgerald, Lord Offaly, Lord Gerald (d.1580); Sir Philip Boteler (d.c.1592).

Knollys, Lettice, Viscountess Hereford, Countess of Essex/Leicester (1543–1634): GPC 1558–1560, LOH Funeral. (P) Sir Francis Knollys and Kathryn Carey*. (H) (m.1560) Walter Devereux, 2nd Viscount Hereford (f.1572) 1st Earl of Essex (d.1576); (m.1578) Robert Dudley, 1st Earl of Leicester (d.1588), Master of the Horse 1558–1588, Lord Steward 1584–1588; (m.1589) Sir Christopher Blount (ex.1601).

Knyvett, Elizabeth, Lady Knyvett (1575–1630): LPCU by 1603. (P) Sir Rowland Hayward and Joan Tyllesworth. (H) Thomas Knyvett (k.c.1602) (d.1622), Groom of the Privy Chamber. (NB) Another Elizabeth Knyvett, the daughter of Nathaniel Bacon, was 'sworn the Queen's woman' in June 1602, according to Philip Gawdy, but he does not say in what role and she does not appear on the 1603 Funeral list.

Knyvett, Catherine, Baroness Howard de Walden, [Countess of Suffolk] (1564–1638): LPC 1599–1603 (probably ordinary), LOH Funeral. (P) Sir Henry Knyvett and Elizabeth Stump. (H) Richard Rich; (m.c.1584) Lord Thomas Howard, (f.1597) Baron Howard de Walden (f.1603) Earl of Suffolk. (NB) According to Rowland Whyte 'Lady Katren Howard' was sworn of the Privy Chamber on 12 September 1599.

Knyvett, Katheryn, Baroness Paget (c.1547–1622): MOH c.1560–1567, LPCH 1569–1603, LOH Funeral. (P) Sir Henry Knyvett and Anne Pickering*. (H) (m.1567) Henry Paget, 2nd Baron Paget (d.1568); (m.c.1569) Edward Carey (k.1596) (d. 1618) Groom of the Privy Chamber.

Leigh, Katherine, [Lady Darcy] (c.1569–1625): MOH 1589–1591. (P) Sir Edward Leigh and Anne Fermor. (H) (m.1592) Sir Francis Darcy (d.1641).

Leigh, Catherine, Baroness Mountjoy (c.1539–1576): LOH Coronation. (P) Sir Thomas Leigh and Joanna Cotton. (H) (m.1558) James Blount, 6th Baron Mountjoy (d.1582).

Lennard, Margaret, Lady Waller (1578–af.1613): LPCU by 1603. (P) Sampson Leonard and Margaret Fiennes (later 11th Baroness Dacre of the South). (H) (m.1593) Thomas Waller (k.1597).

Le Strange, Catherine, Lady Clarke (c.1521–c.1559): LPCE 1558–c.1559. (P) Sir Thomas Le Strange and Anne Vaux. (H) Sir Rowland Clarke.

Lichfield, Margaret (–): GPCE *c.*1574–*c.*1582 (probably). (P) Sir Thomas Pakington and Dorothy Kitson. (H) Thomas Lichfield (d.1586), Groom of the Privy Chamber.

Lucy, Frances (–): GPCU by 1603. (H) Edmund Lucy, Esquire of the Body.

Lyfeld, Frances (d.1597): GPCE or GOTH/QW *c.*1583–*c.*1590. (P) Edmund Bray, 1st Baron Bray and Jane Haliwell. (H) Thomas Lyfeld.

MacWilliam, Cecilia, [Countess of Londonderry] (*c.*1565–1627): MOH 1589–*c.*1590. (P) Henry MacWilliam MP and Mary Hill*. (H) (m.*c.*1590) Thomas Ridgeway (k.1600) (f.1622) 1st Earl of Londonderry.

MacWilliam, Margaret, Lady Stanhope (*c.*1560–1640): MOH *c.*1580–1589, GPCE 1589–1596, LPCE 1596–1603, Vice-Chamberlain's wife 1601–1603. (P) Henry MacWilliam and Mary Hill*. (H) (m.1589) John Stanhope (k.1596) (f.1605) 1st Baron Stanhope (d.1621) Groom of the Privy Chamber, Vice-Chamberlain 1601–1603.

Mainwaring, Lady (–): LPCU by 1603. (NB) She is probably Anne More, Lady Mainwaring, wife of Sir George More and sister of Elizabeth Wolley.*

Manners, Lady Frances, Baroness Abergavenny (*c.*1537–1576): LOH Coronation. (P) Thomas Manners, 1st Earl of Rutland and Eleanor Paston. (H) Henry Neville, 6th Baron Abergavenny (d.1587).

Manners, Lady Gertrude, Baroness Talbot, Countess of Shrewsbury (*c.*1523–1567): LOH Coronation. (P) Thomas Manners, 1st Earl of Rutland and Eleanor Paston. (H) (m.1539) George Talbot, 12th Baron Talbot, (f.1560) 6th Earl of Shrewsbury.

Mansell, Mary (*c.*1538–1564): MOH 1558–1563. (P) Sir Rhys Mansell and Cecily Dabridgecourt. (H) (m.1563) Thomas Southwell (d.1567).

Marbury, Elyzabeth (d.*c.*1591): CHA by 1554, with Elizabeth at Woodstock, CHA 1554–1558, CHA 1558–*c.*1580. (P) Possibly Thomas Marbury and Agnes Lynn. (H) (by 1554) Thomas Marbury, Sergeant of the Pantry. (NB) She is probably the 'Mistress Morberye' featured in the household accounts of Princess Elizabeth (1551–1552). She seems to have retired *c.*1580.

Mewtas, Frances, Viscountess Howard of Bindon (*c.*1548–*c.*1595): MOH *c.*1561–*c.*1565 (retired a few months before her marriage). (P) Sir Peter Mewtas and Jane Astley. (H) (m. 1566) Henry Howard (f.1582) 2nd Viscount Howard of Bindon (d.1590); Edmund Stansfield.

Milborne, Blanche, Lady Herbert of Troy Parva (*c.*1470–*c.*1557): Lady Governess 1537 to at least 1539, Lady Attendant (probably) *c.*1544–*c.*1547. (P) Simon Milborne and Jane Baskerville. (H) Robert Whitney (d.1500); Sir William

Herbert of Troy Parva (d.1524). (B) Probably in Monmouth Parish Church (now lost). (NB) Lady Troy may have been Elizabeth's official Lady Governess from 1537 until 1547 (or later). It is also possible that Lady Troy was attending upon Elizabeth before 1537, perhaps as Baroness Bryan's deputy in the nursery.

Montague, Alice (d.1582): Silkwoman *c*.1570–1582. (H) (m.1562) Roger Montague.

Morgan, Anne, Lady Carey, Baroness Hunsdon (*c*.1530–1604): LPCH 1558–1603, Lady Chamberlain 1585–1596, LOH Coronation, LOH Funeral. (P) Sir Thomas Morgan and Elizabeth Whitney. (H) Sir Henry Carey (f.1559) 1st Baron Hunsdon (d.1596), Lord Chamberlain 1585–1596. (B) Chapel of St John the Baptist, Westminster Abbey, London.

Morgan, Lucy (–): GOTH/QW *c*.1580–*c*.1590. (P) Nicholas Sibell and Joan Sommer. (H) Hugh Morgan, apothecary.

Morris, Anne (–): MOM 1558–*c*.1561. (P) Possibly William Isaac and Margery Haute. (H) William Morris MP (d.1554).

Morrison, Bridget, Countess of Sussex (*c*.1575–*c*.1623): LOH Funeral. (P) Sir Charles Morrison and Dorothea Clerke. (H) (m.1592) Robert Radclyffe, 5th Earl of Sussex (d.1629).

Morton, Margaret (–): One of Queen Mary's women chosen to replace Dorothy Broughton at Woodstock. Previously attended Queen Katheryn Howard. Unidentified.

Neville, Lady Adeline (*c*.1547–1613): LOH Funeral. (P) Henry Neville, 5th Earl of Westmoreland and Lady Anne Manners.

Neville, Lady Margaret, Countess of Rutland (d.1559): LOH Coronation. (P) Ralph Neville, 4th Earl of Westmoreland and Katherine Stafford. (H) (m.1536) Henry Manners, 2nd Earl of Rutland (d.1563).

Neville, Mary, [Countess of Norwich] (*c*.1585–1648): MOH 1601–1603. (P) Edward Neville, 6th Lord Abergavenny and Rachel Lennard. (H) (m.*c*.1608) George Goring (f.1628) Baron Goring, (f.1644) 1st Earl of Norwich (d.1663).

Newton, Nazareth, Baroness Paget (*c*.1541–1583): CHA 1564–1573. (P) Sir John Newton and Margaret Poyntz. (H) (m.1565) Thomas Southwell of Woodrising (d.1568); (m.*c*.1573) Thomas Paget, 3rd Baron Paget (d.1590), separated in 1582.

Newton, Frances, Baroness Cobham (*c*.1539–1592): CHA *c*.1555–1558, CHA 1558–*c*.1564, LOB *c*.1564–1571 (probably), LOB 1574–1592 (possibly Chief LOB). (P) Sir John Newton and Margaret Poyntz. (H) (m.1560) William Brooke, 10th Baron Cobham (d.1597), Lord Chamberlain (1596–1597). (B): St Mary Magdalene Church, Cobham, Kent.

Norris, Mary, [Lady Carew, Lady Champernon] (*c.*1521–1570): Gentlewoman by 1538 to *c.*1539. (P) Sir Henry Norris and Mary Fiennes. (H) (m.*c.*1541) Sir George Carew (d.1545); (m.*c.*1546) Arthur Champernon (k.1548) (d.1578).

Norris, Mistress (–): GOTH 1559. Unidentified.

North, Christiana, Countess of Worcester (**d.1563**): LOH Coronation. (P) Edward North, 1st Baron North and Alice Squire. (H) William Somerset, 3rd Earl of Worcester (d.1589).

Norwich, Elizabeth, Lady Carew (*c.*1530–1594): Maid by 1547 to 1554, 1555–1558 (possibly a Gentlewoman 1556–1558), GOB/LOB 1558–1594. (P) Probably John Norwich of Brampton (d.1557) and Anne Cobham. (H) (m.*c.*1560) Sir Gawain Carew (d.1585). (B) Exeter Cathedral, Devon.

Nott, Elizabeth (**d.1597**): GPCE *c.*1574–*c.*1587 (possibly). (H) William Nott.

Ogle, Catherine, Lady Cavendish (*c.*1569–1629): LPCU by 1603. (P) Cuthbert Ogle, 7th Baron Ogle and Catherine Carnaby (H) (m.1591) Sir Charles Cavendish (d.1617).

Oglefield, Katherine (–): Servant by 1603. Unidentified.

Otemore, Mistress: GPCU by 1603. Unidentified.

Oxenbridge, Elizabeth, Lady Tyrwhit (**d.1578**): Lady Governess 1549. (P) Sir Goddard Oxenbridge and Anne Fiennes. (H) (*c.*1539) Robert Tyrwhit (k.1543) (d.1572). (B) Church of St Mary the Virgin, Leighton Bromswold, Cambridgeshire.

Parker, Alice (or Anne), Lady Brouncker (*c.*1553–1612): LPCU by 1603. (P) Henry Parker, 11th Baron Morley and Lady Elizabeth Stanley. (H) (m.*c.*1584) Sir Henry Brouncker (d.1607).

Parry (Ap Harry), Blanche (*c.*1507–1590): Rocker/Nursemaid f.1533–*c.*1539 (possibly), Gentlewoman *c.*1539–1556 (probably in the Tower and Woodstock with Elizabeth), Chief Gentlewoman 1556–1558 (probably), GOB 1558–1590, Chief GPC 1565–1590, KHMJ 1558–1571, ast. KHMJ 1571–1587. (P) Harry Myles and Alicia Milborne. (B) St Margaret's Church, Westminster Abbey, London. Her heart or bowels may be in St Faith's Church, Bacton, Herefordshire.

Paston, Kattrin, Lady Newton (*c.*1547–1615): CHA 1577–1603. (P) Sir Thomas Paston and Anne Leigh. (H) (m.1578) Henry Newton (k.1592) (d.1599). (B) Bristol Cathedral, Bristol.

Pemberton, Susan, [Lady Pemberton] (–): QW by 1603. (P) Henry MacWilliam and Mary Hill*. (H) Edward Saunders (d.1599); Goddard Pemberton (k.1603) (d.1616); Thomas Ireland (d.1625).

Pendred, Agnes (–): Wet Nurse 1533–*c*.1535. (H) David Pendred.

Penn, Sybil (d.1562): GOTH/QW 1559–1562. (P) Uncertain. (H) David Penn (d.1564). (NB) Sybil must have been born early 1500s not late 1400s if, as the evidence suggests, she was Prince Edward's wet nurse not dry nurse.

Pickering, Anne, Lady Knyvett (d.1582): LOTH 1559. (P) Sir Christopher Pickering and Jane Lewknor. (H) Sir Francis Weston (d.1536); Sir Henry Knyvett (d.1548); John Vaughan (d.1577).

Pole, Katherine, Countess of Huntingdon (1519–1576): LOH Coronation. (P) Henry Pole, 1st Baron Montagu; Jane Neville. (H) (m.1532) Francis Hastings, 2nd Earl of Huntingdon (d.1560).

Poole, Margaret: QW by 1603. Probably Margaret Neville, daughter of George Neville, Baron 5th Abergavenny and Mary Stafford. (H) John Cheney; Henry Poole (d.1580). (NB) First cousin of Dorothee Stafford*.

Poore, Mistress (–): CHA (probably) by 1547. Unidentified. Perhaps the wife, daughter or sister of Robert Poore, one of Elizabeth's gentlemen by 1547.

Powell, Mary (–): QW by 1603. Unidentified.

Poyntz, Anne, Lady Heneage (*c*.1530–1593): Maid *c*.1550–1554, GPCE 1558–1577, LPCE 1577–1593, Vice-Chamberlain's wife 1587–1593. (P) Sir Nicholas Poyntz and Joan Berkeley*. (H) (m.1554) Sir Thomas Heneage (k.1577) (d.1595), Gentleman of the Privy Chamber, Vice-Chamberlain 1587–1595. (B) St Paul's Cathedral, London (destroyed in the Fire of London).

Pranell, Frances, Countess of Hertford, [Duchess of Lennox/Richmond] (1578–1639): LOH Funeral. (P) Thomas Howard, 1st Viscount Howard of Bindon and Mabel Burton. (H) (m.1592) Henry Pranell (d.1599); (m.1601) Edward Seymour, 1st Earl of Hertford (d.1621); (m.1621) Ludovic Stewart, 2nd Duke of Lennox and 1st Duke of Richmond (d.1624).

Quadring, Dorothy (*c*.1520–*c*.1576): GPCE 1558–*c*.1576. (P) Sir Robert Hussey and Anne Saye. (H) Ralph Quadring (d.1554).

Radclyffe, Lady Frances, Lady Mildmay (c–1544–1602): MPC *c*.1561–1566 (possibly). (P) Henry Radclyffe, 2nd Earl of Sussex and Anne Calthorpe. (H) (m.1566) Sir Thomas Mildmay (d.1608).

Radclyffe, Margaret (1573–1599): MOH *c*.1592–1599. (P) John Radclyffe and Anne Ashawe.

Radclyffe, Mary (c.1545–1618): MOH c.1561–1585, GPCE c.1567–1585 (probably), GOB c.1585–1603, Acting Chief GPC 1590–1603, KHMJ 1587–1603. (P) Sir Humphrey Radclyffe and Isabella Harvey*.

Rainsford, Elizabeth Norton (c.1577–?): GPCE c.1597–1603. (P) Thomas Norton and Alice Cranmer. (H) (m.1600) Myles Rainsford (d.c.1603); (m.c.1604) Simon Bassell. (NB) Her sister, Anne, may also have served the Queen.

Randall, Elizabeth Smallpage (–): GOTH/QW 1560s. (P) Robert Collier and Elizabeth Holwood. (H) Smallpage; Vincent Randall.

Rede, Anne, Lady Parry (c.1510–1585): LPCH 1558–c.1566, LOH Coronation Eve. (P) Sir William Rede and Anne Warham. (H) Sir Giles Greville (d.1528); Sir Adrian Fortescue (d.1539); Sir Thomas Parry (d.1560), Comptroller of the Household. (NB) Retired from court c.1566 and received an annuity from the Queen. (B) St Gregory's Church, Welford, Berkshire.

Roberts, Jane, Lady Fitzwilliam (d.c.1565): LOTH 1558. (P) John Roberts and Mary Sackville. (H) Sir William Fitzwilliam (d.1559).

Robinson, Mistress (–): GOTH 1559. Unidentified.

Russell, Anne, [Countess of Worcester] (1578–1639): MOH 1595–1600. (P) John Russell, 3rd Baron Russell and Elizabeth Cooke*. (H) (m.1600): Henry Somerset, 7th Baron Herbert, (f.1628) 5th Earl of Worcester (d.1646).

Russell, Elizabeth (1575–1600): MPC 1594–1600. (P) John Russell (f.1572) 3rd Baron Russell and Elizabeth Cooke*.

Russell, Lady Anne, Countess of Warwick (c.1548–1604): MPC c.1561–1565, LPCH 1565–1603, LOH Funeral. (P) Francis Russell, 2nd Earl of Bedford and Margaret St John*. (H) (m.1565) Ambrose Dudley, 3rd Earl of Warwick (d.1590). (B) St Michael's Church, Chenies, Buckinghamshire.

Russell, Lady Margaret, Countess of Cumberland (1560–1616): LOH Funeral. (P) Francis Russell, 2nd Earl of Bedford and Margaret St John*. (H) (m.1577) George Clifford, 3rd Earl of Cumberland (d.1605).

Russell, Mistress (–): Servant by 1603. Unidentified.

Sackville, Anne, Lady Glemham (c.1565–af.1602): LOH Funeral. (P) Thomas Sackville, (f.1567) 1st Baron Buckhurst, (f.1604) 1st Earl of Dorset and Cicley Baker*. (H) (m.1585) Sir Henry Glemham (d.1632).

Sackville, Anne, Baroness Dacre of the South (*c.*1540–1595): LOH Coronation. (P) Sir Richard Sackville and Winifred Brydges*. (H) Gregory Fiennes, 10th Baron Dacre of the South (d.1594).

Saville, Mistress: GPCU by 1603. Perhaps the wife of Mr Saville, Gentleman of the Privy Chamber, who has been identified as Henry Saville, the Queen's Greek tutor.

Seckford, Alice (*c.*1535–*c.*1582): GOTH/QW *c.*1563–*c.*1582 (probably). (P) Sir Henry Bedingfield and Katherine Townsend. (H) Thomas Kervill; Henry Seckford (k.1603) (d.1610), Groom of the Privy Chamber, Keeper of the Privy Purse.

Seckford, Helen (d.*c.*1593): GOTH/QW *c.*1583–*c.*1593 (probably). (H) Henry Seckford, (k.1603) (d.1610), Groom of the Privy Chamber, Keeper of the Privy Purse.

Seckford, Rebecca, [Lady Seckford] (d.af.1619): QW *c.*1597–1603. (P) Robert Brandon and Katherine Barber. (H) John Rowe; Henry Seckford (k.1603) (d.1610), Gentleman of the Privy Chamber, Keeper of the Privy Purse.

Seycolle, Agnes, Lady Benger (d.*c.*1568): LOTH 1559. (H) Sir Thomas Benger (f.1560), Master of the Revels (d.1572).

Seymour, Mary (*c.*1528–a.1579): GPCE 1558–*c.*1560. (P) Nicholas Woodhull (Odell) and a daughter of William Parr, 1st Baron Parr of Horton. (H) (m.1550) David Seymour (d.*c.*1558).

Seymour, Lady Jane (1537–1561): MOH 1558–1561, LOH Coronation. (P) Edward Seymour, 1st Duke of Somerset and Anne Stanhope*.

Sheffield, Elizabeth, Countess of Ormond (1561–1600): LPCH (probably) and LOH *c.*1582–1600. (P) John Sheffield, 2nd Baron Sheffield and Dougles Howard*. (H) Thomas Butler, 10th Earl of Ormond (d.1614).

Sheffield, Mistress (–): Servant by 1603. Probably a relation of Dougles Howard, Baroness Sheffield*.

Shelton, Amy (d.1579): GPC *c.*1561–1579. (P) Probably Sir John Shelton and Anne Boleyn.

Shelton, Audrey (Ethelreda), Lady Walsingham (1568–1624): G/LPCE *c.*1587–*c.*1601 (probably), LPC 1601–1603 (possibly a CHA or LOB). (P) Sir Ralph Shelton; Mary Woodhouse. (H) Sir Thomas Walsingham (k.1597)(d.1630). (B) St Nicholas Church, Chislehurst, London.

Shelton, Elizabeth (–): GPC *c.*1561–*c.*1568. (P) Probably Sir John Shelton and Anne Boleyn.

Shelton, Mary, Lady Heveningham (*c.*1512–1571): LOTH 1558. (P) Sir John Shelton and Anne Boleyn. (H) (m.*c.*1535) Sir Anthony Heveningham (d.1557); (m.*c.*1558) Philip Appleyard.

Shelton, Mary, Lady Scudamore (*c.*1553–1603): CHA *c.*1570–1603. (P) Sir John Shelton and Margaret Parker. (H) (m.1574) John Scudamore (k.*c.*1592) (d.1623). (B) St Cuthbert's Church, Holme Lacy, Herefordshire (probably).

Sidney, Elizabeth, Countess of Rutland (1585–1612): LOH Funeral. (P) Sir Philip Sidney and Frances Walsingham*. (H) (m.1599) Roger Manners, 5th Earl of Rutland (d.1612).

Sidney, Frances, Countess of Sussex (1531–1589): LOH Coronation, LPCH *c.*1572–1589 (likely), Lady Chamberlain 1572–1583. (P) Sir William Sidney and Anne Packenham. (H) (m.1555) Thomas Radclyffe, 3rd Earl of Sussex (d.1583), Lord Chamberlain 1572–1583. (B) St Paul's Chapel, Westminster Abbey.

Sidney, Mary, Countess of Pembroke (1561–1621): MPC 1575–1577, LOH Funeral. (P) Sir Henry Sidney and Lady Mary Dudley*. (H) (m.1577) Henry Herbert, 2nd Earl of Pembroke (d.1601).

Skipwith, Margaret, Baroness Tailboys (*c.*1520–1583): LOH Coronation. (P) Sir William Skipwith and either his first wife, Elizabeth, or his second, Alice. (H) (m.1539) George Tailboys, 2nd Baron Tailboys of Kyme (d.1540); (m.1547) Sir Peter Carew (d.1575); (m.1579) Sir John Clifton of Barrington.

Skinner, Mistress: QW by 1603. Probably Elizabeth Skinner daughter of Robert Fowkes. (H) Henry Middlemore, Gentleman of the Privy Chamber (d.*c.*1592); (m.*c.*1594) Vincent Skinner (k.1603) (d.1616).

Smallpage, Elizabeth (–): GOTH 1559. (P) Robert Collier and Elizabeth Holwood. (Husband) Smallpage; Vincent Randall.

Smith, Alice, Lady Fortescue (d.1621): LPCU by 1603. (P) Christopher Smith. (H) John Fortescue (k.1592) (d.1607), Keeper of the Great Wardrobe (1559–1603), Privy Councillor (1589–1603), Chancellor of the Exchequer (1589–1603).

Smith, Anne, Lady York (*c.*1526–1575): LPCE *c.*1560–1575 (possibly). (P) Robert and Annie Smith. (H) Paget; Sir John York (d.1569).

Smith, Elizabeth Gorges, [Lady Smith] (*c.*1578–*c.*1659): GPCU by 1603. (P) Sir Thomas Gorges and Helena Snakenborg*. (H) (m.*c.*1596) Hugh Smith (k.1603) (d.*c.*1627); (m.1629) Ferdinando Gorges (d.1647). (NB) Elizabeth is probably the 'Lady Smith' and 'Smith' listed in the funeral records as her husband was knighted before they were completed.

Smythson, Elyzabeth (d.1593): Laundress of the Board 1558–c.1560, Mistress Laundress c.1560–1575. (H) John Smythson (d.c.1589), Master Cook. (NB) The Smythsons were also known as 'alias Taylor' (NYGE).

Snakenborg, Helena, (Elin Ulfsdotter), Marchioness of Northampton, Lady Gorges (1549–1635): MPC 1566–1571, LPCH 1571–1603, Chief LOH 1571–1603, Chief Mourner Funeral. (P) Ulf Henrikson von Snakenborg and Agnetta Knutsdotter. (H) (m.1571) William Parr, 1st Marquess of Northampton (d.1571); (m.1576) Thomas Gorges, gentleman of the robes (d.1610). (B) Salisbury Cathedral, Wiltshire.

Snow, Elyzabeth Cavendish (d.1587): Attending to c.1539 (possible dry nurse), GPCE 1558–1587. (P) Thomas Cavendish and Agnes Gernon. (H) (c.1539) Richard Snow. (NB) According to the *Visitation of Bedfordshire 1634* Elyzabeth was the aunt of the 'old Countess of Shrewsbury' who was probably Mary Cavendish.* Elyzabeth was not mentioned in her father's will, which has led to some confusion over her identity, but in his will he only mentions one daughter, Maud, who was evidently his only daughter from his first marriage and he wanted to make sure she was provided for. Emmy Snow (nee Byne), Elyzabeth's daughter-in-law, may have been in the Queen's household as she received 'ten yards of black damask and three yards of black velvet' in the May of 1580 for a gown. As this was the month she married Edward Snow the gown may have been for her wedding.

Snow, Sara (–): CHA c.1566–c.1567 (possibly). (P) Richard Snow and Elyzabeth Cavendish*.

Somerset, Lady Anne, Countess of Northumberland (1536–1596): named a LOH in the coronation but probably did not attend as no livery is recorded against her name. (P) Henry Somerset, 2nd Earl of Worcester and Elizabeth Browne*. (H) (m.1558) Thomas Percy, 7th Earl of Northumberland (ex.1572), co-leader of the Northern Rebellion (1569).

Somerset, Lady Elizabeth, Lady Guildford (1572–1627): MPC 1594–1596, LPCE 1596–1603, LOH Funeral. (P) Edward Somerset, 4th Earl of Worcester and Lady Elizabeth Hastings*. (H) (m.1596) Sir Henry Guildford.

Somerset, Lady Katherine, [Baroness Petre] (1574–1624): MOH 1594–1596, LOH Funeral. (P) Edward Somerset, 4th Earl of Worcester and Lady Elizabeth Hastings*. (H) (m.1596) William Petre (k.1603), (f.1613) 2nd Baron Petre (d.1637).

Somerset, Lady Lucy, Baroness Latimer (c.1524–1583): LOH Coronation. (P) Henry Somerset, 2nd Earl of Worcester and Elizabeth Browne*. (H) John Neville, 4th Baron Latimer (d.1577).

Sondes, Elizabeth, Lady Berkeley (1532/3–1585): CHA (probably) by 1554, in the Tower with Elizabeth until dismissed, at Woodstock until dismissed, CHA *c.*1560–1585. (P) Anthony Sondes and Anne Mann. (H) (m.1562) Sir Maurice Berkeley (k.1544) (d.1581).

Southwell, Bridget (*c.*1520–af.1583): Possible tutor to Elizabeth at Woodstock. (P) Sir Roger Copley and Elizabeth Shelley. (H) Richard Southwell aka Darcy (d.1600). (NB) Bridget's sister 'Mary Shirley' was already a widow in 1534 so their parents probably married earlier than is thought (LPH8, V.7, 1534).

Southwell, Elizabeth, [Lady Moleyns] (*c.*1566–1606): MOH *c.*1587–1595. (P) Thomas Southwell and Nazareth Newton*. (H) (m.1599) Sir Barentine Moleyns.

Southwell, Elizabeth, [Duchess of Northumberland] (1584–1631): MOH 1600–1603. (P) Sir Robert Southwell and Elizabeth Howard*. (H) Sir Robert Dudley (d.1649). (NB) Elizabeth and Robert lived in exile abroad and styled themselves Duke and Duchess of Northumberland.

Speckard, Dorothy (d.1656): Silkwoman (in the Wardrobe of Robes) *c.*1593–1603 (may have been a MOH *c.*1591–1593). (H) Abraham Speckard.

Spencer, Alice, Countess of Derby (1559–1637): LOH Funeral. (P) Sir John Spencer and Katherine Kitson. (H) (m.1579) Ferdinando Stanley (f.1593) 5th Earl of Derby (d.1594); (m.1600) Thomas Egerton (f.1603) 1st Baron Ellesmere, (f.1616) 1st Viscount Brackley (d.1617).

Spencer, Anne, Baroness Compton, Lady Sackville, [Countess of Dorset] (*c.*1554–1618): LOH Funeral. (P) Sir John Spencer and Katherine Kitson. (H) William Stanley, 3rd Baron Monteagle (d.1581); Henry Compton, 1st Baron Compton (d.1589); (m.1592) Robert Sackville (f.1603) 2nd Earl of Dorset (d.1609).

Spencer, Elizabeth, Lady Carey, Baroness Hunsdon (1552–1618): LPC *c.*1574–1603, Lady Chamberlain 1597–1603, LOH funeral. (P) Sir John Spencer and Katherine Kitson. (H) (m.1574) Sir George Carey (f.1596) 2nd Baron Hunsdon (d.1603), Lord Chamberlain 1597–1603; Ralph Eure, 3rd Baron Eure (d.1617). (B) Westminster Abbey.

Stafford, Dorothee, Lady Stafford (*c.*1526–1604): LPC 1559–1603, LOH Funeral. (P) Henry Stafford, 1st Baron Stafford and Lady Ursula Pole. (H) Sir William Stafford (d.1556) widower of Mary Boleyn.

Stafford, Elizabeth, Lady Drury, Lady Scott (*c.*1554–1599): CHA 1568–1599. (P) Sir William Stafford and Dorothee Stafford*. (H) (m.1573) William Drury (k.*c.*1576) (d.1590); (m.*c.*1591) Sir John Scott (d.1616). (B) St Margaret's Church, Westminster Abbey.

Stanhope, Anne (*c.*1560–*c.*1616): GPCU by 1603. (P) Sir William Read and Gertrude Paston. (H) (m.1597) Michael Stanhope, Groom of the Privy Chamber (k.1603) (d.*c.*1621). (NB) Anne is probably the 'Stanhope' listed in the funeral accounts.

Stanhope, Anne, Duchess of Somerset (d.1587): LOH Coronation, Chief LOH 1558–1587 (probably). (P) Sir Edward Stanhope and Elizabeth Bourchier. (H) (m.*c.*1553) Edward Seymour (f.1547) Duke of Somerset (d.1552); (m.*c.*1558) Francis Newdigate (d.1582).

Stanhope, Jane, Baroness Berkeley (*c.*1547–1618): LOH Funeral. (P) Sir Michael Stanhope and Anne Rawson. (H) (m.*c.*1564) Sir Roger Townshend (d.1590); (m.1598) Henry Berkeley, 7th Baron Berkeley (d.1613).

Stanley, Lady Elizabeth, Baroness Morley (d.*c.*1589): LOH Coronation. (P) Edward Stanley, 3rd Earl of Derby and Dorothy Howard. (H) Henry Parker, 11th Baron Morley (d.1577).

Sterne, Mistress (–): QW by 1603. Unidentified.

St John, Ann, Baroness Howard of Effingham (*c.*1575–*c.*1638): LOH Funeral. (P) John St John, 2nd Baron St John of Bletso and Katherine Dormer*. (H) William Howard, 3rd Baron Howard of Effingham (d.1615).

St John, Margaret, Countess of Bedford (*c.*1524–1562): LOH Coronation, LPCH *c.*1560–1562 (possibly). (P) Sir John St John and Margaret Waldegrave. (H) (m.*c.*1540) William Gostwick (d.1545); (m.*c.*1546) Francis Russell, 2nd Earl of Bedford (d.1585).

St Loe, Elyzabeth (d.af.1566): Maid *c.*1550–1554 and 1555–1558, GPC 1558–*c.*1566. (P) Sir John St Loe and Margaret Kingston.

Tailboys, Elizabeth, 4th Baroness Tailboys (suo jure) (*c.*1520–1563): LOH Coronation. (P) Gilbert Tailboys, 1st Baron Tailboys of Kyme and Elizabeth Blount. (H) Thomas Wymbush (d.1553); (m.1553) Ambrose Dudley, (f.1564) 1st Earl of Warwick (d.1590).

Talbot, Lady Alethea, [Countess of Arundel] (*c.*1585–1654): LOH Funeral. (P) Gilbert Talbot, 7th Earl of Shrewsbury and Mary Cavendish*. (H) (m.1606) Thomas Howard (f.1595) 14th Earl of Arundel (d.1646).

Talbot, Lady Anne, Countess of Pembroke (*c.*1515–1588): LOH Coronation. (P) George Talbot, 4th Earl of Shrewsbury and Elizabeth Walden. (H) (m.1537) Sir Peter Compton (d.1540); William Herbert, 1st Earl of Pembroke (d.1570).

Talbot, Lady Elizabeth, [Countess of Kent] (*c.*1582–1651): MPC *c.*1600–*c.*1601, LOH Funeral. (P) Gilbert Talbot, 7th Earl of Shrewsbury and Mary Cavendish*.

(H) (m.*c.*1601) Henry Grey (f.1623) 8th Earl of Kent (d.1639). (NB) Although her marriage is usually dated to 1601 she was still listed as 'Lady Elizabeth Talbot' in the funeral accounts.

Talbot, Lady Katherine, Countess of Pembroke (*c.*1542–1575): LPCH 1563–1575 (possibly). (P) George Talbot, 6th Earl of Shrewsbury; Gertrude Manners*. (H) (m.1563) Henry Herbert, 2nd Earl of Pembroke (d.1601).

Talbot, Lady Mary, [Countess of Pembroke] (*c.*1580–1649): LOH Funeral. (P) Gilbert Talbot, 7th Earl of Shrewsbury and Mary Cavendish*. (H) (m.1604) William Herbert, 3rd Earl of Pembroke (d.1630). (NB) Possibly a MPC 1600s.

Teerlinc, Levina (*c.*1515–1576): GPCE *c.*1559–1576 (possibly), Queen's Painter 1558–1576. (P) Simon Bening and Katherine Scroo. (H) George Teerlinc (d.1578), Gentleman Pensioner. (NB) In receipt of a £40 annuity for her service to Henry VIII, Edward VI, Queen Mary. On 28 November 1546 she had been appointed Henry VIII's nurse (CPR, Elizabeth, Vol.1, p.41).

Thomazine, Mistress (–): GOTH/QW *c.*1577–1603. (NB) She is better known as Thomazine Muliercula, the Queen's dwarf.

Thomeo, Mary (–): One of Queen Mary's GPC chosen to attend Elizabeth at Woodstock (and possibly the Tower). (H) 'Master Thomeo' also attending upon the princess.

Throckmorton, Elizabeth, Lady Raleigh (1565–1647): GPCE *c.*1584–1592, LPCU by 1603. (P) Sir Nicholas Throckmorton and Anne Carew*. (H) (m.1591) Sir Walter Raleigh (ex.1618).

Thynne, Gresham (*c.*1580–?): MOH *c.*1601–1603, MOH Funeral. (P) Sir John Thynne of Longleat and (probably) Dorothy Wroughton.

Thynne, Katherine, [Lady Long, Lady Fox] (d.1613): MOH 1591–1593, LPCE 1593–1603 (possibly). (P) Sir John Thynne of Longleat and (probably) Dorothy Wroughton. (H) (m.1593) Sir Walter Long of Wraxhall (d.1610); Sir Edward Fox (d.1629).

Tilney, Agnes, Duchess of Norfolk (*c.*1477–1545): Chief Godmother, Christening. (P) Sir Hugh Tilney and Eleanor Tailboys. (H) Thomas Howard, 2nd Duke of Norfolk (d.1524).

Trevanion, Elizabeth, Lady Carey, [Countess of Monmouth] (d.1641): LPCU by 1603. (P) Sir Hugh Trevanion and Sybilla Morgan. (H) (m.1593) Sir Robert Carey (f.1626) Earl of Monmouth (d.1639).

Trevor, Margaret (*c.*1571–1646): QW by 1603. (P) Sir Hugh Trevanion and Sybilla Morgan. (H) (m.1592) John Trevor (k.1603) (d.1630).

Trentham, Elizabeth, Countess of Oxford (*c.*1563–1612): MOH 1581–1591, LOH Funeral. (P) Thomas Trentham and Jane Sneyd. (H) (m.1591) Edward de Vere, 17th Earl of Oxford (d.1604).

Tuchet, Maria (*c.*1579–1611): MOH *c.*1592–1595. (P) George Tuchet, 11th Baron Audley, (f.1616) 1st Earl of Castlehaven and Lucy Marvyn (see Clarke, Amy, Lady Marvyn). (H) (married in secret 1594) Thomas Thynne (d.1638) of Longleat.

Twist, Anne (d.1612): Mistress Laundress 1575–1603. (H) Thomas Twist. (NB) Anne had at least one daughter, Winnifred Twist, who was gifted a loose gown of black grosgrain by the Queen in 1584 along with a partlet and a forepart of taffeta.

Tyrwhit, Lady Bridget Manners (*c.*1575–1604): MPC 1589–1594, LOH Funeral. (P) John Manners, Earl of Rutland and Elizabeth Charlton. (H) (m.1594) Robert Tyrwhit (d.1617). (B) All Saints Church, Bigby, Lincolnshire.

Vaughan, Frances, Baroness Burgh (*c.*1562–1647): MOH *c.*1578–1580, LOH Funeral. (P) John Vaughan and Anne Pickering*. (H) (m.1580) Thomas Burgh (f.1584) 3rd Baron Burgh (d.1597).

Vaughan, Margaret, Lady Hawkins (*c.*1560–*c.*1622): CHA 1589–1603. (P) Charles Vaughan of Hergest and Margaret Vaughan. (H) (m.*c.*1592) Sir John Hawkins (d.1595). (NB) Margaret's parents had married by 1552 so Roger Vaughan of Clyro, Justice of the Peace and Lieutenant of Radnorshire by 1601, was her half-brother, not her mother's first husband, and he was the full brother of Catherine Vaughan, Margaret's half-sister, who married John Price of Pilleth (in her will Margaret refers to Stephen Price of Gray's Inn, their son, as 'my nephew'). (B) Church of St Dunstan in the East, London.

Vavasour, Anne (*c.*1561–*c.*1650): MOH 1580–1581. (P) Henry Vavasour and Margaret Knyvett. (H) John Finch; John Richardson.

Vavasour, Anne, [Lady Warburton] (d.1646): CHA 1601–1603. (P) Sir Thomas Vavasour and Mary Dodge. (H) (m.1603) Sir Richard Warburton (d.1610).

Vavasour, Frances, Lady Sherley (1568–1606): MOH *c.*1591–1591, LPCU by 1603. (P) Henry Vavasour and Margaret Knyvett. (H) (m.1591) Sir Thomas Sherley (d.*c.*1634).

Vernon, Elizabeth, Countess of Southampton (1569–1655): MOH *c.*1593–1598, LOH Funeral. (P) Sir John Vernon and Elizabeth Devereux. (H) (m.1598) Thomas Wriothesley, 3rd Earl of Southampton (d.1624).

Wake, Elizabeth (b.c.1526): QW by 1603. (P) Edward Gorges and Mary Poyntz. (H) (m.c.1540) John Wake.

Walsingham, Frances, Countess of Essex/Clanricarde (1567–1633): LOH Funeral. (P) Sir Francis Walsingham and Ursula St Barbe. (H) (m.1583) Sir Philip Sidney (d.1586); (m.1590) Robert Devereux, 2nd Earl of Essex (ex.1601); (m.1603) Richard Burke, 4th Earl of Clanricarde (d.1635).

Wayneman, Mistress (–): GOTH 1559. Possibly a member of the Wenman family.

West, Joan (d.af.1577): GOTH/QW c.1562–c.1577. Unidentified. Possibly the wife of John West, yeoman and tailor. (NB) Joan received several loose gowns and kirtles of grosgrain camlet from the Queen over the years.

West, Kathryn (d.af.1591): GOTH/QW or G/MPC c.1584–c.1591. Unidentified. Possibly a second (or more) wife of John West, yeoman and tailor, or his daughter. (NB) Kathryn received several loose gowns from the Queen between 1585 and 1591 that were made of black damask or black taffeta and fancifully adorned with 'lace and fringe of black silk'. While unlikely, it is also possible that Kathryn was an unrecorded daughter of Anne Knollys and Thomas West, 2nd Baron De La Warr, born c.1572, and was a MPC.

Weston, Mistress: GOTH 1559. Unidentified.

Wharton, Margaret, [Baroness Wotton] (1581–1659): MOH 1602–1603. (P) Philip Wharton, 3rd Baron Wharton and Lady Frances Clifford. (H) (m.1603) Edward Wotton, (f.1603) 1st Baron Wotton of Marley (d.c.1625).

Widowed Gentlewoman (–): Governess 1556. Unidentified.

White, Lady (–): LPCE 1601–1603. (H) Sir Richard White of South Warnborough (d.1613).

Whitney, Blanche (c.1525–c.1556): Gentlewoman by 1547; probably in the Tower and Woodstock with Elizabeth; probably the gentlewoman who died of smallpox in 1556. (P) Robert Whitney and Margaret Wye. (NB) The 'Mistress Whitney' attending in 1547 and the 'Blanche Qwrtnaye' attending in 1551/2 are probably one and the same (LC 2/2, folio 48.v; HEPE). While 'Qwrtnaye' may be 'Courtenay' it is probably a transcript or clerical error for 'Whitney'. In his will of 1541 Robert Whitney mentions two unmarried daughters: Blanche and Mary Whitney (TNA PROB 11/28/519).

Willoughby, Katherine, Duchess of Suffolk and 12th Baroness Willoughby de Eresby (suo jure) (1519–1580): Chief LOH 1559–1580 (probably). (P) William Willoughby, 11th Baron Willoughby de Eresby and Maria de Salinas. (H) Charles Brandon, 1st Duke of Suffolk (d.1545); Richard Bertie (d.1582).

Willoughby, Margaret, Lady Arundel (c.1540–1584): Maid 1555–1558, GPC 1558–1574, LPC 1574–1584. (P) Sir Henry Willoughby and Lady Anne Grey. (H) (m.1559) Sir Matthew Arundel (k. 1574) (d.1598).

Windebank, Jane, Lady Palmer (d.c.1584): LOTH 1559. (P) Richard and Margaret Windebank. (H) Sir Henry Palmer (d.1559).

Windsor, Anne, [Baroness Grey of Groby] (c.1549–c.1612): MOH c.1561–c.1568. (P) William Windsor, 2nd Baron Windsor and Margaret Sambourne or their son Sir Thomas Windsor and Dorothy Dacre. (H) (m.c.1568) Henry Grey (k.1587) (f.1603) 1st Baron Grey of Groby (d.1614).

Wingfield, Anne (d.c.1571): GPC 1558–c.1571. (P) said to be Sir Anthony Wingfield and Elizabeth de Vere but may have been Sir Charles Wingfield and Joan Knollys, sister-in-law of Kathryn Carey, Lady Knollys.*

Wingfield, Elizabeth (c.1510–c.1600): GPCE c.1562–1600, MOM 1591–1593, 1597–1600. (P) Probably Ralph Leche and Elizabeth Leche Hardwick. (H) Anthony Wingfield (d.c.1593), gentleman usher.

Winter, Mistress: GOTH 1559. Possibly Elizabeth Winter who is said to have served pre-accession.

Wolley, Elizabeth, Lady Wolley, Lady Egerton (1552–1600): LPCE c.1595–1600. (P) Sir William More and Margaret Daniel. (H) (m.1567) Richard Polsted (d.1576); (m.c.1577) Sir John Wolley (k.1592) (d.c.1596), Queen's Latin Secretary; (m.1597) Sir Thomas Egerton, Lord Chancellor (d.1617).

Wotton, Margaret, Marchioness of Dorset (c.1485–c.1535): Godmother, Christening. (P) Sir Robert Wotton and Anne Belknap. (H) William Medley; Thomas Grey, 2nd Marquess of Dorset (d.1530).

Wye, Mistress (–): Servant by 1603. Unidentified.

Yetsweirt, Mary (d.1568): GOTH 1559. (P) James Bourchier. (H) Nicasius Yetsweirt (d.1584).

Zouche, Mistress: MOH Funeral. Possibly Mary Zouche (1582–1652) daughter of Edward Zouche, 11th Baron Zouche of Haryngworth and Eleanor Zouche. (H) Thomas Leighton; William Connard. (NB) Sources differ on the date of Mary's first marriage. If she was the 'Mistress Zouche' serving as a MOH at the Queen's funeral then her marriage cannot have taken place before this date.